Introduction to

Web 2.0

Second Edition

Introduction to

Web 2.0

Second Edition

Diane Coyle

PEARSON

Boston   Columbus   Indianapolis   New York   San Francisco   Upper Saddle River
Amsterdam   Cape Town   Dubai   London   Madrid   Milan   Munich   Paris   Montreal   Toronto
Delhi   Mexico City   São Paulo   Sydney   Hong Kong   Seoul   Singapore   Taipei   Tokyo

Editor in Chief: Michael Payne
Executive Editor: Jenifer Niles
Product Development Manager: Laura Burgess
Editorial Project Manager: Meghan Bisi and Anne Garcia
Development Editor: Karen Misler
Editorial Assistant: Carly Prakapas
Director of Digital Development: Zara Wanlass
Executive Editor, Digital Learning & Assessment: Paul Gentile
Director, Media Development: Cathi Profitko
Senior Editorial Media Project Manager: Alana Coles
Production Media Project Manager: John Cassar
Director of Marketing for Business & Technology: Patrice Jones
Marketing Coordinator: Susan Osterlitz
Marketing Assistant: Darshika Vyas
Senior Managing Editor: Cynthia Zonneveld
Associate Managing Editor: Camille Trentacoste
Manager of Rights & Permissions: Hessa Albader
Operations Specialist: Renata Butera
Production Manager: Renata Butera
Creative Art Director: Jayne Conte
Interior Design: Anthony Gemmellaro
Cover Design: Anthony Gemmellaro
Manager, Cover Visual Research & Permissions: Karen Sanatar
Full-Service Project Management: Saraswathi Muralidhar
Composition: PreMediaGlobal
Printer/Binder: Banta Menasha
Cover Printer: Banta Menasha
Text Font: 10.5/12 Garamond3

All screenshots are reused by permission of Google, Inc.

Library of Congress Cataloging-in-Publication Data

Coyle, Diane
   Introduction to Web 2.0 / Diane Coyle.—2nd ed.
      p. cm.
   Previous edition cataloged under: Alan Evans. c2010.
   Includes index.
   ISBN-13: 978-0-13-284015-6
   ISBN-10: 0-13-284015-4
 1. Web 2.0.   I. Evans, Alan (Alan D.) Introduction to Web 2.0.   II. Title.
   TK5105.88817.E93 2012
   006.7—dc23
                                          2011037949

10 9 8 7 6 5 4 3 2 1

ISBN 13: 978-0-13-284015-6
ISBN 10:   0-13-284015-4

About the Author

Diane Coyle is a faculty member at Montgomery County Community College and also teaches computer literacy courses for at-risk and unemployed clients for several social service programs. She often incorporates Web 2.0 projects into her classes in computer concepts, Microsoft Office, Internet research, and Web design. She also has a successful freelance business providing marketing, editorial, and computer training services. Diane values networking and interacting with other educators and students—both face-to-face and through the use of Web 2.0 tools.

Dedicated with love and affection to my parents, Don and Cass, who have always been there for me, and to my children, Amy and Steven, for their support and encouragement.

Contents

Visual Walk-Through

Many of today's introductory computing courses are moving beyond coverage of just the traditional Microsoft® Office applications. Instructors are looking to incorporate newer technologies and software applications into their courses, and on some college campuses new alternative courses based on emerging technologies are being offered.

The NEXT Series was developed to provide innovative instructors with a high-quality, academic teaching solution that focuses on the next great technologies. There is more to computing than Microsoft® Office, and the books in *The NEXT Series* enable students to learn about some of the newer technologies that are available and becoming part of our everyday lives.

The NEXT Series…making it easy to teach what's *NEXT!*

▶ Whether you are interested in creating a new course or you want to enhance an existing class by incorporating new technology, *The NEXT Series* is your solution.

Included in this series are books on alternative productivity software application products, Google Apps—Productivity Apps, Google Apps—Personal Apps, and OpenOffice.org, as well as new technologies encompassed in Web 2.0 and Social Networking.

▶ *Introduction to Web 2.0,* Second Edition, is a teaching and learning tool that was designed for use in a classroom setting, encouraging students to learn by using these new technologies hands-on.

The text includes in-chapter Hands-On Exercises, end-of-chapter exercises, and instructor supplements.

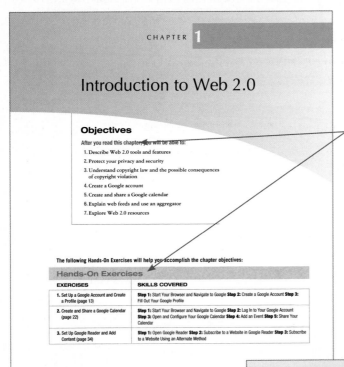

Each chapter opens with a list of numbered **Objectives**, clearly outlining what students will be able to accomplish after completing the chapter. The **Hands-On Exercises** are also outlined at the beginning of the chapter, letting students know what they will be doing in each chapter.

Learn-by-doing approach
Students learn how to use *Web 2.0* by completing a series of **Hands-On Exercises**. These exercises are clearly distinguished from the explanatory text because the pages are shaded in green.

Hands-On Exercises

Professor Schmeckendorf likes the idea of having a calendar that his students can view. He thinks this will be helpful because he will be able to list due dates for homework assignments, projects, and tests. In addition, he would like to make his calendar available to his lab assistant, Hannah Grindeldorf, so that she can add events and update his schedule for him.

2 | Create and Share a Google Calendar

Steps: 1. Start Your Browser and Navigate to Google; **2.** Log In to Your Google Account; **3.** Open and Configure Your Google Calendar; **4.** Add an Event; **5.** Share Your Calendar.

Use Figures 1.20 through 1.31 as a guide to the exercise.

Step 1 Start Your Browser and Navigate to Google

Refer to Figure 1.7 as you complete Step 1.

If you logged out of your Google account and shut your computer down after the previous exercise, follow the directions in Steps 1 and 2. If you have not logged out of your Google account, proceed to Step 3.

a. If necessary, turn on the computer and start your preferred browser (Internet Explorer, Firefox, Chrome, Safari, etc.). Type **www.google.com** in the address bar of your browser and press **Enter**.

b. Click the **Sign in** link at the top-right corner of the Google homepage.

Step 2 Log In to Your Google Account

Refer to Figure 1.20 as you complete Step 2.

a. Google identifies you by the email address you used to create your account. To log in to your Google account, you must use your complete email address and the password you selected. In the **Email** text box, type the email address.

b. In the **Password** text box, type your password.

Be sure the **Stay signed in** checkbox is unchecked, especially if you are using a public computer.

c. Click the **Sign in** button.

Alert

If you are having trouble signing in to your account, the **Can't access your account?** link will take you to a page where you can reset your password or retrieve your username.

Question & Answer Format

Each section begins with a question, engaging students in a dialog with the authors and drawing them into the content.

Key terms are defined in the margins.

Objective 3

Understand copyright law and the possible consequences of copyright violation

Many people think that because it is easy to find an image or a video on the web, they are free to use it for their own purposes. This might include posting someone else's videos or photos on a social networking site or copying blog entries found on other blogs and displaying them on their own blog verbatim. However, the creators or owners of written works and digital media (such as photographs, graphics, and videos) have legal rights. There can be serious consequences to violating these rights.

What legal rights do creators of web content have?

Under U.S. laws, and the laws of many other nations, *copyright* is the legal protection granted to authors of "original works of authorship." In the United States and the European Union, copyrightable works include the following:

- Literary works, including computer software
- Musical works, including any accompanying words
- Dramatic works, including any accompanying music
- Pantomimes and choreographic works

Copyright The legal protection granted to authors of "original works of authorship."

Tip boxes provide students with useful tips and tricks.

When you first create your Twitter account, you will see two other tabs for your Twitter settings. You can use the **Password** tab to create and confirm a new password and the **Mobile** tab to set up your Twitter account to use text messaging on your mobile phone. Professor Schmeckendorf does not intend to use Twitter on his phone and does not need to change his password, so he won't use these tabs now. However, you may want to review the information on each of these tabs for future reference. The **Applications** tab (shown in Figure 6.13) will not appear until you authorize a third-party application to access your Twitter account.

If you added a profile picture, website address, or bio, or if you changed your theme, you should see these changes on your profile page. Professor Schmeckendorf's profile page is shown in Figure 6.14. When you are done viewing your profile page, click on your username at the top right of the page and click **Sign out** to log out of your account and then close your browser.

Alert

Due to the ever-changing nature of Twitter, some of the Twitter accounts used in this exercise may be listed in a different order or may have been closed. If you don't see a specific account, try to locate something similar and use that instead.

Alert boxes call attention to items that might cause students to get hung up.

The left side of the page displays the expanded category list containing links to the Twitter accounts in the category, including the **Safety** account you just selected. If a user has uploaded a photo or added a bio, this information is also displayed on this side of the page. The **Follow** button allows you to quickly select those users you'd like to follow. To the right of the **Follow** button is a button showing the profile of a person, known as the **Person** icon. Clicking this icon displays a drop-down menu with options for that user account, including mentioning the user in a tweet, adding the user to a list, blocking the user, and reporting the user for spam.

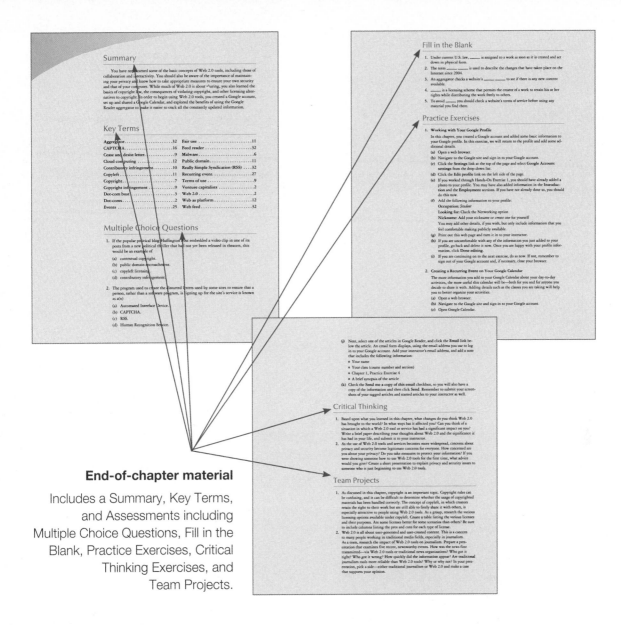

End-of-chapter material

Includes a Summary, Key Terms, and Assessments including Multiple Choice Questions, Fill in the Blank, Practice Exercises, Critical Thinking Exercises, and Team Projects.

Supplements for Instructors

Online Instructor Resource Center with:

- Instructor's Manual
- Solution Files

www.pearsonhighered.com/nextseries

Supplements for Students

Companion Website with:

- Objectives
- Glossary
- Chapter Summary
- Student Data Files

www.pearsonhighered.com/nextseries

Introduction to Web 2.0

Objectives

After you read this chapter, you will be able to:

1. Describe Web 2.0 tools and features

2. Protect your privacy and security

3. Understand copyright law and the possible consequences of copyright violation

4. Create a Google account

5. Create and share a Google calendar

6. Explain web feeds and use an aggregator

7. Explore Web 2.0 resources

The following Hands-On Exercises will help you accomplish the chapter objectives:

Hands-On Exercises

EXERCISES	SKILLS COVERED
1. Set Up a Google Account and Create a Profile (page 13)	**Step 1:** Start Your Browser and Navigate to Google **Step 2:** Create a Google Account **Step 3:** Fill Out Your Google Profile
2. Create and Share a Google Calendar (page 22)	**Step 1:** Start Your Browser and Navigate to Google **Step 2:** Log In to Your Google Account **Step 3:** Open and Configure Your Google Calendar **Step 4:** Add an Event **Step 5:** Share Your Calendar
3. Set Up Google Reader and Add Content (page 34)	**Step 1:** Open Google Reader **Step 2:** Subscribe to a Website in Google Reader **Step 3:** Subscribe to a Website Using an Alternate Method

Objective 1

Describe Web 2.0 tools and features

What is meant by Web 2.0?

Web 2.0 An expression
that is used to describe the
changes that have taken place
in the usage and applications
available on the Internet
(specifically the World Wide
Web) since 2004.

Web 2.0 is an expression that is used to describe the changes that have taken place in the usage and applications available on the Internet—specifically the World Wide Web—since 2004. The phrase "Web 2.0" began to gain public notice when it was used as the title for a conference meant to explore the changes and future of the World Wide Web, but has since evolved to encompass a whole new outlook on the web and its use. Sometimes referred to as the "Social Web," Web 2.0 refers to the fact that creativity, collaboration among users, and information sharing are now driving the creation of web applications and services available on the web. This has led to the creation of many new types of applications, including social networks, blogs, podcasts, wikis, and video sharing sites. The map shown in Figure 1.1 was created for the 2010 Web 2.0 Summit and provides a visualization of many of the key Web 2.0 entities and their areas of involvement. In true Web 2.0 fashion, this map is interactive—go to **http://map.web2summit.com** to see the entire map, and add your input.

Figure 1.1 Created for the 2010 Web 2.0 Summit, produced by Federated Media, O'Reilly Media, and UBM TechWeb, this interactive map portrays many of the key Web 2.0 entities as countries.

What exactly was Web 1.0 (and how did I miss it)?

There never really was a Web 1.0—at least no one called it by that name. The World Wide Web was invented primarily by Tim Berners-Lee in the early 1990s, with the original intent of fostering better communication between scientific researchers. But as the web gained popularity in the latter half of the 1990s, most people driving web development were businesspeople and **venture capitalists** (investors who specialize in funding new, high-growth ventures in exchange for shares of stock in a company). The focus was to use the web as a source of providing products and services to consumers—and other businesses—in an efficient and cost-effective manner. Amazon.com was started during this period and eventually became a very profitable company, based on its original idea of selling books without having a physical bookstore.

Venture capitalists Investors
who specialize in funding
new, high-growth ventures in
exchange for shares of stock in
a company.

Unfortunately, many of the first businesses that were started on the Internet suffered from flawed business designs and never became profitable. Eventually, all the enthusiasm over the web being new and cool waned, and most of the **dot-coms**

Dot-coms Companies that do
most or all of their business on
the Internet.

Dot-com bust A period of time from late 2000 through 2002 during which many dot-com companies with unworkable business ideas went out of business.

(companies that do most or all of their business on the Internet) with unworkable business ideas went out of business. This was known as the bursting of the Internet bubble, or the *dot-com bust*, and took place in late 2000 through 2002. Clearly, a better way to use the Internet and make it commercially profitable had to be found.

So how did Web 2.0 develop?

Venture capitalists and investors became more cautious after the dot-com bust and began to concentrate their funding on Internet businesses that had solid, feasible business plans leading to eventual profitability. At the same time, the costs of establishing Internet companies declined due to falling prices of hardware, software, and telecommunications lines—the medium needed to carry the vast amounts of information across the Internet. The decline in costs made it easier to experiment with revolutionary ideas, with less risk to investors.

What is the essence of a Web 2.0 application?

Web 2.0 sites get back to the original ideas of the World Wide Web: individuals sharing information with each other efficiently and effectively. Effective Web 2.0 ventures rely on user creativity to create and distribute an individual's intellectual property, such as videos, photos, or writing. Many successful Web 2.0 products include a social component that fosters interaction between individuals, either for the purpose of sharing information or just to chat and swap ideas or opinions. Social networking sites that encourage online communication between members (such as Facebook or LinkedIn), video sharing sites (such as YouTube), blogs (such as Blogger or WordPress), wikis that enable many people to collaborate and contribute to the development of a document (such as Wikipedia, shown in Figure 1.2), and social bookmarking sites that use tags to manage and categorize web content (such as Digg or Delicious) are all examples of Web 2.0 applications. The hallmarks of a Web 2.0 site are collaboration and interactivity. The best Web 2.0 sites are those which develop an active community with members who generate content and interact with one another. In contrast to a traditional website, which is static and relatively unchanging, a Web 2.0 site constantly has fresh, up-to-date content, with more information being added on a regular basis.

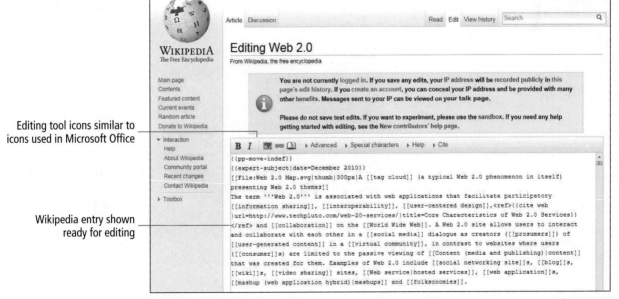

Editing tool icons similar to icons used in Microsoft Office

Wikipedia entry shown ready for editing

Figure 1.2 A Wikipedia page shown in editing mode. Anyone can create or edit a page in Wikipedia, which is a very efficient way to collaborate on the creation of an information document.

Are Web 2.0 companies more likely to survive and remain in business than earlier web ventures?

If the owners of Web 2.0 sites can figure out how to make money from user-generated content and social interaction, they will fare better than the early web companies that went bankrupt. Consider YouTube, the video sharing site. It is free to view videos on YouTube, and it costs nothing to establish an account and post a video you make on the site. So how does YouTube make money? So far, its main method of revenue generation is advertising. Millions of people visit YouTube every day to view videos, providing Google (the owner of YouTube) with a vast audience for advertising. You may have clicked on an ad you saw while on YouTube, which generated revenue for Google. Even if you've never clicked on an ad while viewing videos on YouTube, many other people are clicking, which allows YouTube to make money and survive.

Is advertising the only way for Web 2.0 companies to make money from their websites?

Advertising is by far the biggest source of revenue for most Web 2.0 sites, but some companies are finding other ways to convert user interaction and creativity into dollars. Threadless.com is a Web 2.0 company that has found a way to make money by selling tangible products (Figure 1.3). Threadless runs art contests on a regular basis. Anyone can submit a design to a Threadless contest. Threadless has built a vast online community of artists and people who appreciate clever design. The community votes on the art submitted to the contests to determine the winners. The winners receive $2,500 in cash and merchandise, and their designs are printed on T-shirts that Threadless then sells. Because the customers (the community) are essentially telling Threadless what they want to purchase by voting for designs, Threadless always has exceptionally strong demand for any products it produces.

Figure 1.3 The Threadless community can rate and comment on potential T-shirt designs. Sales from the winning designs generate profit for both Threadless and the artists.

Objective 2

Protect your privacy and security

What can I do to maintain my privacy and use Web 2.0 tools safely?

As identity theft and other Internet security issues become more prevalent, the necessity of protecting your privacy and using Web 2.0 tools safely becomes even more important. Every Web 2.0 tool has a different set of features and privacy options available. As we look at these tools individually, we'll explore that site's options, but there are still some overall steps and precautions you can take, regardless of the site you're on or the tool you are using. One of the easiest things you can do is to use common sense. Everyone has a different comfort level when it comes to disclosing personal information. You will need to decide how much or how little information you want to share with others. Sometimes it can help to think about the way you share information with others in face-to-face situations. You probably would feel more comfortable sharing information with someone who is in your class or is a friend of a friend, whereas you might not be as forthcoming with someone you meet at a store or concert. You might not mind giving your friend's friend your phone number or home address, but chances are you might think twice about giving the same information to a total stranger. It turns out that those rules you learned as a child about never talking to strangers or divulging personal information such as addresses, phone numbers, or email addresses are just as true for online sites. Although using Web 2.0 tools is all about communication and collaboration, it is still important to recognize that you may really know very little about the people with whom you are connecting. Using some discretion and common sense when disclosing personal information can help keep you safe and protect you from cybercrimes such as identity theft, stalking, and bullying.

A key rule is that you should never share your password with others. Before you post anything to your network, think about what this information reveals about you. If you wouldn't give this information to a stranger, you shouldn't post it online. Many people use Web 2.0 tools such as blogs and social networks to post their thoughts, write about their activities, or issue group invitations. Predators and stalkers may strike up an online friendship or lurk in the background, reading your contributions over time and developing a good idea of your daily routine from these types of posts. Posting general updates that include few details is a safer way to use these areas. The same concept holds true when posting photos or videos. As a general rule, you should avoid publishing images that easily identify where you live, work, or go to school. Although you have less control over items your friends might post, you should make your wishes known to them. If a friend posts something with which you are uncomfortable, you shouldn't hesitate to ask him or her to remove it from his or her site. In return, you should also respect your friends' privacy and avoid posting personal information about them without their permission. Remember also that the information and images you post online can be copied and reused—either by well-meaning friends or by unscrupulous individuals. Once you've posted something online, it can be difficult, if not impossible, to get it back. The images that seem funny now could be rather embarrassing a few years down the road when you are trying to impress a potential employer or convince a new romantic interest that your wild streak is years behind you.

Sites such as Stay Safe Online (**www.staysafeonline.org**), OnGuard Online (**www.onguardonline.gov**), and Microsoft Safety and Security Center (**www.microsoft.com/security**) provide plenty of advice and information about safeguarding your privacy and using the Internet safely (Figure 1.4).

Figure 1.4 Sites such as Stay Safe Online (**www.staysafeonline.org**) from the National Cyber Security Alliance provide useful information about security topics.

What other types of risks are there?

Unfortunately, Web 2.0 sites are not immune from the dangers that exist elsewhere on the Internet. You should make sure that you are using up-to-date antivirus and anti-spyware software and scan your computer regularly. Just like email, messages and posts on social networks, comments on blogs, and other forms of communication all have the potential to contain viruses, spyware, worms, or links to malicious sites. You should be very careful about opening messages, clicking on hyperlinks, viewing videos, or downloading files from people you don't know. Even if a message appears to come from a friend, it could easily have been spoofed, or your friend's computer might have been infected. You should exercise caution if you receive a message asking you to download a file. Often, these files contain Trojan horses or other types of malware. *Malware*, or malicious software, is designed to damage or disrupt a computer, often leaving it vulnerable to hackers, thereby compromising your computer's security and threatening your privacy. Malware includes viruses, spyware, worms, and Trojan horses. Data breaches such as the one that shut down the PlayStation Network in April 2011 allowed hackers to obtain personal information such as names, addresses, passwords, credit card numbers, and email addresses belonging to members of the PlayStation Network community. Even if you weren't affected, there's a good chance someone you know may have been. It's possible that some of these people may find that their computers have been infected with some type of malware. Infected computers may help spread virus-infected messages, direct users to unsafe websites, or relay personal information to hackers.

What else can I do to protect myself?

In addition to making sure that your computer is protected against viruses and spyware, you should make it a habit to install all the latest security updates released for your computer hardware and software. You should use the same safe computing practices that you use elsewhere on the Internet. Here are some other steps you can take:

- Check to see if the Web 2.0 site you are visiting has a safety or security page that provides information about current threats or viruses, and visit it regularly to stay updated.

Malware Malicious software designed to damage or disrupt a computer, often leaving it vulnerable to hackers; includes viruses, spyware, worms, and Trojan horses.

- Read the site's privacy policy, and be sure you understand it.

- Carefully review your privacy settings to be sure they reflect your preferences.

- Create a strong password that is easy for you to remember but hard for others to guess. Change your password periodically, and don't use the same password for other sensitive areas such as financial sites, email accounts, or your school or work network. To check the strength of your own passwords, or for more tips about creating strong passwords, visit Microsoft's Safety and Security Center (**www.microsoft.com/security/online-privacy/passwords-create.aspx**).

- Upgrade to the latest version of Windows Internet Explorer, currently Internet Explorer 9.0 (IE9), or consider using an alternate browser such as Mozilla Firefox or Google Chrome. Although alternate browsers are not invulnerable, much malware is still designed to work best with Internet Explorer, so using another browser might thwart an attack. However, Microsoft continues to take steps to improve the security of its products and protect its users, and IE9 has received good reviews for some of its new safety features.

Objective 3

Understand copyright law and the possible consequences of copyright violation

Many people think that because it is easy to find an image or a video on the web, they are free to use it for their own purposes. This might include posting someone else's videos or photos on a social networking site or copying blog entries found on other blogs and displaying them on their own blog verbatim. However, the creators or owners of written works and digital media (such as photographs, graphics, and videos) have legal rights. There can be serious consequences to violating these rights.

What legal rights do creators of web content have?

Copyright The legal protection granted to authors of "original works of authorship."

Under U.S. laws, and the laws of many other nations, *copyright* is the legal protection granted to authors of "original works of authorship." In the United States and the European Union, copyrightable works include the following:

- Literary works, including computer software

- Musical works, including any accompanying words

- Dramatic works, including any accompanying music

- Pantomimes and choreographic works

- Pictorial, graphic, and sculptural works

- Motion pictures and other audiovisual works

- Sound recordings

- Architectural works

Current copyright law in the United States grants copyright for the life of the author or creator, plus 70 years for original works. And copyright occurs automatically as soon as a work is created and set down in physical form. For written works, this would include publishing an entry on a blog, wiki, social network, or other website. For images or videos, this occurs as soon as the image is saved to the memory card or hard drive of a camera or computer. So if you have written material that has been posted to a website, you already own copyright to that work and are protected legally from someone stealing your ideas and using them as his or her own.

Copyright laws can be rather complex. The information presented here should be used as a guideline, but for more specific information, the U.S. Copyright Office has a website devoted to copyright issues—**www.copyright.gov** (Figure 1.5). Detailed information about copyright laws and the processes, rules, and responsibilities of copyright issues can be found there.

Figure 1.5 The U.S. Copyright Office's website **www.copyright.gov** is an excellent resource for learning about copyright laws.

If someone owns copyright to a work, what exactly does he or she own?

Copyright holders own a bundle of rights that grant them the ability to exclusively do the following things with the copyrighted work:

- Reproduce the work—This means copying the entire work or just part of the work. Violations of this right might involve burning a copy of a music CD or a video DVD, photocopying a magazine article, copying software DVDs, printing a cartoon character on a T-shirt, or copying an online article and posting it elsewhere.

- Prepare derivative works based upon the original work—This means developing any media based on the original work, regardless of what form the original is in. The X-Men were originally characters in a comic book, but they now appear in movies and video games thanks to licensing agreements. You can't develop a derivative work without the copyright holder's permission, so you cannot develop a blog or wiki dedicated to the X-Men that includes images of the X-Men you have copied from other sources.

- Distribute the work to the public—This means any method of distribution but usually involves selling the work. However, the copyright holder could also loan, rent, or give away the work. Copying a music CD and selling it—or even giving it—to your friend would be a violation of this right. However, if you post a video that you made of your cat on YouTube and allow anyone to access it, you have essentially given away this work to the public for free. You still own the copyright to the video, but you have given up your rights to control who views it.

- Perform the work publicly—Obviously, this applies to any audiovisual work such as plays, movies, songs, choreographic works, and literary readings. You can't put a copy of the latest Harry Potter movie up on YouTube without the permission of the copyright holder, because that would constitute a public performance. If you posted a video of your cat on YouTube that anyone can access, you have essentially given permission for people to publicly exhibit your work by showing it to others through an Internet browser.

- Display the work publicly—This usually applies to works of art such as paintings, photographs, and sculpture. Putting copies of photographs that someone else holds copyright to on your site is a violation of this right.

Under what circumstances can I use copyrighted material on my blog?

Many websites that contain copyrighted material also contain lengthy legal documents that define the *terms of use* (the terms governing your use of material) for the material that you download from the site. It is important for you to find and read the terms of use *before* using any copyrighted material on the site. Failure to read the terms of use does not absolve you from liability for using copyrighted material without permission.

What if a website does not have terms of use?

Locating the terms of use on a particular site can sometimes be tricky. Look for links such as Terms of Use, Restrictions, Copyright, Rules, FAQ, or even Contact Us. Sometimes, the usage terms are not displayed until you attempt to download copyrighted material. If you have done a thorough search and can't find them, then follow the instructions for contacting the organization that maintains the website and ask about the terms of use.

Can you use copyrighted material if it isn't permitted in the terms of use or if there are no terms of use?

Copyright holders can always grant permission to use copyrighted material to an individual or organization. Depending upon the material used and the specific nature of the usage, there may be a fee required to secure the rights to the copyrighted work. Sometimes, though, simply asking permission is enough to obtain the rights to use the work free of charge for a specific purpose, though you should be sure to obtain this permission in writing.

Who do you contact for permission?

Who to contact to obtain permission depends on the nature of the intellectual property. Sometimes it can be difficult to tell who actually owns the copyright—or the particular rights you need—to a piece of media. The creator may not be the copyright holder any longer. He or she may have sold his or her rights to another party. For materials you find online, if the copyright owner is not clearly stated, check out the site's contact information. You might look for the webmaster or an individual involved with press releases or marketing.

What happens if you use copyrighted material without the permission of the copyright holder?

A violation of the copyright holder's rights is known as *copyright infringement*. By infringing copyright, the violator risks a potentially long and costly legal battle. At best, you might receive a slap on the wrist, but the worst-case scenarios can involve large fines and jail time. Additionally, you may find that the material in question has been removed or that your site has been shut down—either temporarily or permanently. Sites such as YouTube and Facebook regularly respond to complaints of copyright violation by taking these steps immediately and then notifying you. They do not have to ask for your permission, and getting your account reinstated can be difficult.

How will you know if someone thinks you have infringed on his or her copyright?

If you used a picture of Mickey Mouse on your website without permission, you might receive a *cease and desist letter* from The Walt Disney Company. A cease and desist letter is a request to immediately stop the alleged copyright infringement. The letter should describe the alleged infringement and require you to reply by a certain date to indicate that the infringement has ceased. If you receive such a letter, you should take it seriously. You should immediately remove the material in question from your website and send written documentation by the due date indicating what you have done to stop the infringement.

What if you don't believe that you have committed copyright infringement?

If you don't think you've done anything wrong, you should seek competent legal advice from an attorney specializing in intellectual property law. Have the attorney assist you in crafting a reply to the cease and desist letter, explaining your side of the story. You may be able to prove that you did not infringe if you have proof that you received permission to use the material. Because the next step taken against you might be formal legal action, the help of an attorney is critical at this stage.

Is posting a URL that points to a copyrighted website on your site considered copyright infringement?

A URL is a specific direction for finding a particular web page on the Internet. It is not debatable or open to interpretation and, therefore, is considered a fact. Because facts cannot be copyrighted, you can list all the textual URLs you want on your website without committing copyright infringement. However, be sure you do not take copyrighted material (such as a logo or character) to use as a picture link to a website (such as using a picture of Mickey Mouse to link to the Disney website), as this may constitute infringement.

Does embedding a video from YouTube on your site constitute copyright infringement?

When you embed video from YouTube on your site, you are actually only creating a link to the video. The video is still stored on YouTube. Therefore, although there has not been a definitive court case on this issue, it appears that you would not be held liable for infringing copyright for embedding video in a blog, wiki, or social network post. However, you would still need to comply with a request from the owner of the copyrighted video to take down the link if he or she alleged that his or her copyright was being infringed.

Contributory infringement A type of infringement in which you do not commit the original copyright infringement, but you link to copyrighted material that you are aware has been infringed upon and your link to the content materially contributes to the infringement.

You should still be careful when embedding video on your site. Even if you aren't the one who committed the original infringement by posting copyrighted material on YouTube, you could still be found guilty of *contributory infringement*. Contributory infringement takes place if

- You know that a video you are linking to is infringing—For example, your friend posted a portion of a *Law and Order* episode to YouTube.

  or

- Any reasonable person would have known that the video is infringing—For instance, when you find a portion of the *Late Show with David Letterman* on YouTube that was not posted by CBS, it is pretty obvious that this is a copyright infringement.

  and

- Your link to the video materially contributes to the infringement—This would probably be the case only with a site that is exceptionally popular (for example, tens of thousands of people see the video through the link on your site).

So linking to a video of the *Late Show with David Letterman* posted by CBS would probably be fine, but linking to a portion of a *Law and Order* episode that your friend posted could be problematic.

So what should I do to avoid copyright infringement?

Following a few simple rules should keep you out of most sticky situations.

- Write your own blog entries—Do not plagiarize the work of others.

- Use your own digital images and video—You know you own copyright to media that you have created. However, if your media includes images of other people or the work of other individuals, make sure that you obtain their written permission before posting the media on your blog.

- Respond quickly to requests to cease infringement—Follow the directions in the letter, and consult an attorney as soon as you are contacted.

Are there alternatives to avoid copyright infringement?

Fair use Permits the use of portions of copyrighted material for the purpose of commentary and criticism.

As mentioned previously, creating and using your own materials is probably the best way to avoid copyright infringement. But there are other options. One of these options is the doctrine of fair use. *Fair use* permits the use of portions of copyrighted material for the purpose of commentary and criticism. There are four factors to be considered when determining whether the proposed usage qualifies as fair use.

- The purpose and character of the work—Will the material be used for commercial or nonprofit educational purposes?

- The nature of the copyrighted work—In general, it is more acceptable to use information from published, factual works (such as biographies) than from fiction or nonpublished work.

- The amount and substance of work used—Reproducing an entire episode of *American Idol* would not be considered fair use.

- The effect upon the value of the copyrighted work—Giving away the twist ending of a movie, thereby discouraging people from going to see it, would not be considered fair use.

  It can be tricky to decide whether the use of copyrighted material falls within fair use guidelines, and sometimes the courts will make the final decision. In general, if you are using a small portion of copyrighted material for a nonprofit purpose, such as a review, a news commentary, or a parody, and this usage will not have an impact on the creator's ability to earn money from his or her work, then your usage may be within the fair use guidelines and you may avoid copyright infringement charges.

What is the public domain?

Public domain The realm containing works that are not protected by intellectual property laws.

It is also possible to avoid copyright issues by using works that fall within the public domain. Works that are not protected by intellectual property laws are considered to be in the *public domain*. These include the following:

- Works for which the copyright has expired or was not renewed

- Works that were never copyrighted

- Works that were deliberately added to the public domain by their creator

- Works for which copyright does not apply, such as facts and figures, and material created by U.S. government employees in their official capacities

How can I share my work but still retain my rights?

Copyleft A licensing scheme that permits the creator of a work to retain the copyright while distributing the work freely to others with restrictions to limit the use of the work.

Some people believe that current copyright laws are too restrictive for the collaborative and sharing environment inherent in most Web 2.0 tools. As a result, a new alternative known as copyleft has developed. *Copyleft* allows the creator to license his or her work to permit others to make use of it at no charge. The creator can include restrictions to limit the use of the work. People who make use of such material must use the same copyleft licensing process for any work resulting from it, which means they cannot use something that was freely shared and convert it to a proprietary product for their own benefit. Using the traditional copyright scenario, a creator must either prohibit all use of a work and grant permission to use it on a case-by-case basis, or submit the work to the public domain and permanently relinquish all rights. With copyleft, the creator still retains copyright to the work, but he or she can make the work freely available to others as long as specified conditions are met.

GNU (**www.gnu.org/licenses/licenses.html**) and Creative Commons (**http://creativecommons.org/licenses**) are two nonprofit organizations that provide copy-left licensing options, although there are others as well. The GNU General Public License (GNU GPL) was one of the first examples of copyleft licensing and is still widely used for software licensing. For most other types of work, the Creative Commons licensing schemes have become quite popular. Creative Commons offers several different levels of licensing and also includes tools and information on its website to help implement these licenses. Currently, Creative Commons offers six different licensing schemes with increasing levels of restrictions. The least restrictive, Attribution—CC BY, permits others to use your work in whatever way they wish, as long as they credit you for the original creation. The most restrictive, Attribution-NonCommercial-NoDerivs—CC BY-NC-ND, permits others to use your work as long as they credit you, but they cannot change the work in any way or distribute it commercially. The Creative Commons licensing structure also permits you to change the level of license for your work. For instance, you might initially use the CC BY license, but later change your mind and decide to use a more restrictive license. Anyone who obtained your work under the CC BY license can continue to use it according to those rules, but anyone who obtains it under the stricter licensing must abide by the new regulations. Sites such as the Public Library of Science advocate open access for all the scientific and medical literature published on the site and therefore use the Creative Commons licensing structure to keep these works freely accessible (Figure 1.6).

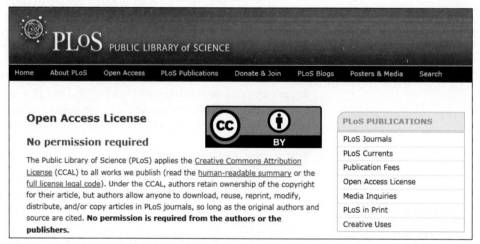

Figure 1.6 The Public Library of Science uses a Creative Commons license for all the works it publishes on its site (**www.plos.org**). This page provides additional details for site visitors.

Objective 4

Web as platform, cloud computing A concept in which users are not tied to a specific application or computing device; rather, users access their information via services available over the Internet.

Create a Google account

From the very beginning, Google has been an important entity in Web 2.0 applications. You may have heard the terms *Web as platform* or *cloud computing*. At their simplest, both of these terms refer to using the World Wide Web for all your computing tasks, rather than being tied to one specific device. Instead of having software installed on your laptop, desktop computer, or mobile device, and being limited to accessing it from that location only, you can store, access, and work with your information via services available over the Internet. Google offers a number of services that allow you to do this. For instance, Google Docs is a suite of web applications used to create and share online documents, spreadsheets, and presentations. Google also owns YouTube (video sharing), Blogger (blog hosting), Picasa (photo sharing and editing), Gmail (email service), and a number of other useful services. Because we will be using several of these services throughout this textbook, it will be helpful to create a Google account.

Hands-On Exercises

For purposes of the Hands-On Exercises, we are assuming that Professor Schmeckendorf, a computer science professor at Ginormous State University (GSU), is setting up a Google account to begin making use of the many services Google offers. This Hands-On Exercise will create an account using Professor Schmeckendorf's information; you will be creating an account for yourself and should add your own information where appropriate.

1 | Set Up a Google Account and Create a Profile

Steps: 1. Start Your Browser and Navigate to Google; **2.** Create a Google Account; **3.** Fill Out Your Google Profile.

Use Figures 1.7 through 1.19 as a guide to the exercise.

Step 1 Start Your Browser and Navigate to Google

Refer to Figures 1.7 and 1.8 as you complete Step 1.

If you already have a Google account, you can skip Steps 1 and 2 and proceed to Step 3. If you would prefer to create a new Google account for these exercises, you should sign out of your current account, if necessary. You will also need to sign up with a different email address than the one you used for your original Google account.

a. Turn on the computer.

b. Start your preferred browser (Internet Explorer, Firefox, Chrome, Safari, etc.). Type **www.google.com** in the address bar of your browser and press **Enter**.

c. Click the **Sign in** link at the top-right corner of the Google homepage.

C – Click the Sign in link

Figure 1.7 Hands-On Exercise 1, Step 1c.

d. On the next page, click the **Create an account now** link. (If you already have a Google account, check with your instructor to see if you should create a new account for this exercise.)

If you wish to use your existing account, uncheck the **Stay signed in** checkbox and sign in using your email address and password, and proceed to Step 3.

If you already have a Google account, uncheck the Stay signed in checkbox and sign in here

D – Click the Create an account now link

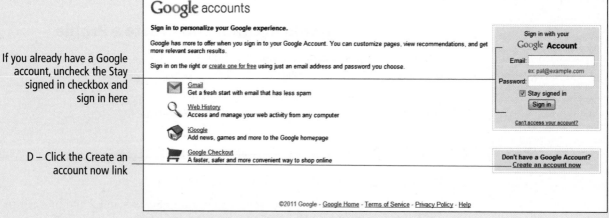

Figure 1.8 Hands-On Exercise 1, Step 1d.

 Step 2 **Create a Google Account**

Refer to Figures 1.9 through 1.12 as you complete Step 2.

a. Type a valid email address where indicated.

You will be required to validate this email address after signing up for a Google account; therefore, the email account needs to already exist before you begin this process.

b. Type a password that is at least eight characters long.

Notice the password strength meter next to the password text box. Creating a password that uses a mixture of uppercase and lowercase letters, combined with numbers or other symbols, and that is at least 8 to 12 characters long, will result in a stronger, more secure password.

c. Type the password again to check for typing errors; both passwords must match exactly.

d. If necessary, uncheck the **Stay signed in** and **Enable Web History** checkboxes. Both of these boxes can create privacy conflicts, especially if you are using a public computer such as those found in your school's computer lab. Checking the **Stay signed in** checkbox allows you to access your Google account without needing to enter your username and password. Google will remember this information for up to two weeks. While this might be convenient for you, it also means that anyone else with access to your computer can easily access your Google account. Checking the **Enable Web History** checkbox allows Google to provide you with more relevant search results and information based upon the sites you have visited in the past. Google stores this information on its servers for up to 180 days. Although some people like this personalization feature, others have concerns about how Google might handle this tracking information and believe it is an intrusion of their privacy.

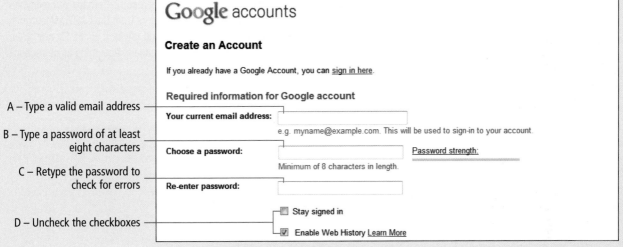

A – Type a valid email address

B – Type a password of at least eight characters

C – Retype the password to check for errors

D – Uncheck the checkboxes

Figure 1.9 Hands-On Exercise 1, Steps 2a through 2d.

e. Uncheck the **Default Homepage** checkbox. Leaving this box checked will change the default homepage for your browser, which means the Google site will be the first page you see when you open your browser. While you may wish to use this page on your computer, many schools prefer to have their own website be the default homepage when the browser is opened.

f. Use the **Location** drop-down arrow to select your country.

g. Type your birthdate in the **Birthday** text box. Some people are reluctant to provide this information due to privacy concerns and may create a false birthdate to prevent hackers from obtaining their true information. Google does not verify your birthdate, but you may be required to provide it if you have forgotten your username or password. If you choose to create a false birthdate, be sure that you will remember it. Also, note that according to Google's Terms of Service, you must be "of legal age to form a binding contract with Google." In most areas, this means you must be at least 18 years of age.

h. Type the distorted letters shown above the **Word Verification** text box. Note that the appearance of the letters on your screen will be different than those shown in Figure 1.10.

The computer program used here is known as a *CAPTCHA* (Completely Automated Public Turing Test to Tell Computers and Humans Apart). A CAPTCHA is a program that helps protect websites by preventing software programs (known as bots) from executing procedures on the sites (in this case, signing up for a Google account). The CAPTCHA program generates a test that humans can pass but automated computer programs will fail. Although it may be somewhat troublesome, humans can usually read the distorted text—shown here in red. However, computer programs cannot read the text and will be unable to enter it accurately. Google does not want automated programs setting up thousands of Google accounts that could then be used for nefarious purposes such as spamming and malware distribution.

i. Review the **Terms of Service** displayed in the text box. You should also click the **Privacy Policy** link to review that as well. The Privacy Policy will open in a new browser tab or browser window. You can close this tab or window after you've reviewed the information.

j. After you've reviewed the Terms of Service and the Privacy Policy, click the **I accept. Create my account.** button to indicate your agreement with these terms.

If you were not taken to the next page, the Google accounts page will redisplay. There will be notes on the page indicating which sections were not completed properly. Perhaps you mistyped your password the second time. Or maybe you didn't type the letters from the CAPTCHA correctly. For security purposes, you will need to re-enter your password and retype it again. Fix any other errors you may have made and then accept the Terms of Service again. Assuming all corrections have been made, you should then be taken to the next page.

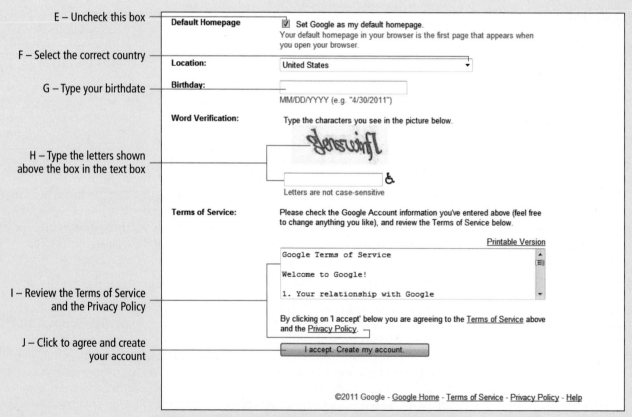

Figure 1.10 Hands-On Exercise 1, Steps 2e through 2j.

k. The next page confirms that your account has been set up. Depending upon the email address you provided, you may be able to verify your account by clicking the link or button on this page. However, in some instances, you may need to verify your Google account by going to your email account and following the instructions in the email Google will send you. Regardless of which verification method you use, Google will still send a message to your email account. This security measure helps to ensure that you are actually the person who has requested the Google account. Figure 1.12 shows the verification email received by Professor Schmeckendorf.

K – Click to verify your
email address

Click here to request a
verification email

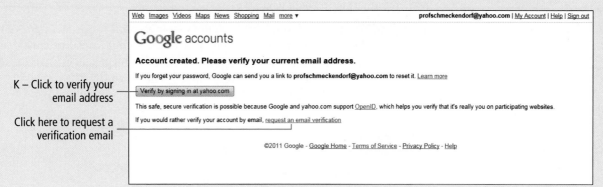

Figure 1.11 Hands-On Exercise 1, Step 2k.

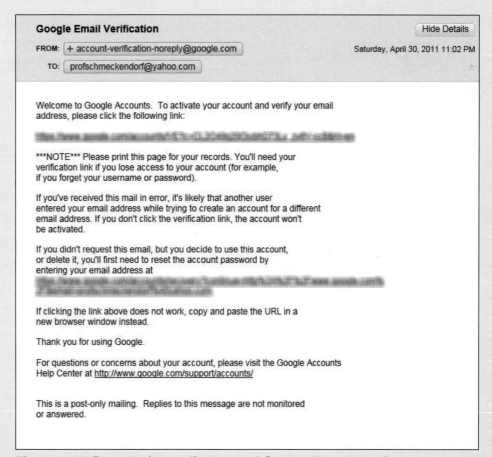

Figure 1.12 Example of the verification email Google will send to confirm your account.

 Step 3 **Fill Out Your Google Profile**

Refer to Figures 1.13 through 1.19 as you complete Step 3.

Your Google profile can be used to provide information about yourself to others and can make it easier for other people to find you. You may want to create a bio, provide your contact information, or include links to other sites. You can choose whether or not to include a public profile. At a minimum, your first name, your last name, and your photo (assuming you submit one) will be included in your public profile. However, you will still be able to decide what other details you want to share publicly. The profile page is also where you can manage security issues, such as changing your password or the email address associated with your Google account, connecting to accounts from other services, and selecting other Google services that you want to use. Since some Google tools require you to have a public profile, you will set up some basic information in these next steps.

a. Depending upon how you verified your Google account in the last step, you may be at the Google homepage, or you may be at the Google accounts email verification page. To access your profile from the Google homepage, click your username at the top of the page and click **Account settings** from the drop-down list. From the email verification page, click the **click here to manage your account profile** link.

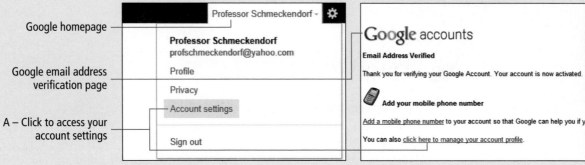

Figure 1.13 Hands-On Exercise 1, Step 3a.

b. Click the **Create a profile** link.

Figure 1.14 Hands-On Exercise 1, Step 3b.

c. The next page may ask you to verify your identity. Google wants to be sure that no one else is trying to sign up for this service using your identity. Select the **Verification Options** to receive a text message or an automated phone call.

d. Select your country from the drop-down list.

e. Type your mobile phone number in the text box. If you don't have a mobile phone or are having trouble with the verification process, click the **contact support** link.

f. Click the **Send verification code to my mobile phone** button to complete the process.

Use this link if you are having a problem verifying your identity

C – Select the desired verification method

D – Select your country

E – Type your mobile phone number

F – Click to complete the process

Figure 1.15 Hands-On Exercise 1, Steps 3c through 3f.

g. On the next page, you will need to enter the verification code sent to you by Google. Type the number in the text box.

h. Click the **Verify** button to proceed.

G – Enter verification code here

H – Click to proceed

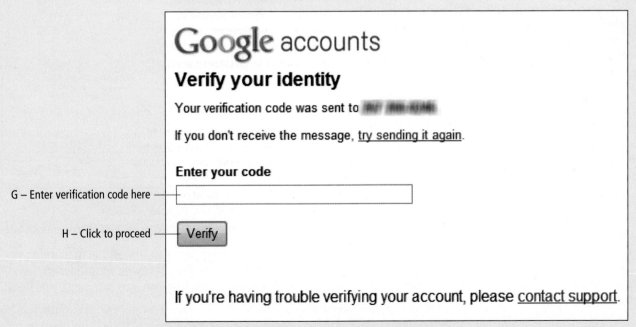

Figure 1.16 Hands-On Exercise 1, Steps 3g and 3h.

i. On the **Create a public profile** page, type your first and last names in the appropriate text boxes.

j. If you wish to add a photo, click the **Add photo** link. A dialog box will open giving you the option to select a photo from a Picasa Web Album or from your computer.

I – Type your name here

J – Click to add a photo

Figure 1.17 Hands-On Exercise 1, Steps 3i and 3j.

k. Click the **Upload from my computer** option and click **Browse** to choose a picture. If you do not have a suitable picture or are reluctant to use a photo of yourself, you can navigate to the **Pictures** library on your computer and select a photo from the **Sample Pictures** folder.

l. Once you've selected a photo, you may be prompted to size the image accordingly and click the **Set as profile** button, or you may just need to click the **Upload** button to add the photo to your profile.

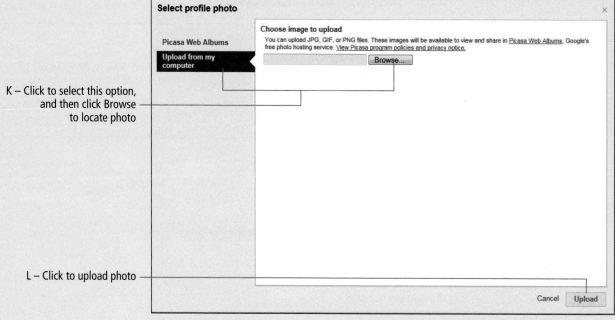

K – Click to select this option, and then click Browse to locate photo

L – Click to upload photo

Figure 1.18 Hands-On Exercise 1, Steps 3k and 3l.

m. On the **Create a public profile** page, click the **Create profile & continue** button.

n. The **Google profiles** page includes a number of areas that you may wish to personalize. Add the information you want to include, keeping in mind that this information will be available to anyone on the Internet.

Professor Schmeckendorf does not want to include a lot of personal information in his profile. He has chosen to add a brief introduction and his place of employment. Notice the **Search visibility** option near the bottom of the list. If you would prefer not to be listed in search results, you can turn this feature off by clicking it and following the instructions that appear. Similarly, the **Delete profile** link can be used to remove your Google profile.

o. When you are done editing your profile, click the **Done editing** button at the top of the page. The resulting page will display the information you have added.

If you wish to change anything, simply click the **Edit profile** button at the top of the page or the **Edit your profile** link to return to the previous screen.

If you are taking a break after this exercise, you should log out of your Google account by clicking your name in the top-right corner and selecting **Sign out** from the drop-down list. You may also want to close your browser window and turn off your computer.

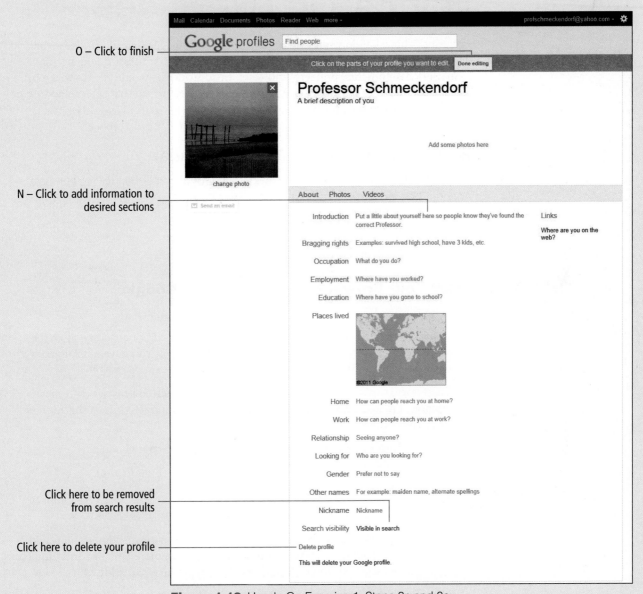

Figure 1.19 Hands-On Exercise 1, Steps 3n and 3o.

Objective 5

Create and share a Google calendar

Now that you have a Google account, it is time to begin using some of Google's tools. One tool that is of particular interest is the Google Calendar. Not only can the calendar be used to keep track of your appointments and activities, it is possible to share the calendar with others. You can make your calendar public or choose to share it only with specified friends, family, or coworkers. You can also choose the level of access someone has to your calendar, so while some people may only be able to view the calendar, others may be able to add, edit, or delete events.

Hands-On Exercises

Professor Schmeckendorf likes the idea of having a calendar that his students can view. He thinks this will be helpful because he will be able to list due dates for homework assignments, projects, and tests. In addition, he would like to make his calendar available to his lab assistant, Hannah Grindeldorf, so that she can add events and update his schedule for him.

2 | Create and Share a Google Calendar

Steps: 1. Start Your Browser and Navigate to Google; **2.** Log In to Your Google Account; **3.** Open and Configure Your Google Calendar; **4.** Add an Event; **5.** Share Your Calendar.

Use Figures 1.20 through 1.31 as a guide to the exercise.

Step 1 Start Your Browser and Navigate to Google

Refer to Figure 1.7 as you complete Step 1.

If you logged out of your Google account and shut your computer down after the previous exercise, follow the directions in Steps 1 and 2. If you have not logged out of your Google account, proceed to Step 3.

a. If necessary, turn on the computer and start your preferred browser (Internet Explorer, Firefox, Chrome, Safari, etc.). Type **www.google.com** in the address bar of your browser and press **Enter**.

b. Click the **Sign in** link at the top-right corner of the Google homepage.

Step 2 Log In to Your Google Account

Refer to Figure 1.20 as you complete Step 2.

a. Google identifies you by the email address you used to create your account. To log in to your Google account, you must use your complete email address and the password you selected. In the **Email** text box, type the email address.

b. In the **Password** text box, type your password.

Be sure the **Stay signed in** checkbox is unchecked, especially if you are using a public computer.

c. Click the **Sign in** button.

If you are having trouble signing in to your account, the **Can't access your account?** link will take you to a page where you can reset your password or retrieve your username.

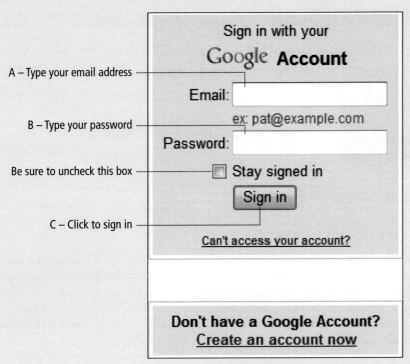

A – Type your email address

B – Type your password

Be sure to uncheck this box

C – Click to sign in

Figure 1.20 Hands-On Exercise 2, Steps 2a through 2c.

Step ③ Open and Configure Your Google Calendar

Refer to Figures 1.21 through 1.24 as you complete Step 3.

a. If you had to sign in to your Google account, you may see the iGoogle page or you may see the Google homepage, as shown in Figure 1.21. From either page, click the **more** link at the top of the page and then click **Calendar** from the drop-down list. Proceed to Step 3c.

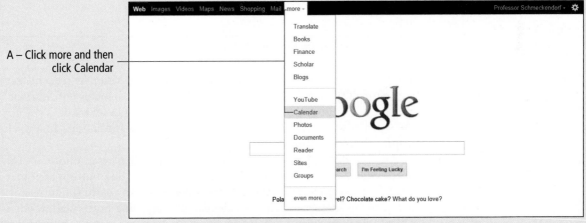

A – Click more and then click Calendar

Figure 1.21 Hands-On Exercise 2, Step 3a.

b. If you did not sign out of Google after the last exercise, you should still be on the Google profiles page, as shown in Figure 1.22. From the list of choices at the top of the page, click **Calendar**.

B – Click to open the calendar

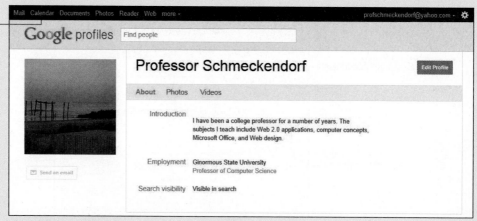

Figure 1.22 Hands-On Exercise 2, Step 3b.

c. If this is your first time using Google Calendar, the **Welcome to Google Calendar** screen appears next, with a section allowing you to add or update some of your personal information. Check to be sure this information is correct and make any desired changes. Be sure that you have the correct time zone displayed for your location so the calendar will display your events correctly and then click the **Continue** button.

Make any necessary changes here

C – Click to continue

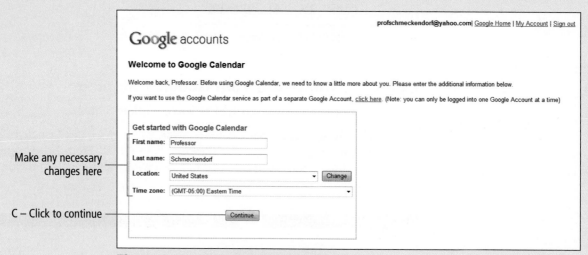

Figure 1.23 Hands-On Exercise 2, Step 3c.

The Google Calendar is now displayed (Figure 1.24). You may see a message bar at the top of the screen. Google occasionally provides alerts or notifications to let you know about problems or changes that you should be aware of. Typically the message bar will include a link for more information and another link to close, dismiss, or hide the message.

The calendar typically opens in Week view and displays a column for each day of the current week. The **Today** button and two scrolling buttons appear at the top left of the calendar. The **Today** button will return you to the current date if you are on another date in the calendar. The scrolling buttons allow you to quickly scroll backward or forward in time to view other dates. Buttons at the top right of the calendar permit you to change the calendar view. You can select **Day**, **Week**, **Month**, 4 **Days**, or **Agenda**. You will probably switch views from time to time, depending upon what type of information you want to see. For instance, to check your daily schedule, the Day view might be your best option; to get an overview of the next few weeks, you might want to select the Month view; to see what's coming up in the next few days, you could select the 4 Days view; and to view a list of your events, select the Agenda view.

On the left side of the calendar, you will see the calendar for the current month, with the **Create** button and the **Quick Add** drop-down button above it. Note that Google

Events Used to identify Google calendar entries, regardless of the duration or frequency of occurrence.

refers to all calendar entries, no matter how long their duration or how often they occur, as *events.* Below this you will see sections for **My calendars** and **Other calendars**. You can create multiple calendars for yourself to organize your life. For instance, you might create one calendar for your school activities, another for personal activities, and a third for work activities. And, you can share calendars with others, which can be helpful for organizing group activities such as a sports team or book club or a group vacation.

You can also make a number of customizations to your Google Calendar, by clicking the gear-like **Options** button at the top right of your screen next to your name and clicking **Calendar settings**. You can select your language, adjust the way Google displays dates and times, set up notification preferences, and so on. At this time, we will use the default settings.

Click to change calendar settings

Go to the current date

Use to scroll through calendar

Manage your calendars

View calendars belonging to others

Click to change the calendar view

Figure 1.24 Features of the Google Calendar.

Step 4 Add an Event

Refer to Figures 1.25 through 1.28 as you complete Step 4.

There are three ways to add an event to the Google Calendar. You can click a location on the calendar itself to display a pop-up window with some details already included (Figure 1.25). Clicking the **Create event** button will add the event to the calendar. Another way to add an event is to click the **Quick Add** drop-down button, next to the **Create** button, on the left side of the screen. A text box appears and you can simply type in your event details (Figure 1.26). You can include what, who, where, and when (i.e., Lunch with Amy at her house Wednesday at noon) and click the **Add** button; Google will add the information accordingly. Although the "who" and "where" are optional, you must include the "what" and "when." The third option, using the **Create** button, will be explored in the next step.

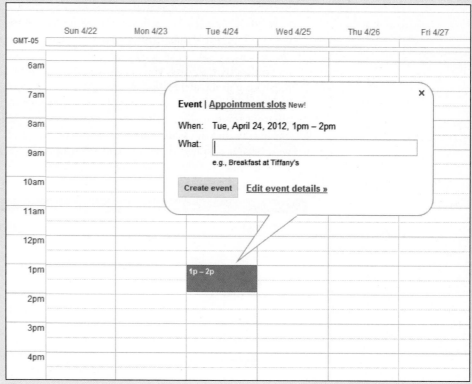

Figure 1.25 You can add an event by clicking the desired date and time on the Google Calendar.

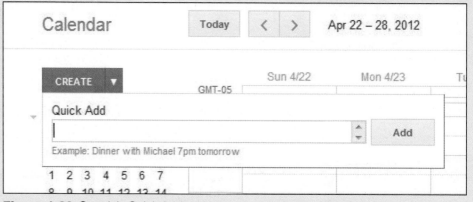

Figure 1.26 Google's Quick Add drop-down button lets you quickly type in your event details.

For this exercise, Professor Schmeckendorf will begin adding events to his primary calendar and will share it with his assistant, Hannah. You will be adding this same information to your own calendar.

a. Click the **Create** button to begin adding an event. A new screen will appear.

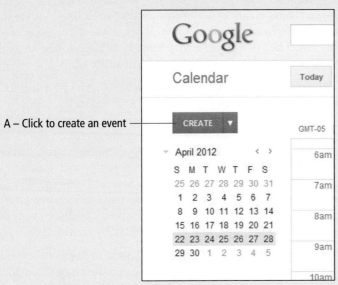

A – Click to create an event

Figure 1.27 Hands-On Exercise 2, Step 4a.

b. The top half of the event screen allows you to add the basic details of your calendar entry—the name of the event, the date, and the time. The bottom half of the screen gives you options for adding additional details. Professor Schmeckendorf wants to add the final exam for his class to his calendar. At the top of the screen, in the **Click to add a title** text box, type **Final Exam – CIS 110**.

c. Notice that the date boxes below the event title box already have a date and time in them. These boxes are used to set up the start and end dates and times for events. This information may coincide with the current date and time, or it may reflect the calendar date you were on before you clicked the **Create** button. If this is the date/time you need, you've already got the basics done. If this information is not correct, it can be revised. Clicking in the date boxes displays a monthly calendar, while clicking in the time boxes reveals a drop-down list of times in half-hour increments. You can select your choices from the calendar and list of times, or you can delete the displayed dates and times and type the correct information. For this calendar entry, add the following information:

- Click in the first **date** box and delete the existing date. Type ~~5/11/2012~~ 9/30/2014 and press **Tab**.

- The time in the first **time** box will already be highlighted. Type **12:30pm** and press **Tab**.

- In the next **time** box, type **2:30pm**. There is no need to adjust the date in the last date box, since Professor Schmeckendorf's final exam will start and end on the same day.

Below the start and end date/time boxes, there are two checkboxes. To identify an event that will last all day, such as a vacation day, birthday, or holiday, you can check the **All day** checkbox. Doing this will remove the time text boxes and the end date text box. For an event that takes place more than once, known as a *recurring event*, such as a class that runs for the semester or a meeting that occurs once a month, check the **Repeat** checkbox. This will open a pop-up window that allows you to indicate how often the event will occur and when the final event will take place. Neither of these checkboxes should be checked for this event.

The second half of the event window, below the two checkboxes, has two tabs: **Event details** and **Find a time**. The **Find a time** tab is useful when you are trying to coordinate schedules with other people, but is not needed right now.

d. On the **Event details** tab, in the **Where** text box, type **Lab 331**.

e. If you have more than one Google Calendar, the Calendar drop-down list is used to select the correct calendar to which to add your event. In this case, you should choose your primary calendar, most likely the one that is currently displayed.

Recurring event An event that takes place more than once.

f. In the **Description** text box, it can be useful to add some brief information about the event. You might want to add directions to a location, the names of people you will be meeting, the URL of a website with more information, and so on. For this event, type **Final exam will cover Chapters 7 through 12**.

Google Calendar can remind you of any events you've added. The **Reminders** section of the **Event details** tab allows you to receive a reminder by email, by pop-up, or by both methods. If you need, or want, multiple reminders, the **Add a reminder** link will give you additional reminder text boxes. If you choose to receive reminders by email, the notice is sent to the email address associated with your Google account. If you choose the pop-up option, a notice will appear on-screen, but you must be logged in to your Google account and have the Calendar open for the message to appear. The email and pop-up reminders are available by default, but it is also possible to have Google send a text message to your cell phone via SMS, if you have configured your calendar settings accordingly.

g. Professor Schmeckendorf would like to receive an email notification to remind him about the exam the day before it is scheduled. He would also like to receive a pop-up notification 30 minutes before the exam begins. As shown in Figure 1.28, Professor Schmeckendorf has an **Email** and **Pop-up** notification displayed. Your page may vary. Use the drop-down boxes to choose the type of notification you wish to receive.

- For the email notification, click the **time** text box, delete the default time interval (10) and type 1 and then click the drop-down arrow and click **days**.

- For the pop-up notification, click the **time** text box, delete the default time interval (10) and type 30. Be sure the time designation is still set for **minutes**.

h. The **Show me as** section is used to identify your availability. The default option is **Busy**, but you can choose to be **Available**. These choices are especially useful when you are sharing your calendar with others. If you have a firm commitment, such as a doctor's appointment, a class, or a job interview, that prevents you from doing something else, you should select the Busy option. However, there are times when you will add events to your calendar that may be more flexible. For instance, you might want to block out time on your calendar to study for your finals, perform household chores, or go food shopping. But, if something more important or interesting comes along, these plans can be changed. For these types of events, you might want to choose the Available option. Because Professor Schmeckendorf will need to be at the exam and cannot be anywhere else at that time, you should click the **Busy** option button.

i. The **Privacy** section has three choices: **Default**, **Public**, and **Private**. The Default option corresponds with the privacy setting of your calendar. If you have set your calendar to private, the event will also be private. Similarly, if your calendar is public, your event will be also. The Public option allows anyone with access to your calendar to see all the details of the event. The Private option allows only you and anyone to whom you have given permission to make changes to your calendar the ability to view the event details. Professor Schmeckendorf wants to ensure that his students can see this event; therefore, you should click the **Public** option button.

The **Add guests** area on the right side of the screen can be used when you create an event, such as a party or meeting, to which you'd like to invite others. Google will send out invitations by email to the people you designate and keep track of their responses and comments. Guests do not have to have access to your calendar and don't even need to have a Google account. Since Professor Schmeckendorf will not be sending out invitations for the final exam, no information needs to be entered in this area.

j. Review the information you've entered and click the **Save** button to add the event to your calendar and return to the main calendar. Since the main calendar displays the current date, you may need to scroll through the calendar to view the event you just added.

J – Click to save event

B – Add event title

C – Add event date(s) and time(s)

D – Add event location

E – Select the calendar for the event

F – Add event description

G – Set reminders

H – Select your availability

I – Set privacy option

Figure 1.28 Hands-On Exercise 2, Steps 4b through 4j.

Step 5 Share Your Calendar

Refer to Figures 1.29 through 1.31 as you complete Step 5.

Google has many different options for sharing your calendar. You can share your calendar with the public or with only those people you specify. You can even share your calendar with people who don't use Google Calendar by giving them your calendar's URL. If you choose to make your calendar public, you can allow people to see the details of your events, or set it to show only whether you are free or busy. Information added to a public calendar may also appear in Google search results. Professor Schmeckendorf has decided that he wants to share his calendar only with his lab assistant, Hannah Grindeldorf, at this time. You should select a classmate with whom to share your calendar. You can add more than one person if you wish. You will need the email address of each person you wish to invite.

a. From the **My calendars** section on the left side of the screen, locate your calendar and click the drop-down arrow.

   Notice that the resulting menu offers a number of options for working with your calendar, such as choosing which calendar to display, adjusting your calendar settings, creating events, and working with notifications. The color palette at the bottom of the menu can be used to change the color of the events displayed on your calendar or events displayed on a shared calendar.

b. Click **Share this Calendar** to open the **Details** window.

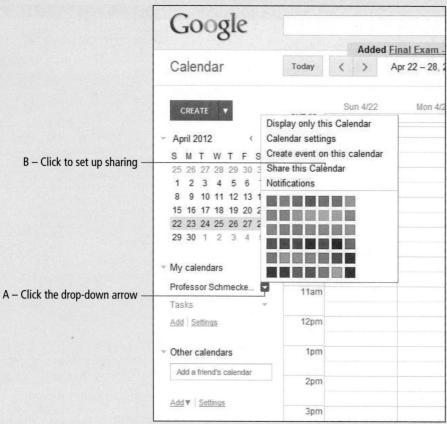

B – Click to set up sharing

A – Click the drop-down arrow

Figure 1.29 Hands-On Exercise 2, Steps 5a and 5b.

c. The **Details** window has three tabs, **Calendar Details**, **Share this Calendar**, and **Notifications**, each of which can be used to customize your calendar. The **Share this Calendar** tab should be active.

d. In the **Share with specific people** section, notice that your email address and permission level is already listed. In the **Person** text box, type the email address of the classmate with whom you will share your calendar.

e. Click the **Permission Settings** drop-down arrow to choose a permission level. Google has four permission levels available. Following is a description of the permission levels, listed from least restrictive to most restrictive:

- Make changes AND manage sharing—This is the highest permission level and is automatically given to the owner of a calendar. If you assign this permission to someone, he or she will be able to view your calendar; add, change, or delete events; and share your calendar with others. You should assign this level of permission only to someone you trust.

- Make changes to events—Assign this level to allow someone to view your calendar and add, change, or delete events.

- See all event details—This permission level allows someone to view the events on your calendar, but does not permit this person to make any changes to the events.

- See only free/busy (hide details)—This is the most restrictive permission level. At this level, people can see only if you have available time (free) on your calendar or if you have blocked out time (busy). They will not be able to see any of your event details. The exception would be if you have changed the privacy level for an individual event when you were setting it up.

Choose the permission level you wish to use. Professor Schmeckendorf wants Hannah to be able to add events to his calendar, so he assigns her the **Make changes to events** level.

f. Click the **Add Person** button to share your calendar. A new line for this person appears below your email address and permission level. It is possible for you to modify this person's permission level if you change your mind. You can also remove someone from your calendar by clicking the trash can icon at the right of the line.

g. Click the **Save** button to save your changes.

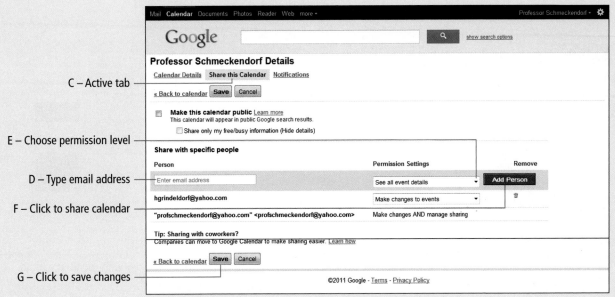

C – Active tab

E – Choose permission level

D – Type email address

F – Click to share calendar

G – Click to save changes

Figure 1.30 Hands-On Exercise 2, Steps 5c through 5g.

Alert!

If you receive a message indicating that the person you've invited does not have a Google Calendar, click the **Invite** button. An invitation to join Google Calendar will be sent.

You may also receive an email inviting you to share someone's calendar. Click the link in the email and follow the instructions. Figure 1.31 shows how Hannah's calendar looks once she has accepted Professor Schmeckendorf's invitation. Shared calendars appear in the **Other calendars** section. Notice that events are color-coded depending upon whose calendar they are from. In this case, Hannah has added a reminder to make copies of the exam on her calendar, which appears in blue. The final exam event that was previously added to Professor Schmeckendorf's calendar appears in red.

Shared calendars appear here

Events are color-coded to identify the calendar to which they belong

Figure 1.31 A Google Calendar showing a shared calendar with multiple events.

Objective 6

Explain web feeds and use an aggregator

One of the biggest benefits of Web 2.0 is the amount of new content that is generated on an ongoing basis. But, this is also one of its biggest drawbacks. With so much information, people can easily become overwhelmed. How do you keep up with all this constantly changing information? One way to do this is through the use of web feeds. A *web feed* is a specialized type of web page written in XML code, enabling it to be updated whenever the website's content is updated. Unlike regular HTML code, which is the coding language most web pages are written in, a web feed page needs to be read by an aggregator, also known as a feed reader. An *aggregator*, or *feed reader*, is a type of software that is specially designed to go out and check the Internet for new content from sites that use web feeds and to which you have subscribed, such as websites, blogs, podcasts, and wikis. Aggregators gather this information in one central location for your viewing convenience. Aggregator software can be installed on your computer, or it can reside on the web. Examples of installed aggregators include iTunes, FeedDemon, and Xnews, while Google Reader, Bloglines, and Netvibes are examples of web-based aggregators.

When you subscribe to a site using your aggregator, the software checks the web feed to see if any new content is available whenever you launch (or log in to) your aggregator software. Once you have an aggregator set up to check web feeds, you are relieved of the tedium of checking numerous favorites or bookmarks in your browser to determine if a site has been updated with new content.

Really Simple Syndication (RSS) is a popular type of web feed used to syndicate content on the Internet. Feed pages look like abbreviated text versions of the original site and usually contain a portion of the site's most recent entries or articles (Figure 1.32). Some browsers, including IE9 and Firefox 4.0, support RSS and web feed technology and may include an icon or other feature to make it easier to subscribe to a site's web feed.

Web feed A specialized type of web page written in XML code, enabling it to be updated whenever the website's content is updated.

Aggregator, feed reader Software designed to check the Internet for new content from sites that use web feeds and to which you have subscribed, and to gather the information in one central location for subsequent viewing.

Really Simple Syndication (RSS) A popular type of web feed used to syndicate content on the Internet.

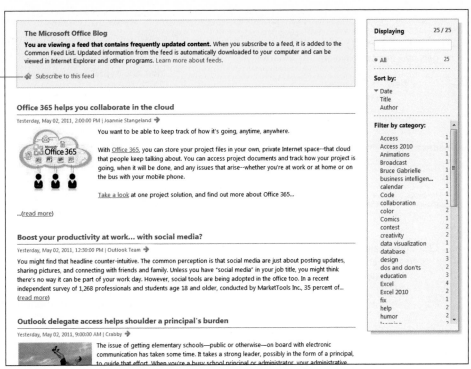

Clicking here allows you to subscribe to this blog in an aggregator

Figure 1.32 An excerpt of the web feed from the Microsoft Office blog.

Sites that make use of RSS or web feeds may indicate this by using a symbol or link. Unfortunately, not every site is consistent in the way this is handled. Figure 1.33 shows several frequently used icons, but some sites may use different icons or may simply use a textual hyperlink such as "Subscribe."

Figure 1.33 A site might indicate the presence of a web feed using one of these symbols.

Since you already have a Google account, we'll use the Google Reader aggregator to start tracking some sites that might be of interest to you. Google Reader, shown in Figure 1.34, is a free tool that provides you with an easy way to manage your subscriptions to websites, blogs, podcasts, wikis, and other sites as well. By clicking on the title of the site shown in the pane on the left side of the reader, the newest entries are displayed in the large window on the right. You can choose to see all entries or only new entries. Depending on the way the web feed has been set up, you may see only the title of the article, the title and a brief blurb from the article, or the entire article. After viewing these articles in the Reader window, they will be marked as read and will no longer be displayed in Google Reader. You can easily mark an article as "Unread" if you want it to remain in the reader for future viewing. You can also share an interesting article with a friend or colleague by emailing the link from within Reader. To read the complete article, simply click on the headline to be transferred to the actual website where the content is located. In the following Hands-On Exercise, you'll learn how to access Google Reader and subscribe to a blog.

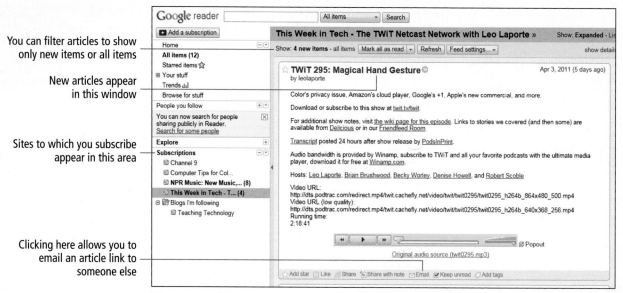

You can filter articles to show only new items or all items

New articles appear in this window

Sites to which you subscribe appear in this area

Clicking here allows you to email an article link to someone else

Figure 1.34 Google Reader is a useful tool for managing your web feed subscriptions.

Hands-On Exercises

3 | Set Up Google Reader and Add Content

Steps: 1. Open Google Reader; **2.** Subscribe to a Website in Google Reader; **3.** Subscribe to a Website Using an Alternate Method.

Use Figures 1.35 through 1.43 as a guide to the exercise.

 Step 1 **Open Google Reader**

Refer to Figures 1.35 and 1.36 as you complete Step 1.

If you logged out of your Google account and shut your computer down after the previous exercise, follow the directions in Hands-On Exercise 2, Steps 1 and 2, before beginning here. If you are still viewing your Google Calendar from the previous exercise, go to the Google homepage by clicking the **Web** link at the top of the page.

a. From the Google homepage, click the **more** link at the top of the page and then click **Reader** from the drop-down list.

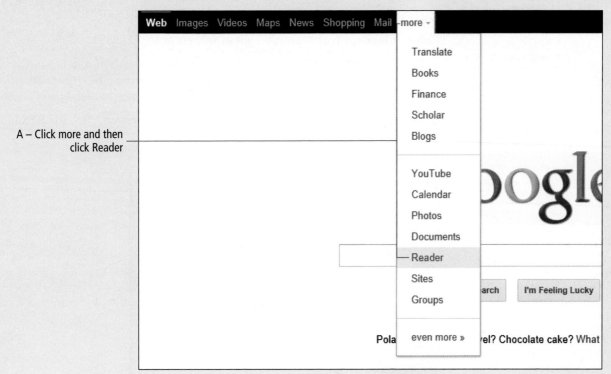

A – Click more and then click Reader

Figure 1.35 Hands-On Exercise 3, Step 1a.

If you have never used Google Reader on this Google account before, your reader should look like the one in Figure 1.36. The content in the window on the right acts as a tour to take you through some of the most common Reader features. As you scroll down, you will also see an entry containing a link for a video tutorial and another entry explaining the various buttons you'll see on the screen. You should take a few moments to review this information before proceeding to the next step.

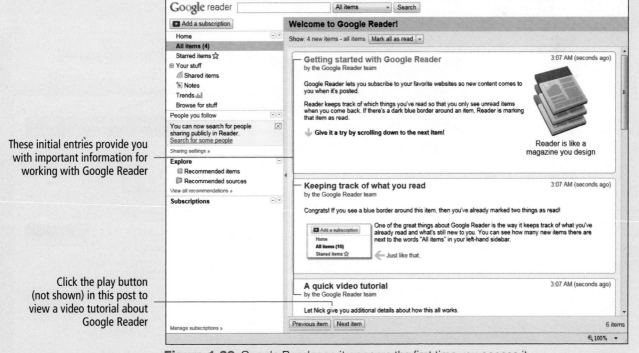

These initial entries provide you with important information for working with Google Reader

Click the play button (not shown) in this post to view a video tutorial about Google Reader

Figure 1.36 Google Reader as it appears the first time you access it.

Step 2 Subscribe to a Website in Google Reader

Refer to Figures 1.37 through 1.40 as you complete Step 2.

a. Leave Google Reader open in your browser. Open a new tab in your browser, or open a new browser window. Type **http://technologyinstruction.blogspot.com** in the address bar of your browser to go to the *Teaching Technology* blog and press **Enter**.

b. On the right side of the blog, below the **Subscribe** section, click the **RSS icon** next to **Posts** to display a list of feed reader choices.

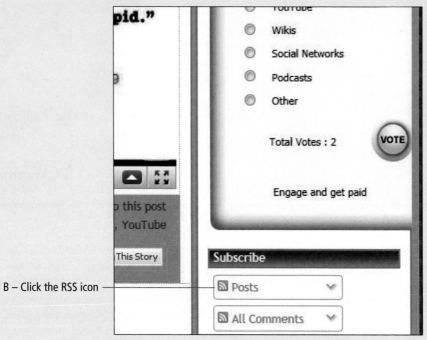

B – Click the RSS icon

Figure 1.37 Hands-On Exercise 3, Step 2b.

c. Click the **Add to Google** link.

C – Click to select a feed reader

Figure 1.38 Hands-On Exercise 3, Step 2c.

d. A new page displays giving you the option to add this blog to your Google homepage or to Google Reader. Click the **Add to Google Reader** button. If you are asked to log in to your Google account on the next page, add the required information and click **Sign in** to continue.

D – Click to add to Google Reader

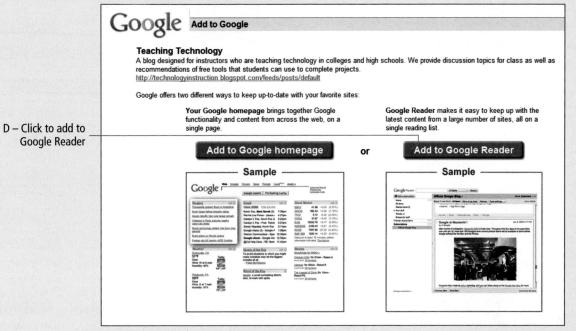

Figure 1.39 Hands-On Exercise 3, Step 2d.

Google Reader should now display with the entries from the *Teaching Technology* blog appearing in the main window, as shown in Figure 1.40. The blog title is listed in the Subscriptions section on the left side of the screen. Review the posts you are interested in and then click the **Mark all as read** button. This indicates to Google Reader that you no longer consider these posts to be new. They will not appear the next time you click the blog's title, unless you click the **all items** link at the top of the window. Similarly, if you wish to see only articles that you haven't read, click the **new items** link. This makes it very easy to review only the newest entries from the site to which you've subscribed and can save you from spending time looking at previous entries. Below each entry is a bar containing tools you can use to help customize your Reader experience. These include the following:

- Add star—Starring an entry is similar to flagging it. Doing so can let you easily find the entry at a later time by clicking the **Starred items** link on the left side of the screen.

- Like—Click this to send a notification back to the author of the entry to let him or her know you liked this article.

- Share—You can create a public page, viewable by anyone, with links to items by clicking this link. Each item you share will appear on the public page.

- Share with note—This option allows you to add your own comments about the item that you are sharing.

- Email—Use this option to share an item privately.

- Keep unread—Check this box to mark an individual item as unread and keep it available for future reading. Note, if you click the **Mark all as read** option at the top of the window, this option will go away and cannot be restored.

- Add tags—Add your own tags to help locate articles on specific subjects.

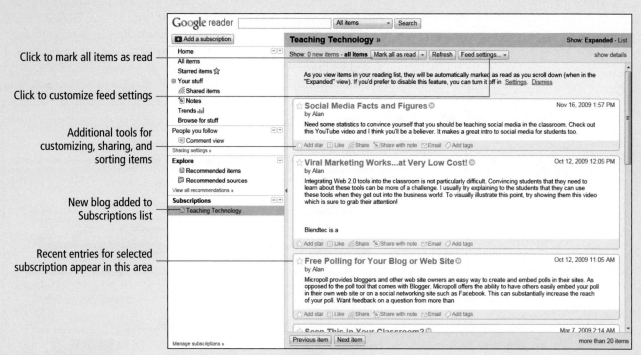

Click to mark all items as read

Click to customize feed settings

Additional tools for customizing, sharing, and sorting items

New blog added to Subscriptions list

Recent entries for selected subscription appear in this area

Figure 1.40 Features of Google Reader.

Step 3 Subscribe to a Website Using an Alternate Method

Refer to Figures 1.41 through 1.43 as you complete Step 3.

Some websites and browsers handle RSS feeds differently than others. If you are using IE9 as your browser when you attempt to subscribe to a web feed, you might find that the only available subscription option is to use the browser's feed reader feature. Fortunately, there is another way to add a subscription to Google Reader.

a. Leave Google Reader open in your browser. Open a new tab in your browser, or open a new browser window, and type **http://windowsteamblog.com/ windows/b/bloggingwindows/** in the address bar. Press **Enter** to go to Microsoft's Blogging Windows blog.

b. Locate the Syndication heading on the right side of the page. Click the **RSS for Posts** icon to subscribe.

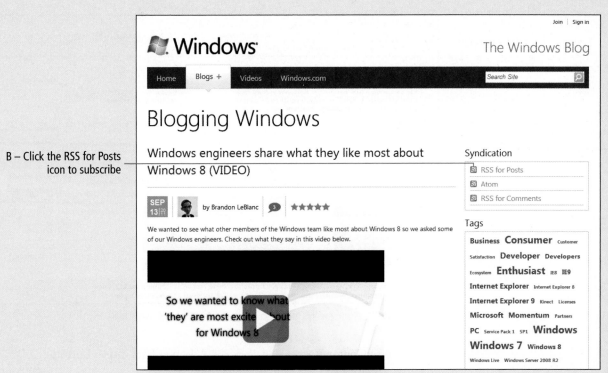

B – Click the RSS for Posts icon to subscribe

Figure 1.41 Hands-On Exercise 3, Step 3b.

c. The web feed page appears with a brief synopsis of current articles. Click the **Subscribe to this feed** link and the dialog box shown in Figure 1.42 displays.

d. The IE9 dialog box is useful if you want to subscribe to a site's web feed and add it to IE9's Favorites Center. However, it doesn't provide an option to subscribe using Google Reader, or any other aggregators. Click **Cancel** to dismiss this dialog box.

e. You can add a subscription directly to Google Reader if you have the URL for the feed page. Often, clicking the RSS icon will take you to this page. The URL for a feed page will typically include "rss," "xml," or "feed" as part of the format. The complete URL for Microsoft's Blogging Windows web feed page is **http://windowsteamblog.com/windows/b/bloggingwindows/rss. aspx,** and includes "rss" in the URL. Select the URL in the address bar, right-click, and select **Copy.**

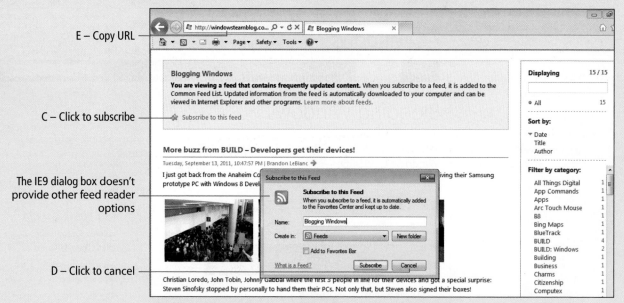

E – Copy URL

C – Click to subscribe

The IE9 dialog box doesn't provide other feed reader options

D – Click to cancel

Figure 1.42 Hands-On Exercise 3, Steps 3c through 3e.

f. Return to Google Reader and click the **Add a subscription** button.

g. Paste the URL from the Blogging Windows page into the resulting text box and click **Add**. The Blogging Windows subscription should now appear in the **Subscriptions** section, and you should see the most recent entries in the main window.

Once you've reviewed this new addition, you can log out of Google Reader and close your browser.

F – Click to add a subscription

G – Paste web feed URL and click Add

Figure 1.43 Hands-On Exercise 3, Steps 3f and 3g.

Objective 7

Explore Web 2.0 resources

Because of the ever-changing nature of Web 2.0 tools and services, it is important to stay in touch with new developments. Here are some resources to help you keep up-to-date:

- **Mashable (http://mashable.com)**—This is one of the premier sites for news about social media and Web 2.0 tools and services. With everything from resources and guides to trends analysis and site reviews, this is one site you'll want to add to your Google Reader.

- **ReadWriteWeb (www.readwriteweb.com)**—This technology blog offers a wide array of information about all things Web 2.0. Topics include posts about mobile devices, business, enterprise applications, venture capital, and start-up organizations.

- **O'Reilly Radar—Web 2.0 Coverage and Insight (http://radar.oreilly.com/web2)**—Billed as a site featuring "insight, analysis, and research about emerging technologies," and backed by Tim O'Reilly, a long-standing leader in the Web 2.0 community, this site features posts from a variety of authors on Web 2.0 technologies.

- **Google Calendar Help (www.google.com/support/calendar)**—Visit the Google Help Center to learn about other features available for your calendar.

- **Google Reader Help (www.google.com/support/reader)**—Explore the Google Help Center and see what else you can do with Reader.

Summary

You have now learned some of the basic concepts of Web 2.0 tools, including those of collaboration and interactivity. You should also be aware of the importance of maintaining your privacy and know how to take appropriate measures to ensure your own security and that of your computer. While much of Web 2.0 is about sharing, you also learned the basics of copyright law, the consequences of violating copyright, and other licensing alternatives to copyright. In order to begin using Web 2.0 tools, you created a Google account, set up and shared a Google Calendar, and explored the benefits of using the Google Reader aggregator to make it easier to track all the constantly updated information.

Key Terms

Multiple Choice Questions

1. If the popular political blog Huffington Post embedded a video clip in one of its posts from a new political thriller that had not yet been released in theaters, this would be an example of

    (a) contextual copyright.

    (b) public domain encroachment.

    (c) copyleft licensing.

    (d) contributory infringement.

2. The program used to create the distorted letters used by some sites to ensure that a person, rather than a software program, is signing up for the site's service is known as a(n)

    (a) Automated Interface Device.

    (b) CAPTCHA.

    (c) RSS.

    (d) Human Recognition Service.

3. What type of software would you use to check the Internet for new content from the sites to which you have subscribed?

   (a) Web sniffer

   (b) Locator program

   (c) Feed reader

   (d) XML finder

4. Which of the following terms refers to the practice of using the web for all your computing tasks?

   (a) Sky writing

   (b) Web as initiator

   (c) Cloud computing

   (d) Venture computing

5. When does a copyrighted work enter the public domain?

   (a) A copyrighted work is not eligible to be in the public domain.

   (b) Immediately upon creation

   (c) When the copyright expires

   (d) Ten years after its creation date

6. The legal documents found on websites that help explain how to handle copy-righted materials are known as

   (a) creative policies.

   (b) terms of use.

   (c) security notices.

   (d) liability exemptions.

7. An appointment that appears multiple times on a calendar is known as a(n)

   (a) repetitive object.

   (b) enduring appointment.

   (c) special event.

   (d) recurring event.

8. Collectively, programs such as viruses, spyware, and worms are known as

   (a) malware.

   (b) nuisance software.

   (c) invasive software.

   (d) intruders.

9. Which of the following is not an example of a copyleft licensing scheme?

   (a) Attribution—CC BY

   (b) Fair use

   (c) Attribution-NonCommercial-NoDerivs—CC BY-NC-ND

   (d) GNU GPL

10. Companies that do most or all of their business on the Internet are known as

    (a) venture capitalists.

    (b) dot-coms.

    (c) virtual enterprises.

    (d) cyber-coms.

Fill in the Blank

1. Under current U.S. law, _____ is assigned to a work as soon as it is created and set down in physical form.

2. The term _____ is used to describe the changes that have taken place on the Internet since 2004.

3. An aggregator checks a website's _____ to see if there is any new content available.

4. _____ is a licensing scheme that permits the creator of a work to retain his or her rights while distributing the work freely to others.

5. To avoid _____ you should check a website's terms of service before using any material you find there.

Practice Exercises

1. **Working with Your Google Profile**

   In this chapter, you created a Google account and added some basic information to your Google profile. In this exercise, we will return to the profile and add some additional details.

   (a) Open a web browser.

   (b) Navigate to the Google site and sign in to your Google account.

   (c) Click the **Settings** link at the top of the page and select **Google Account settings** from the drop-down list.

   (d) Click the **Edit profile** link on the left side of the page.

   (e) If you worked through Hands-On Exercise 1, you should have already added a photo to your profile. You may have also added information in the **Introduction** and the **Employment** sections. If you have not already done so, you should do this now.

   (f) Add the following information to your profile:

   Occupation: *Student*

   Looking for: Check the Networking option

   Nickname: Add your nickname or create one for yourself

   You may add other details, if you wish, but only include information that you feel comfortable making publicly available.

   (g) Print out this web page and turn it in to your instructor.

   (h) If you are uncomfortable with any of the information you just added to your profile, go back and delete it now. Once you are happy with your profile information, click **Done editing**.

   (i) If you are continuing on to the next exercise, do so now. If not, remember to sign out of your Google account and, if necessary, close your browser.

2. **Creating a Recurring Event on Your Google Calendar**

   The more information you add to your Google Calendar about your day-to-day activities, the more useful this calendar will be—both for you and for anyone you decide to share it with. Adding details such as the classes you are taking will help you to better organize your activities.

   (a) Open a web browser.

   (b) Navigate to the Google site and sign in to your Google account.

   (c) Open Google Calendar.

(d) Click the **Create** button and begin to add the information for your next class meeting. (For example, your class details might be: *Thursday, January 19, 2012, 9:05am–11:00am*.)

(e) Check the **Repeat** checkbox.

(f) A pop-up window displays allowing you to select the appropriate details for your recurring event. From the **Repeats** drop-down list, choose the appropriate class meeting pattern. The remaining choices in the pop-up window will vary depending upon the meeting pattern you choose. If your class meets once a week, you will have the option to designate which day of the week the class meets and then select the start and end dates for the class. If your class meets two or three times a week, you won't need to pick a day for the class, but you will need to specify the start and end dates. No matter what your class meeting pattern may be, in the **Starts on** date box, add the first class meeting date for the semester. Note that if you already added your start date in Step d, this date will already appear in the date box and does not need to be entered again. The **Ends** section has three option buttons. The **Never** choice will add this recurring event to your calendar without an end date. The **After ___ occurrences** option lets you add the exact number of times an event will happen. The **On ___** option allows you to set an end date. You should use this option to add the date for the last time your class will meet this semester. Notice that the **Summary** at the bottom of the pop-up window provides you with an overview of the recurring event. Click **Done** to return to the main event window.

(g) Add the remainder of the event details, including the location of your class. Set up reminders and adjust your availability and privacy options. Print out this page and then click **Save** to add this event to your calendar. Give the page with your event information to your instructor.

(h) If you are continuing on to the next exercise, do so now. If not, remember to sign out of your Google account and, if necessary, close your browser.

3. **Adding Other Calendars to Google Calendar**

   In this chapter, you shared your calendar with a classmate. You can also ask other people to share their calendars with you and add other types of calendars as well.

   (a) Open a web browser.

   (b) Navigate to the Google site and sign in to your Google account.

   (c) Open Google Calendar.

   (d) In the **Other calendars** section, click the **Add** button. From the drop-down menu, click **Add a friend's calendar**.

   (e) In the resulting pop-up window, type the email address of one of your classmates. Alternately, your instructor may want you to send this email to him or her. Check with your instructor to determine his or her preferences. If you are emailing a classmate, it should not be the same person with whom you shared your calendar previously. Click **Add**. The pop-up window expands to show the sample text of your request. You can modify the default text if you wish. Depending upon your friend's email address and whether or not he or she already has a Google calendar, the message and action button you see may vary slightly. Click whichever button is displayed: **Send Request** or **Send Invite**.

   (f) Your friend (or instructor) will have to accept your request. You will not have access to his or her calendar until this happens. Additionally, this person will also be able to choose your permission level for his or her calendar. You may be given full rights or only the ability to see if he or she is free or busy, or some level in between.

   (g) If your classmate has accepted your request, you will receive an email to notify you. Print out this email, and hand it in to your instructor to confirm that you completed this portion of the exercise (or forward the email to your instructor, depending upon his or her preferences). Your classmate's calendar will be automatically added, but in order to see it, you will need to log out of Google Calendar and then log in again.

(h) Next, you will explore some of the other calendars Google provides. In the **Other calendars** section, click the **Add** button. From the drop-down menu, click **Browse Interesting Calendars**.

(i) A new window will open, displaying a lengthy list of calendars that you can choose to include in your calendar. You can select a calendar displaying holidays in various countries, select the schedule for your favorite sports team (or teams), or investigate other calendars. When you find one you like, click the **Subscribe** link to add it to your calendar.

(j) When you are done selecting calendars, click the **Back to calendar** link to return to your calendar. You'll see the calendars you've added listed in the **Other calendars** section, and any events will appear on your calendar in the color associated with each new calendar.

(k) Print out the main window of your calendar, with the newly added calendars displayed, and turn this in to your instructor.

(l) If you are continuing on to the next exercise, do so now. If not, remember to sign out of your Google account and, if necessary, close your browser.

4. **Tagging, Starring, and Sharing Items in Google Reader**

In this chapter, you set up Google Reader and began adding content to it. In this exercise, you'll explore some of the other things you can do with Reader.

(a) Open a web browser.

(b) Navigate to the Google site and sign in to your Google account.

(c) Open Google Reader.

(d) In the pane on the left side, under **Subscriptions**, click the **Blogging Windows** subscription. The newest articles will appear in the main window.

(e) From the Google Reader window, review the first item in the list. Recall that below each article are a series of links that allow you to organize and share articles. Click the **Add star** link to star this article. Notice that the star turns yellow and the link changes to **Remove star**, so you can easily un-star an item if you wish. The star feature can be used to identify favorite articles or simply to identify an article that you want to read when you have more time.

(f) Next, click the **Add tags** link. This gives you the ability to add descriptive keywords to an article. What is the main topic of this article? Does it involve a specific company (or companies) or country? Is it about a product or type of technology? As you begin to develop a tagging scheme, you should try to remain consistent. For instance, decide whether you want a tag to be "computer" or "computers" and try not to use both terms. Add the tags that apply to this article, and separate each tag with a comma. Once you're done, click **Save**.

(g) Notice that the tags you selected now appear at the bottom of the article. They are also listed in the **Subscriptions** section, below the list of sites you've subscribed to. Go through your articles, and tag several more to see how this list changes. Add a star where appropriate as well.

(h) Now that you've marked some of your content, let's take a look at how you can use these markers. First, in the pane on the left, click the **Starred items** link. Notice that the content in the main window changes—only the articles that you have starred appear here now. Take a screenshot of this window (press **PrtSc**, open a Word document, and press **Ctrl+V**) to print it out, and submit it to your instructor.

(i) At the bottom of the **Subscriptions** section, you'll see a list of the tags you've created. Click one of the tags, and all the articles that have that tag will appear in the main Reader window. Again, take a screenshot of the window, print it out, and submit it to your instructor.

(j) Next, select one of the articles in Google Reader, and click the **Email** link below the article. An email form displays, using the email address you use to log in to your Google account. Add your instructor's email address, and add a note that includes the following information:

- Your name
- Your class (course number and section)
- Chapter 1, Practice Exercise 4
- A brief synopsis of the article

(k) Check the **Send me a copy of this email** checkbox, so you will also have a copy of the information and then click **Send**. Remember to submit your screenshots of your tagged articles and starred articles to your instructor as well.

Critical Thinking

1. Based upon what you learned in this chapter, what changes do you think Web 2.0 has brought to the world? In what ways has it affected you? Can you think of a situation in which a Web 2.0 tool or service has had a significant impact on you? Write a brief paper describing your thoughts about Web 2.0 and the significance it has had in your life, and submit it to your instructor.

2. As the use of Web 2.0 tools and services becomes more widespread, concerns about privacy and security become legitimate concerns for everyone. How concerned are you about your privacy? Do you take measures to protect your information? If you were showing someone how to use Web 2.0 tools for the first time, what advice would you give? Create a short presentation to explain privacy and security issues to someone who is just beginning to use Web 2.0 tools.

Team Projects

1. As discussed in this chapter, copyright is an important topic. Copyright rules can be confusing, and it can be difficult to determine whether the usage of copyrighted materials has been handled correctly. The concept of copyleft, in which creators retain the right to their work but are still able to freely share it with others, is especially attractive to people using Web 2.0 tools. As a group, research the various licensing options available under copyleft. Create a table listing the various licenses and their purposes. Are some licenses better for some scenarios than others? Be sure to include columns listing the pros and cons for each type of license.

2. Web 2.0 is all about user-generated and user-created content. This is a concern to many people working in traditional media fields, especially in journalism. As a team, research the impact of Web 2.0 tools on journalism. Prepare a presentation that examines five recent, newsworthy events. How was the news first transmitted—via Web 2.0 tools or traditional news organizations? Who got it right? Who got it wrong? How quickly did the information appear? Are traditional journalism tools more reliable than Web 2.0 tools? Why or why not? In your presentation, pick a side—either traditional journalism or Web 2.0 and make a case that supports your opinion.

Credits

Figure 1.1, Courtesy of Web 2.0 Summit.
Figure 1.3, Courtesy of www.threadless.com.
Figure 1.4, Courtesy of The National Cyber Security Alliance.
Figure 1.6, Courtesy of the Public Library of Science.
Figures 1.7–1.11, 1.35–1.36, 1.40 and 1.43, Courtesy of Google.
Figures 1.33a–1.33c, Courtesy of the Wikimedia Foundation.
Figures 1.37–1.38, Courtesy of Diane Coyle.
Figures 1.41–1.42, Courtesy of Brandon LeBlanc.

CHAPTER 2

Social Networks

Objectives

After you read this chapter, you will be able to:

1. Explain what a social network is, what social networks are used for, and the typical features of social networks

2. Describe the advantages and disadvantages of social networks

3. Set up a LinkedIn account and create your profile

4. Add a connection to your LinkedIn network

5. Modify your LinkedIn account settings

6. Investigate other types of social networks

7. Explore social networking resources

The following Hands-On Exercises will help you accomplish the chapter objectives:

Hands-On Exercises

EXERCISES	SKILLS COVERED
1. Set Up a LinkedIn Account and Create a Profile (page 58)	**Step 1:** Start Your Browser, Navigate to LinkedIn, and Create Your Account **Step 2:** Create Your LinkedIn Profile **Step 3:** Change Contact Settings and Add a Position to Your LinkedIn Profile
2. Add a Connection to Your LinkedIn Network (page 70)	**Step 1:** Review the Add Connections Page **Step 2:** Add a Connection **Step 3:** Create and Apply Tags and View a Connection
3. Modify LinkedIn Account Settings and Get Help (page 76)	**Step 1:** Share an Update **Step 2:** Edit Your Settings and Save Your Changes **Step 3:** Access Help

Objective 1

Explain what a social network is, what social networks are used for, and the typical features of social networks

What is a social network?

Social network A community made up of people, groups, or organizations that are connected by one or more common interests.

A *social network* is a community made up of people, groups, or organizations that are connected by one or more common interests. Social networks are not new; communities are the building blocks of society. In fact, you are already a member of at least one social network. Take a look at the people with whom you interact regularly. Chances are that you have at least one best friend and several other good friends, as well as your immediate family members. From there, your network begins to branch out to include casual friends and acquaintances, classmates, teachers, coworkers, neighbors, and others. Some of these people may know each other, while others may be strangers to one another, but they all have one thing in common: they know you! With the advent of Web 2.0, social networking has moved online. In this chapter, we will explore the various types of online social networks that currently exist.

What are social networks used for?

The primary purpose of online social networks is to help people make connections within a community and to put those connections to good use. For example, Steve had two tickets to see the band Soundgarden, but his friend had to cancel at the last minute. Steve called several of his friends, but everyone already had plans. Luckily, Steve is a member of an online social networking site and he posted a comment there about his extra ticket. Several of Steve's friends commented on his page, and their friends saw the post too. In a short while, Steve had heard from several people, all of whom were either going to the concert or wanted to go. Steve's friend Jessie is friends with Scott, who was happy to buy Steve's extra ticket. As a result of Steve's posting, they made plans to meet up with their other friends who were also going to the concert, and everyone had a great time. By using the social networking site to make connections, Steve was able to find someone with similar interests to accompany him to the concert.

What types of social networks are there?

There are many different types of social networks. Some—such as Facebook (**www.facebook.com**), MySpace (**www.myspace.com**), Bebo (**www.bebo.com**), and Orkut (**www.orkut.com**)—are used to create communities of friends and people with similar interests (Figure 2.1). These social networks help members to communicate with one another in many different ways. Many organizations and groups have also created social networking sites as a way to interact with current members and attract new members. Some of the earliest examples of social networks included Friendster and Classmates.com. Friendster helped people to connect with their friends, while Classmates.com enabled users to identify their high schools and years of graduation so that they could reconnect with former classmates. Over the years, these sites changed and many users lost interest and moved away as newer and more enticing sites appeared.

Figure 2.1 Social networks create communities by helping people to connect to their friends and colleagues and allowing them to see their connections as well.

Are there other types of social networks?

Some sites—such as LinkedIn (**www.linkedin.com**) or Plaxo (**www.plaxo. com**)—are referred to as professional networks. A *professional network* connects businesspeople and other professionals in an online community and allows them to showcase their talents and skills. Rather than being used for entertainment purposes, such sites are used to manage and develop professional relationships with colleagues and potential employers. Other sites—such as YouTube (**www.youtube.com**), Twitter (**www.twitter.com**), Flickr (**www.flickr.com**), and Match.com (**www.match.com**)—are also considered to be social networks. Although not always as full-featured as sites such as Facebook or MySpace, these sites also give people the opportunity to become part of an online community and share videos, photos, opinions, information, and other personal details about themselves with other members. On a more serious note, sites such as Change.org (**www.change.org**) and Jumo (**www.jumo.com**) are examples of *issues-focused networks*: social action networks that provide members with information and opportunities to help with causes that range from global warming and animal rights to fair trade and peace in the Middle East. Additionally, some sites—such as Ning (**www.ning.com**), Spruz (**www.spruz.com**), Enter The Group (**www. enterthegroup.com**), and Grou.ps (**http://grou.ps**)—allow members to create their own online communities.

Can anyone join a social network?

Social networks can be open or closed communities. In an *open community*, anyone is free to join, regardless of his or her interests or who he or she might know. Most social networking sites fall into this category. However, to connect with other members on these sites, you may still need to obtain a member's permission before adding him or her to your network. In a *closed community*, members typically must be invited by the site organizer or pre-existing members. Closed communities often represent special interest groups or may be used in corporate or educational settings.

Professional network A social network that connects businesspeople and other professionals in an online community and allows them to showcase their talents and skills.

Issues-focused network A social action network that provides members with information and opportunities to help with causes that range from global warming and animal rights to fair trade and peace in the Middle East.

Open community A social network in which anyone is free to join, regardless of his or her interests or who he or she might know.

Closed community A social network to which members typically must be invited by the site organizer or pre-existing members.

What are the features of a social network?

Although each social network tries to differentiate itself from its competitors, most sites have some similar features (Figure 2.2); they may, however, refer to those features using different names. To a first-time user, the vast array of features available on a social network can be overwhelming, but here are some of the typical features you might find:

- Homepage—Once you've logged in, this page provides an overview of your activities within the network.

- Profile—A *profile* is used to provide information about a member. Although some details may be mandatory, such as your name or email address, many can be added or skipped at your discretion.

- Friends—A social network may have millions of members. The individuals with whom you have connected are often identified as *friends*, *colleagues*, or *contacts*. These are the people who make up your portion of the online community. Typically, this area will display your friend's name and an image selected by that person. Clicking the name or image will take you to your friend's homepage.

- Communication areas—Depending upon the site, there may be several different types of communication areas. Many sites include one or more sections—such as a message wall, discussion forum, or comments area—to allow members to leave messages and comments for one another. News feeds, status updates, activity streams, and other areas often allow you to see when others have made changes to their pages (such as posting a photo or video) or posted comments on the sites of mutual friends. These areas also allow you to update your own status to let others know what you are doing. Some networks include an icon to indicate when you are online and enable live chatting through the use of an instant-message application. Message and notification areas provide ways to communicate privately—similar to email messages—and are not visible to others in the network.

- Video and pictures—Part of the fun of social networks is the ability to post pictures and videos to share with your friends. Members of your network can view and comment on the media you post and may also be able to view items your friends have posted.

- Groups—In addition to your friends and contacts, many organizations have become involved with social networking. You can join one of these groups or create your own special-interest group. Some groups are open to everyone, while others are by invitation only.

- Applications—There are a number of other features, known as applications, *apps*, or *widgets*, which you can add to your social network. *Internal applications* are developed by the creators of the network, while *external applications* are created by third-party developers, sometimes for commercial purposes. Some applications are for entertainment purposes and allow you to play games, send virtual hugs, take quizzes, poke your friends, or listen to music. Still other apps have more practical uses and allow members to track events, organize website bookmarks, or coordinate schedules. Others have been developed to promote special causes. For instance, in March 2011 the Earth Day Network and Facebook created a new app called A Billion Acts of Green. Released just in time for Earth Day, the app encouraged people to announce their intentions to help the environment on Facebook in the hopes that other Facebook users would be inspired to take similar steps.

Profile A feature of a social network that is used to provide information about a member.

Apps, widgets Applications or features that you can add to your social network.

Internal applications Features that can be added to a social network that are developed by the creators of the network.

External applications Features that can be added to a social network that are created by third-party developers, sometimes for commercial purposes.

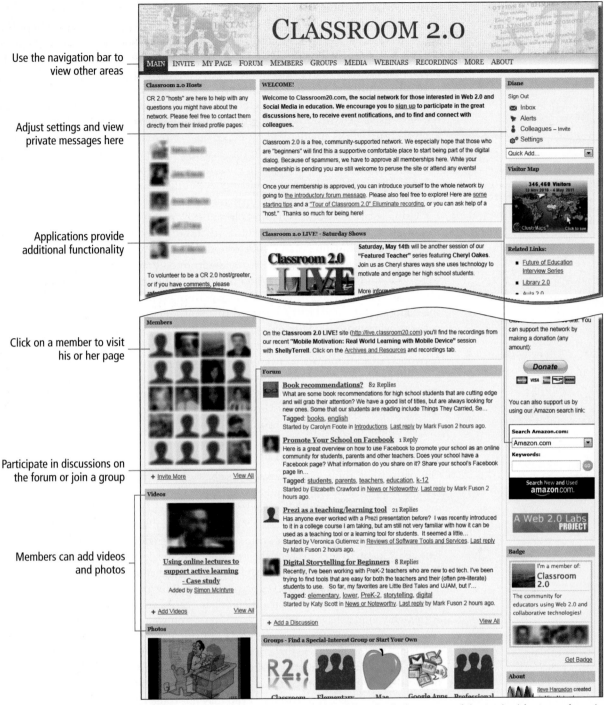

Use the navigation bar to view other areas

Adjust settings and view private messages here

Applications provide additional functionality

Click on a member to visit his or her page

Participate in discussions on the forum or join a group

Members can add videos and photos

Figure 2.2 Classroom 2.0, hosted by Ning, includes some of the typical features found on many social networking sites.

Objective 2

Describe the advantages and disadvantages of social networks

What are the advantages of a social network?

There are many reasons why you might want to join a social network. As with most Web 2.0 applications, one of the primary reasons for using a social network is the ability to easily and affordably communicate with others. Although some sites offer advanced capabilities and features for a fee, most of the basic services are free. Most social networks are fairly straightforward, so members can develop an online presence without any knowledge of web design or coding. Because the learning curve is not steep, new members can begin connecting with others right away. Another advantage is the ability to add new people to your network, reconnect with old friends, and continue to expand your circle of friends and colleagues over time. Some people have extensive networks consisting of hundreds of contacts, while others prefer to keep their networks smaller and more personal. No matter what size your network is, each new contact can put you in touch with others who have similar interests. It's not unusual for new college students to check out potential roommates on social networking sites ahead of time. Starting an online friendship can help to make the transition from home to dorm (or apartment) an easier and smoother process.

Using social networks can also help to develop and improve your writing and technical skills. A study of low-income urban high school students conducted by the University of Minnesota in 2008 found that 77 percent of the respondents were members of social networks. The study determined that students using such sites were developing communication and technical skills that could help them to become successful in the future. In 2009, a study performed in the United Kingdom by the National Literacy Trust confirmed that teenagers who had a profile on a social network were more likely to enjoy writing, thought they were better writers, and wrote more often and more prolifically than those who did not participate in social networks. In addition, social networks are good tools for promoting your own business and expanding your professional networking opportunities. No matter what type of business you are in, chances are that there's a group of like-minded individuals on a social network site. Because most social networks are global in scope, you can also develop friendships with people all over the world.

What are some disadvantages of a social network?

One of the most immediate disadvantages of a social network that you might encounter is the amount of time you'll spend there. Social networking sites can quickly become a distraction. In fact, a recent Pew Internet Project survey reported that 48 percent of teens visit social networking sites at least once a day, with nearly half of them reporting multiple visits. Some users actually report symptoms resembling addiction, including the need to repeatedly log in to sites to check their profile pages, neglecting other responsibilities and activities, and experiencing distress and anxiety when they are unable to access their sites.

Another disadvantage involves privacy issues. Information, photos, and videos posted to your profile page or on a friend's page can have far-reaching consequences. Although you may have enabled privacy settings on your own page, it is very easy for someone who has access to your site to copy materials and post them elsewhere. Once this happens, you may have little or no control over how this information is used (Figure 2.3). Sadly, what you may have posted all in good fun can easily be misinterpreted by people who don't know you, and this can lead them to form a negative impression before they ever meet you. Although you may not think that those silly party pictures or sarcastic comments on your site are inappropriate, many colleges and employers may disagree. College admissions personnel and human resource managers are beginning to use social networking sites to screen potential candidates, and the information they find could easily lead them to change their minds about you. In fact, a recent CareerBuilder survey indicated that 56 percent of employers regularly search, or plan to begin searching, sites such as Facebook and MySpace when screening prospective employees, with one-third reporting that the information they have found has caused them to drop a candidate from consideration for a position. Items that caused the most concern included information about alcohol and drug use, inappropriate text or photos, poor writing and communication skills, and bashing former employers or coworkers.

Figure 2.3 As shown in the popular cartoon *Zits*, it can be difficult to maintain your privacy on social networking sites.

Cyberstalking Threatening or harassing behavior that is facilitated by the use of the Internet and online tools such as email and online social networks.

Cyberbullying Limited to children, preteens, or teens, this type of bullying takes place via online tools such as email or social networks, as opposed to occurring face-to-face.

Cyber predator An adult who uses the Internet to prey on children or other hapless individuals, attempting to lure them into a sexual, or otherwise unsafe, situation.

Another concern surrounding social networks involves their use of unethical or illegal activities, such as cyberstalking and cyberbullying. *Cyberstalking* is defined as threatening or harassing behavior that is facilitated by the use of the Internet and online tools such as email and online social networks. *Cyberbullying* is similar to cyberstalking but involves children, preteens, or teens rather than adults. A recent McAfee/Harris survey reported that 20 percent of teens have engaged in some form of cyberbullying behavior. Individuals who are victims of cyberstalking or cyberbullying may report being teased, humiliated, threatened, or frightened. They may receive intimidating emails or instant messages, become the victims of online rumors or cyberpranks, or be threatened by humiliating or disturbing pictures. This behavior may not be limited to an online presence and can escalate to real-world situations as well.

A *cyber predator* might also be a cyberstalker and is typically an adult who preys on children or other hapless individuals, attempting to lure them into sexual—or otherwise unsafe—situations. Cyberbullying has been attributed to a number of suicides in recent years, including those of Megan Meier in 2006 and Tyler Clementi and Phoebe Price in 2010. Currently, at least 44 states have laws concerning bullying and 30 of these states mention bullying through the use of online tools. Although very few of these laws include any form of criminal punishment for the perpetrators, the laws surrounding cyberbullying are still evolving. Various surveys reveal that parents consider online predators to be as much of a threat to children as drinking and drugs; however, new reports indicate that this belief may be highly exaggerated. According to a recent study, only two children out of 1,500 interviewed reported being sexually victimized by someone they met online. In contrast, nearly one-fifth of teen or young-adult drivers involved in fatal traffic accidents had blood alcohol levels above the legal limit. Ultimately, although online behaviors can have very real and tragic results, it appears that these high-profile cases tend to be the exception rather than the rule. While online safety is a valid concern, statistics show that drugs and alcohol represent a much greater risk for teens and young adults.

What can I do to use social networks safely?

You can take several actions to help make your experience with social networks a positive one. First and foremost, use common sense and be careful about what you post online, especially when it involves personal information such as addresses, phone numbers, and other easily identifiable details. Think about how your comments, photos, and videos might influence someone's opinion of you—either positively or negatively.

Describe the advantages and disadvantages of social networks **55**

Remember that information and items you post online can remain there indefinitely and may be passed along to many other people, without your consent. It can be difficult, and is often impossible, to retrieve this information once it is out of your control.

Is there a way to limit access to my social network?

Most social networks provide several levels of privacy options. You can usually choose to allow anyone to view your information or limit access to just your contacts (Figure 2.4a and 2.4b). Another option might provide access to your friends' contacts also. And you can often apply different privacy levels to different features. For instance, you might let anyone view your profile page but only allow trusted friends to view your photos. You should adjust your privacy settings to match your comfort level.

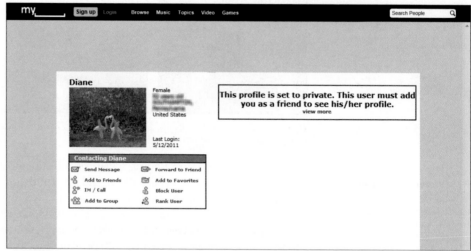

Figure 2.4a The privacy options for this user's MySpace page prevent unauthorized individuals from viewing personal data.

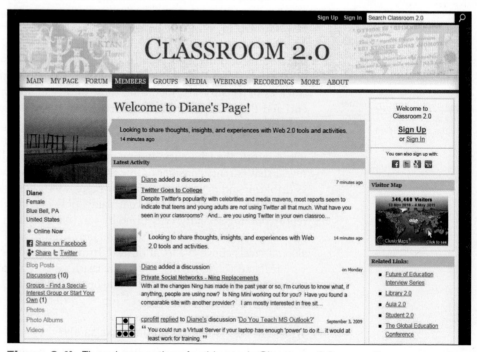

Figure 2.4b The privacy options for this user's Classroom 2.0 page allow everyone to view the information posted there.

What other types of risks are there?

Unfortunately, malware isn't limited to email and disreputable websites. Viruses and Trojan horses can be sent through the messaging systems of social networks; links in wall posts might be *phishing* attempts, leading you to fake websites that attempt to trick you into revealing private information to facilitate identity theft or links to download malware; and seemingly innocent apps can reveal your private information to others. These attempts aren't just limited to the social networking sites either. Scammers frequently send emails purporting to be from your social network. As with any other type of email scam, responding to the message by clicking a link or opening an attachment launches the malware.

Reports indicate that 70 percent of phishing attempts now occur on social networks and 20 percent of Facebook's newsfeed posts contain harmful content, with one in 10 hyperlinks leading to spam. In addition, those fun applications that you can add to your network page could be a security risk. Security experts claim that external applications written by third-party developers are responsible for 60 percent of threatening Facebook apps. Malicious applications have the potential to compromise your privacy and access confidential data on your computer. These applications are especially dangerous for two reasons. First, users tend to trust social networking sites and feel safe because they are in a closed environment, so they are more likely to download these programs without considering the consequences. Second, there is no easy way for a member to determine if an application is legitimate or malicious. Some of the most popular scams to avoid include the following:

- Offers to show who has been viewing your profile

- Claims that your access to the site has been restricted or your password has been changed

- Opportunities to win free prizes, such as laptop computers or iPhones

- Links leading to videos or photos of questionable subjects or shocking events

What else can I do to protect myself?

In addition to making sure that your computer is protected against viruses and spyware and has all the latest security updates, you should use the same safe computing practices on a social network that you use elsewhere on the Internet. Here are some other steps you can take:

- Check to see if your social network has a safety or security page that provides information about current threats or viruses, and visit it regularly to stay updated.

- Read your social network's privacy policy and be sure you understand it.

- Change your password periodically and don't use the same password for other sensitive areas such as financial sites, email accounts, or your school or work network.

- Carefully review your privacy settings to be sure they reflect your preferences.

- Consider using an alternate browser—such as Mozilla Firefox or Google Chrome—rather than Internet Explorer. Although alternate browsers are not invulnerable, much malware is still designed to work best with Internet Explorer, so using another browser might thwart an attack.

- Don't be lulled into a false sense of security if you're using a Mac or Linux computer. As more people use iPhones and iPads, malware creators are beginning to target these operating systems too. And phishing attempts, which trick you into revealing personal information, are web-based and don't depend on the type of computer or device you are using.

Phishing A type of social engineering in which a fake website attempts to trick you into revealing private and personal information, such as passwords and account numbers, in order to steal your identity.

Objective 3

Set up a LinkedIn account and create your profile

LinkedIn (www.linkedin.com) is a free professional networking site. Launched in 2003, LinkedIn has over 100 million members and reports that approximately 1 million new members join the site each week. While many of these members are seasoned professionals, LinkedIn members also include over 11 million recent college graduates. Establishing a professional profile now can help you develop a network of resources and contacts for your intended career. As your work experience grows, you will be able to update your LinkedIn profile to reflect your expertise and skills.

Hands-On Exercises

For purposes of the Hands-On Exercises, Professor Schmeckendorf has asked his lab assistant, Hannah Grindeldorf, to set up a LinkedIn account to demonstrate the benefits of belonging to a professional network. This Hands-On Exercise will create an account using Hannah's information; you will create your own account and should add your own information where appropriate.

1 | Set Up a LinkedIn Account and Create a Profile

Steps: 1. Start Your Browser, Navigate to LinkedIn, and Create Your Account; **2.** Create Your LinkedIn Profile; **3.** Change Contact Settings and Add a Position to Your LinkedIn Profile.

Use Figures 2.5 through 2.18 as a guide to the exercise.

Step 1 ▶ **Start Your Browser, Navigate to LinkedIn, and Create Your Account**

Refer to Figure 2.5 as you complete Step 1.

a. If necessary, turn on your computer.

b. Start your preferred browser (Internet Explorer, Firefox, Chrome, Safari, etc.). Type **www.linkedin.com** in the address bar of your browser and press **Enter**. If you already have a LinkedIn account, proceed to Step 3 in this exercise.

c. Locate the **User Agreement** and **Privacy Policy** links at the bottom of the page. By joining LinkedIn, you are confirming that you agree with the information on these two pages. Click each of these links and review the information to ensure you are comfortable with these terms. Return to the sign up page at **www.linkedin.com** to continue.

d. Locate the **Join LinkedIn Today** box and enter the required information. You will need to use a valid email address since LinkedIn will use it to verify your account request. Additionally, LinkedIn will send notifications, contact requests, and other messages to this email address. You should also create a strong password. LinkedIn requires your password to be at least 6 characters, but a password with 8 to 12 characters is better; including upper- and lowercase letters, numbers, and symbols will make your password even more secure.

e. Click the **Join Now** button to create your LinkedIn account.

D – Enter your first name, last name, email address, and password in the boxes

E – Click this button to proceed

C – Click the links to review this information

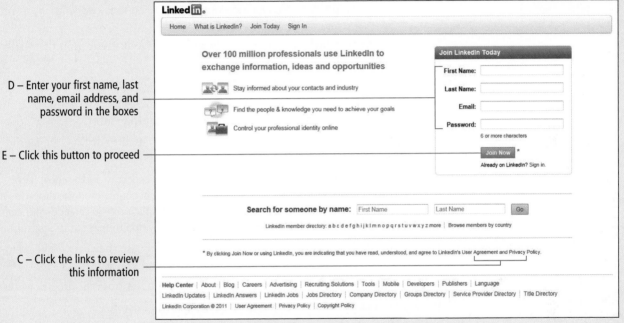

Figure 2.5 Hands-On Exercise 1, Steps 1c through 1e.

 Create Your LinkedIn Profile

Refer to Figures 2.6 through 2.12 as you complete Step 2.

On the next screen, you will begin to develop your professional profile. By default, LinkedIn shows you the profile screen for someone who is currently employed, as shown in Figure 2.6. LinkedIn also provides options for business owners, people who are looking for work, people who work independently, and students. Selecting the appropriate status will change the available text boxes accordingly. Since Hannah is still a student, this exercise will use the options available for the student profile.

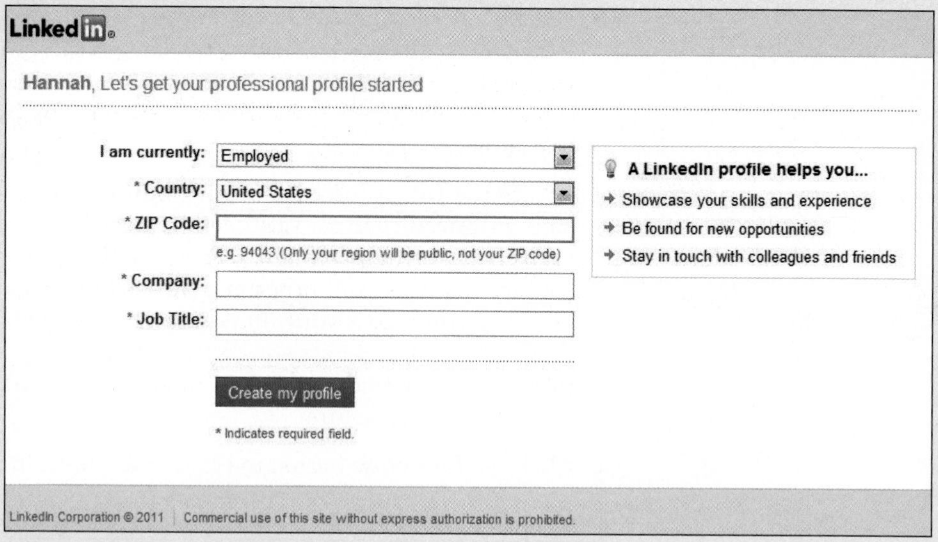

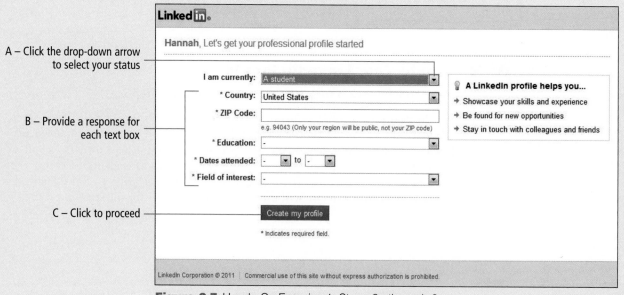

Figure 2.6 LinkedIn profile screen for individuals who are currently working.

a. Click the **I am currently** drop-down arrow and select **A student** from the available choices.

b. Each of the remaining text boxes is a required field. You must provide a response for each one.

   Country: Select the appropriate country from the drop-down list.

   ZIP Code: Type your zip code here. Note that this is used to display the region you are in, rather than your specific location.

   Education: This text box is a bit misleading. You might expect to add a school name or field of study here, but instead LinkedIn provides a list of countries in the drop-down menu. If you choose **United States**, a second text box displays so you can add your state. Once you've added a state, a third text box provides the option to select your institution.

   Dates attended: These two text boxes allow you to choose the year you began your education and the year you graduated or expect to graduate.

   Field of interest: Select your area of study or field of interest from the drop-down list.

c. Review your choices and click the **Create my profile** button.

A – Click the drop-down arrow to select your status

B – Provide a response for each text box

C – Click to proceed

Figure 2.7 Hands-On Exercise 1, Steps 2a through 2c.

d. The next screen displays a status bar at the top of the page indicating that you are now on Step 2 of 6 in the profile creation process. The email address you used to sign up for your account should appear in the text box. LinkedIn can view your email address book and check to see if anyone you know is already a member of the site. However, this can be done later once you are more familiar with the site. For now, click the **Skip this step** link to go to the next screen.

Status indicator

Your email address displays here

D – Click this link to proceed to the next step

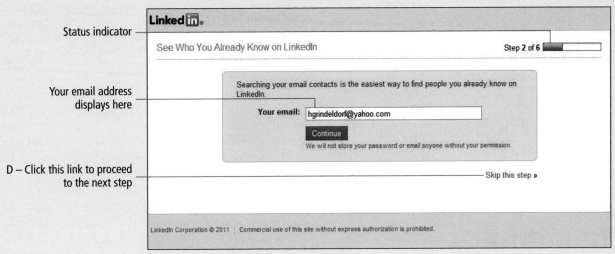

Figure 2.8 Hands-On Exercise 1, Step 2d.

e. For this step, you will need to confirm your email address. LinkedIn attempts to automate this process for some of the popular email providers, such as Gmail, Yahoo!, and AOL. Depending upon the email address you used, the screen you see may vary from the one shown in Figure 2.9. Hannah used her Yahoo! email account so she has the option of simply clicking the **Confirm my Yahoo! Account** button. If you do not have a Yahoo! account, this will not be an option for you. Regardless of the email account you used, you should also see a **Send a confirmation email instead** link on this screen. Click this link to have LinkedIn send you a message to confirm your email account.

E – Click to send an email to your account

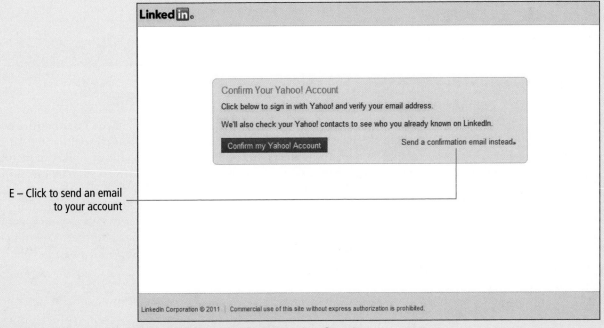

Figure 2.9 Hands-On Exercise 1, Step 2e.

f. As in Step 2e, the next screen may vary depending upon the email account you used. It might display a button leading to your email provider's website or include a message telling you to check your email. You can click the button, if applicable, or open a new browser tab or window and navigate to your email account.

g. Check your email account for a message from LinkedIn and follow the instructions in the email. Typically, the email message will include a link you can click to return to the LinkedIn site, as well as a link you can cut and paste into a browser window. Either method will open a new LinkedIn screen asking you to confirm your email address. Click the **Confirm** button to proceed.

Although this seems like a circular step, LinkedIn and many other sites use this method to confirm that you are actually the person creating the account. If you were attempting to create an account using someone else's information, theoretically you would not have access to that person's email account. Without access to the account, you would be unable to confirm the email address or to continue with the LinkedIn account creation process.

G – Click to confirm your email address

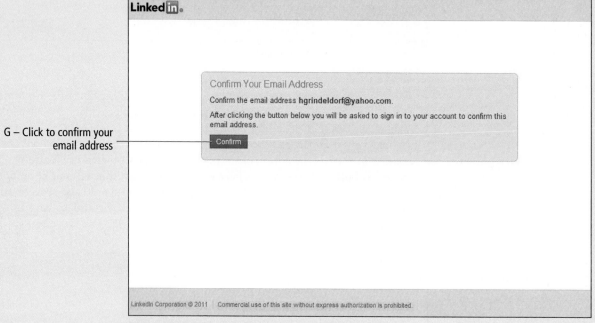

Figure 2.10 Hands-On Exercise 1, Step 2g.

h. Now that you've verified your email account, you just need to log in to LinkedIn. Your email address should already appear in the **Email address** text box. In the **Password** text box, type the password you created in Step 1d and then click **Sign In**. If any of your email contacts are already LinkedIn members, you may see a page asking if you want to connect with them. You can skip this step for now. If you arrive at a page showing Step 5 of 6 on the status bar, asking you to connect with others by adding their email addresses, you can skip this step as well. The next page to appear may be an offer to choose your plan level. The basic account is free and will be sufficient for our purposes. You can click the **Choose Basic** button, or click the **Skip this step** link to go to your LinkedIn Welcome page.

H – Enter your password and click Sign In

Figure 2.11 Hands-On Exercise 1, Step 2h.

Congratulations! You now have a LinkedIn account. You may see a message at the top of the Welcome page asking you to confirm your email address. Since you have already done this in the previous steps, you can safely ignore this message. The Welcome page provides you with several ways to begin interacting with other members of LinkedIn. You can search your email contacts for people who are already on LinkedIn, update your status, check your network activity, see who else has just joined LinkedIn from your school, upgrade to a premium account (for a fee), explore job listings, or join a group.

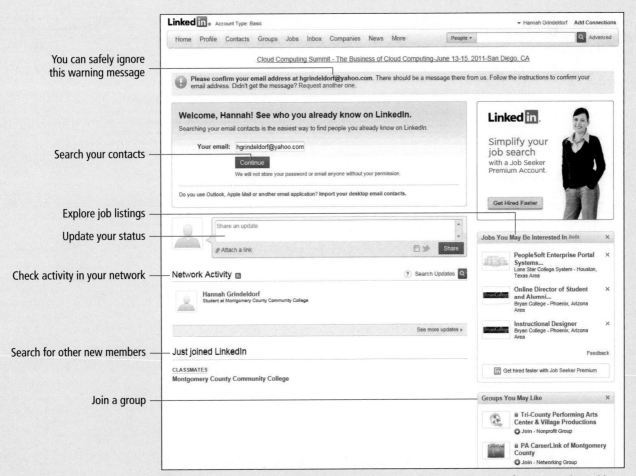

You can safely ignore this warning message

Search your contacts

Explore job listings

Update your status

Check activity in your network

Search for other new members

Join a group

Figure 2.12 The LinkedIn Welcome screen provides suggestions for connecting with other members.

Step 3   Change Contact Settings and Add a Position to Your LinkedIn Profile

Refer to Figures 2.13 through 2.18 as you complete Step 3.

In Step 2, you created a basic LinkedIn profile. But, to get the most impact from LinkedIn, you should provide more information and customize the site for your purposes.

a. To see how your profile currently appears, go to the menu bar at the top of the page, hover over the **Profile** link, and click **View Profile** from the drop-down menu.

Currently, Hannah's profile shows her name, the school she is attending, the area she lives in (based on the zip code entered previously), her field of interest, and that she has not yet connected with anyone. The menu bar at the top of the page leads to many different areas of the LinkedIn network. The **Contact Settings** area at the bottom of the screen shows the default contact choices and can be revised. Hannah's recent activity is displayed in the activity box on the right side of the page. In the case of a new account, it is possible that there may be no information here. That will change as you begin to use LinkedIn and make changes to your account. Take some time to explore the LinkedIn site and return to the **View Profile** page when you are done.

b. By default, the **Contact Settings** area is set to indicate you are interested in being contacted for a wide variety of reasons. Since some of these reasons may not be relevant, click the **Change your contact settings** link at the bottom of the screen to go to the **Account & Settings** page.

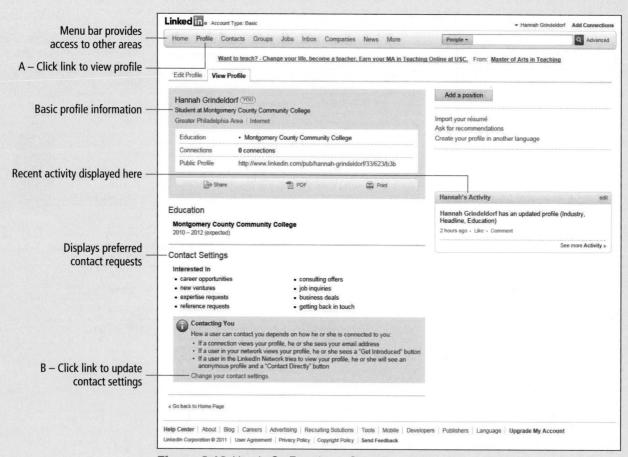

Figure 2.13 Hands-On Exercise 1, Steps 3a and 3b.

The **Account & Settings** page allows you to modify many different areas of your account. You can change your primary email address or password; upgrade from the free, basic account to a premium account; and adjust the settings for your

Profile, Email Preferences, Groups, Companies & Applications, and Account. You can also purchase one or more *InMails*, which allows you to send private messages through LinkedIn to someone with whom you are not connected, or pay to increase the number of *Introductions* available to you. Introductions allow you to contact people who are connected to people with whom you are already connected. Essentially, you are asking your contact to introduce you to his or her contact (or contacts). Currently, the basic account permits you to use five Introductions per month at no charge.

c. The **Accounts & Settings** page should have the **Email Preferences** section open. If not, click **Email Preferences** to display the choices and then click **Select the types of messages you're willing to receive**.

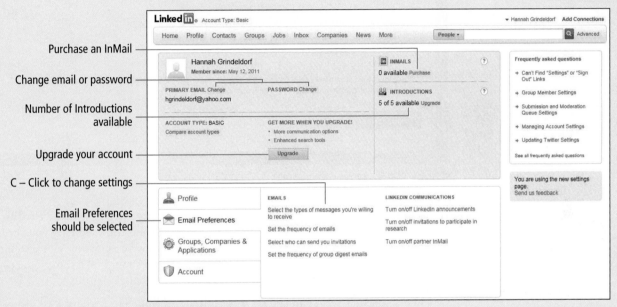

Figure 2.14 Hands-On Exercise 1, Step 3c.

d. The **Types of messages you're willing to receive** pop-up window appears with a number of options. Under the **Messages** section, the default choice is **Introductions and InMail only (Recommended)**. Hannah will leave this unchanged.

e. In the **Opportunities** section, you will see a number of checkboxes that provide reasons for people to contact you. Since Hannah is still a student, she has chosen to uncheck **Expertise requests** and **Business deals**. You should uncheck any boxes that do not apply to you.

f. The **Advice to people who are contacting you** text box allows you to leave a brief message indicating why you would welcome their interest. Hannah is currently attending school in Pennsylvania, but would like to relocate to the Silicon Valley in California. She will add the message *Interested in opportunities on the West Coast, relocating in June 2012.* You can leave this text box blank or add a message that is relevant to your situation. If you are not sure what to write, click the **See examples** link below the text box. Be sure to proofread your message to avoid any embarrassing errors or typos.

g. Review your choices and your message. Click the **Save changes** button to close the pop-up window and return to the **Accounts & Settings** page. After saving your changes, you may notice a green message bar at the top of the page indicating that your settings were updated successfully.

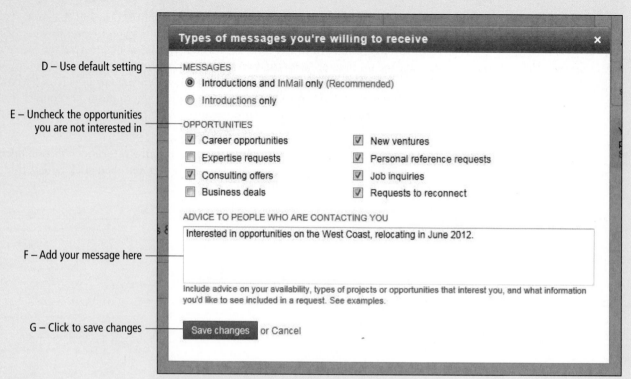

D – Use default setting

E – Uncheck the opportunities you are not interested in

F – Add your message here

G – Click to save changes

Figure 2.15 Hands-On Exercise 1, Steps 3d through 3g.

h. From the menu on the left of the **Accounts & Settings** page, click the **Profile** link. You will modify some of your privacy settings and begin editing your profile from this area. In this Hands-On Exercise, we will not be adjusting all these settings; however, at the conclusion of this exercise, you should take some time to look through them and adjust the ones you wish to change.

i. Click the **Select who can see your activity feed** link. The activity feed shows any changes you've made to your LinkedIn account, such as updating your profile, adding a contact, or joining a group. A pop-up window displays when you click the link.

j. To determine who will have access to this information, click the drop-down arrow. Your choices, ranging from least private to most private, are **Everyone, Your network, Your connections,** or **Only you.** LinkedIn defines your network as those individuals who are a first-degree, second-degree, or third-degree connection, as well as anyone who is a member of a group to which you belong. First-degree connections are those people to whom you are directly connected. Second-degree connections are the contacts of your first-degree connections and third-degree connections are the contacts belonging to second-degree connections. At this time, Hannah wants only people with whom she is directly connected to see her activity, so she selects **Your connections,** which is also the default selection. You may choose this option or pick another.

k. Click the **Save changes** button when you are done to return to the **Accounts & Settings** page.

l. Click the **Edit your profile** link to display the **Edit Profile** page and begin editing your profile.

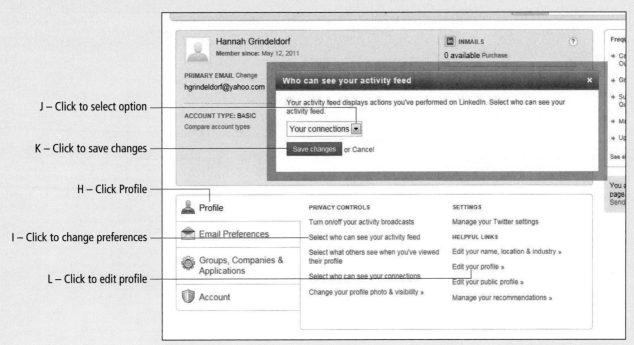

Figure 2.16 Hands-On Exercise 1, Steps 3h through 3l.

The **Edit Profile** page has many sections that you can edit. Notice the status bar on the right side of the screen indicating that Hannah's profile is 15 percent complete. Below the status bar are a number of suggestions you can follow to complete your profile. One of the quickest ways to add information to your profile is to import your resume. However, Hannah does not feel that the information from her current resume reflects her skills and abilities. Rather than importing the resume, she is going to select several sections to modify individually. Remember that you will be adding your own information in these steps, so your page will vary from the one shown in the following figures.

m. The **Profile Completion Tips** box shows that adding a position will contribute greatly to completing your profile. There are several links on this page that will allow you to add a position. You can click the link in the **Profile Completion Tips** box, the links next to the **Current** and **Past** sections, or the **Add a position** button on the top right of the page. Each of them will lead you to the **Add Position** page.

Profile completion status bar —

M – Click any one of these to add a position

Figure 2.17 Hands-On Exercise 1, Step 3m.

n. Since Hannah is currently working at Ginormous State University as Professor Schmeckendorf's lab assistant, she wants to list this position. You can add your own information or copy Hannah's if necessary. In the **Company Name** text box, type the name of the company you work for, or type *Ginormous State University*. As you type a company name, LinkedIn may display a list of matching company names. If your company is on the list, you can click it to add it. If your company is not on the list, LinkedIn may ask you to provide the company's website address and the industry. You should add the appropriate details. Hannah will leave the website address blank and select *Higher Education* as the industry.

o. In the **Title** text box, add the name of your position. Hannah's official title is *Computer Lab Assistant.*

p. The **Time Period** section will vary depending upon whether or not you check the **I currently work here** checkbox. If you leave this unchecked, you will need to select a start and end date for your job by clicking the drop-down arrows for the months the job began and ended and typing the appropriate years into the year text boxes. If you check the **I currently work here** checkbox, you will need to add only the starting month and year. Hannah will check the checkbox, select May from the drop-down list, and type 2011.

q. By checking the **I currently work here** checkbox, another option displays. The information added to the **Headline** text box will display at the top of your LinkedIn profile and replace the text indicating you are a student. If you wish to have this information appear, simply leave the checkbox checked. Otherwise, uncheck the box or modify the information shown in the **Headline** text box.

r. In the **Description** text box, type a brief description of your job. Click the **See examples** link if you are not sure what to put here. Hannah will type *"Providing lab assistance for computer science instructors at a large state university. Duties include care and maintenance of printers and computers and hands-on assistance for students during class."*

s. Once you've added this information, click the **Save Changes** button to return to your profile page. Notice that your new position has been added and your headline—the line below your name—has been updated.

Add details of your position ——

S – Click to save changes ——

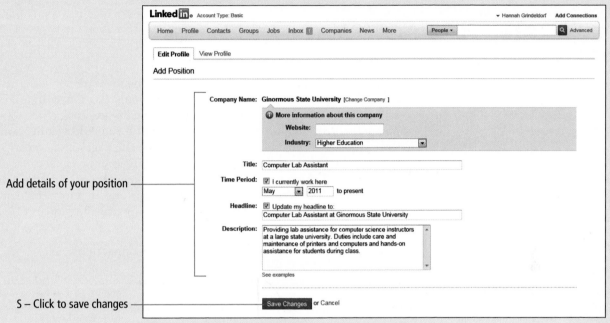

Figure 2.18 Hands-On Exercise 1, Steps 3n through 3s.

Leave your LinkedIn account open to complete the next exercise.

Objective 4

Add a connection to your LinkedIn network

LinkedIn provides several ways to add people to your network. Depending upon the email account you used when you signed up, LinkedIn may be able to import your contacts from your address book and then locate those individuals who are already LinkedIn members. LinkedIn can do this for a number of the larger email service providers, including Gmail, Yahoo!, Hotmail, and AOL. If you choose not to import your contact information, or if you use a different email account, such as your school email account, you can also use LinkedIn's search feature to locate individuals. LinkedIn also allows you to search for people you may know from companies at which you've worked and schools you've attended. LinkedIn will also suggest people you may know, based upon connections you already have. These three features will be more useful once you have added more information to your profile and begun connecting with people. One of the easiest, and most direct, ways of connecting with someone is to send him or her an email from within LinkedIn.

Hands-On Exercises

2 | Add a Connection to Your LinkedIn Network

Steps: 1. Review the Add Connections Page; **2.** Add a Connection; **3.** Create and Apply Tags and View a Connection.

Use Figures 2.19 through 2.25 as a guide to the exercise.

Step 1 Review the Add Connections Page

Refer to Figure 2.19 as you complete Step 1.

While it is important to provide accurate information about yourself on LinkedIn, the real strength of networking lies in the connections you make. LinkedIn makes it very easy for you to add connections from anywhere on its site. Look at the top-right corner of the website. Next to your name, you will see an **Add Connections** link. Your name and this link will appear on every LinkedIn page on the site as long as you are logged in. You can click on your name to adjust your profile settings or sign out of the site. Clicking the **Add Connections** link will take you to the **Add Connections** page where you can import email contacts or search for people in a variety of ways. At this time, Hannah will invite only specific individuals to join her network.

a. Click the **Add Connections** link to go to the **Add Connections** page.

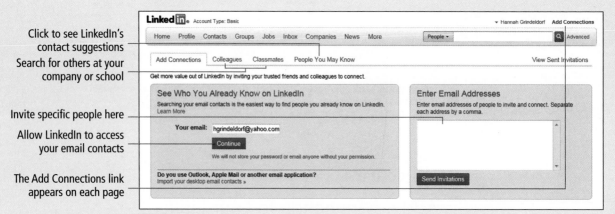

Figure 2.19 Hands-On Exercise 2, Step 1a.

Step 2 Add a Connection

Refer to Figures 2.20 through 2.22 as you complete Step 2.

You may already have an account with a social networking site like Facebook or MySpace and are accustomed to inviting friends to join your network. However, inviting someone to connect with you on a professional network like LinkedIn may take a bit more thought. It's wise to think of LinkedIn as an online resume and reference tool. Prospective employers do check sites like LinkedIn when they are researching job candidates. While some employers may be more tolerant of frivolous postings and comments on Facebook, they would expect your presence on LinkedIn to reflect a more mature and professional attitude. Your friend Crazy Jay might be a fun contact on Facebook, but he may not be the right person to connect with on LinkedIn. Whether or not it is fair, people really do judge you by the company that you keep. With that in mind, your connections on LinkedIn should be business-like and professional. People you should consider adding to your network include employers, managers, supervisors, coworkers, mentors, and instructors. You might also want to connect with friends who will take your invitation seriously, and other people you know and respect from other areas of your life.

Hannah has decided that she would like to ask Professor Schmeckendorf to connect with her. You should select one or more individuals to invite to join your LinkedIn network. Be sure to invite at least one other person from your class to ensure that you can continue with this exercise.

a. In the **Enter Email Addresses** text box, add the email address of one of your classmates. You may invite more than one person by adding a comma after each email address.

b. Click the **Send Invitations** button. Using this method, LinkedIn sends an automated email with a default message to the person whose email address you entered. A green notification bar will appear at the top of the window to show that your invitation has been sent.

Some schools or instructors may have policies that prohibit instructors from accepting requests from students to join their social network. Such policies have been instituted to protect students and instructors from potentially troublesome situations. Check with your instructor to see if such a policy exists at your institution.

c. To check the status of your invitation, click the **View Sent Invitations** link on the right side of the page. This will take you to the **Sent Invitations** section of your LinkedIn Inbox.

C – Click to view invitation status

A – Add email addresses here

B – Click to send invitation

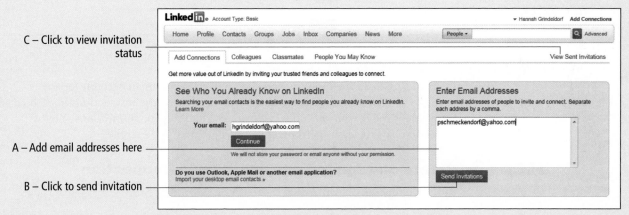

Figure 2.20 Hands-On Exercise 2, Steps 2a through 2c.

d. The **Sent Invitations** tab in the Sent folder of your Inbox displays the invitations you have sent. Depending upon whether the person you invited has a LinkedIn account, the text may appear slightly different. Typically, people with existing LinkedIn accounts will be identified by their name and profile picture (if they have one). If the person you invited does not have a LinkedIn account, you may see only his or her email address. Once someone accepts your invitation, the word "Accepted" will appear next to the name in green text. To review the automated message LinkedIn sent, click the **Invitation to connect on LinkedIn** link below the name or email address of the person you invited.

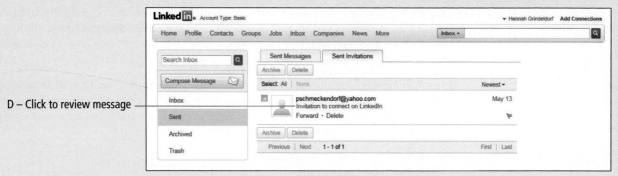

D – Click to review message

Figure 2.21 Hands-On Exercise 2, Step 2d.

e. The Inbox in LinkedIn works similarly to other email systems. You can reply to a message or forward it. If you want to save a message and remove it from your Inbox, you can archive it. This moves the message to the **Archived** section of your Inbox. You can also delete a message once you no longer need it. In the case of invitations, if you've changed your mind about inviting someone, you can withdraw the invitation. And, if you haven't received a response and want to try again, you can use the **Resend** button to send another request.

Default invitation message

E – Use buttons to resend or withdraw invitation

Figure 2.22 Hands-On Exercise 2, Step 2e.

At this point in the exercise, you should check your email account for any LinkedIn invitations you may have received. Follow the instructions in each email to accept the invitation and add this individual to your connections. You will need to have at least one contact to continue with the exercise.

Step 3 Create and Apply Tags and View a Connection

Refer to Figures 2.23 through 2.25 as you complete Step 3.

a. Click the **Contacts** link on the menu bar to proceed to your **Connections** page.

The **Connections** page allows you to view and manage your connections in LinkedIn. Assuming you have accepted someone's invitation or that someone has accepted yours, you should have at least one contact on this page. The **Connections** page has three columns. The first column includes a list of categories that can be used to filter your connections. Currently, the **Tags** category is expanded, showing a list of tags. Since you have not tagged any of your contacts yet, only the **Untagged** choice has a number next to it. Once you have more contacts, clicking on a tag, or one of the choices from the other categories, will display a subset of your connections. The number displayed next to the choice you select indicates how many of your contacts will be included in this subset. The second column lists your connections in alphabetical order by last name. The **ABC** link at the top of this column allows you to quickly navigate through your list of connections.

Clicking on a contact will display additional information in the third column. In this column, you will see your contact's name and image (if a profile picture has been added), the number of connections he or she has, any tags that you have assigned, the email address, your contact's title, and the company name.

You can interact with your connections directly through LinkedIn. In essence, the **Connections** page acts as an address book. Initially, the only information you will see about a specific contact is the information he or she has chosen to display on LinkedIn. However, when your contact's information is displayed in the third column, the **Edit details** link allows you to add additional information such as phone numbers, addresses, birthdays, and notes. Any information you choose to add in this column will be visible only to you. From this column, you can also access your contact's profile page. If your contact allows others to see his or her connections, you will be able to view those from this column as well.

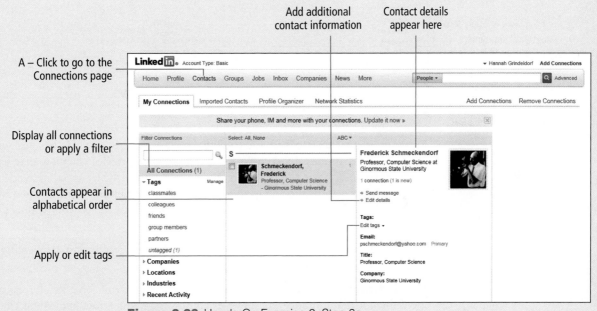

Figure 2.23 Hands-On Exercise 2, Step 3a.

Professor Schmeckendorf has accepted Hannah's invitation, so his information is now visible on her **Connections** page. The following steps will show you how to add a tag to your contact and access your contact's profile page and connections.

b. If necessary, click the desired connection in the second column to display the details in the third column.

c. To apply a tag, click the **Edit tags** link in the third column. A new box appears below the link. The box includes a selection of default tags provided by LinkedIn. It also includes a text box in which you can enter a new tag of your choice. For instance, you might want to create a tag for instructors or relatives.

d. Hannah would like to create a new tag, called *instructor*, to identify Professor Schmeckendorf. Type the new tag name in the text box and click the plus symbol next to it to add the tag. This tag will also be available to apply to other connections.

e. Click as many of the other tag checkboxes as you need to identify your contact. You can apply as many as you want, or not use any at all. You can modify your tags at any time by coming back to this detail view and changing your selections.

f. Click the **Save** button when you are finished tagging your contact. Notice that the tags you applied now appear in the details column and the list of tags in the first column has been updated accordingly.

g. Notice that in the details column, your contact's name is a hyperlink. Click this link to go to his or her profile page.

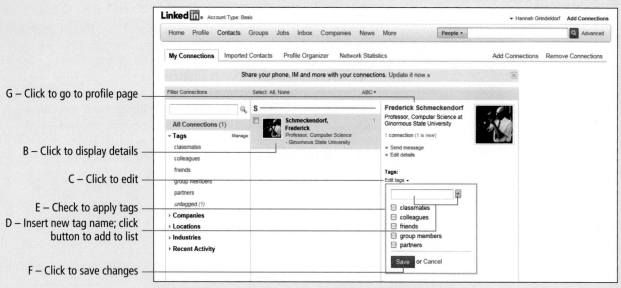

G – Click to go to profile page

B – Click to display details

C – Click to edit

E – Check to apply tags
D – Insert new tag name; click button to add to list

F – Click to save changes

Figure 2.24 Hands-On Exercise 2, Steps 3b through 3g.

Professor Schmeckendorf's profile page is shown in Figure 2.25. He has just joined LinkedIn and has not fully completed his profile. The profiles you view may have more or less information than what is shown here. As with any social network, each member has the ability to add as much or as little information as he or she wishes to share. Following are some of the items you will usually see on your connections' profiles:

Relationship to you—LinkedIn indicates whether the profile you are viewing is a first-, second-, or third-degree connection.

Profile synopsis—This section provides a brief summary of some key information including current employer(s), previous employer(s), education, and connections.

In-depth information—Expanded details appear below the profile synopsis.

Recent activity—Updates on your contact's recent LinkedIn activity are displayed here.

Contact information—This area includes information provided by your contact and any additional information you may have added.

Connections—If your contact has made it possible for others to view his or her connections, this area will display some or all of those individuals.

How you're connected—This area is especially useful when viewing the profiles of second- or third-degree contacts to see which LinkedIn members you have in common.

h. Not everyone wants to make his or her connections available for viewing. By default, LinkedIn has this feature turned on to make networking easier, but it can be turned off from the **Settings** page on the **Profile** tab. Assuming your contact has not disabled this feature, in your contact's profile synopsis section, click the link next to **Connections** to see who your contact has connected with on LinkedIn. To see more information about anyone on your contact's connection list, simply click on that person's name to be taken to his or her profile page.

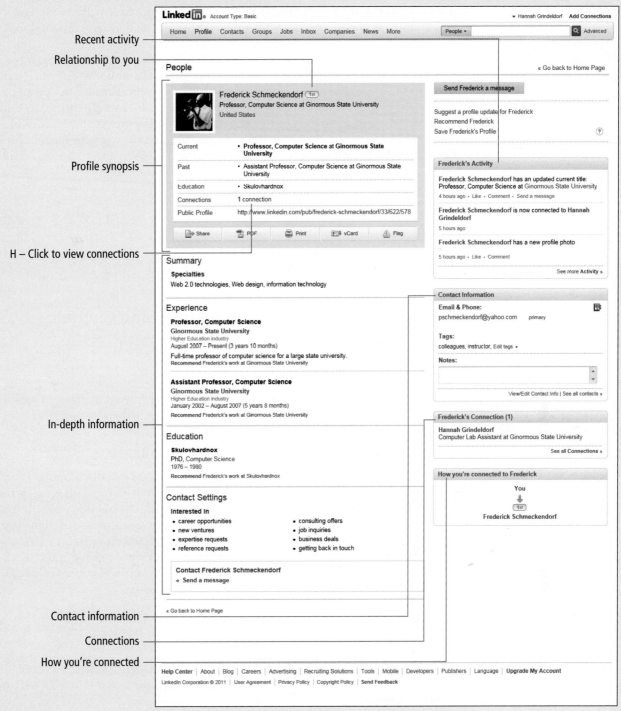

Recent activity

Relationship to you

Profile synopsis

H – Click to view connections

In-depth information

Contact information

Connections

How you're connected

Figure 2.25 Hands-On Exercise 2, Step 3h.

Objective 5

Modify your LinkedIn account settings

Like many other social networks, it is possible to add a brief statement to your profile, indicating your current status. This might be an accurate reflection of what you are currently doing, or it could be a comment on current events, a link to a website or item of interest, or some other sort of observation. Such a statement is optional and can be updated whenever you choose. Additionally, LinkedIn gives you the opportunity to create a very detailed profile. Although you may have provided some information when you originally created your profile, there is much more that you can add if you choose to do so. Whatever you decide to post, you should remember to review your privacy settings to be sure you are comfortable with who can view your information. Typically, LinkedIn offers four levels of privacy. Setting your privacy level to **Everyone** makes your information accessible to all LinkedIn members. **Your network** provides access for all first-, second-, and third-degree connections, while **Your connections** allows only your first-degree contacts to view your content. Setting your privacy level to **Nobody** (or **Only me**) will prohibit anyone but you from seeing the information.

Hands-On Exercises

3 | Modify LinkedIn Account Settings and Get Help

Steps: 1. Share an Update; **2.** Edit Your Settings and Save Your Changes; **3.** Access Help.

Use Figures 2.26 through 2.36 as a guide to the exercise.

Step 1 Share an Update

Refer to Figures 2.26 and 2.27 as you complete Step 1.

a. If necessary, open your web browser and sign in to your LinkedIn account. Your LinkedIn account opens with the homepage displayed. If you are still viewing the profile page of a connection from the previous exercise, click **Home** on the menu bar. Near the top of the page, a **Share an update** text box appears. In addition to adding a comment, you can also click **Attach a link** to direct viewers to an item of interest on another site. If you use Twitter, you can place a check in the checkbox to have LinkedIn's Twitter app send your update to your Twitter account as well.

> **Alert!**
>
> Your homepage may still display a box encouraging you to allow LinkedIn to search your email contacts. At some point, possibly after you have acquired a sufficient number of contacts, this box will stop appearing.

b. Type a brief comment of your choice in the **Share an update** text box. Notice that as you begin to enter text in this text box, the **visible to** option appears below it.

c. Click the **visible to** option and select whether you want your status to be visible to anyone or only to your connections.

d. Click the **Share** button to post the update.

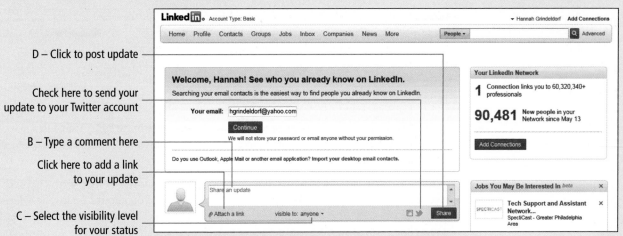

D – Click to post update

Check here to send your
update to your Twitter account

B – Type a comment here

Click here to add a link
to your update

C – Select the visibility level
for your status

Figure 2.26 Hands-On Exercise 3, Steps 1a through 1d.

e. To view your update, point to **Profile** on the menu bar and click **View Profile**. Your update appears below your name at the top of the page and also appears in the activity area on the right side of the page.

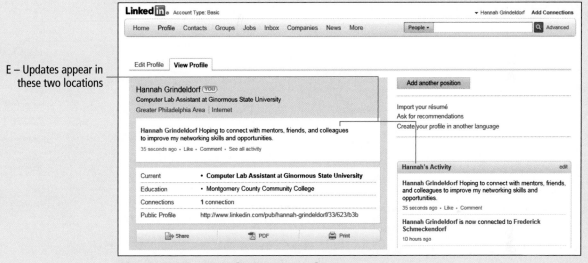

E – Updates appear in
these two locations

Figure 2.27 Hands-On Exercise 3, Step 1e.

Step 2 Edit Your Settings and Save Your Changes

Refer to Figures 2.28 through 2.33 as you complete Step 2.

As with any social networking site, it is important to periodically review your settings and ensure that you are displaying only the information you want to share to the people with whom you want to share it. From LinkedIn's **Account & Settings** page, you can adjust these four categories:

- Profile
- Email Preferences
- Groups, Companies & Applications
- Account

a. To access your settings, hover over your name at the top right of the page and from the drop-down menu, click **Settings**.

A – Click to adjust settings

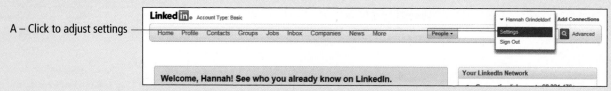

Figure 2.28 Hands-On Exercise 3, Step 2a.

The **Account & Settings** page appears with the **Profile** category choices displayed. Recall that some of these settings were previously modified in Hands-On Exercise 1.

b. In the **Profile** category, under **Privacy Controls,** click the **Select who can see your connections** link. As with all privacy settings, you should make the selection that best suits your comfort level. A pop-up window appears from which you can choose to allow your connections to see who you are connected to or keep your connections private and allow them to be visible only to yourself. Hannah chooses **Your connections** and clicks the **Save changes** button. The pop-up window closes and a notification bar appears at the top of the screen indicating that your update was successful.

c. Next, click the **Change your profile photo & visibility** link. This will take you to a new page where you will be able to upload a profile photo.

B – Click to adjust connections visibility

C – Click to add a profile photo

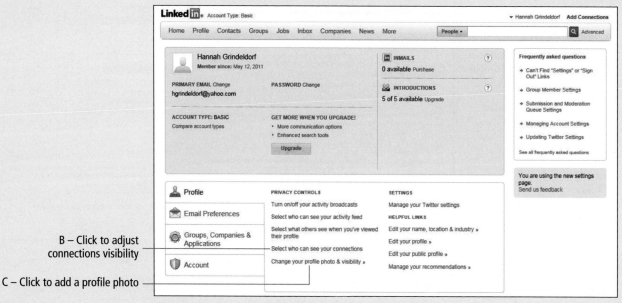

Figure 2.29 Hands-On Exercise 3, Steps 2b and 2c.

Displaying a profile picture on your LinkedIn page is not mandatory, but surveys of LinkedIn users reveal that people are more inclined to link to you if you have a profile picture. This is especially true if the person is not a close acquaintance. Seeing your picture might help to jog someone's memory or confirm that you are who he or she thought you were. Because LinkedIn is a professional network, the picture you choose to display should reflect that fact. While you do not have to have a professional portrait taken, the picture your friend took last summer on his or her cell phone may not be the one you want to use. You should consider using a headshot—a photo that shows just your head and shoulders. A photo that shows you smiling or looking approachable is good. The image should be clearly focused with a neutral background and good lighting. You may decide to wear business attire for your photo or dress in business casual—but wearing your favorite heavy metal T-shirt is probably not a good idea! You should also avoid photos that are abstract, show you in an unprofessional setting, or aren't current. So, if you recently changed your hairstyle or started wearing glasses, it's probably time for a new picture. The image you choose to upload should be a JPG, GIF, or PNG file and must be less than 4MB in size.

d. The photo you upload must be yours to distribute and must comply with LinkedIn's User Agreement. If you are unsure about this, click the **User Agreement** link before uploading your picture. Click your browser's back button to return to the photo upload page.

e. Click the **Browse** button to locate the image you want to use for your profile picture. Note: If you do not have a suitable image at this time, skip this step and proceed to Step 2g.

f. Click the **Upload Photo** button to upload your picture.

D – Click to review User Agreement

E – Click to locate the image file

F – Click to upload the image

Figure 2.30 Hands-On Exercise 3, Steps 2d through 2f.

g. Before your photo is uploaded, a new window appears allowing you to adjust the size and positioning of your photo. The small photo at the top of the window displays how your profile picture will appear. The larger image includes a yellow square that you can resize and reposition to obtain the best possible photo. Once you've adjusted the image, click the **Save Photo** button to proceed.

G – Click to save photo

Use the yellow square to select the best size and position for your photo

Figure 2.31 Hands-On Exercise 3, Step 2g.

h. The **Edit My Profile** page displays with a notification at the top indicating your photo has been saved. Your profile photo appears on the left side of the screen with links to edit or delete it. You can also select who will be able to see your picture—**My Connections, My Network,** or **Everyone.** Click the option button for your choice and then click **Save Settings.**

Notification that photo was saved

H – Select photo visibility level and then save

Figure 2.32 Hands-On Exercise 3, Step 2h.

i. You will return to the **Account & Settings** page after you've uploaded your photo. Click the **Groups, Companies & Applications** choice from the list on the left side of the page.

A new selection of settings appears to help you manage groups, companies, and applications. Many social networks allow their members to utilize applications created by third-party developers. These tools can provide additional features and greater functionality, such as the application that permits your shared updates to be sent to your Twitter account, but they also allow third-party developers to access your information. LinkedIn states that "applications are contractually obligated to respect privacy settings," but if you install an application, you must agree to the application developer's terms of use and privacy policy. You should use care when installing and using an application and be sure that you understand how the application's developers will use your personal information.

j. Because Hannah does not want to allow third-party applications to be able to access her information, she has decided to turn off data sharing. Click the **Turn on/off data sharing with 3rd party applications** link.

k. A pop-up window appears. Uncheck the checkbox to prevent data sharing and click **Save changes.**

K – Uncheck the checkbox and click to save

I – Click to display options

J – Click to adjust data sharing

Figure 2.33 Hands-On Exercise 3, Steps 2i through 2k.

Step 3 Access Help

Refer to Figures 2.34 through 2.36 as you complete Step 3.

From time to time, you may have a question about how to use one of LinkedIn's features or have a problem setting something up. LinkedIn has several different ways to obtain help. You can ask a question of LinkedIn members, visit the Learning Center, or go to the Help Center.

a. On the menu bar, point to **More** and click **Answers** to open the **Answers Home** page. The **Answers Home** page lets members ask questions about how to use LinkedIn or ask for advice on a variety of career-related topics. You can decide whether the entire LinkedIn membership can read and reply to your question or if you just want a response from your connections. Conversely, you can also answer questions that others have posted from this page.

b. Once you have reviewed the **Answers Home** page, return to the menu bar, point to **More**, and click **Learning Center**. The **Learning Center** page opens and displays a list of resources on the left side of the page. You can take a tour of the site, learn about LinkedIn features, and access User Guides from the Learning Center.

A – Click to ask a question

B – Click to view resources

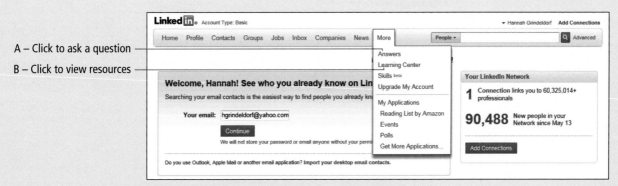

Figure 2.34 Hands-On Exercise 3, Steps 3a and 3b.

c. Once you have reviewed the Learning Center, click the **Go to LinkedIn.com** link at the top right of the page to return to your homepage. Scroll down to the bottom of the page and click the **Help Center** link.

d. The Help Center has an **Answers** tab and a **Contact Us** tab. On the **Answers** tab, you can type a phrase or keyword in the **Get Started Here** search box and click the **Search** button to display a list of links. This page already has a list of links for various topics and a **Recommended Answers** section as well.

Figure 2.35 Hands-On Exercise 3, Step 3d.

e. If you are unable to find an answer to your question using any of the tools shown so far, click the **Contact Us** tab. On this page, you can add your contact information and provide a subject and detailed description of the question or problem you have. If necessary, you can also attach a document to help describe your problem. LinkedIn's Customer Service department will respond to the email address you provide.

f. At the top of the **Help Center** page, click the **Go to LinkedIn.com** link to return to your account. To log out of LinkedIn, hover over your name at the top right of the page and click **Sign Out** from the drop-down menu.

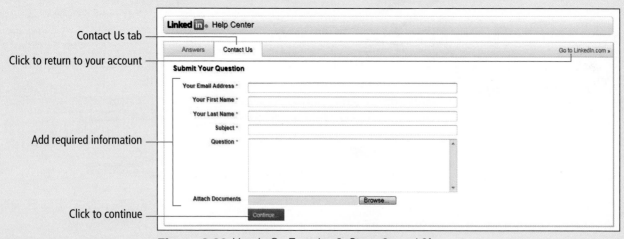

Figure 2.36 Hands-On Exercise 3, Steps 3e and 3f.

Objective 6

Investigate other types of social networks

Can I create my own social network?

Sites such as LinkedIn, Facebook, and MySpace are good for interacting with a wide variety of people and groups. It's possible to connect with people you already know, make new friends, or join groups of people with similar interests. But what if you'd like to be part of a smaller community? Sites such as Ning (**www.ning.com**), Spruz (**www.spruz.com**), Enter The Group (**www.enterthegroup.com**), and Grou.ps (**http://grou.ps**) provide site hosting and tools to help you develop your own social network. Most of these sites don't require you to have any web design experience, but if you do, it's often possible to tweak your online community. Some of these sites are fee-based, while others may be free. Although there may be no charge to create your own community, many hosting companies will place ads on your network as a way for them to generate revenue. For a fee, you can eliminate the ads (or sponsor your own), obtain your own customized website address, or access other premium features.

What do I need to do to create my social network?

Success is often in the details. Take some time before you begin to determine the objectives for your network and plan accordingly. By doing so, you'll improve your chances of creating a useful online community that people will want to join and participate in. Following are some of the things you should consider:

- **Who will host the social network?** As mentioned previously, there are a number of sites from which you can choose, so you should explore your options carefully. Some sites are good for beginners, while others are geared toward professional or business uses, and still others are meant to be used with existing websites. Check the **About Us** or **Company Info** pages for sites you are considering, review their privacy policies, and, if possible, examine some of the networks already using their services. Don't forget to think ahead: If your social network becomes successful, will the site you've selected still be able to support your members? Does it offer advanced features and, if it does, at what price?

- **Who will join the community?** You should have a clear idea of the people for whom you are building the community. Will it be for people who share an affinity for a particular hobby or sport? Will it be a professional network for coworkers or your colleagues in a specific industry? Will it be a social network for your friends? In each instance, knowing who the members of your social network will be and considering their needs and preferences ahead of time can help you decide how you'd like your site to appear and what features you'd like to include. A casual, fun type of theme may be fine for a social group but might prevent your site from being taken seriously if you were hoping to attract professional colleagues.

- **What features should be included?** You can add a variety of features to your social network: message areas, discussion forums, blogs, chats, photo and video sharing, and so on. Explore the hosting site you have selected to see what's available for your network. You might decide to start out with just a few basic features and add more as the site grows.

- **How will the site be moderated?** How can you protect your site from unwanted visitors such as hackers and spammers? What privacy levels are available to your members? It can be difficult to balance the desire to share information and ideas with the need for privacy and security, but you should have a plan in place to protect your members. Be sure you know how to work with the hosting site to handle any problems that might arise.

How do I moderate and promote my social network?

As a member of a social network, your responsibilities are relatively few. Most likely, you only need to follow the rules of the site and be a good Internet citizen, which means don't send spam or knowingly spread any type of malware, be polite to the other members, provide useful information when appropriate, and have fun participating in the network. However, as the creator of a social network, your responsibilities are greater because it is up to you to moderate, or maintain, the site. As the social network's *site administrator*, you can determine what features appear on the site, approve photos and videos before they are posted, approve members before allowing them to join, delete offensive comments, and ban members who act in an inappropriate way on your network. You can also assign individuals to act as *moderators* and help you maintain the standards you have set for your site.

Another role for the creator of a social network is *promoter*. In order for your social network to be successful, you need to attract members. As the creator of your network, you can take actions to promote your site and to encourage others to help you spread the word.

Methods for promoting social networks may include the following:

- **Sending an invitation**—This is the easiest and quickest way to spread the word about your site. Use your social network's invitation feature to enter the email addresses of your friends and colleagues, and invite them to join your network.

- **Sharing network content**—When a video, photo, discussion thread, or blog post is added to the network, it often includes a Share link. You can click the link to email it to individuals who are not on the network. This is a good way to let others see what your network is all about.

- **Embedding content**—Some items include code that can be embedded in other sites, such as a blog, website, or another social networking site. This provides another way to generate interest in your online community.

- **Creating a Facebook application**—This feature may be a bit more advanced, but some social networks may provide assistance for developing applications that will promote your social network on Facebook.

- **Creating a badge or widget**—Similar to embedding code on a website, badges and widgets provide icons that you can post on other websites or social networking sites to improve your network's visibility. A *badge* is a small graphic that links to your social network. A widget is a small application that displays video or photos—or that plays music—and that also links back to your site when it is clicked.

Objective 7

Explore social networking resources

The collaboration and communication features of a social network give you more ways than ever to interact with people all over the world. Whether you decide to participate in a social network or create your own, there are a number of resources that can provide additional information to help you get the most from this experience. Some of the following sites may be of interest:

- **David Lee King** (www.davidleeking.com)—This blog from David Lee King, a public librarian in Topeka, Kansas, explores emerging digital technologies as they relate to libraries. His blog includes a number of posts on social networking.

Site administrator A social network role with responsibilities for determining which features appear on the site, approving photos and videos prior to posting, approving member requests to join the site, deleting offensive comments or materials, and banning members who act inappropriately.

Moderator A social network role responsible for maintaining the network's standards.

Promoter A person who actively markets and promotes a social networking site, encouraging others to help spread the word.

Badge A small graphic or icon posted on a website or social networking site that links to another social network site.

- **Ning: Network Creators** (http://networkcreators.ning.com/notes/The_Perfect_Social_Network)—This social network hosted by Ning provides advice and tutorials for individuals who have created their own social networks on Ning.

- **Mashable: 5 Fun and Safe Social Networks for Children** (http://mashable.com/2010/10/11/social-networks-children/)—Mashable has created a list of social networks that are specially designed for younger children. With tighter privacy controls and family-friendly designs, these offer a safer alternative for kids than sites like Facebook or MySpace.

- **Social Networking** (www.whatissocialnetworking.com)—This site provides a simple primer that explains the basics of social networking in a clear and easy-to-understand manner.

- **Social Networking Privacy: How to be Safe, Secure and Social** (www.privacyrights.org/social-networking-privacy)—This scholarly article from the Privacy Rights Clearinghouse provides useful information about privacy and security for social networks.

- **Social Networking in Plain English** (www.youtube.com/watch?v=6a_KF7TYKVc)—The folks at Common Craft have created an entertaining video that explains the concepts of social networking.

- **Microsoft Safety & Security Center** (www.microsoft.com/security)—Hosted and funded by Microsoft to promote online safety and security, this site covers various topics, including social networking.

- **LinkedIn Learning Center** (http://learn.linkedin.com/students)—This site contains a number of videos to help you explore the many features available on LinkedIn.

Summary

In this chapter, you learned a number of basic skills needed to participate in a social network and to create your own network. We've looked at the advantages and disadvantages of social networking and provided information on how to maintain your safety and security as a member of a network, as well as how to help maintain your members' privacy if you create your own network. To be successful, social networks need to attract members who will participate and add value, because collaboration and communication are the key features of social networks.

Key Terms

Multiple Choice Questions

1. A form of social engineering designed to trick you into revealing personal information in order to commit identity theft is known as

    (a) phishing.

    (b) cyberbullying.

    (c) profiling.

    (d) spamming.

2. Which of the following activities is *not* the responsibility of a moderator on a social network?

    (a) Removing objectionable content

    (b) Deleting the network

    (c) Approving new members

    (d) Approving photos and video

3. Which of the following is an example of a professional network?

    (a) LinkedIn

    (b) Orkut

    (c) Twitter

    (d) Digg

4. The main difference between cyberbullying and cyberstalking is

    (a) cyberstalking never involves email.

    (b) cyberbullying is less serious than cyberstalking.

    (c) cyberbullying involves children, preteens, or teens rather than adults.

    (d) cyberstalking only involves adults.

5. Widgets that are created by third-party developers are known as

    (a) internal applications.

    (b) moderated applications.

    (c) profile applications.

    (d) external applications.

6. Which of the following is an example of an issues-focused social network?

    (a) Bebo

    (b) Change.org

    (c) Flickr

    (d) Plaxo

7. Which of the following sites can be used to create your own social network?

    (a) Twitter

    (b) YouTube

    (c) Facebook

    (d) Enter The Group

8. Which of the following is *not* a way to get help on the LinkedIn network?

    (a) Use the Tutorial page

    (b) Use the Learning Center

    (c) Use the Help Center

    (d) Ask a question on the Answers Home page

9. Which of the following is *not* a method used to create awareness of a social network?

    (a) Issue invitations

    (b) Set the privacy settings so that only invited individuals can see the content

    (c) Share network content

    (d) Post a badge on another website or social network

10. A social network that requires its members to be invited by the site organizer or a pre-existing member is an example of a(n)

    (a) hybrid community.

    (b) open community.

    (c) private community.

    (d) closed community.

Fill in the Blank

1. A(n) _____ is the feature of a social network that provides information about a member.

2. A social network that is visible to anyone and permits people to join without being invited is a(n) _____ _____.

3. The creator of a social network can assign an individual to act as the _____ to help maintain the network's standards.

4. _____, also known as apps, are applications that can be added to your social network and allow you to do things such as play games, listen to music, promote causes, and track events.

5. An adult who uses social networks and other online tools to lure children or adults into unsafe situations of a sexual or illegal nature is known as a(n) _____ _____.

Practice Exercises

1. **Develop Your Connections on LinkedIn**

   As discussed in this chapter, connecting with people on a professional network may take more thought than connecting to friends on a social network. For this exercise, take some time to consider to whom you would like to be connected on LinkedIn. Create a list of ten names and provide a reason why you think each of these individuals would be a valuable connection. Submit this paper to your instructor.

2. **Add More Connections to LinkedIn**

   Using the list you developed in Practice Exercise 1 and the skills you learned in this chapter, invite each of the ten people on your list to become one of your connections on LinkedIn. Monitor the status of your requests. After one week, open your **Connections** page and print a copy for your instructor to show who has accepted your request. If necessary, if someone did not accept your request, provide a brief explanation for why this may have happened.

3. **Join a Group in LinkedIn**

   In addition to adding connections to your LinkedIn account, you can also join groups in a variety of areas and fields of interest. For this exercise, you will explore the groups to find one that might be of interest to you and join it.

   (a) Open a web browser and navigate to **www.linkedin.com**.

   (b) Log in to LinkedIn, using the email address and password you used to create your account.

   (c) On the menu bar, point to **Groups** and click **Groups You May Like** from the drop-down menu. LinkedIn generates this list based upon the information that is in your profile.

   (d) Notice that some groups display a padlock icon next to their name. This means the group is a members-only group. Members may need to be pre-approved and this approval is up to the group leader. Additionally, the discussions in a members-only group will not be seen by anyone who is not a member of the group. Groups that do not display a padlock are open groups. Anyone can join an open group and read the discussions. If you see a group that interests you, click the group name to view additional details. If you don't see anything of interest, use the **Search Groups** tool on the left side of the screen to search for a group.

   (e) Once you've found a group you'd like to join, click the **Join Group** button.

(f) If you've selected an open group, you will already have access to the group's information. If you selected a members-only group, you may need to wait for your request to be approved. Once your membership is approved, your group will appear on your **Profile** page.

(g) Print out a copy of your **Groups** page showing your group or capture it by taking a screenshot.

(h) Submit the printout or screenshot you produced in Step g to your instructor.

(i) Log out of LinkedIn and close your browser.

4. **Follow a Company on LinkedIn**

   It is possible to locate companies that you are interested in on LinkedIn and to connect to them as well. You can follow a company to receive notifications of new developments, job openings, changes in personnel, and so on. In this exercise, you will locate a company for which you might want to work and follow it.

   (a) Log in to your LinkedIn account.

   (b) On the menu bar, point to **Companies** and click **Find Companies** from the drop-down menu.

   (c) Review the information displayed on the **Companies** page. LinkedIn provides suggestions for companies you might like and also provides a list of the most-followed companies. If you are interested in one of these, click the company to see its page. If you want to follow a company that doesn't appear on this page, use the search text box at the top of the page.

   (d) Once you've found a company of interest, click the **Follow Company** button. Once clicked, the button will change to **Following**.

   (e) Print out a copy of this page or capture it by taking a screenshot.

   (f) Submit the printout or screenshot you produced in Step e to your instructor.

   (g) Log out of LinkedIn and close your browser.

Critical Thinking

1. Are you a member of one or more social networks, other than the LinkedIn network you worked on for this chapter? If so, in which networks do you participate? Why did you choose to join? How much time do you spend on social networks? What do you think is the greatest advantage of a social network? What is the biggest disadvantage? Answer these questions in a brief one- or two-page paper explaining your reasons, and submit it to your instructor.

2. Before you read this chapter, were you aware that various types of malware and scams existed on social networking sites? Security experts are concerned about the threats posed by social networks. Because members are receiving information from people they "know," they may not exercise the same level of caution when opening messages, clicking on hyperlinks, or following directions. Have you experienced any trouble with a virus, spyware, or a scam resulting from your use of a social network? Do you think this is a serious problem? Research this issue on the Internet and locate an article discussing a current security threat on a social network (within the last six months or as determined by your instructor). Write a synopsis of the article and your responses to these questions and then submit the paper to your instructor.

Team Projects

1. As discussed in this chapter, it is possible to find social networks developed for a wide range of topics and interests. Split your group into two teams and visit the issues-focused social networks on Change.org (**www.change.org**). Each team should pick two topics and review the associated networks. Compare and contrast the two networks and create a chart listing your findings. Consider items such as included features, number of members, site design, and ease of use. Include a brief review of your impression of each network.

2. As a team, explore the professional networks LinkedIn (**www.linkedin.com**) and Plaxo (**www.plaxo.com**). Sign up for Plaxo and explore the features offered by each. As a college student, how would you use these sites? Conduct a search on each and see if anyone you know is a member of one of the sites. Do you think that one of these sites is better than the other? If so, why? Would you consider inviting an instructor to be your contact? Do you think an instructor would be more inclined to accept your invitation from a professional networking site than from a site like Facebook or MySpace? Create a brief paper that explains your team's findings on each site and that supports your opinions.

Credits

CHAPTER **3**

Blogs

Objectives

After you read this chapter, you will be able to:

1. Explain what a blog is, the popular types of blogs, and the typical features of a blog

2. Identify the characteristics of successful blogs

3. Plan a blog and identify a free blog hosting service

4. Set up an account at Blogger.com and create a blog

5. Create a blog post, publish your blog, and edit a post

6. Add images and video to a blog post

7. Add features to your blog

8. Explain how to publicize a blog

9. Explore blogging resources

The following Hands-On Exercises will help you accomplish the chapter objectives:

Hands-On Exercises

EXERCISES	SKILLS COVERED
1. Set Up a Blogger Account and Create a Blog (page 97)	**Step 1:** Start Your Browser and Navigate to Blogger **Step 2:** Create a Blogger Account **Step 3:** Name Your Blog, Select a URL and a Template, and Create the Blog
2. Create, Publish, and Edit a Blog Post (page 104)	**Step 1:** Start Your Browser and Sign In to Blogger **Step 2:** Write a Blog Post and Publish It to Your Blog **Step 3:** Select a Blog Post to Edit **Step 4:** Add a Hyperlink and Change Text Formatting **Step 5:** Correct a Mistake and Add Text to a Post
3. Add an Image and a Video to Blog Posts (page 114)	**Step 1:** Download an Image **Step 2:** Log In to Blogger and Add an Image to a New Blog Post **Step 3:** Add a Video to a New Blog Post
4. Add Features to a Blog (page 127)	**Step 1:** Add Labels to a Published Blog Post **Step 2:** Modify a Blog Layout **Step 3:** Add a Subscription Links Gadget to a Blog

Objective 1

Explain what a blog is, the popular types of blogs, and the typical features of a blog

What is a blog?

Blog Short for *web log*, a type of web page featuring multiple entries providing commentary on a topic of interest or a particular genre.

Blogger A person who creates and maintains a blog.

A *blog* (short for *web log*) is a type of web page featuring multiple entries that provide a commentary on a single subject (the benefits of recycling household garbage, for instance) or a particular genre (politics, religion, green living, fashion, etc.). A blog is essentially an online journal, often written by a single person. The topic of an individual entry often reflects what a *blogger* (a person who creates and maintains a blog) was thinking about at the time it was written. Today's blogs evolved from the personal online diaries that early Internet users maintained for others to access and read. Although these early diaries were primarily text-based, modern blogs often contain images and video. Blogging is quite popular, with a recent survey showing that the average blogger maintains three or more blogs. Although it is difficult to calculate the exact number, it is estimated that there are over 150 million blogs in existence.

Blogosphere The entire collection of all blogs on the web.

Bloggers often enjoy reading other people's blogs and frequently write about their favorite bloggers in their own blogs. Therefore, many blogs contain references or hyperlinks to other blogs. The entire collection of all blogs on the web is known as the *blogosphere*.

What does a typical blog look like?

Whereas conventional websites have many pages, most of the action on a blog occurs on the blog's main web page, as shown in Figure 3.1. In addition to the main page, blog sites may include other pages that usually contain older blog entries. Features you will find on most blogs include the following:

Blog posts The text, images, and/or videos that provide information to blog readers; appearing in reverse chronological order, each post includes a title and the date it was added to the blog.

- Posts—*Blog posts* are the text, images, and/or videos that provide information to blog readers. Posts contain a title and the date they were posted to the blog site. Blog posts are listed in reverse chronological order (i.e., the newest entries appear first).

Blog comments Written commentaries left by blog readers pertaining to a specific blog post.

- Comments—*Blog comments* are written commentaries left by readers pertaining to a specific blog post. Not every blog permits readers to post comments. Comments are typically displayed directly below a post or may be accessed through a link located next to or below the post.

Blog archive A list of the posts added to a blog, organized by date.

- Archive—A *blog archive* is a list of the posts that have been added to the blog, organized by date—usually by week or month. This provides readers the ability to quickly navigate to a specific point in time on the blog to locate an item.

Blogroll A list of hyperlinks to other blogs that the blog creator believes will be of interest to his or her readers.

- Blogroll—A *blogroll* is a list of hyperlinks to other blogs that the blog creator feels will be of interest to his or her readers.

- Topic list—In addition to an archive, many blogs include a list of topics for the blog posts. This makes it easier for a reader to find relevant information on blogs that have a large number of postings.

- Subscription links—Many blogs provide readers with an option to subscribe to their blogs through the use of RSS feeds. These subscription links give readers an easy way to be notified when a blog has been updated.

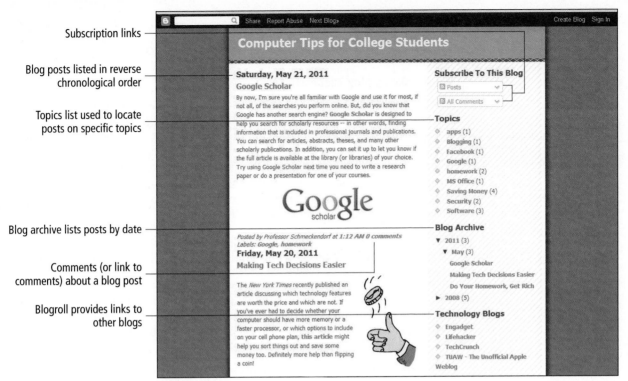

Subscription links

Blog posts listed in reverse chronological order

Topics list used to locate posts on specific topics

Blog archive lists posts by date

Comments (or link to comments) about a blog post

Blogroll provides links to other blogs

Figure 3.1 Components of a typical blog.

What types of blogs are there?

Blogs may be written for many different purposes and are created and maintained by a wide variety of people and organizations. The most common categories are the following:

- Personal blogs—These are blogs created and maintained by a single individual and are by far the most common type of blog. They most often resemble a personal diary in which the creator shares his or her thoughts about a particular subject—or sometimes almost anything that comes to mind—in a running commentary. Personal blogs can have many purposes, such as

  - keeping friends and family informed of events in the blogger's life
  - offering opinions on political and social issues
  - informing others of a hobby about which the blogger is knowledgeable

- Political blogs—Political candidates discovered the power of communicating through blogs during the campaigns preceding the 2004 presidential election, and political blogs continue to be influential today.

- Social awareness blogs—Many nonprofit organizations or groups promoting social causes (such as recycling, gun control, or animal rescue) use blogs to disseminate their message.

- Media blogs—Many blogs (such as the Huffington Post at **www.huffingtonpost. com**) have become media outlets in their own right. Bloggers often report breaking news events before traditional media outlets (like television and newspapers) pick up on the stories. An interesting subcategory of media blogs is the expert or celebrity blog. Many journalists have their own blogs, apart from their regular news jobs. Similarly, quite a few celebrities of movie, TV, music, or sports fame have begun blogging.

- Corporate blogs—Businesses use blogs to reach their customers and to inform them of new products and product enhancements. Small businesses especially like using blogs, because the cost is very reasonable, and may even be free, if you use the right blogging website.

Objective 2

Identify the characteristics of successful blogs

What makes a blog successful?

The best measure of a blog's success is the number of people who read it on a regular basis. The common measure that blog owners use to gauge their sites' popularity is how many *unique visitors* (different people who visit a website) and *page views* (each time a web page is loaded in a browser) their blogs generate each day. The ultimate goal for your blog is to establish a dedicated base of readers who regularly visit your blog and recommend your blog to others, thereby increasing your readership. You can encourage readers to return to your blog by providing them with compelling information and by following these guidelines:

■ Update the blog frequently—If a visitor to your blog comes back and does not find any new content, he or she will be much less likely to visit your blog in the future.

■ Keep blog posts on topic—All blog posts should relate to the topic of your blog. If you are blogging about cool, new rock bands, don't suddenly start posting entries about the funny thing your cat did today. Irrelevant posts will make readers search for other sources of information.

■ Maintain a professional-looking blog—Having a clean, organized design for your blog and blog posts that are free of grammatical errors and misspellings helps to establish and maintain your credibility. Blog readers often equate sloppiness with inaccuracy.

■ Be innovative—Your blog should have a unique slant to it that sets it apart from other blogs. Often, this is the creative writing style of the blogger. In other instances, a blog approaches a topic in a unique way that other bloggers have not yet thought about. Cartoonist Dave Walker writes "the dullest blog in the world" (**www.dullestblog.com**), and although it isn't updated frequently (which is part of the joke), it still generates a lot of visitors because of its unique, humorous nature (Figure 3.2).

■ Connect with others—Bloggers often permit readers to leave comments on a blog post to encourage interaction. The comments are visible to all readers of the blog. Blog authors can also reply to their readers' comments to encourage even more participation. Successful bloggers also connect with other bloggers whom they admire or who maintain blogs that would be of interest to their readers. Links to these other sites are a common feature on blogs.

■ Become indexed in search engines and blog directories—Your blog will get visitors only if people can find it. Having your blog indexed in search engines and *blog directories*, which are listings of blog sites usually organized by topic, will help people find your blog. If you are blogging about restoring your 1968 Mustang to original factory condition, you certainly want your site to appear in the results list when someone conducts a search for "*restoring 1968 Mustangs.*"

Unique visitors The number of different people, as identified by their IP addresses, who visit a website within a specific time period.

Page views The number of times a web page is loaded in a browser.

Blog directories Listings of blog sites, usually organized by topic.

Figure 3.2 The dullest blog in the world (**www.dullestblog.com**) is pretty unexciting, but it is a unique idea and still generates a lot of visitors and comments.

Objective 3

Plan a blog and identify a free blog hosting service

What steps should I take when planning my blog?

Although you may be eager to start generating posts for your blog, you should step back and think carefully about your blog before you begin. Addressing the following issues up front can save you a lot of time and prevent you from having to make extensive changes to your blog—or possibly start over—in the future.

- What is your topic?—You obviously need a topic, and careful thought needs to go into the subject areas your blog will encompass. If your topic is too broad (e.g., saving energy), you may not attract much readership because people searching the web are often looking for specific information. Conversely, if your topic is too narrow (e.g., compact fluorescent lamps), you may quickly run out of things about which you can blog. A happy medium might be energy-saving tips for the home and office. After you hit all the basic tips (installing automatic thermostats to control the temperature, putting adequate insulation in your attic, etc.), you should still have plenty to write about, because new energy-saving appliances and products are released all the time.

- What will you call your blog?—Selecting a title is important because it sets the tone for your blog. Additionally, because visitors often find a blog by using a search engine, the right title is critical for directing this search engine traffic to your blog. You should avoid using cutesy names or clever plays on words unless you are creating a personal blog. If you are developing a blog for commercial purposes, think about the keywords someone would type into a search engine (such as Google), and then work those keywords into your blog title. Green Computing Tips would be a better title for a blog than Techno Green. Although Techno Green sounds cool, few people are likely to type that phrase in a search engine.

- What will you choose for your URL?—The Uniform Resource Locator (URL) is your blog's website address; it's what people will type into the browser's address bar to reach your site. Ideally, your URL should be the same as, or similar to, your blog's title. However, it is best if the URL is concise and easy to remember. Your URL also needs to be unique—something that no one else has chosen. Keywords can be helpful in this situation too. If you are using a blogging tool such as Blogger or WordPress to host your blog, part of the address may also include the hosting site's domain name. Blogs created on Blogger typically include blogspot.com as the final part of the URL, so the full URL for your blog might be http://mythoughts.blogspot.com.

- How often will you post?—This is often determined by how much time you have to devote to your blog. If you are blogging solely for personal fulfillment or to communicate with family and friends, the frequency of your posts may not be that important. However, if you are trying to build a community and generate lots of visitors to your blog—perhaps in the hopes of making money from it—you need to be prepared to blog on a regular basis (several times per week or even daily).

- Will you accept comments?—When you set up your blog, you can select whether or not to allow readers to leave comments on posts. Some bloggers choose not to allow comments because managing comments can be time consuming. You need to review posts to delete inappropriate comments or offensive remarks. You also will need to manage *blog spam*, which are comments that are posted to your blog by automated programs to specifically promote a product or website. If building a community is critical to the theme of your blog, you should probably allow comments. But you need to allow time to manage comments as well as create new posts.

- Will you accept posts written by others?—On a personal blog, you may want friends and family to be able to post entries. Corporate blogs may have several authors, each writing about a specific topic or area of interest. If you are trying to have your blog become a major web destination, you may not be able to keep up with the demand for content. You may need to take on other blog authors to generate posts.

Blog spam Comments designed to promote an often undesirable product or website that are posted to a blog by automated programs.

Where can I set up a blog?

There are numerous websites that provide free hosting for blogs, including Blogger (www.blogger.com), WordPress (www.wordpress.com), and Tumblr (www.tumblr.com). Starting off your personal blog on a free site is usually a good idea. If you lose interest in your blog or lack the time to maintain it properly, you won't have invested any money in it. However, if you are considering launching a commercial blog site, you may want to locate a hosting service and register a domain name there instead of on one of the free sites. Free sites usually provide a URL for your blog that includes the site's domain name. Having your own domain name makes your site appear more credible and professional. It also implies that you are serious about your topic and not just creating a blog on a whim. Hosting service fees vary depending upon the features you want to include in your plan, but many are quite affordable. The free hosting sites do impose some limitations on the features you can have on your blog, and you may not want these restrictions if your blog becomes very popular.

In the next section, we'll use Blogger.com to set up an account and create your first blog.

Objective 4

Set up an account at Blogger.com and create a blog

Blogger.com is a site owned by Google where anyone can set up a blog for free. In the following Hands-On Exercises, you will set up your first blog and launch yourself into the blogosphere!

Hands-On Exercises

For purposes of the Hands-On Exercises in this chapter, we are assuming that Professor Schmeckendorf is setting up a blog for his computer literacy students to inform them about aspects of information technology that can make their lives easier.

1 | Set Up a Blogger Account and Create a Blog

Steps: 1. Start Your Browser and Navigate to Blogger; **2.** Create a Blogger Account; **3.** Name Your Blog, Select a URL and a Template, and Create the Blog.

Use Figures 3.3 through 3.10 as a guide to the exercise.

Step 1 | Start Your Browser and Navigate to Blogger

Refer to Figure 3.3 as you complete Step 1.

To complete this exercise, you will need to use the Google account you created in Chapter 1. If you have not yet created a Google account, follow the instructions in Chapter 1, Hands-On Exercise 1, and then return to this exercise.

a. Turn on the computer.

b. Start your preferred browser (Internet Explorer, Firefox, Chrome, Safari, etc.). Type **www.blogger.com** in the address bar of your browser and press **Enter**.

c. Sign in to Blogger using the email address and password you created for your Google account in Chapter 1. If necessary, you should uncheck the **Stay signed in** checkbox, especially if you are on a public computer. Click the **Sign in** button to proceed to the **Create Blogger Account** page.

Keep unchecked ———

C – Enter the email address and password used to create your Google account and then click Sign in

Figure 3.3 Hands-On Exercise 1, Step 1c.

> **Tip ☆**
>
> If you are the only person using your computer, you may wish to select the checkbox next to the words **Stay signed in** before clicking the **Sign in** button. This creates a cookie file on your computer that will automatically sign you in to Blogger when you return to the site. The cookie will be effective for up to two weeks, after which time you will need to sign in again. You should not select the **Stay signed in** feature when you are using a public or shared computer, such as one in a computer lab at your school. If you do, any person using that same computer will have access to your blog.

Step 2 Create a Blogger Account

Refer to Figures 3.4 and 3.5 as you complete Step 2.

a. The **Sign up for Blogger** screen is the first step in the Blogger account creation process. You should see the email address you signed in with and your name on this screen. In the **Display name** text box, add the name you wish to use as the author of your blog posts. You do not have to use your full name; in fact, you can even create a pseudonym if you prefer to retain your anonymity while blogging.

b. If you wish to receive email from Blogger with blogging advice, announcements, and tips, click the **Email notifications** checkbox. If you do not wish to receive email, leave this box unchecked.

c. The **Gender** drop-down list allows you to choose your gender. You may also leave this blank if you wish.

d. In the **Acceptance of Terms** section, click the **Terms of Service** link to review this information. Assuming you agree with these terms, click the **I accept the Terms of Service** checkbox.

e. Click the **Continue** arrow to proceed to the next step.

[handwritten note in margin: Send MsV e-mail of url for blogging]

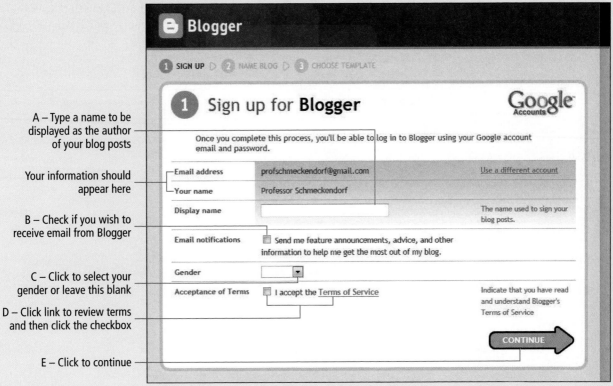

A – Type a name to be displayed as the author of your blog posts

Your information should appear here

B – Check if you wish to receive email from Blogger

C – Click to select your gender or leave this blank

D – Click link to review terms and then click the checkbox

E – Click to continue

Figure 3.4 Hands-On Exercise 1, Steps 2a through 2e.

The Blogger **Dashboard** page appears (Figure 3.5). The Dashboard is a summary screen where you can see and manage all the blogs in your account. This is the first page you will see each time you log in to Blogger. The top of the Dashboard page frequently displays system messages from Blogger administrators, which may or may not be relevant to your account. You can click on the messages that interest you and ignore those that don't. Below the messages are two sections. The upper section lists any blogs you are currently authoring. It is possible to create multiple blogs and manage them from a single Blogger account. You can also create a new blog from within this section. Below this section is the **Reading List** section, which displays a list of any blogs you have chosen to follow. You also have the option to view the blogs you are following in Google Reader. The **Blogger Buzz**, which is Blogger's own blog, is included in the Reading List by default and often contains useful tips and updates.

Alert!

If you see a message on your Dashboard that says you have not verified your email address, you should log in to the email account that you used when you created your Blogger account. There should be an email message from Blogger that contains a hyperlink for you to click to verify your email account. Blogger wants to ensure that your email account is valid. If you can't find the email message, be sure to check your spam or junk mail folder. If you never received the message, click the **Resend Verification Email** link on your Dashboard to receive a new verification email and follow the instructions it contains.

f. If necessary, you can click the **Language** drop-down button to select your preferred language for your blog. English is the default choice and is what Professor Schmeckendorf will use.

g. Click the **New Blog** button.

F – Select language,
if necessary

G – Click to create a blog

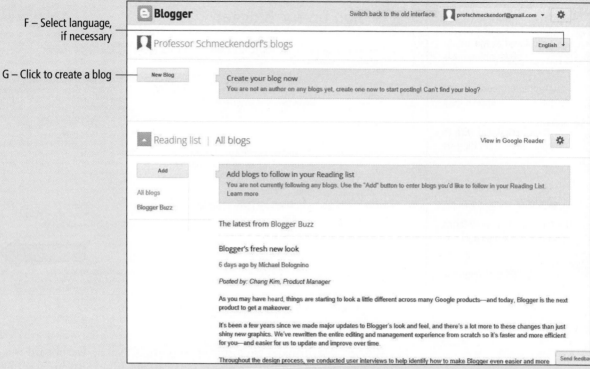

Figure 3.5 Hands-On Exercise 1, Steps 2f and 2g.

The Blogger user interface was recently updated. If your Dashboard doesn't look the same as the one shown in Figure 3.5, check the top of the page for the **Try the updated Blogger interface** link. Click the link to begin using the new interface.

Step 3 Name Your Blog, Select a URL and a Template, and Create the Blog

Refer to Figures 3.6 through 3.10 as you complete Step 3.

a. On the **Blogs List > Create a new blog** window, in the **Title** text box, type a title for your blog. Professor Schmeckendorf has decided to name his blog "Information Technology Resources for GSU Students."

Remember that the name of your blog should help define the topic of your blog. You can always change the name later if you decide something else would be more appropriate.

b. In the **Address** text box, type a URL for your blog. Professor Schmeckendorf has selected *gsustudentitresources* for his portion of the blog's URL.

The URL for your blog is very important because this is what people will type into their browser's address bar to navigate to your blog. All blogs hosted by Blogger will use a URL that ends in *blogspot.com*, but Blogger permits you to define the first part of the URL for your blog. Be sure to choose a URL that contains keywords that someone would use in a search engine when looking for a blog about your chosen topic.

As you type your proposed URL, Blogger checks within the blogspot.com domain and displays a message to indicate whether or not it is available. Someone else may already be using the URL that you have chosen. If so, you will need to select another URL and check again to see if your new choice is available. You may need to repeat this step more than once until you find a URL that is available.

c. To make designing your blog easier, Blogger provides several standard templates. These templates can be used to help you create a blog with a professionally designed appearance, even if you don't have great design skills. You can always change or modify your blog's template later. Changing the template for your blog at a later point in time will not remove any existing blog posts. Click one of the templates to select it. Professor Schmeckendorf has selected the **Simple** template.

 Tip

What if you don't like any of the templates that Blogger offers? There are plenty of free templates available on the web, designed for people to use with Blogger. Just go to Google and search with the keywords *Blogger templates;* you should find plenty to choose from.

d. Once you've selected a URL and a template, click the **Create blog!** button.

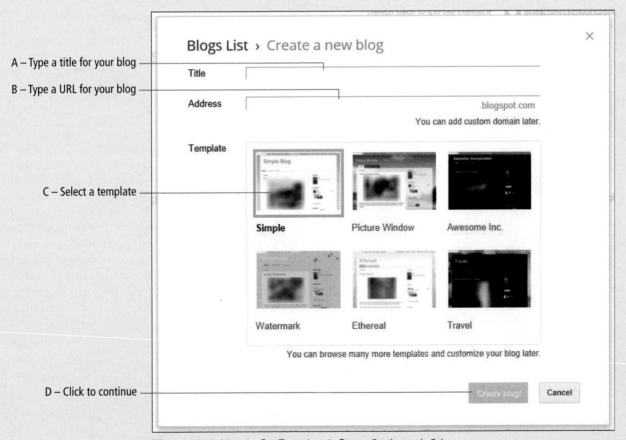

Figure 3.6 Hands-On Exercise 1, Steps 3a through 3d.

e. The Dashboard screen appears with a message indicating that the blog has been created. Click the **Start posting** link to proceed to the next step.

E – Click to continue

Figure 3.7 Hands-On Exercise 1, Step 3e.

Your blog appears with the **Create Post** screen displayed. There is a row of editing tool buttons at the top of the page and a column of options that can be used to modify your post on the right. We'll cover creating blog entries in Hands-On Exercise 2. For now, we'll only view the blog we just created.

f. On the **Create Post** screen, at the top left of the screen, click the title of your blog to go to the **All posts** page.

F – Click to go to the All posts page

Editing tools

Post settings options

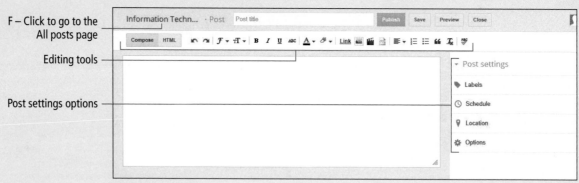

Figure 3.8 Hands-On Exercise 1, Step 3f.

The **All posts** page should look similar to what is shown in Figure 3.9. At the top of the page are navigation buttons to take you back to your list of blogs (if you have more than one), create a new post, view existing posts, and view your blog. The right side of the page displays your user name and a gear icon. Click your name to update your Blogger profile, edit your account settings, and log out of Blogger. Click the gear icon to access Google's help feature. On the left side of the page is a list of tabs that can be used to customize and modify your blog and work with various features. The main section of this page is blank right now, but will eventually list all of the posts that you publish to your blog.

g. Click the **View blog** button to display your blog.

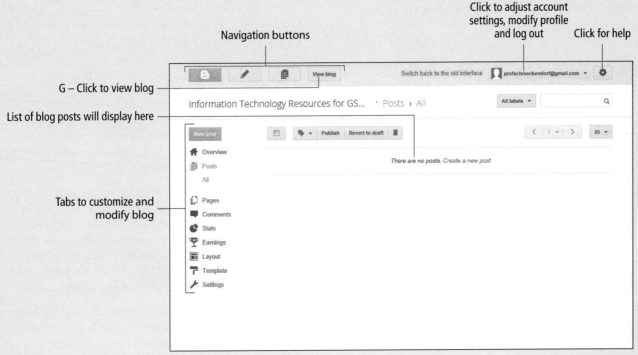

Figure 3.9 Hands-On Exercise 1, Step 3g.

Your blog may appear different because of the template you selected in Step 3c. Obviously, the blog's title will display the title you chose and the information in the **About Me** section will show your name and not Professor Schmeckendorf's.

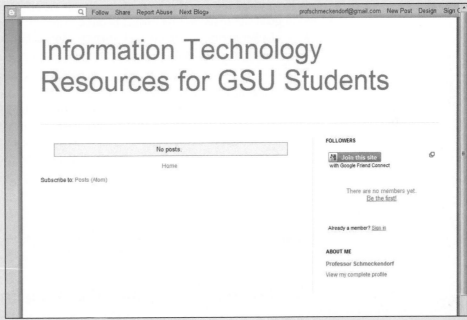

Figure 3.10 The blog you created should look similar to the one shown here. Your blog is now set up and ready for your first post.

You may now sign out of Blogger by clicking the **Sign Out** link in the upper right corner of the screen. You can also close your browser.

Objective 5

Create a blog post, publish your blog, and edit a post

Now that you have your blog set up, you are ready to write your first blog post. To generate effective blog posts, you should keep these guidelines in mind:

- Stay on topic—Be sure that all blog posts are related to the theme of your blog. Professor Schmeckendorf's blog is designed to provide his students with useful resources and tips about computing; therefore, a good first post for his blog would be to direct students to a good source of information about Microsoft Office.

- Keep it short—Given the vast amount of information available on the Internet and the limited time many web surfers have to find and use this information, you should try to keep your blog posts concise and to the point. A good target is 75 to 175 words, depending on the information you are conveying. Posts that direct someone to another site might be rather short, while a post that conveys a great deal of important information may be considerably longer. However, if your post exceeds 300 words, you might want to consider breaking it up into several smaller posts.

- Link to other blogs and websites—Many posts reference information on other blogs or other websites. When appropriate, you should include clickable links in your blog post to make it easy for your readers to navigate to other relevant sites.

- Use media appropriately—Many beginning bloggers get carried away with video and images in their posts. A blog conveys information primarily through the use of text. Don't overwhelm your audience by the use of gratuitous multimedia. Also, make sure you have permission to use the images and video you place on your blog. Most media is copyrighted and requires the permission of the copyright holder before you can use it. Don't just copy images you find on the web and post them on your blog site; this is often a copyright violation. Flickr (**www.flickr.com**) is a good site to use to find images because many Flickr posters, although not all, grant blanket permission to use their images. MorgueFile (**www.morguefile.com**) is another site that features free, high-resolution digital stock photography.

- Create effective titles—The post title is extremely important because search engines index the titles of blog posts. Therefore, to drive traffic to your blog, use keywords in your post titles that people might use to search for information on the topic of your post. A post titled "My Summer Vacation" might not generate much traffic, but one titled "Hiking in the Grand Canyon – Bright Angel Trail" is much more descriptive and includes more words that someone might enter into a search engine.

Hands-On Exercises

2 | Create, Publish, and Edit a Blog Post

Steps: 1. Start Your Browser and Sign In to Blogger; **2.** Write a Blog Post and Publish It to Your Blog; **3.** Select a Blog Post to Edit; **4.** Add a Hyperlink and Change Text Formatting; **5.** Correct a Mistake and Add Text to a Post.

Use Figures 3.11 through 3.24 as a guide to the exercise.

Step Start Your Browser and Sign In to Blogger

Refer to Figure 3.11 as you complete Step 1.

a. Start your preferred browser. Type **www.blogger.com** in the address bar of your browser and press **Enter**.

b. Sign in to Blogger using the email address and password you created for your Google account and then click the **Sign in** button to go to the **Dashboard** page of your Blogger account.

> **Alert!**
>
> In addition to the system messages that appear at the top of the Dashboard, Blogger will occasionally display a callout box to point out a particular feature or new item of interest. You can choose to explore this information or close the box to dismiss it.

c. Notice that the top section of the Dashboard now displays information about the blog you created in the previous exercise. Click the **Create new post** button to navigate to the **Create post** screen.

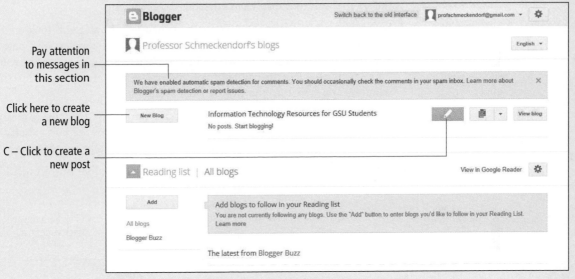

Figure 3.11 Hands-On Exercise 2, Step 1c.

Step 2 Write a Blog Post and Publish It to Your Blog

Refer to Figures 3.12 through 3.14 as you complete Step 2.

The **Create post** screen opens with a blank blog post text box displayed. To the right of the text box is a list of **Post settings** you can use to add additional details to your blog post. Adding a blog post to your blog is very much like creating an email message. The post title is similar to the Subject line of an email and the blog post itself resembles the email message. For this exercise, Professor Schmeckendorf wants to inform his students about the Microsoft Office blog. You may create your own blog post, or you can copy the information Professor Schmeckendorf will post, as shown in the following steps. If you choose to create your own post, keep the blog posting guidelines discussed earlier in mind.

a. In the **Post title** text box, type the following text: **Improve Your Microsoft Office Skills**.

b. Add the text for your post in the large text box in the center of the screen, below the **Title** text box. Type the following text: **If you have recently made the transition from an older version of Microsoft Office to Microsoft Office 2010, you may find you have a lot of questions about how things work. In addition to Microsoft's Help and Support areas on its website, Microsoft also publishes the Microsoft Office Blog. This blog is a team effort, containing posts from a number of different individuals. The blog's primary purpose is to provide you with tips and information to help you become a better Microsoft Office user. The blog posts cover the full range of Microsoft Office products and are designed to help you get the most of these software programs.**

c. The toolbar at the top of the text box includes a number of buttons that will probably be familiar to most users. Click the **Check spelling** button to review the contents of your post for any spelling errors. Misspelled words are highlighted. Click on any highlighted words to display a pop-up list of correct spelling suggestions. If the correct word is in the list, simply click it to replace the misspelled word. If you don't see the word you need, you can click **Ignore** and revise your text by deleting it and retyping it correctly.

Although the spell-check tool in Blogger will find spelling errors, it is not perfect and may not catch everything. Also, it does not check your entry for proper grammar. Make sure to review your post carefully for any typos or grammatical errors the spell-check tool may have missed.

d. Before publishing your entry, you may want to see how it will look on your blog. Click the **Preview** button above the text box to display your post in a new browser tab (or new browser window). The entry will appear in your blog's template with a *Preview* banner displayed in the top-left corner. Close this tab (or window) and return to the **Create post** screen.

e. If you aren't ready to publish your post, but want to save the work you've done so far, you can click the **Save** button above the text box to save it as a draft. Draft posts are not visible on your blog. Blogger will also periodically save your posts for you.

f. Once you're ready to publish your post, click the **Publish** button to add your entry to your blog and return to the **All Posts** page.

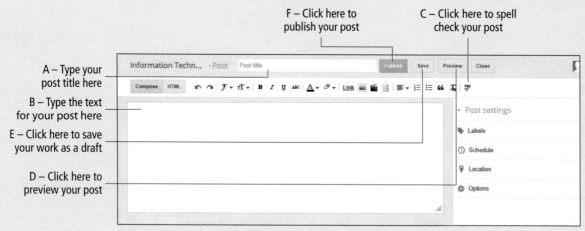

Figure 3.12 Hands-On Exercise 2, Steps 2a through 2f.

g. In the column on the left side of the **All posts** page is the **Posts** tab. This section displays the total number of posts you have written for your blog, as well as how many have been published successfully. The title of your post appears in the center of the screen, along with the blog post author's name, icons indicating the number of comments and views for the post, and, depending upon how recently the post was published, the time or date of publication. You should now view your blog to ensure the entry looks the way you wish it to appear on your blog. Click the **View blog** button at the top of the page to go to your blog page.

G – Click here to view your blog post

Figure 3.13 Hands-On Exercise 2, Step 2g.

Figure 3.14 shows Professor Schmeckendorf's blog with the first post added. When you post an entry to a blog, the date and time you created it are assigned to the post. The date is displayed above the title of the blog post and, depending on the template that is selected, the time may appear at the end of the post, along with the name of the post's author. Remember that blogs display posts in reverse chronological order, so your most recent posts will always appear at the top of your blog. By default, Blogger includes a blog archive on your blog, grouping your posts by year and then by the months in which they were created. Notice that your first post now appears in the blog archive.

You should now practice making posts to your blog. Click the **New Post** link located at the top right of the blog to navigate back to the **Create post** page in Blogger. Repeat Steps 2a through 2g to create and publish at least two more posts to your blog before proceeding to Step 3.

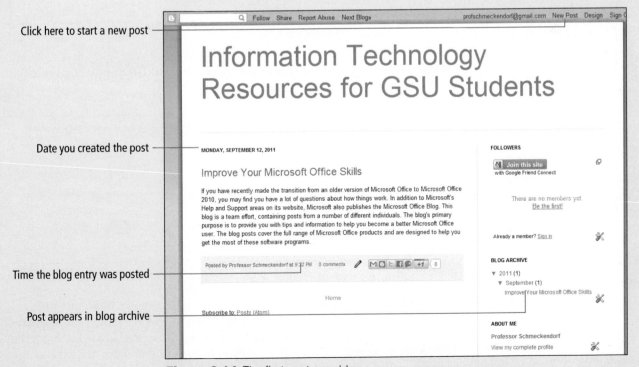

Click here to start a new post

Date you created the post

Time the blog entry was posted

Post appears in blog archive

Figure 3.14 The first post on a blog.

Step ③ Select a Blog Post to Edit

Refer to Figures 3.15 through 3.17 as you complete Step 3.

After publishing a post, you might think of additional information that you need to add. Or you might spot a spelling or grammar error in the post that you missed earlier. Fortunately, Blogger makes it easy to edit previously published blog posts.

How you will select your post for editing depends upon where you currently are. If you are logged in to Blogger and are viewing your blog, begin with Step 3a. However, if you have logged out of Blogger, you will need to log back in and start from your Dashboard. If you are anywhere else on your blog, click the **Blogger** button at the top of the page to go to your blog list on the Dashboard. If you are starting from the Dashboard, begin with Step 3b.

a. If you are still logged in to Blogger and are viewing your blog, you should see a pencil icon at the bottom of each post. Click the pencil icon for the post you want to edit to go directly to the **Edit post** page with the text of the post displayed and then proceed to Step 4.

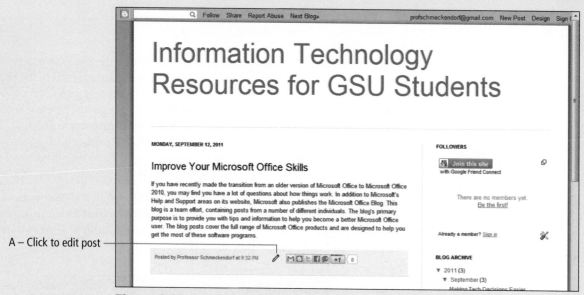

A – Click to edit post

Figure 3.15 Hands-On Exercise 2, Step 3a.

b. If you are starting from the **Dashboard** page, click the **Go to post list** button to go to the **All posts** page.

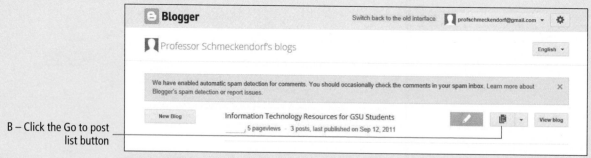

B – Click the Go to post list button

Figure 3.16 Hands-On Exercise 2, Step 3b.

The **All posts** page lists all the posts on your blog. As shown in Figure 3.17, there are currently three posts on Professor Schmeckendorf's blog; your blog may have more or less, depending on how many posts you created in Step 2. From the **All posts** page, you can manage your posts by hovering over the desired post to display the **Edit**, **View**, and **Delete** options.

c. If you created the same post as Professor Schmeckendorf did in Step 2—*Improve Your Microsoft Office Skills*—click the **Edit** link below this post. If you created your own posts, select one that may need some revisions and could also benefit from the addition of a hyperlink. Clicking the **Edit** link will open your post in the editing mode.

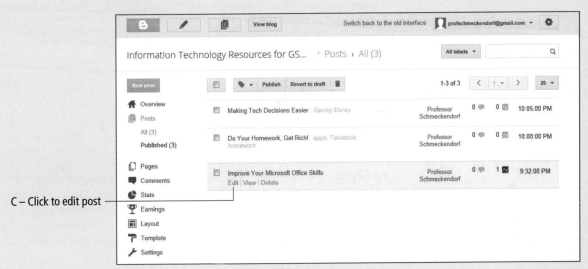

C – Click to edit post

Figure 3.17 Hands-On Exercise 2, Step 3c.

Step 4 Add a Hyperlink and Change Text Formatting

Refer to Figures 3.18 through 3.22 as you complete Step 4.

The **Edit post** screen looks almost identical to the **New Post** screen and it provides the same functionality, although two of the buttons at the top of the page have changed. The **Save** button has been replaced by the **Revert to draft** button. This allows you to undo any changes you might make and return your post to its last published version. The **Publish** button has been changed to the **Update** button. Clicking this button will publish any changes you make to the existing post. It would be helpful to add a hyperlink to Professor Schmeckendorf's post about the Microsoft Office blog so that students can easily find it. If you have created your own post, you should review it and identify a website that can provide some additional value for your readers. Blog readers appreciate links that make it easy for them to navigate to relevant pages. You should locate a word or phrase in your post that can be converted to a live hyperlink. In the case of Professor Schmeckendorf's post, we will turn the phrase *Microsoft Office Blog* in the second sentence into a live hyperlink.

a. Locate the phrase *Microsoft Office Blog* in the second sentence of the blog post (or the phrase of your choice in your own post). Select the phrase by left-clicking and dragging the mouse to highlight it.

b. Click the **Add or remove link** button on the toolbar to display the **Edit Link** dialog box.

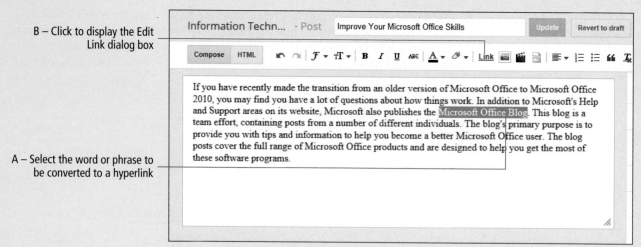

B – Click to display the Edit
Link dialog box

A – Select the word or phrase to
be converted to a hyperlink

Figure 3.18 Hands-On Exercise 2, Steps 4a and 4b.

c. In the **Edit Link** dialog box, the **Text to display** text box should display the text you have already selected. The **Link to** section allows you to add a link to either a **Web address** or an **Email address**. Make sure the **Web address** option button is selected and type the URL of the website that you wish to link to. To create a link to the Microsoft Office Blog, type **http://blogs.office.com/** in the **Web address** text box.

If you are creating a link to a website that has a lengthy URL, open a new tab or window in your browser and locate the website to which you want to link. Highlight the URL in the address bar of your browser and press **Ctrl+C** to copy the address. Return to your blog and follow the steps to open the **Edit Link** dialog box. Click in the **Web address** text box and press **Ctrl+V** to paste the URL there. This will ensure you have entered the URL correctly.

d. To ensure you've added the link correctly, click the **Test this link** link. If you've typed the URL correctly, the website will open in a new tab or window in your browser. If you don't reach the website you expected, check the URL and correct it if necessary.

e. After you've confirmed that the URL is correct, close the browser tab or window to return to the **Edit Link** dialog box and click **OK**.

Selected text displays here

C – Type the URL for the
desired website here

D – Click to ensure the
link is correct

E – Click to create the link

Figure 3.19 Hands-On Exercise 2, Steps 4c through 4e.

f. The selected text has been converted to a hyperlink. A toolbar appears below the link providing the option to see the actual URL and go to the site, or to change or remove the link from the post. Click the **Close** button in the upper right corner to close the toolbar.

Selected text is now a hyperlink ——

F – Click to close the toolbar ——

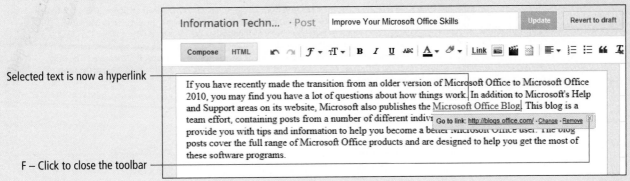

Figure 3.20 Hands-On Exercise 2, Step 4f.

Sometimes you will need to change the formatting of text in your post to add emphasis or draw attention to certain key phrases. Blogger provides a toolbar with formatting options that should be familiar to most users, since the buttons use many of the same icons you see when working with other tools, such as Microsoft Office or email. If a button is not familiar to you, simply hover over it to display a screen tip that identifies the button's purpose. You should use these formatting options carefully. Using too many colors, fonts, or other effects may actually be distracting for your viewers and make your blog appear amateurish.

In Professor Schmeckendorf's current post, he wants to emphasize the phrases *Microsoft Office 2010* and *Help and Support* by changing the font color for the first phrase to blue and making the second phrase bold. Use the following techniques to apply your choice of formatting to your blog post as well.

g. In the first sentence of the post, select the phrase *Microsoft Office 2010*.

h. Click the **Text color** button to display a color palette and then click the color of your choice to apply it to the selected text. Click away from the highlighted text to unselect it and view the change.

H – Click to change text color ——

G – Select text to be formatted ——

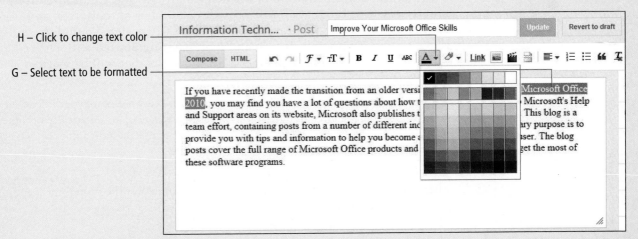

Figure 3.21 Hands-On Exercise 2, Steps 4g and 4h.

i. In the second sentence, select the phrase *Help and Support*.

j. Click the **Bold** button to apply bolding to the selected text.

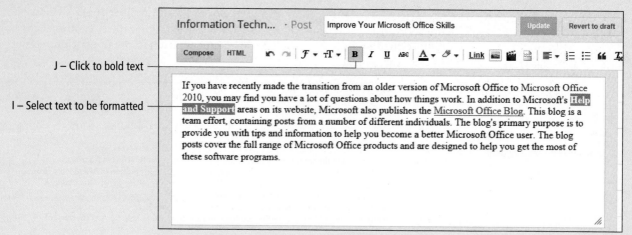

J – Click to bold text

I – Select text to be formatted

Figure 3.22 Hands-On Exercise 2, Steps 4i and 4j.

Step 5 | Correct a Mistake and Add Text to a Post

Refer to Figures 3.23 and 3.24 as you complete Step 5.

Professor Schmeckendorf has noticed that he omitted the word *out* in the last sentence of his post—it should read "to help you get the most *out* of these software programs." He also wants to provide some additional information to help students make the transition from older versions of Office to Office 2010. You may find that you need to make changes to your blog post as well. You can use many of the same editing techniques for blog posts that you use with Microsoft Office to delete, revise, or add text. The following steps describe how to modify Professor Schmeckendorf's blog post—you can apply the same techniques to revise and add text to your own post.

a. Position your insertion point after the word *most* in the last sentence of the post. Type **out** to correct the sentence.

b. Position your insertion point at the end of the blog post after the word *programs*. Press **Enter** twice to begin a new paragraph. Type the following text into the blog post text box: **In addition to the helpful articles you will find on the Microsoft Office Blog, Microsoft provides a number of tools, tips, and articles to help make the transition to Office 2010 easier. To find these tools, go to www.microsoft.com and type "Getting Started with Office 2010" in the search box. You'll get a list of results that will be worth exploring.**

Notice that Blogger automatically converts *www.microsoft.com* to a hyperlink when you type it. URLs that begin with either *www* or *http://* will automatically become hyperlinks once you've typed them. You only need to use the Edit Link tool when you want to convert a word or phrase to a hyperlink.

c. Remember to proofread your changes and use the spell-check tool. Once you've finished editing your blog post, click the **Update** button to post the revised entry and return to the **All posts** page.

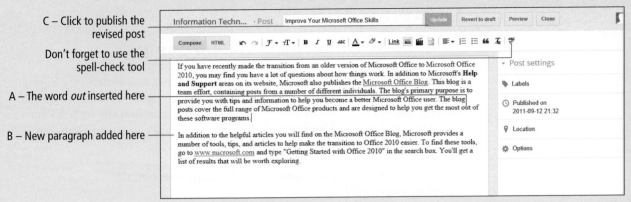

C – Click to publish the revised post

Don't forget to use the spell-check tool

A – The word *out* inserted here

B – New paragraph added here

Figure 3.23 Hands-On Exercise 2, Steps 5a through 5c.

d. On the **All posts** page, locate the title of the post you just updated in the post list. Click the **View** link below the post title to view your blog with the revised blog entry (see Figure 3.24). Your blog may open in a new tab or new browser window. Notice that the post still shows the date and time that this entry was originally posted. Blogger does not update this information; therefore, the post will still be in the same order as it originally appeared on the blog, it will not move to the top. You might also notice that your hyperlinks may not look as expected. A hyperlink that has never been clicked is formatted differently than an active one. Similarly, an *active* hyperlink is one that a cursor is pointing to and is formatted differently. Links that have been clicked are referred to as *visited*. Depending on the status of the links whether none of them have been clicked, all of them have been clicked, or not. Also, depending upon the template you chose, your links may vary from the ones used here. In Professor Schmeckendorf's blog post in Figure 3.24, you can see both an active hyperlink and the visited hyperlink.

e. Click the **X** in the upper right corner of the

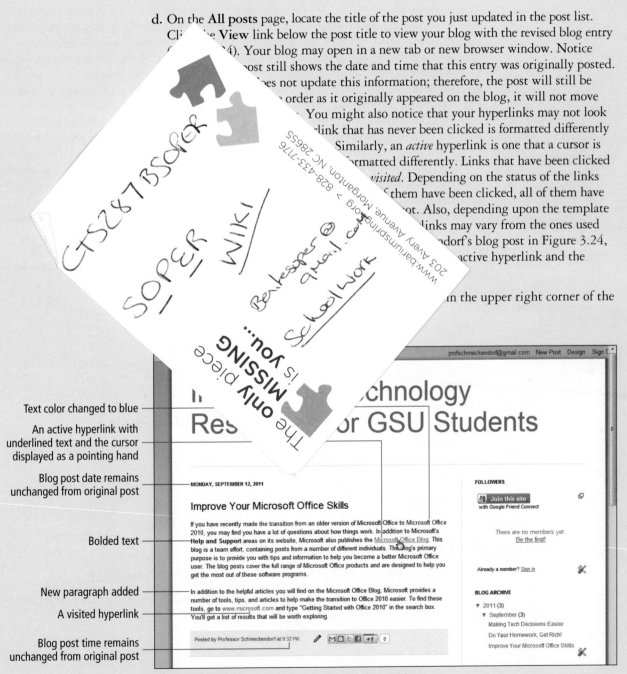

Text color changed to blue

An active hyperlink with underlined text and the cursor displayed as a pointing hand

Blog post date remains unchanged from original post

Bolded text

New paragraph added

A visited hyperlink

Blog post time remains unchanged from original post

Figure 3.24 Blog post's appearance after editing.

Objective 6

Add images and video to a blog post

A blog comprised of posts that contain only text is going to look pretty boring. However, a blog that is filled only with digital images and video might be distracting and not particularly informative. The trick is to find the right balance and integrate images and video into your blog posts so they can serve to enhance or clarify your message.

If I need a specific image, where can I obtain one without violating copyright?

Not everything is covered by copyright laws. A work such as a book, painting, photograph, or video that is created but not covered by copyright is considered to be in the public domain. There are several reasons why a work may be in the public domain—it may never have been copyrighted or the work's creator may have elected to add it to the public domain. Similarly, if the copyright expires and is not renewed, the work enters the public domain. Works that are in the public domain may be reproduced, distributed, or modified by anyone for any type of use, including commercial purposes.

There are numerous websites that provide public domain photos and images for your use, including sites such as Public-Domain-Photos.com (**http://public-domain-photos.com**), PD Photo (**www.pdphoto.org**), and Public Domain Pictures (**www.publicdomainpictures.net**). You should be sure to review the information on these sites carefully, since not everything that is there may meet the public domain criteria.

You may also want to search for works that are covered by Creative Commons licensing schemes. Creative Commons licenses allow the creator to relinquish some, but not all, of their rights, and may be just what you need.

In the following Hands-On Exercise, you'll be recreating two blog posts—which include pictures and video—that Professor Schmeckendorf used on his blog.

Hands-On Exercises

3 | Add an Image and a Video to Blog Posts

Steps: 1. Download an Image; **2.** Log In to Blogger and Add an Image to a New Blog Post; **3.** Add a Video to a New Blog Post.

Use Figures 3.25 through 3.41 as a guide to the exercise.

 Step 1 **Download an Image**

Refer to Figures 3.25 through 3.28 as you complete Step 1.

a. Start your preferred browser. Type **www.pearsonhighered.com/nextseries** in the address bar of your browser and press **Enter**.

b. From the list of books provided, locate this textbook and click the **Companion Website** link. This will take you to the companion website for this book.

c. Click the **Student Data Files** link and then click the **Chapter 3** link to start the download process.

d. In the **Windows Internet Explorer** dialog box, click the **Save as** button to display the **Save As** dialog box.

Alert

When downloading a file, if you click **Save**, Internet Explorer 9 (IE9) saves the downloaded file to the Users\username\Downloads folder by default. Change IE9's default location for all downloaded files before you begin the download process by pressing **Ctrl+J** and clicking the **Options** link to select the desired location. To change the download location for an individual file, use the **Save as** option.

D – Click to save the file to a location of your choice

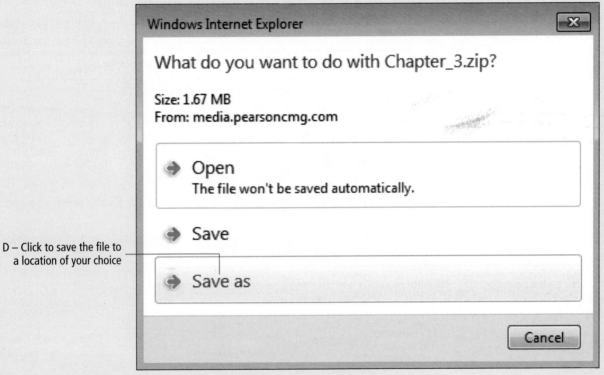

Figure 3.25 Hands-On Exercise 3, Step 1d.

e. Browse through the folders (or create a new folder) on your computer's hard drive or your flash drive to find an appropriate place to save the file.

f. Click the **Save** button to download the file and save it to your computer. Be sure to remember where you saved the file.

g. A message bar may appear at the bottom of your screen indicating the status of the download. Once the download is complete, you can click the **Close** button to dismiss this message.

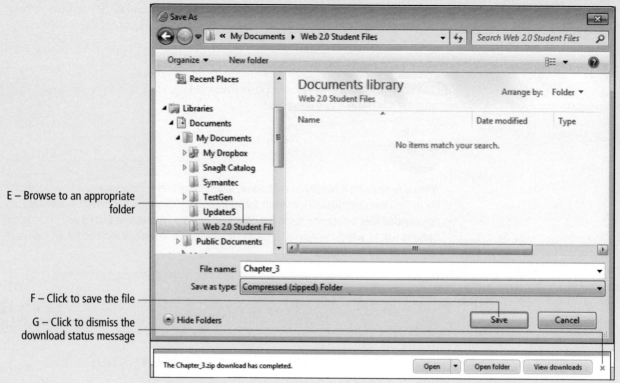

E – Browse to an appropriate folder

F – Click to save the file

G – Click to dismiss the download status message

Figure 3.26 Hands-On Exercise 3, Steps 1e through 1g.

h. You can close all the Companion Website tabs or windows in your browser, but leave your browser open for Step 2.

i. The file you just downloaded is a zipped folder. Open Windows Explorer and browse to the location where you saved this file.

j. Right-click the zipped folder and select **Extract All** from the shortcut menu.

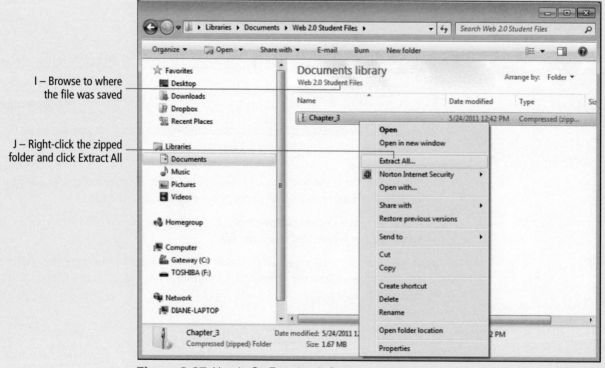

I – Browse to where the file was saved

J – Right-click the zipped folder and click Extract All

Figure 3.27 Hands-On Exercise 3, Steps 1i and 1j.

k. In the **Extract Compressed (Zipped) Folders** dialog box, there may already be a file path displayed in the **Files will be extracted to this folder** text box. If this is the location to which you wish to extract the file or files, go to the next step. If this is not the correct location, click the **Browse** button to locate the correct location.

l. If necessary, ensure there is a check in the **Show extracted files when complete** checkbox.

m. Click the **Extract** button to proceed. A new window appears showing the extracted folder.

K – File location for extracted
file; click Browse to select a
different location

L – Check this box, if necessary

M – Click to proceed

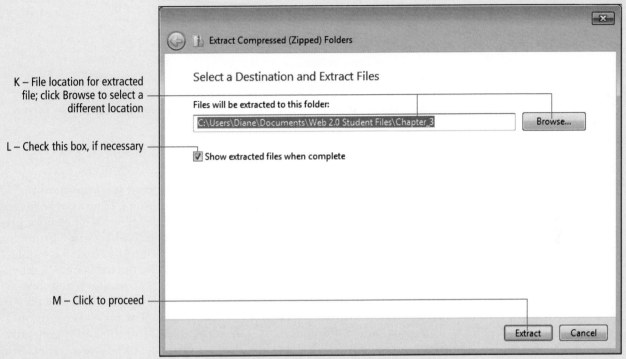

Figure 3.28 Hands-On Exercise 3, Steps 1k through 1m.

Step ❷ Log In to Blogger and Add an Image to a New Blog Post

Refer to Figures 3.29 through 3.36 as you complete Step 2.

a. Go to **www.blogger.com** and log in to your Blogger account.

b. On the Blogger **Dashboard** page, click the **Create new post** button to go to the **Create post** page.

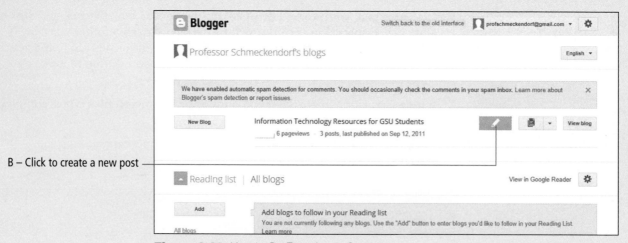

B – Click to create a new post

Figure 3.29 Hands-On Exercise 3, Step 2b.

Professor Schmeckendorf has created a post about whole-house surge protectors for his students. You will recreate this post on your blog now, using the picture you downloaded in Step 1, Ch_3_Exercise_3.jpg.

c. On the **Create new post** page, in the **Post title** text box, type **Whole-House Surge Protection**.

d. In the main text box for the post, type the following text: **It's important to protect all your electronic devices, not just computers, from power surges. Printers, televisions, appliances, and computer peripherals all require protection. However, it can be inconvenient to use individual surge protectors on all the devices that need protection. One solution is to install a whole-house surge protector, as shown in this photo. The device is installed by an electrician and is attached to your circuit breaker panel. Whole-house surge protectors work just like other surge protection devices, but they protect all electrical devices in the house at once. The typical cost to buy and install one of these devices ranges from $200 to $300 and is generally less than the cost of buying individual surge protectors for every electrical device in your home.**

e. Position your insertion point at the beginning of the text for this post (before the word *It's*).

f. Click the **Insert image** button to display the **Add Images** dialog box.

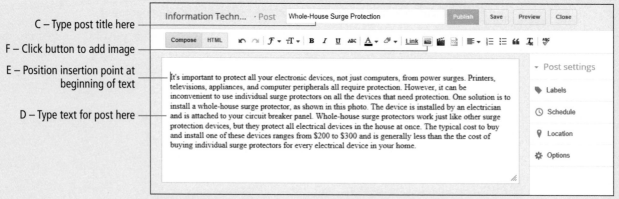

C – Type post title here

F – Click button to add image

E – Position insertion point at beginning of text

D – Type text for post here

Figure 3.30 Hands-On Exercise 3, Steps 2c through 2f.

The **Add Images** dialog box provides several options for working with images. You can select an image from a location on your computer (or network, flash drive, etc.) to upload to the blog. You can reuse an image that has already been added to your blog. You can also select images from a Picasa Web Album (a product that is owned by Google, the owner of Blogger), or use an image from a website.

g. From the **Add Images** dialog box, if necessary, select the **Upload** option.

h. Click the **Browse** button to open the **Choose File to Upload** dialog box.

H – Click to locate the image file

G – Click to select Upload

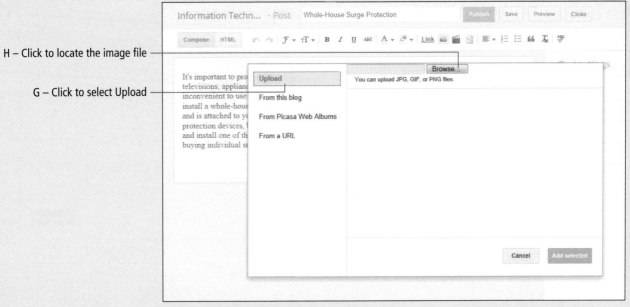

Figure 3.31 Hands-On Exercise 3, Steps 2g and 2h.

i. Navigate to the folder you selected in Step 1k when you extracted the image file and select the **Ch_3_Exercise_3.jpg** file.

j. Click **Open** to return to the **Add Images** dialog box.

I – Navigate to the appropriate folder and select the file

J – Click to proceed

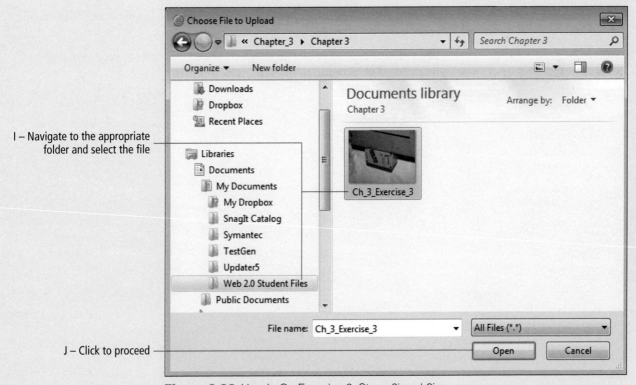

Figure 3.32 Hands-On Exercise 3, Steps 2i and 2j.

k. Once you've located the image, it will appear in the **Add Images** dialog box. Click the **Add selected** button to insert the image into your blog.

Selected image appears here —

K – Click to insert image —

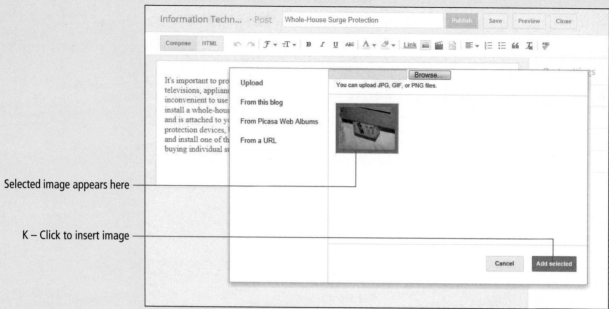

Figure 3.33 Hands-On Exercise 3, Step 2k.

l. The image appears centered above the text of the blog post. Click the image to display a toolbar with various editing options below the image. You can change the image size, change the placement of the image, add a caption, or remove the image from the post. Take a few moments to experiment with these choices, but don't remove the image! If you click away from the image, the toolbar will close—to display it again, simply click on the image.

m. If necessary, click the **Medium** link to adjust the size of the image. The Medium option usually works well with most blog post images.

n. Click the **Left** link to place the image on the left side of the blog post and wrap the text around it on the right.

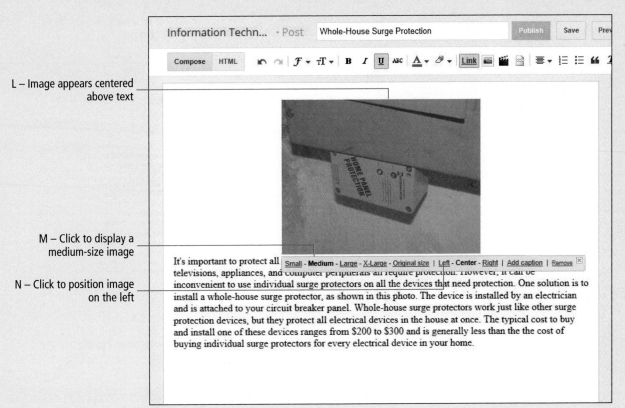

L – Image appears centered above text

M – Click to display a medium-size image

N – Click to position image on the left

Figure 3.34 Hands-On Exercise 3, Steps 2l through 2n.

When inserting images into blog entries, Blogger often inserts one or more blank lines. These should be deleted before publishing your post.

o. If you have a blank line above the text of your post, click in the blank line and press the **Delete** key to remove it.

p. Deleting the blank line may also change the alignment of your text. If necessary, click the **Alignment** drop-down button and choose **Align left**.

q. Click the **Preview** button to see how your post will look on your blog. When you are done, close the browser tab or window for the Preview and return to your post.

r. Click the **Publish** button to publish this entry to your blog.

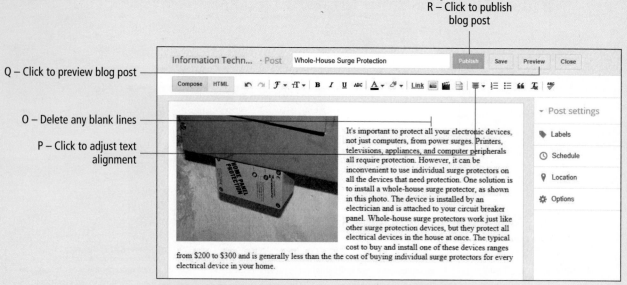

R – Click to publish blog post

Q – Click to preview blog post

O – Delete any blank lines

P – Click to adjust text alignment

Figure 3.35 Hands-On Exercise 3, Steps 2o through 2r.

s. On the **All posts** page, click the **View** link for the Whole-House Surge Protection post to view the newest entry to your blog.

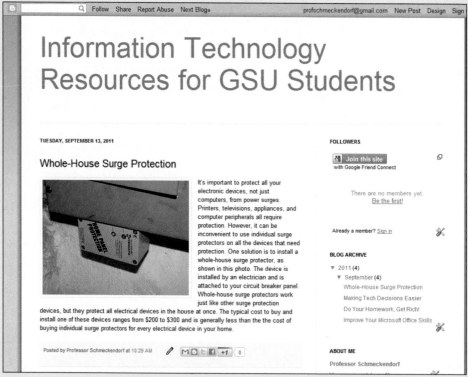

Figure 3.36 A blog post with a photograph included for illustration purposes.

Step 3   Add a Video to a New Blog Post

Refer to Figures 3.37 through 3.41 as you complete Step 3.

Adding a video to a blog post is even easier than inserting a picture into a blog post. Since Google owns both Blogger and YouTube, the process for including a YouTube video in your Blogger blog is quite simple. Professor Schmeckendorf has found a video on YouTube that provides a clear and entertaining explanation of blogging. He would like to share this video with his students, so he is going to embed it in a new blog post.

a. At the conclusion of Step 2, you were logged in to your Blogger account and viewing your most recent blog post. If you are not at this point, log in to Blogger and view your blog. Click the **New Post** link at the top of the blog to go to the **Create post** page.

A – Click to create a new blog post

Figure 3.37 Hands-On Exercise 3, Step 3a.

b. In the **Post title** text box, type **New to Blogging? Watch This Video!**

c. Type the following text in the main text box window: **If you are not sure what a blog is or how it works, this video, called "Blogs in Plain English," will help. Created by the folks at CommonCraft, this video explains why blogs are such a "big deal." To view the video, just click on the large arrow in the middle of the video window below.**

d. Press **Enter** twice after this text to add a blank line between the text and the video.

e. Click the **Insert a video** button to open the **Add a Video** dialog box.

B – Type post title here
E – Click button to insert video
C – Type text for post here
D – Press Enter twice to create a blank line

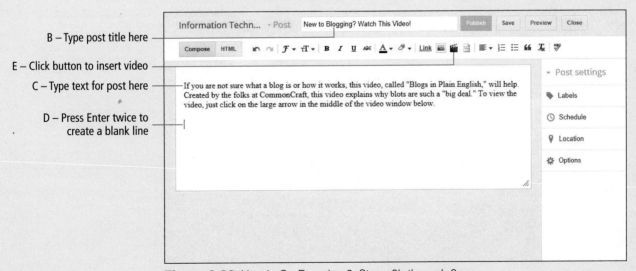

Figure 3.38 Hands-On Exercise 3, Steps 3b through 3e.

The **Add a Video** dialog box provides several options for working with videos. You can upload a video from a location on your computer (or network, flash drive, etc.), you can select a video that has already been published on YouTube, or you can access the videos on your own YouTube account (if you have one).

f. From the **Add a Video** dialog box, select the **From YouTube** option.

g. In the search text box, type **blogs in plain english** and click the search button.

h. The results of your search will appear as a list below the search text box. If the list is quite large, a scroll bar appears so you can scroll through the list. The video Professor Schmeckendorf wants to use—**Blogs in Plain English**—should be at or near the top of the list.

When you use the **Add a Video** dialog box to perform your own searches, you might not be sure which video to select from the results that display. Fortunately, Blogger has made it easy to check. Simply click the video once to play it within the **Add a Video** dialog box. You can also click the video a second time to go directly to YouTube and play the video there.

i. Click the **Blogs in Plain English** result to select it. A blue border will appear around the video you have chosen.

j. Click the **Select** button to insert the video into your blog post.

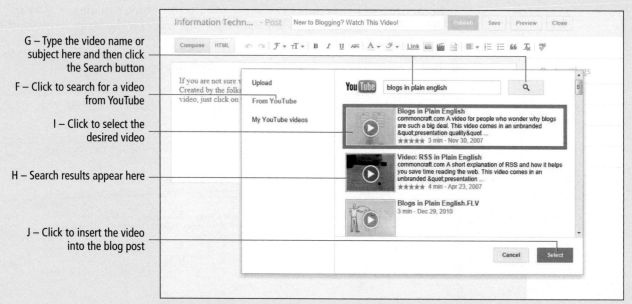

G – Type the video name or subject here and then click the Search button

F – Click to search for a video from YouTube

I – Click to select the desired video

H – Search results appear here

J – Click to insert the video into the blog post

Figure 3.39 Hands-On Exercise 3, Steps 3f through 3j.

Although YouTube is a very popular video sharing site, it is not the only one out there. What do you do if the video you want to add to your blog post isn't on YouTube? First, you need to find the embed code for the video. The embed code is an HTML tag that you can copy from the site. Most sites make this fairly easy to find by using a **Share** or **Embed** button or link, and often include helpful tips about how to use this feature. Once you've copied the embed code, return to the **Create post** page. Notice that there are two buttons at the top left of the text box— **Compose** and **HTML**. You've been working in the **Compose** mode throughout these exercises, but to work with the embed code, you need to click the **HTML** button. Add your blog text the same as always and then paste the HTML for the embed code in the location you want your video to appear. Once that's done, use the **Preview** and **Publish** buttons as usual to check your post and publish it.

An icon representing the video will appear below the text. Unlike the photo you added previously, there are no editing options for the video. However, you can click on the video icon and drag it to a new location in the post if you wish.

k. Click the **Preview** button to see how your post will look on your blog. When you are done, close the browser tab or window for the Preview and return to your post.

l. Click the **Publish** button to publish this entry to your blog.

L – Click to publish blog post

K – Click to preview blog post

Video icon

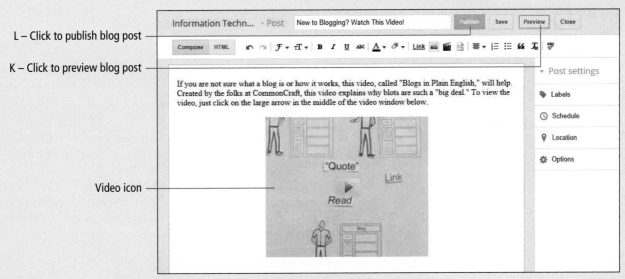

Figure 3.40 Hands-On Exercise 3, Steps 2k and 2l.

m. On the **All posts** page, click the **View** link below the post title to view the newest entry to your blog. To view the video, click the play button in the center of the video.

You may now sign out of Blogger by clicking the **Sign Out** link in the upper right corner of the screen. You can also close your browser.

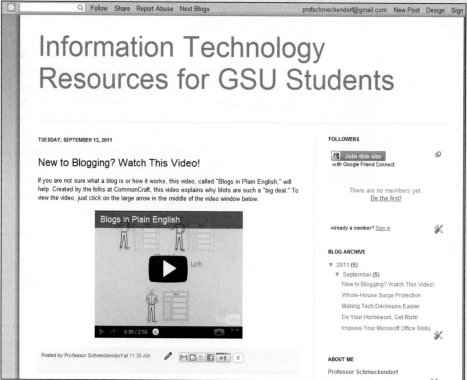

Figure 3.41 A blog post with a video inserted.

Objective 7

Add features to your blog

So far, we've concentrated on creating and formatting blog posts and adding images and video to them. But, there are many more things you can do to make your blog more useful for your readers and encourage collaboration. Blogger has over 1,000 items you can add to your blog, including items such as blogrolls, polls, subscription links, blog statistics, and newsreels. We'll look at a few of these and add some to the blog in the next Hands-On Exercise, but you should take some time to explore Blogger's offerings and see which features appeal to you.

How can I help readers find information on my blog?

Although Blogger automatically includes a blog archive of your posts, organized by date, readers often need a better way to find the material that they are interested in on your blog. Once a blog has many posts, it can be tedious to wade through date archives, reading blog post titles to sort out which entries are relevant. Organizing your posts by topic gives your readers a quick way to zero in on information that is relevant to them and makes your blog much more user-friendly.

Labels Topics or categories, similar to keywords, created by a blog's author and assigned to a blog post to help readers locate information on the blog.

Blogger makes it easy to assign labels to your blog posts. *Labels* are topics or categories, similar to keywords, which are created by you to describe your blog posts. Currently, Blogger allows users to create up to 5,000 labels, so you can create as many different labels as you need to categorize your blog. You should assign at least one label to every blog entry and the same label can be used on multiple blog posts. You can add labels to a post as you are creating it, or you can edit posts that have already been published and assign labels then.

Hands-On Exercises

4 | Add Features to a Blog

Steps: 1. Add Labels to a Published Blog Post; **2.** Modify a Blog Layout; **3.** Add a Subscription Links Gadget to a Blog.

Use Figures 3.42 through 3.57 as a guide to the exercise.

Step 1 Add Labels to a Published Blog Post

Refer to Figures 3.42 through 3.45 as you complete Step 1.

a. Go to www.blogger.com and log in to your Blogger account.

b. On the Blogger **Dashboard** page, click the **Go to post list** button to go to the **All posts** page.

B – Click to go to the list of blog posts

Figure 3.42 Hands-On Exercise 4, Step 1b.

Blogger keeps track of any labels you create. When you assign a label to a blog post, it will appear next to the title of the post on the **All posts** page. In Figure 3.43, you will see that Professor Schmeckendorf has already created labels for some of his posts.

Your blog probably does not have any labels yet, unless you have assigned some to posts on your own. The example blog shown here already uses the labels *apps*, *Facebook*, *homework*, and *Saving Money*. You should think about whether a post falls into any of these previously defined label categories. Because this post is about using Microsoft Office and how to improve your skills, *homework* might be an appropriate label to assign. You might also decide to create two new labels—one called *Microsoft Office* and another called *software*—because Professor Schmeckendorf expects to provide his students with lots of tips on how to use Microsoft Office and other types of software too.

c. Locate the first blog post you created about improving your Microsoft Office skills. Click the **Edit** link below the title of the post to enter edit mode.

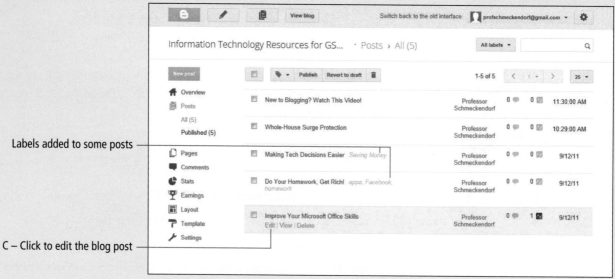

Labels added to some posts ⎯

C – Click to edit the blog post ⎯

Figure 3.43 Hands-On Exercise 4, Step 1c.

d. To the right of the blog post text window, under **Post Settings**, you will see the **Labels** setting option. Click the **Labels** option to expand the setting and display a text box and a list of labels currently in use for your blog.

It is easy to create a new label on Blogger. Just type the new label in the **Labels** text box for the post. Once the post is published, the new label is applied and will be available for use on other posts as well.

e. In the **Labels** text box, type the labels **homework, Microsoft Office**, and **software** for this post. When adding multiple labels, separate them by adding a comma and a space after each one in the list. If you are adding a label that already exists, as you start to type it, a screen tip displays. You can click the screen tip to add the label, rather than typing the full word. Doing this helps to keep your labels consistent. If you reuse existing labels, it helps to prevent having similar labels, such as *MS Office* and *Microsoft Office*, or *blog* and *blogs*. Having too many labels that are too specific can be as frustrating to your readers as not having any labels at all. Click **Done** to close the **Labels** option.

f. Click the **Update** button to republish the post with the labels assigned to it and return to the **All posts** page.

F – Click to republish the blog post with assigned labels

D – Click to hide or display the labels currently in use

E – Add new labels and then click Done

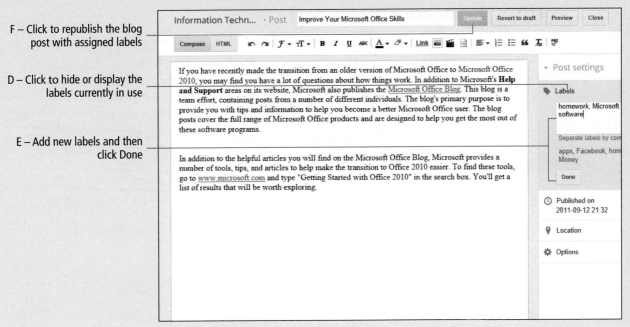

Figure 3.44 Hands-On Exercise 4, Steps 1d through 1f.

Repeat Steps 1c through 1f to assign labels to all the posts on your blog. Figure 3.45 shows an example of how a blog post appears once labels have been assigned to it. Now that you have assigned labels to your blog, it is time to modify the blog's design by adding a category archive.

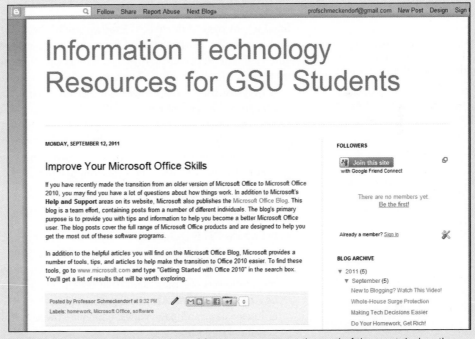

Figure 3.45 Labels assigned to a blog post appear at the end of the post, below the author's name.

Step 2 Modify a Blog Layout

Refer to Figures 3.46 through 3.53 as you complete Step 2.

The blog layout controls what is visible on the blog. The **Layout** option can be found on the **All posts** page and is used to add or remove features from your blog. In this step, you will modify the layout of your blog to add the category archive and you will also delete some unnecessary default features that Blogger places on all blogs.

a. From the **All posts** page click the **Layout** option on the left side of the page to go to the **Layout** page.

A – Click to modify the blog's layout

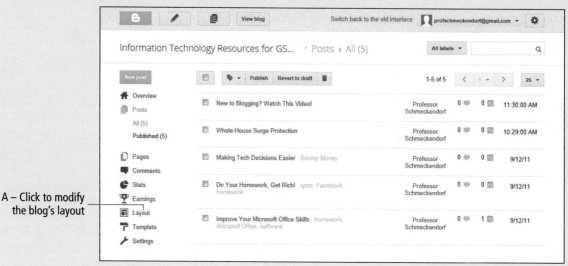

Figure 3.46 Hands-On Exercise 4, Step 2a.

Header A section of a blog that contains the title of your blog and possibly a subtitle.

Gadget A section of a blog that contains code resulting in some type of functionality for the blog.

The **Layout** page (Figure 3.47) shows where the main components of your blog are located. The *header* section contains the title of your blog and can also contain a subtitle in certain templates. The **Blog Posts** section is where your posts are positioned on the blog. The various Gadgets sections contain the features of your blog. In Blogger, a *gadget* is a section of your blog that contains code that results in some type of functionality for your blog. You can add blog archives, clocks, calendars, and even virtual pets using a gadget. Blogger provides some pre-made gadgets that you can easily insert into the blog layout. You can also obtain HTML code from third-party websites and place it in a special HTML gadget to further enhance the functionality of your blog.

The current blog template includes three gadgets on the right side that are assigned by Blogger by default. They are the following:

- Followers—This gadget allows registered users to click a link and indicate that they are following (reading) your blog. Because Professor Schmeckendorf doesn't wish to use this gadget, it will be removed from the blog. Using a gadget to track followers of a blog is not that useful. The **Overview** section of your blog can be accessed from the **All posts** page and provides website statistics, such as unique visitors and page views, which are more useful in analyzing the traffic generated by a blog.

- Blog Archive—This gadget provides a list of blog postings, grouped by year and month. Because this gadget is useful to many blog readers, it will remain on the blog.

- About Me—This gadget shows information about the blog author that is drawn from his or her Blogger profile. You can add more information to your Blogger profile whenever you wish. If you don't want to be identified as the author of your blog, you should remove the **About Me** gadget.

b. Click the **Edit** link in the **Followers** gadget box to display the **Configure Followers List** dialog box.

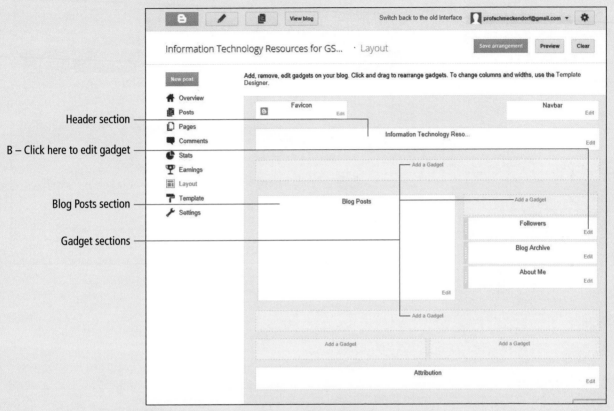

Figure 3.47 Hands-On Exercise 4, Step 2b.

 Alert

If your blog's layout screen doesn't look like the one pictured in Figure 3.47, you may have chosen a different Blogger template than the one used in the example. Your layout should have the same sections as the ones shown here, but they may be positioned differently on the screen. You should be able to follow along with the rest of this section; your gadgets will have the same names as the ones in the book.

c. In the **Configure Followers List** dialog box, click **Remove**. A **Message from webpage** dialog box appears asking you to confirm your deletion request.

d. Click **OK** in the browser dialog box to confirm deletion of the **Followers** gadget.

C – Click to remove gadget

D – Click to confirm deletion

Figure 3.48 Hands-On Exercise 4, Steps 2c and 2d.

Notice that the **Followers** gadget has now been removed from the **Layout page**, and a small orange box briefly appears at the top of the page confirming the change and giving you the option to view the changes to your blog.

e. Click the first **Add a Gadget** link in the column on the right side of the screen to display a list of gadgets that can be added to your blog.

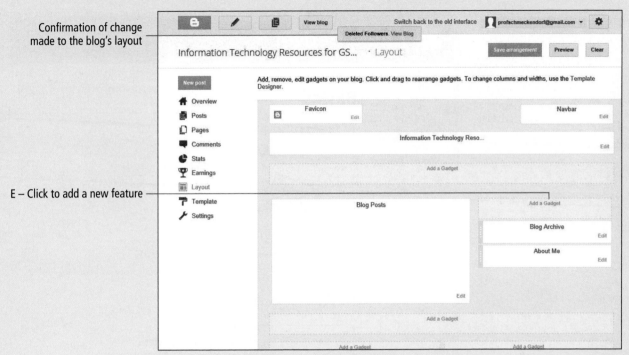

Confirmation of change made to the blog's layout

E – Click to add a new feature

Figure 3.49 Hands-On Exercise 4, Step 2e.

f. The **Add a Gadget** window displays with a list of categories on the left—Basics, Featured, Most Popular, More Gadgets, and Add your own. If necessary, click the **Basics** category to display the list of basic gadgets on the right side of the window.

g. Use the scroll bar to scroll through the **Basics** list until you find the **Labels** gadget.

h. Click the **Add** button—the plus symbol to the right of the gadgets—to display the **Configure Labels** dialog box.

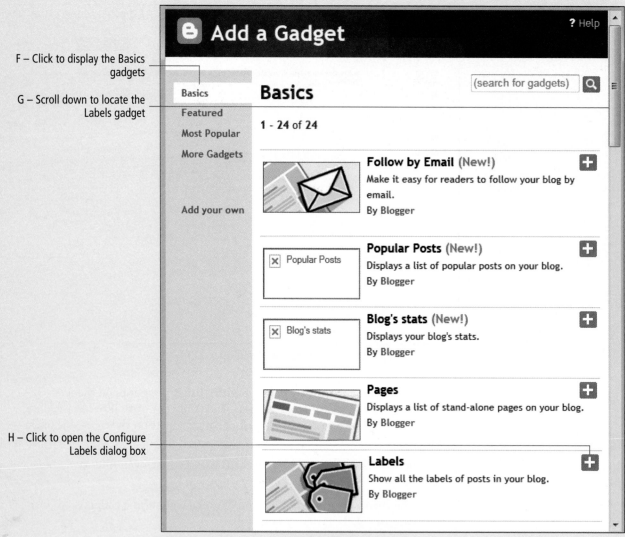

F – Click to display the Basics gadgets

G – Scroll down to locate the Labels gadget

H – Click to open the Configure Labels dialog box

Figure 3.50 Hands-On Exercise 4, Steps 2f through 2h.

i. In the **Configure Labels** dialog box, in the **Title** box, delete the default text and type a title for your list of labels. You should choose something more descriptive than the default "Labels" title that Blogger provides. Professor Schmeckendorf is going to name his list **Blog Topics**.

j. The **Configure Labels** dialog box provides several other options for how your list will appear.

- The **Show** option allows you to display all labels or just a selection of labels that you can specify. Professor Schmeckendorf will choose the **All Labels** option.

- The **Sorting** option allows you to display labels in alphabetical order or by frequency. Frequency is determined by the number of blog posts that use each label. Sorting labels alphabetically usually makes the most sense for your readers, as it is easier to find a topic you are looking for in an alphabetical list.

- The **Display** option allows you to display your labels in a list or as a tag cloud. If you choose the **Cloud** option, your labels will appear clustered in a group, with the most frequently used labels appearing larger than those used less frequently. Professor Schmeckendorf will use the **List** option.

- Check the **Show number of posts per label** checkbox—this makes it easier for your readers to see how many articles use a specific label.

k. Click the **Save** button to add the label archive to your blog.

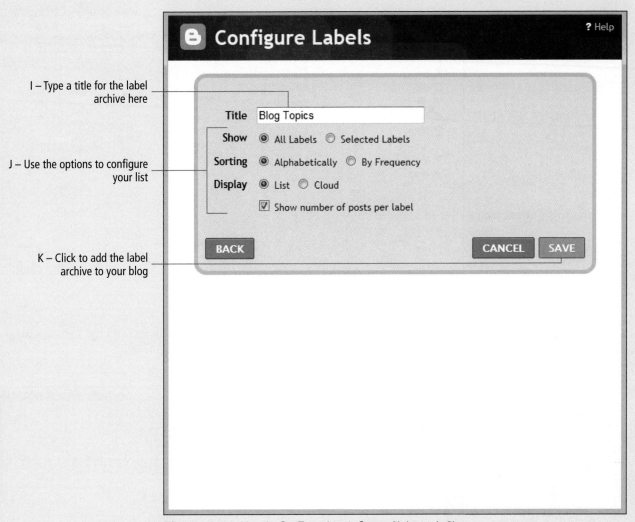

I – Type a title for the label archive here

J – Use the options to configure your list

K – Click to add the label archive to your blog

Figure 3.51 Hands-On Exercise 4, Steps 2i through 2k.

The label archive, titled *Blog Topics*, has been added to the blog layout. Your archive will display using the title you created. At this point, the changes you have made are not yet permanently saved to your blog. You should preview the changes to ensure that your blog looks the way you want it to before making the changes permanent.

l. Click the **Preview** button to display your blog. The blog will open in a new browser tab or window. Review the blog to ensure the changes you made appear as you expected. Notice that the label archive now appears at the top of the page and the **Followers** gadget has been deleted.

m. Once you've reviewed your changes, close the blog preview tab or window and return to the **Layout** page. If you do not want to save your changes, click the **Clear** button and try again, if necessary. If the changes are correct, click the **Save arrangement** button to make the changes permanent and republish your blog.

n. Click the **View blog** button to view your blog with these changes.

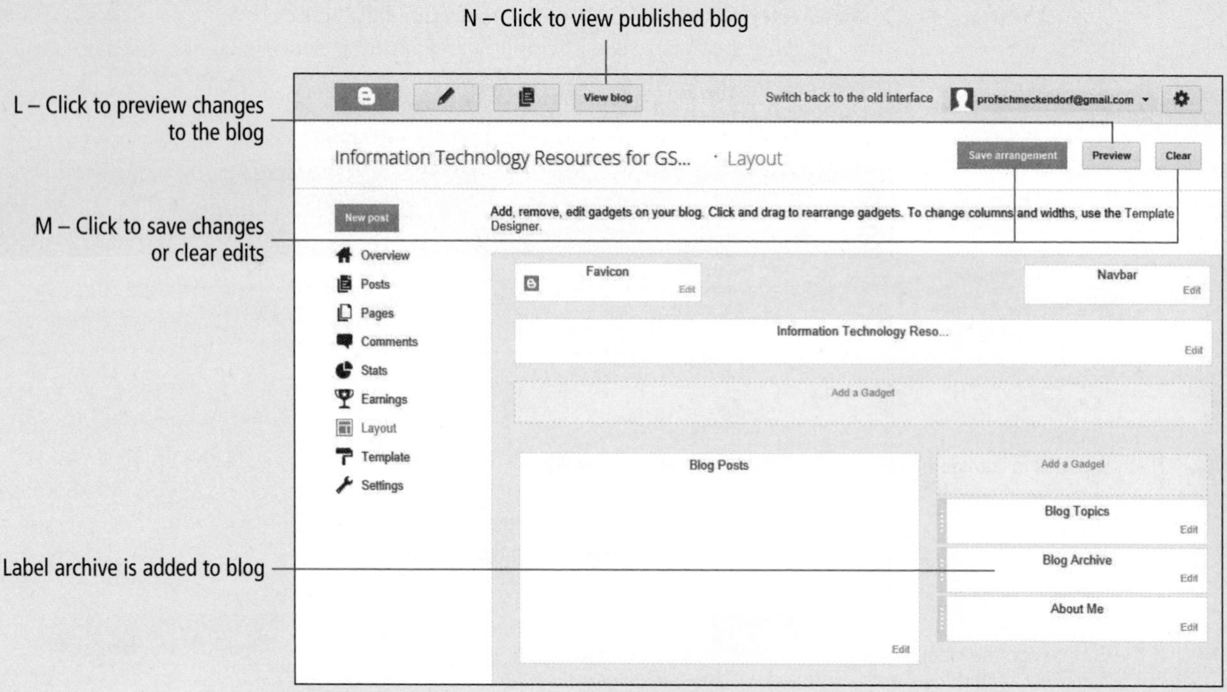

N – Click to view published blog

L – Click to preview changes to the blog

M – Click to save changes or clear edits

Label archive is added to blog

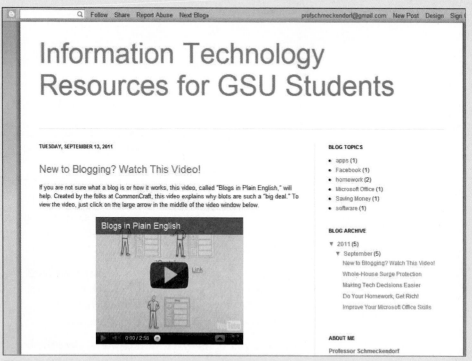

Figure 3.52 Hands-On Exercise 4, Steps 2l through 2n.

Your published blog, with the **Followers** gadget removed and the **Labels** gadget added, should appear similar to the one shown in Figure 3.53.

Figure 3.53 Updated blog with design changes—Followers gadget removed, Labels gadget added.

Step 3   Add a Subscription Links Gadget to a Blog

Refer to Figures 3.54 through 3.57 as you complete Step 3.

Aggregators and feed readers, such as Google Reader, can be used to subscribe to blogs, podcasts, and other sites of interest. Now that you have your own blog, you want to be sure that your readers will be able to subscribe to your content through an RSS feed as well.

Blogger automatically sets up an RSS feed for each blog. All you need to do is add a gadget to your blog that provides a subscription link. Visitors to your blog can simply click this link to subscribe to your blog using their aggregator of choice. You should place the subscription link in a prominent place on your blog so that people can find it easily. A location near the top of the blog, on either the right or left side, is a good place to place the link.

a. If you are viewing your published blog from Step 2n, click the **Design** link at the top-right corner of the page to go to the **Template** page. You can select a new template for your blog from this page, but you can also access the other areas of the blog as well. Click the **Layout** option to go to the **Layout** page. If you are at the Blogger Dashboard, click the drop-down arrow next to the **Go to post list** button and click **Layout** from the menu. If you are somewhere else in your blog, click the **Layout** option to go to the **Layout** page, if necessary.

b. Click the **Add a Gadget** link at the top of the column, above the **Blog Topics** gadget, to display the **Add a Gadget** dialog box. Refer to Figure 3.49 if you need help with this step.

> **Alert**
>
> Depending upon the design template you selected and the gadgets you have added to your blog, your **Layout** screen may differ from the one shown here. You should choose an **Add a Gadget** link that is located in an appropriate place for the **Subscription Links** gadget to appear.

c. In the **Add a Gadget** dialog box, with the **Basics** category displayed, scroll down the list to locate the **Subscription Links** gadget.

d. Click the **Add** button to display the **Configure Subscription Links** dialog box.

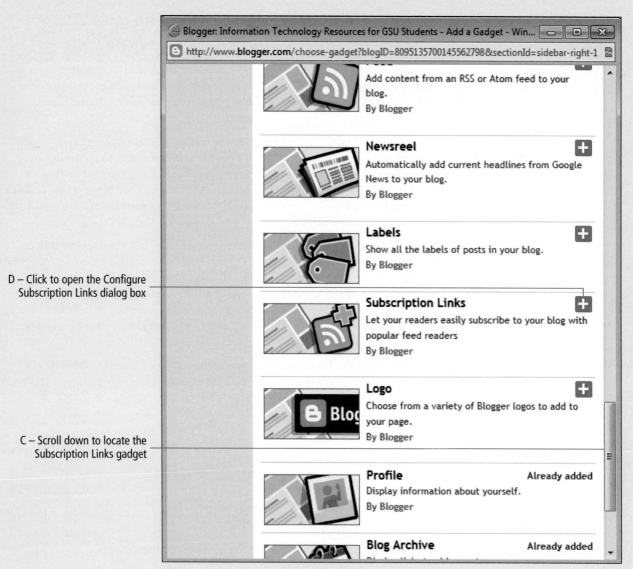

D – Click to open the Configure
Subscription Links dialog box

C – Scroll down to locate the
Subscription Links gadget

Figure 3.54 Hands-On Exercise 4, Steps 3c and 3d.

e. In the **Configure Subscription Links** dialog box, in the **Title** text box, delete
the default text and type **Subscribe to This Blog**.

f. Click the **Save** button to add the **Subscription Links** gadget to your blog.

E – Type a title here

F – Click to save gadget to the blog

Figure 3.55 Hands-On Exercise 4, Steps 3e and 3f.

g. Notice that the gadget has now been added to the design of the blog. Click the **Preview** button to display the blog with the new gadget installed.

h. Close the blog preview tab or window and return to the **Layout** screen. Click the **Save arrangement** button to save the changes to the blog.

i. Click the **View blog** button to view your blog with these changes.

I – Click to view published blog

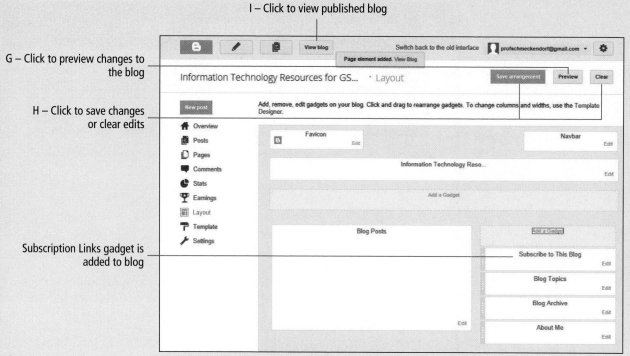

G – Click to preview changes to the blog

H – Click to save changes or clear edits

Subscription Links gadget is added to blog

Figure 3.56 Hands-On Exercise 4, Steps 3g through 3i.

Your published blog, with the **Subscription Links** gadget added, should appear similar to the one shown in Figure 3.57. Readers of your blog now have a handy link they can click to subscribe to your blog posts. This gadget also adds a second subscription link to allow readers to subscribe to any comments on the blog posts. Readers can click either or both of these subscription links.

Figure 3.57 Professor Schmeckendorf's blog with the Subscription Links gadget configured.

You may now sign out of Blogger by clicking the **Sign Out** link in the top-right corner of the screen. You can also close your browser.

Objective 8

Explain how to publicize a blog

Now that you've got the basics of blogging down, you may have some ideas for a really good blog that you would like to continue writing. It might be the most insightful, funny, or informative blog ever written, but if no one is reading it, you really aren't accomplishing your objective. In order to attract people to your blog and begin to develop an audience, you need to publicize your blog.

How do I publicize a blog?

Publicizing a blog is just like marketing any other product or service. Think about the way soft drinks are advertised. An advertisement can be designed to create product awareness of a new type of drink, such as when Coca-Cola first introduced its new Full Throttle line of energy drinks. If a product is new, you need to explain what the product is and where it can be found. Other advertisements are persuasive in nature and are designed to get you to purchase a product. An ad for an energy drink might show tired young people consuming an energy drink and then dancing all night at a party or club. Finally, some advertisements are designed to remind people that the product exists. Displaying banners that advertise an energy drink at the X Games serves to remind the audience that the product is available, but not necessarily to generate an immediate purchase.

These same marketing principles can be applied to promoting a blog. The three basic objectives of marketing, as applied to blogs, are as follows:

- Inform—Build initial awareness of your blog with potential readers.

- Persuade—Convince readers to subscribe to your blog and keep them returning to read new content.

- Remind—*Gently* refresh people's memory about your blog so that they don't forget about it.

Reminding readers really isn't an appropriate option for promoting a blog, unless you want to create an email list and periodically send people email about your blog. This can be rather time consuming, and you may have difficulty getting readers to provide you with their email addresses. But you can certainly inform people and persuade them to visit your blog.

How do I create initial awareness of my blog?

You can take many different approaches to build awareness of your new blog. Fortunately, most of them are relatively simple and cost nothing to implement. Here are a few suggestions to consider:

Leave Comments on Other Blogs Search for other blogs that complement or are related to your blog's topic. If you have a blog about restoring classic cars, chances are that readers who might be interested in your blog are also reading other blogs about cars. Find a blog posting to which you can add relevant information, such as confirming the user's opinion through personal experience, and then post an informative or helpful comment on that blog entry and include a link back to your blog. Readers of blogs often read comments as well as blog entries, and this can help direct readers to your blog.

For example, Professor Schmeckendorf regularly reads and comments on blogs written by other computer science instructors. Recently, he read a post from an instructor discussing the transition to Microsoft Office 2010. In response, Professor Schmeckendorf left a brief comment and included a link to his post about the Microsoft Office blog. Not long after this, he received several comments on his blog from the instructor and some of his students. By providing helpful information, he has gained several new readers for his blog.

Get Your Blog Listed in Search Engines Search engines are websites that are designed to search the web for information and create an index of that information. Users of a search engine can enter keywords and the engine will then return a list of websites that are relevant to the search terms, sometimes referred to as a *hit list*. Popular search engines include Google, Yahoo!, and Bing. If your blog is indexed by major search engines, it can improve the chances that your blog will appear in the search results when people try to find information relating to your blog's topic.

With the vast increase in blogs over the past few years, blog search engines have become popular. A ***blog search engine*** is a specialized type of search engine that focuses on indexing and returning search results for information posted on blogs (Figure 3.58). Popular blog search engines include Technorati (**www.technorati.com**), Google Blog Search (**http://blogsearch.google.com**), and IceRocket (**www.icerocket.com**). It is important to have your blog indexed in these specialized search engines also. Most search engines and blog search engines make it fairly easy to list your blog with them. Check the Help section or look for links for blog publishers or authors to get started.

Figure 3.58 Google Blog Search (**http://blogsearch.google.com**) is a specialized version of the Google search engine that concentrates specifically on information found in blogs.

Enter Your Blog in Blog Carnivals A ***blog carnival*** is a type of online magazine (or newsletter) that is usually published on a blog on a regular basis (weekly, monthly, etc.). Blog carnivals typically have a specific topic and usually contain short descriptions of blog articles with links to those articles. Carnivals are like printed magazines because readers of carnivals browse through blog posts (articles) on related topics. It is a fast way for people to locate blog postings on a specific topic. Each blog carnival is organized by an author who solicits suggestions for content from blog owners and blog readers. Often, various blogs take turns hosting a carnival, so they are said to "travel" from place to place, similar to a real carnival.

Blog Carnival (**www.blogcarnival.com**) is a site that helps carnival hosts solicit articles for inclusion in carnivals. The site provides a searchable listing of carnivals (**http://blogcarnival.com/bc/clist.html**) so that you can find carnivals that cover topics related to your blog. Each carnival has its own description and listing of topics that are acceptable for submission to the carnival. You can submit articles to a carnival and the host of the carnival will decide whether or not to include your article in the next issue. Since there is no charge for participating in carnivals, and since many blog readers consult carnivals for fresh content, this is an excellent way to build your blog's readership.

Blog search engine A specialized type of search engine that focuses on indexing and returning search results from information posted on blogs.

Blog carnival A type of online magazine (or newsletter) that is usually published on a blog on a regular basis (weekly, monthly, etc.).

Let Your Readers Promote Your Blog Some social networking sites like Digg.com (Figure 3.59) encourage their members to find content on the Internet, share it with other community members, and vote on the popularity of the submission. Votes are either positive (digg) or negative (bury). The submissions with the most positive votes are displayed on the front page of various sections on Digg.com.

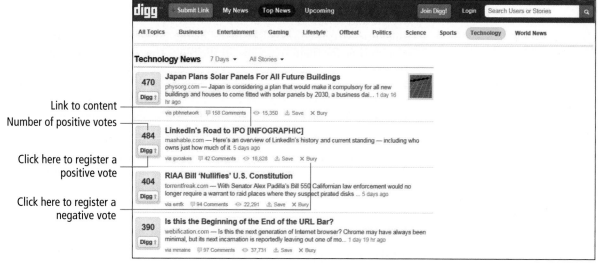

Figure 3.59 Popular content on the Technology page of Digg.com.

Many people visit Digg and other social networking sites with submission and voting systems on a regular basis, so if your article becomes popular, it could be viewed by quite a few people. You can place icons on your blog that make it easy for your readers to recommend your content and share it with others through sites like Digg, Facebook, and Twitter (Figure 3.60).

Figure 3.60 Professor Schmeckendorf added a social networking gadget to enable readers to share his blog with others.

How do I persuade readers to return to my blog?

Once readers have found your blog, you need to develop strategies to keep them coming back for more. There are many approaches you can take to build a loyal following for your blog, and we recommend a few key ones here.

- Create New, Quality Content Regularly—Although this should be obvious, many new blogs fail to follow this strategy. People are looking for information, engaging content, creative discourse, or entertainment when reading blogs. If you don't produce well-written articles that pertain to the topic of your blog, readers will have no incentive to come back.

- Use Images and Multimedia When Appropriate—Although most blog postings contain a great deal of text, the use of visual media can stimulate interest for readers who are visual learners. Appropriate still images and videos also give your blog a more professional, polished feel.

- Make It Easy for Readers to Subscribe to New Content—Your readers may be reading numerous blogs on the Internet besides yours. Having to browse to your website and review it for new content might not seem like it would take much time. But what if your readers are following 50 different blogs? Will there be enough time for them to review all the blogs they are interested in every week? To make it easy to track numerous websites, blogs, and podcasts for new content, many readers use an aggregator, such as Google Reader, to sign up for a site's RSS feed. Using Blogger's **Subscription Links** gadget to add an RSS feed to your blog enables your readers to easily subscribe to your blog.

- Make New Content Obvious—In addition to adding subscription links, you should also consider including a list of the newest posts to your site, formatted as clickable links. This will help visitors find your most recent material.

Objective 9

Explore blogging resources

Because blogging has become quite popular, there is a wealth of information on the Internet that can help you learn more about creating effective blogs. In fact, there are many blogs created solely for the purpose of teaching people how to blog. Here are some resources you may want to explore:

- **Daily Blog Tips (www.dailyblogtips.com)**—A well-written blog by Daniel Scocco, author of several successful blogs. This blog allows Daniel to share the lessons he has learned while blogging. It offers great advice for novice and experienced bloggers in straightforward language.

- **Blogging Tips (www.bloggingtips.com)**—Another well-crafted blog that provides advice for novice and experienced bloggers. It has an entire category of tips just for people using Blogger.

- **YouTube Blogger Help (www.youtube.com/user/BloggerHelp)**—Videos created by the people at Blogger to help you get started blogging. Make sure to search YouTube for other useful blogging videos too. Use search terms that involve the information you are seeking, such as *Blogger templates* or *inserting images*.

- **Pearsonified (www.pearsonified.com)**—The author humbly refers to this as the "Best Damn Blog on the Planet." He provides some useful tips for improving your ranking on search engines, and his insights on website design are very refreshing.

- **Problogger (www.problogger.net)**—This site provides excellent advice on how to make money with your blog. Check the Archive section for "31 Days to Building a Better Blog" containing 31 daily posts that this blogger wrote to provide you with one task you can tackle per day to improve your blog.

- **The Original Blogger Tips and Tricks (www.bloggertipsandtricks.com)**—This blog focuses primarily on improving blogs that are hosted on Blogger. If you are sitting there scratching your head and wondering how you can do something on Blogger—like making a certain post always stay at the top of the screen (which is called a *sticky post*)—try searching on this site for an answer.

- **Personal Development for Smart People (www.stevepavlina.com)**—In this personal development blog, the author shares his experience of creating a blog that earns over $1,000 a day, while spending very little money. He has some unique opinions and ideas, and his content will usually make you think.

Summary

You have now learned many of the basic skills needed to create an engaging blog and promote it to gain an audience. Blogs can be as simple or as complex as you want, but it is important to understand that what draws readers to your blog is interesting content. Creativity spawns readership. Adding cool features to your blog may be fun for you, but won't always appeal to your readers, who are most likely looking for information. Concentrate on writing frequent, informative blog posts that support the topic of your blog. You can always add appropriate gadgets to the blog at a later time.

Key Terms

Multiple Choice Questions

1. To help blog visitors find a blog post on a specific topic, which of the following should be added to a post?

   (a) A label

   (b) A blog directory

   (c) A topic category

   (d) A subscription link

2. Which of the following items are used to measure a blog's popularity?

   (a) Labels and blog comments

   (b) Page views and blog spam

   (c) Unique visitors and page views

   (d) Blog comments and page views

3. What are the three basic marketing objectives that are applied to blogs?

   (a) Inform, entertain, become profitable

   (b) Inform, persuade, remind

   (c) Notify, educate, persuade

   (d) Recommend, become profitable, notify

4. Which of the following is *not* a method used to create awareness of a blog?

   (a) Become listed in search engines

   (b) Change the blog's title and design frequently

   (c) Leave comments on other blogs

   (d) Encourage readers to promote the blog

5. To provide additional functionality to a blog in Blogger, you might add a

    (a) sponsored ad.

    (b) blog carnival.

    (c) screen tip.

    (d) gadget.

6. When using Blogger, which of the following comments about adding a video to a blog post is *not* true?

    (a) Only YouTube videos can be added to a blog post.

    (b) Adding a video can help stimulate interest for a blog's readers.

    (c) Videos on blogs should comply with copyright laws.

    (d) An embed code might be needed to add a video hosted on another site.

7. A tool used to notify you when new blog content has been posted is known as a(n)

    (a) blog archive.

    (b) social network.

    (c) aggregator.

    (d) blog announcement.

8. The entire collection of all blogs on the web is known as the

    (a) blogoverse.

    (b) blog community.

    (c) blog carnival.

    (d) blogosphere.

9. Which of the following items is *not* commonly added to a blog for use by its readers?

    (a) Comments option

    (b) Editing tools

    (c) Archive

    (d) Subscription links

10. When using Blogger, the summary screen from which you can see and manage all the blogs in one account is known as the

    (a) Control Center.

    (b) Homepage.

    (c) Dashboard.

    (d) Welcome screen.

Fill in the Blank

1. _____ _____ measures the number of times a web page is loaded in a browser.

2. Features such as About Me, Blog Archive, and Followers are examples of _____.

3. A(n) _____ _____ is similar to an online magazine and includes short descriptions of blog articles and links leading to those articles. It is often hosted by blogs that take turns publishing it.

4. The section of a blog that contains the blog's title, and possibly a subtitle, is known as a(n) _____.

5. Sites such as Technorati and IceRocket, which are designed to index and return results based on information posted on blogs, are examples of blog _____ _____.

Practice Exercises

1. **Creating a Meaningful Blog Name and Selecting a URL**

   As discussed in this chapter, selecting an appropriate name for a blog and choosing an appropriate URL can help visitors locate your blog more easily. For this exercise, you will go through the initial steps of creating a blog about white water rafting.

   (a) Sign in to your Blogger account and go to the Dashboard.

   (b) Click the **New Blog** button to begin the blog creation process.

   (c) Select a meaningful blog title and type it into the **Title** text box.

   (d) Select an appropriate URL and ensure you can use it. Once you've found an available URL, print out this page or take a screenshot to paste into a Word document.

   (e) Repeat Steps c and d two more times, remembering to print out the results (or take a screenshot) each time.

   (f) Because you do not need to create this blog, click the **Cancel** button to return to the Dashboard and cancel the blog creation process. Log out of Blogger and close the browser window.

   (g) Submit the three printouts (or screenshots) you produced to your instructor.

2. **Creating and Revising Blog Posts**

   Well-respected blogs usually consist of frequent posts that are well-written and contain useful or entertaining information. In this exercise, you will create new posts for your blog and revise them to include several formatting styles.

   (a) Sign in to Blogger and return to the blog you created in this chapter.

   (b) Create three new blog posts. Each post should be about a different aspect of information technology.

   (c) Be sure that each post has a meaningful title relating to the contents of the post.

   (d) Change at least one word or phrase into a hyperlink in each post.

   (e) Apply labels to each post, creating new ones if necessary.

   (f) Publish each post as you complete it.

   (g) View your blog and print out the page or pages showing your new posts or take a screenshot of the new posts on your blog.

   (h) After you have published the posts, return to one of them and edit it. Select a keyword or phrase and change the font color. Apply bold formatting to another selection and apply italic formatting to a third selection.

   (i) Publish the revised post and view the blog. Print out this page or take a screenshot of it. Submit this page and the page(s) you printed out in Step g to your instructor. Log out of your Blogger account and close the browser window.

3. **Inserting and Removing a Gadget**

   Gadgets may be used to provide helpful items on a blog or to provide visual interest. In this exercise, you will practice adding and removing gadgets.

   (a) Sign in to Blogger and return to the blog you created in this chapter.

   (b) Navigate to the **Layout** page to work with the gadgets.

   (c) Previously, you worked with the gadgets in the **Basics** tab and added them to the column on the side of the blog. Depending on the template you chose for your blog, you may be able to add a gadget above or below the **Blog Post** section, as well as next to it. For this exercise, you should explore some of the other gadget categories. Choose a location for your new gadget, locate a gadget you'd like to try, and add it to your blog.

(d) Preview your blog to see the gadget you've added. Print the preview page or take a screenshot of it.

(e) Repeat Steps c and d to add two more gadgets to your blog. After each gadget has been added, preview the blog and print the preview page or take a screenshot of it.

(f) Remove two of the three gadgets you added to the blog.

(g) Save the changes to your blog and view it. Print the blog page or take a screenshot of it and submit it to your instructor along with the printouts of the three preview pages.

4. **Putting a Google Search Box on Your Blog**

As you continue to add posts to your blog, it may become more difficult for readers to find what they are looking for. Adding a search feature to your blog can help visitors locate information in older posts. Fortunately, Blogger has a gadget for this—the **Search Box** gadget is located in the **Basics** category. When your readers perform a search using this tool, the results will return links to your blog posts that match the keywords. In addition to searching your blog posts, readers can choose to search the pages to which you've linked in your posts or the Internet.

(a) Sign in to Blogger and return to the blog you created in this chapter.

(b) Navigate to the **Layout** page to work with the gadgets.

(c) It is a good idea to have the search function be easily visible, so you may want to add it to the top (or near the top) of the side column, or use the **Add a Gadget** box below the header of your blog. Locate the **Search Box** gadget in the **Basics** category and add it to your blog.

(d) Preview your blog to see the gadget you've added.

(e) Save the changes to your blog and view it. Print the blog page or take a screenshot of it and submit it to your instructor.

Critical Thinking

1. Because blogging is relatively easy, many people have blogs and use them to share their news and opinions on the Internet. In some cases, bloggers have been able to share information about current events more quickly than traditional news outlets, such as newspapers or television. Some critics worry that the quality of information that is available online has declined due to the number of bloggers. Others believe that blogging makes information more accessible. How do you feel about this? Is blogging a legitimate way to share information? Write a brief paper discussing the pros and cons of blogging.

2. Many bloggers use their blogs to discuss ongoing events in their daily lives. They may talk about family, friends, and work. Although some bloggers conceal their identities, others are very open about who they are and clearly identify other individuals and companies too. Some individuals have responded by suing bloggers for invasion of privacy or libel. Similarly, some bloggers have faced disciplinary action at work and some have even been fired for their opinions about their company or the company's products. How can bloggers balance their right to free speech with the right to privacy belonging to others? Do companies have a right to prosecute employees who are blogging on their own time? Research these issues and prepare a presentation supporting your views.

Team Projects

1. As a group, locate one blog in each of the following categories:

   ■ Politics

   ■ Social Awareness

   ■ Personal/Hobby

   ■ Corporate

   Create a table that lists the title and URL for each blog, and the category it represents. Review the blogs and evaluate them using the following criteria:

   ■ How long has the blog been in existence?

   ■ When was the most recent post?

   ■ Are the posts relevant to the overall theme of the blog?

   ■ Does the blog have other helpful features—topic lists, labels, archives, other gadgets, and so on? Is it easy to find information?

   ■ What is the average frequency of blog posts—daily, two or more posts per week, three or four posts per month?

   Which of the four blogs do you think is the best? Which is the worst? Explain your reasoning and include your findings on the table and submit it to your instructor.

2. You used Blogger to create blogs in this chapter. Split your team into two groups and explore the WordPress (**www.wordpress.com**) and Tumblr (**www.tumblr. com**) free blogging tools. Compare and contrast each of the three tools (Blogger, WordPress, and Tumblr). How easy is it to set up an account at each site? Are other features available? Put together a brief presentation and share your findings with the class.

Credits

CHAPTER 4

Podcasts

Objectives

After you read this chapter, you will be able to:

1. Explain what a podcast is, what podcasts are used for, and where to find podcasts
2. Describe the software and hardware needed to listen to or view podcasts
3. Describe the software and hardware needed to create podcasts
4. Explain the characteristics of quality podcasts and the preparation needed to create your own podcasts
5. Download and install Audacity software
6. Record an audio podcast
7. Import video to your computer
8. Create a video podcast using Windows Live Movie Maker
9. Upload a podcast to the Internet
10. Explore podcasting resources

The following Hands-On Exercises will help you accomplish the chapter objectives:

Hands-On Exercises

EXERCISES	SKILLS COVERED
1. Download and Install Audacity Software (Page 160)	**Step 1:** Start Your Browser and Navigate to the Audacity Download Page **Step 2:** Download and Install the Audacity Software **Step 3:** Download and Install the LAME MP3 Encoder
2. Record an Audio Podcast (Page 171)	**Step 1:** Ensure That Your Recording and Playback Devices Are Configured **Step 2:** Start Audacity and Set Preferences **Step 3:** Record a Podcast **Step 4:** Export a Podcast to an MP3 File
3. Produce a Video Podcast (Page 185)	**Step 1:** Download the Media Files to Your Computer **Step 2:** Download and Install Windows Live Movie Maker **Step 3:** Start Windows Live Movie Maker and Import the Media Files **Step 4:** Assemble the Components of the Podcast on the Storyboard **Step 5:** Apply an AutoMovie Theme to the Podcast **Step 6:** Export Your Podcast to a WMV File
4. Upload a Podcast to the Internet (Page 198)	**Step 1:** Create an Account at Podbean.com **Step 2:** Upload Podcast Files to Podbean.com

Objective 1

Explain what a podcast is, what podcasts are used for, and where to find podcasts

What is a podcast?

Podcast A group of audio or video files, usually issued in a series or sequence, that can be subscribed to and downloaded from the Internet.

A *podcast* is a group of audio or video files, usually issued in a series or sequence, that can be subscribed to and downloaded from the Internet. The word *podcast* originated from a combination of two words: *iPod* and *broadcast.* One of the first and most popular personal media players (PMPs) is the Apple iPod; because of its popularity, its name was co-opted into the name of this media. While audio podcasts are usually referred to only as podcasts, video podcasts are sometimes called *vidcasts* or *vodcasts.* Many people listen to audio podcasts or watch video podcasts every day on their computers or PMPs.

Vidcast, vodcast A video podcast.

When I download an episode of my favorite television show, am I watching a podcast?

Downloading one episode of a TV show to your iPod or watching the episode online in a streaming format on your computer probably does not fall into the definition of a podcast. However, if you purchase an entire season of a television show and new episodes are downloaded to your computer or PMP when they become available, then you are participating in a podcast.

Web feed A data format for a web page that enables it to provide information when the page's content is updated.

A key component of podcasts is that they can be subscribed to, and followers of a podcast are alerted when new "episodes" are available. This is accomplished by the use of web feeds. A *web feed* is a data format for a web page that enables it to provide information when the page's content is updated. RSS, sometimes referred to as Really Simple Syndication, is a popular type of web feed that is used to syndicate content on the Internet and to notify people when new content is available for podcasts.

Why do people create podcasts?

Podcasts are used mostly to inform or entertain. Podcasts are easy and inexpensive to create and can provide individuals with an outlet for their opinions or creativity. In the past, you needed to be on a broadcast radio or television station to reach a large audience. With podcasting and the Internet, you can reach a wide-ranging audience from the comfort of your own home. Many podcasts are like mini radio or television shows that talk about politics or current events or feature comedy skits.

Other podcasts, like Coffee Break Spanish (**www.coffeebreakspanish.com**), are a series of how-to instructions that teach a skill—in this case, how to speak Spanish. Technical podcasts that provide commentaries on technology, such as This Week in Tech (**http://twit.tv**) or Microsoft's Channel 9 (**http://channel9.msdn.com**), shown in Figure 4.1, are popular with people in technology-related industries. Podcasts that demystify technology for novice users or educate consumers on technical areas, such as the HDTV and Home Theater Podcast (**www.htguys.com**), are quite common. If you look hard enough, you can probably find a podcast on almost any area of interest.

Figure 4.1 Channel 9 connects developers and end users in ongoing conversations about Microsoft products.

Where can I find podcasts that interest me?

There are many good podcast directories that make it easy to find podcasts with content that interests you, including Apple iTunes (**www.apple.com/itunes**), Podcast Alley (**www.podcastalley.com**), and Podcast Pickle (**www.podcastpickle.com**). On sites such as Podcast Pickle (Figure 4.2a), you can often search for specific topics by using the site's search tool. Many podcast directories

Enter keywords here to search for a specific type of podcast

Figure 4.2a Podcast Pickle features a vast array of interesting podcasts.

contain sections on podcasts that are organized by topic, and often the podcasts you will find there are free. Podcast Pickle also provides lists of new and top-rated podcasts, as well as reviews and other helpful items. (Figure 4.2b). You can also use a search engine, such as Google or Bing, to find even more useful content. Simply enter keywords such as *Windows tips* followed by the word *podcast* and check out the results.

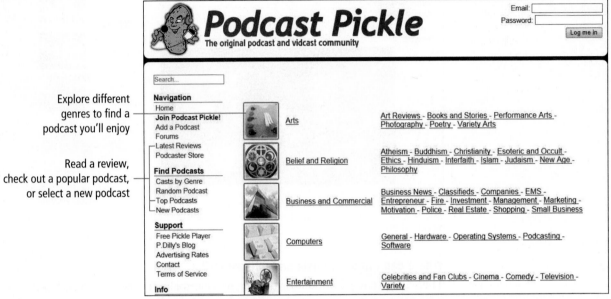

Figure 4.2b Podcast Pickle offers podcasts on a variety of topics. Select a new or popular podcast, or choose one from a topic that interests you.

Objective 2

Describe the software and hardware needed to listen to or view podcasts

Do I need an iPod (or other PMP) to listen to or view podcasts?

You do not need an iPod or any other type of PMP to take part in podcasting. Any software designed to play audio and video files—such as Windows Media Player, iTunes, or RealPlayer—allows you to view or listen to podcasts. Although you don't need a PMP, you will need a computer and a connection to the Internet to download podcasts. And, obviously, you'll need either speakers or headphones to listen to the audio tracks from podcasts.

To subscribe to podcasts, you need software that is specially designed to go out and check the Internet for new episodes of the podcasts to which you subscribe. Software of this type is known as a ***podcatcher*** or an ***aggregator***. Podcatcher software can either be installed on your computer like iTunes or be web-based software like Google Reader (Figure 4.3). When you subscribe to a podcast, your podcatcher software checks the web feed for that podcast whenever you launch—or log in to—your software to see if there are any new episodes available. Then you can easily check if any of those episodes interest you.

Podcatcher, aggregator
Software that is specially designed to go out and check the Internet for new episodes of the podcasts to which you subscribe.

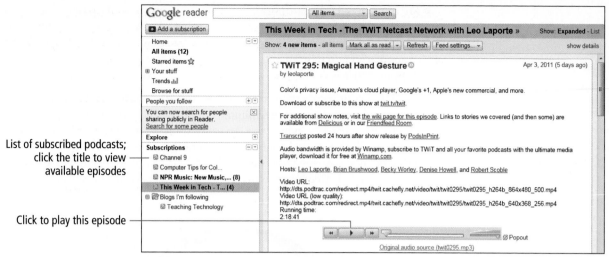

List of subscribed podcasts; click the title to view available episodes

Click to play this episode

Figure 4.3 Google Reader makes it easy to subscribe to podcasts and listen to current episodes.

Where are the podcast files stored?

With web-based solutions such as Google Reader, the podcast files you listen to remain stored on the Internet at the websites that contain the podcasts. In the case of software such as iTunes, which is installed on your computer, the podcasts are downloaded from the Internet and stored on your computer. The podcasts can then be downloaded to your PMP the next time you *sync*, or connect, your PMP to your computer.

Sync The process of connecting your PMP to your computer to update its contents.

Objective 3

Describe the software and hardware needed to create podcasts

What hardware do I need to create my own podcasts?

You may already own all the hardware you need to create your own podcasts. Following is a list of essential equipment:

- Computer with Internet access—You'll need a computer to run the software required to record and edit your podcasts. You'll also need the computer to be connected to the Internet so that you can distribute your podcasts online. This should be a broadband connection (such as cable, FiOS, or DSL) and not a dial-up connection. Video podcast files can be huge, and even audio podcast files can be rather large. Uploading your content with a dial-up connection would be frustrating at best.

- Sound card—All modern computers include a sound card, because the expectation is that users will want a multimedia experience. The sound card should have a microphone input jack and a headphone output jack. If you are using an older desktop computer that does not have a built-in sound card, you can purchase a sound card at your local computer retailer and easily install it.

- Microphone—For recording sound, you need a microphone to input the sound of your voice into the computer. If you own a notebook computer, it may already have a microphone installed in it that may be sufficient for creating podcasts. You can also purchase an external microphone that will plug into a jack on your computer that is connected to the computer's sound card.

- Headphones or speakers—You will need to listen to the playback of podcasts you create, so speakers or headphones are essential. You might even consider purchasing a headset, which is a device that includes both headphones and a microphone (Figure 4.4). An adjustable microphone on a headset allows you to find a microphone position that is optimal for your recording needs and allows you to keep your hands free for working on the computer while you speak.

Figure 4.4 Headsets combine headphones and microphones in one device. Using a headset that includes an adjustable microphone can provide optimal recording results.

Pop filter A mesh screen that is placed directly in front of a microphone to disrupt the fast flow of air as it speeds toward the microphone.

- Pop filter (optional)—Microphones don't react well to the human voice when sounds like the letter *p* are pronounced. The rush of air accompanying these sounds causes popping noises to occur on the recording. To prevent this, you need to use a pop filter. A *pop filter* is a mesh screen that is placed directly in front of a microphone to disrupt the fast flow of air as it speeds toward the microphone. You can buy pop filters from music supply stores or make a homemade one—like the one shown in Figure 4.5—from a wooden embroidery hoop and a pair of pantyhose. Because pops can be quite annoying to listeners, the use of a pop filter is highly recommended if you want to be taken seriously as a podcaster.

Figure 4.5 Even a homemade pop filter like the one shown here will improve the quality of your podcasts.

- Video camera or camcorder—For recording video, you'll need a camera that can capture video (perhaps a cell phone) or a video camera (camcorder). Although most video cameras come with built-in microphones, the sound quality may not be optimal for producing a high-quality video podcast. Most video cameras have a port into which you can plug an external microphone, so a microphone might be a good investment if you are doing serious video podcasting.

- Tripod—Watching a shaky, wobbly video is no fun for anyone. A tripod is a stand that is designed to hold a video camera steady to ensure better-quality video. Tripods are not expensive and will go a long way toward making your videos look more professional.

What software do I need to create my own podcasts?

There are many software packages available that enable you to produce high-quality audio and video podcasts. You may purchase this software, but there are also shareware and freeware options. To start out, free software—or software included with Windows—allows you to begin producing quality podcasts at little or no cost. Consider the following options:

- Sound Recorder—Sound Recorder is a basic sound recording program that is included with Windows. Click the **Start** button, select **All Programs** and then the **Accessories** folder to locate this program. Although it doesn't have many features, you can use it to record simple audio podcasts.

- Audacity (**http://audacity.sourceforge.net**)—This full-featured sound recording package is available for free. Audacity is an open source software package that provides you with many options for recording and editing audio, such as using multiple sound tracks (like music and voice) and adding special effects to recordings. It is available for Windows, Mac OS X, and Linux, and is used by many podcasters.

- Windows Live Movie Maker—This video software tool allows you to import video to your computer from video capture devices and to combine video with still photographs and sound tracks to produce very high-quality video podcasts. Originally known as Windows Movie Maker, this program was included in older versions of Windows, but was removed from Windows 7. However, the newest version—Windows Live Movie Maker—can be downloaded for free from the Windows Live site (http://explore.live.com). Although it doesn't have quite as many features as some high-end video production software suites, it will still allow you to begin producing video podcasts quickly and easily.

- CamStudio (http://camstudio.org)—Sometimes you may want to record video that captures what is happening on your computer screen. This is often useful if you are producing a tutorial to show people how to use a software package or how to navigate around a complex website. CamStudio is a free open source software package that enables you to record all onscreen and audio activity occurring on your computer and export it to video files that can be used as part of a podcast. In combination with a microphone, this software allows you to produce high-quality, narrated tutorials very quickly.

Objective 4

Explain the characteristics of quality podcasts and the preparation needed to create your own podcasts

What makes a podcast high quality?

Exceptional podcasts are entertaining as well as informative. They stick to their topic, and the information they present is well organized. New episodes of the podcast are produced on a regular basis, because listeners appreciate and expect fresh content.

What steps should I take when planning a podcast?

Planning is critical to establishing a successful podcast and accomplishing your objectives, whether they be to inform, to market, or to entertain. Well-designed podcasts are usually more engaging than ones that are haphazardly thrown together. Consider these four basic steps:

1. **Determine a topic for your podcast.** Successful podcasts are created by people who are passionate about their topics. Carefully consider your personal interests. Do you have a hobby that you would like to share with others? If you love seeking out new Indie rock bands that your friends haven't heard about yet, a podcast promoting new bands you have heard could be very engaging. What are your areas of expertise? If you are an avid long-distance bicyclist, your experience and knowledge in selecting appropriate cycling gear could be valuable to others. What topics could you discuss for hours on end? If you love spending time playing fantasy football and discussing key moves that improve your fantasy team, you will probably find others who could benefit from your insights.

   Perhaps you live in an area where there are a lot of leisure activities. You could create a podcast that informs people about what there is to do when they visit your community. The possibilities for topics are endless, but you should pick one and make sure that your podcasts all relate to the core topic so as not to confuse or alienate your loyal listeners.

2. **Pick an appropriate format for your podcast.** Radio and television shows usually have a set format, and podcasts can benefit from a set format as well. Shows are usually divided into segments. Consider the *Late Show with David Letterman*.

David does a monologue (segment 1), comedy bits either at his desk or in the audience (segment 2), the Top Ten List (segment 3), an interview with a guest (segment 4), an interview with a second guest (segment 5), a musical performance (segment 6), and then the show ends. Viewers feel more comfortable when they know what to expect at certain points during a show.

If you were considering doing a podcast about leisure activities in your area, your format might be as follows: Introduction, perhaps with theme music (segment 1), spotlight on the featured location for the week (segment 2), upcoming activities in the local area (segment 3), interview with a special guest (segment 4), and a wrap-up that includes a preview of the next show (segment 5).

You also need to consider whether an audio or a video format is appropriate for your podcast. Audio takes up much less space than video and is much quicker to download from the web. And audio is a great format for many types of podcasts, such as political commentaries and humor. But if the topic of your podcast needs visual images to support its message (such as demonstrating proper waterskiing techniques), video may be the best format for your podcast.

3. **Consider the optimal length for your podcast.** Your podcast needs to be long enough to get your information out to listeners but not so long that you bore them. When in doubt, keep a podcast short (generally under 20 minutes). If you have a particularly long topic to cover, consider breaking the podcast into smaller chunks and creating two or three podcasts that cover all the issues for one topic.

4. **Develop a schedule for new episodes of your podcast.** Regular contact with your listeners is important. They will forget about you and your podcast if new episodes are not released on a regular basis. Many podcasts feature new episodes on a weekly basis. If you don't have the time to produce new episodes regularly, you should really think long and hard about whether podcasting is something that you want to pursue.

Should I write a script for my podcast?

Very few people can produce engaging content spontaneously. Most people benefit from scripting out their ideas ahead of time, which helps determine proper sequencing of ideas. Having a script or an outline also ensures that you will cover all pertinent information and that you don't leave out any critical pieces of data. But if you are using a script, don't read the script word for word as you record the podcast. This usually results in a recording that sounds very mechanical or monotonous. Use the script as a guideline for what you are going to say. And don't worry if you make mistakes—you can always delete your file and start again.

Where should I record my podcast?

You need a quiet room, free of distractions and extraneous noise. Microphones are sensitive and can pick up all sorts of background noise, such as fans, air conditioners, televisions, ringing phones, roommates, and family members. So make sure that there is nothing in the room where you are recording that is generating sound besides you. If you are recording outdoors, you should be aware that your microphone—even one on a camcorder—will probably pick up many extraneous sounds, such as wind noise, street traffic, or birds. You may find that the sound track for a video that you filmed in less than optimal sound conditions might need to be rerecorded in a nice, quiet room in your home.

Objective 5

Download and install Audacity software

You are going to need software to record your audio podcast episodes. Although you could use Sound Recorder—which is included with Windows—you probably want a program that includes more advanced features.

Hands-On Exercises

For purposes of the Hands-On Exercises in this chapter, we are assuming that Professor Schmeckendorf is recording podcasts for his computer literacy students to inform them about aspects of information technology that can make their lives easier.

1 │ Download and Install Audacity Software

Steps: 1. Start Your Browser and Navigate to the Audacity Download Page; **2.** Download and Install the Audacity Software; **3.** Download and Install the LAME MP3 Encoder.

Use Figures 4.6 through 4.21 as a guide to the exercise.

Step 1 Start Your Browser and Navigate to the Audacity Download Page

Refer to Figures 4.6 and 4.7 as you complete Step 1.

a. Turn on the computer.

b. Start your preferred browser (Internet Explorer, Firefox, Safari, etc.). Type **http://audacity.sourceforge.net/download** in the address bar of your browser and press **Enter**.

Beta version Software that is still being tested and evaluated.

Sometimes a *beta version* of the Audacity software will be available for download. Beta software is a computer program that is still being tested and evaluated; therefore, it may not work as expected. In general, unless you are an extremely experienced computer user, you should not download the beta version; you should select a stable version of the software instead. However, if you are using Windows Vista or Windows 7, Audacity recommends using the beta version for these two operating systems. Often, there will be several interim versions of beta software released before the final product, so the version number you see may be higher than the one shown here.

c. You should now click the appropriate link for the operating system you are using. We are assuming that Windows 7 is the OS for the rest of this example, so click the Windows link.

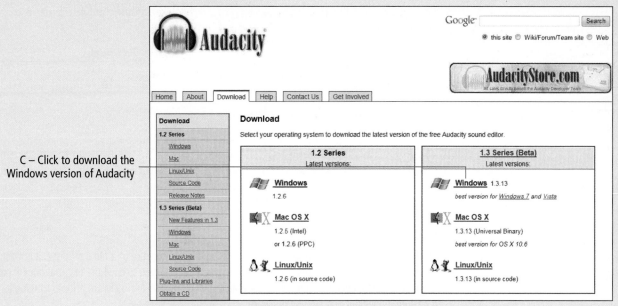

C – Click to download the
Windows version of Audacity

Figure 4.6 Hands-On Exercise 1, Step 1c.

d. Click the correct **Audacity 1.3.13** installer link for your operating system to download the installation file.

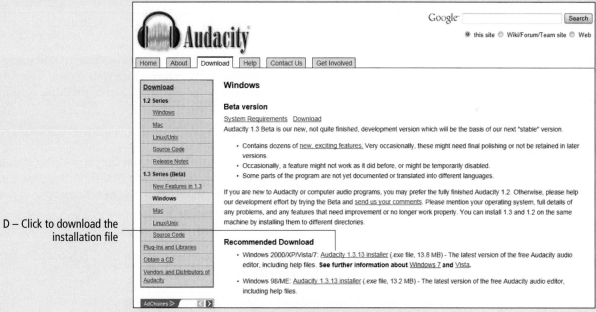

D – Click to download the
installation file

Figure 4.7 Hands-On Exercise 1, Step 1d.

Step 2 Download and Install the Audacity Software

Refer to Figures 4.8 through 4.16 as you complete Step 2.

Depending upon the browser you are using, you might receive a message asking whether you want to run or save the installation file. The following example shows you how to proceed using Internet Explorer 9. You may experience slight differences if you are using another browser. Check with your instructor for additional instructions.

a. On the notification bar at the bottom of the browser, click the **Save** button to download the file.

A – Click Save to download the Audacity installation file

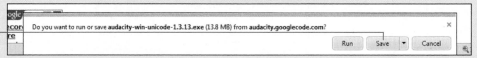

Figure 4.8 Hands-On Exercise 1, Step 2a.

b. Once the download is complete, the notification bar will refresh and indicate that the download has completed. Click the **Run** button to run the installation file for the Audacity software.

> **Alert**
>
> If you are downloading a file from an unknown source, or are unsure of a file's purpose, it is best to choose Save rather than Run. You can select a location in which to save the file and, once it has been downloaded, check the file with your antivirus and antispyware software prior to running it, to be sure it does not contain any malware.

B – Click Run to launch the Audacity installation file

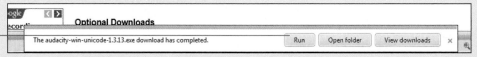

Figure 4.9 Hands-On Exercise 1, Step 2b.

Depending upon the version of Internet Explorer and the version of Windows that you are running, a security warning box may display on your screen. The Audacity installation file is safe to download and install, so you can bypass this warning.

> **Alert**
>
> If you are running Windows 7 or Windows Vista, the **User Account Control** dialog box may appear. This is an additional warning mechanism in Windows 7 and Windows Vista to prevent unauthorized software from being installed on your computer. Click the **Yes** or **Allow** option to proceed with the installation.

c. The **Select Setup Language** dialog box should appear next. Select the appropriate language from the drop-down box and click **OK.**

C – Select the appropriate language

Figure 4.10 Hands-On Exercise 1, Step 2c.

d. The Audacity Setup Wizard dialog box should now be displayed on your screen. Click the **Next** button to continue the installation process.

The next screen in the installation dialog box is the **Information** screen, which includes the GNU General Public License. You should review the license to ensure that you agree with the terms of the agreement before proceeding with the installation.

e. Click the **Next** button to indicate your agreement with the licensing terms and continue the installation process.

Use the scroll bar to review the entire licensing agreement

E – Click Next to accept the licensing agreement and proceed to the next step

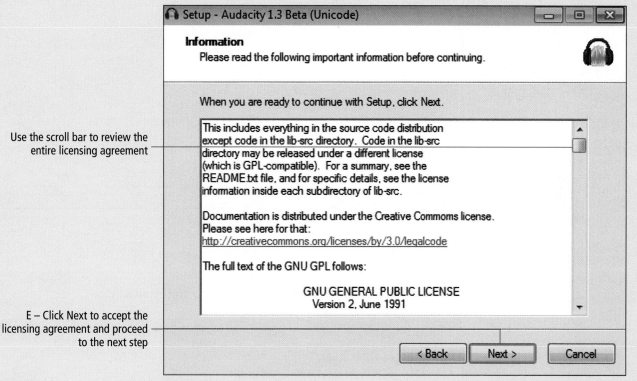

Figure 4.11 Hands-On Exercise 1, Step 2e.

f. Accept the default folder location for installed files (C:\Program Files (x86)\ Audacity 1.3 Beta (Unicode)) or browse to find a different folder to hold the Audacity files. If you are performing this exercise in a computer lab, check with your instructor for the correct location.

g. Click the **Next** button to proceed to the **Select Additional Tasks** screen.

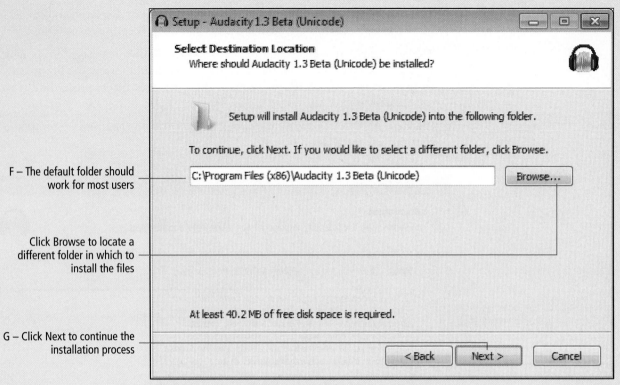

F – The default folder should work for most users

Click Browse to locate a different folder in which to install the files

G – Click Next to continue the installation process

Figure 4.12 Hands-On Exercise 1, Steps 2f and 2g.

h. Confirm that the checkbox next to **Create a desktop icon** is checked. This will ensure the creation of an icon on the desktop to start Audacity.

i. Click the Next button to proceed to the **Ready to Install** screen.

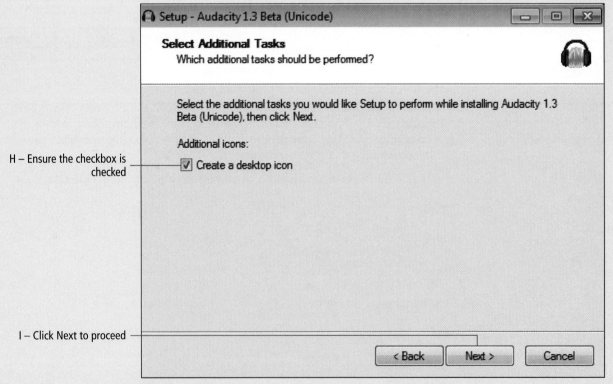

H – Ensure the checkbox is checked

I – Click Next to proceed

Figure 4.13 Hands-On Exercise 1, Steps 2h and 2i.

j. In the **Ready to Install screen,** click the **Install** button to complete the installation of Audacity.

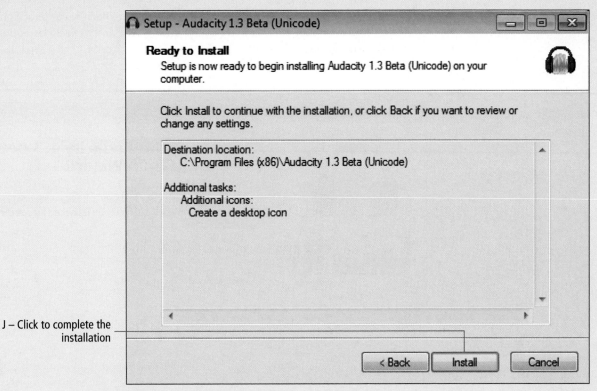

J – Click to complete the installation

Figure 4.14 Hands-On Exercise 1, Step 2j.

k. A second **Information** screen will appear containing the **README** documentation, which provides additional information about licensing, version changes, known issues, and other details that may be of use to the end user. Once you have reviewed this information, click the **Next** button.

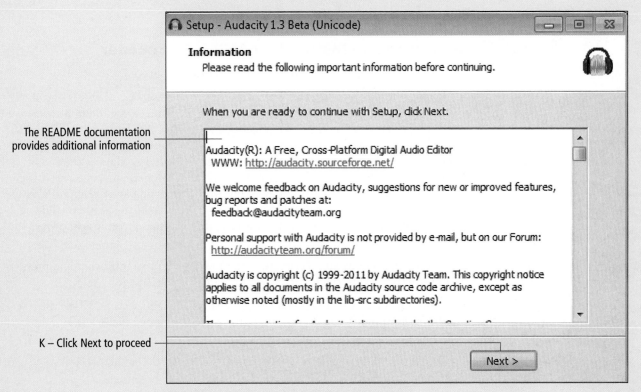

The README documentation provides additional information

K – Click Next to proceed

Figure 4.15 Hands-On Exercise 1, Step 2k.

l. When the installation is complete, you will see a **Completing the Audacity Setup Wizard** dialog box. Uncheck the **Launch Audacity** checkbox and click **Finish** to complete the installation. You will launch Audacity in a separate exercise. Leave your browser open for the next step.

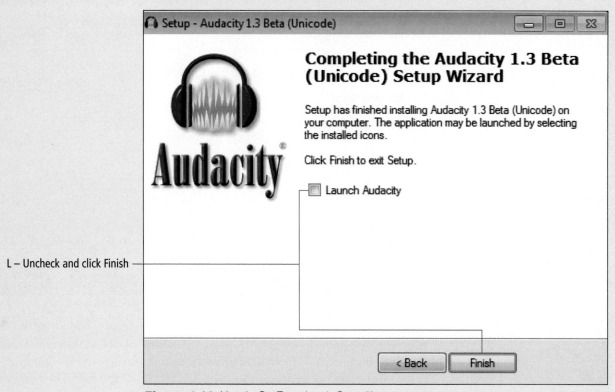

L – Uncheck and click Finish

Figure 4.16 Hands-On Exercise 1, Step.2l.

Step ❸ Download and Install the LAME MP3 Encoder

Refer to Figures 4.17 through 4.21 as you complete Step 3.

You will most likely want to create MP3 files for your podcasts, as this is one of the most popular audio file types on the Internet. When you record a file in Audacity, it uses a proprietary file format called *Audacity Project Files*. An Audacity project consists of a project file (the file extension is *.aup*) and a project data folder. The project data folder has the same name as the project file but includes **_data** at the end of the folder name. It is important that the file and the folder remain together; if they become separated, the Audacity file will not work. Exporting an Audacity file to an MP3 format eliminates this problem. Audacity needs an additional file to allow it to export files to an MP3 format. Fortunately, this file is also free; it is known as the *LAME MP3 Encoder.*

a. Type **http://lame.buanzo.com.ar** in the address bar of your browser and press **Enter** to proceed to the **LAME MP3 Encoder Binaries** page.

b. Scroll down the page until you see the **ZIP OPTION:** section. Click the **libmp3lame-win-3.98.2.zip** link to download the zipped file.

Zipped folders (or *zipped files*) Groups of files that have been compressed using special file compression software to condense the files so that they are smaller in size and can be downloaded quickly.

Extracted Files that have been unzipped, or restored, to their original size.

B – Click the link to download the zipped file

Zipped folders (or *zipped files*) are groups of files that have been compressed using special file compression software to condense the files so that they are smaller in size and can be downloaded quickly. Zipped folders must be *extracted*, or unzipped, to restore the files to their original size before they can be used. Current versions of Windows include file compression utility software. If you have a version of Windows that does not include file compression software, you can download a free program at **www.camunzip.com.**

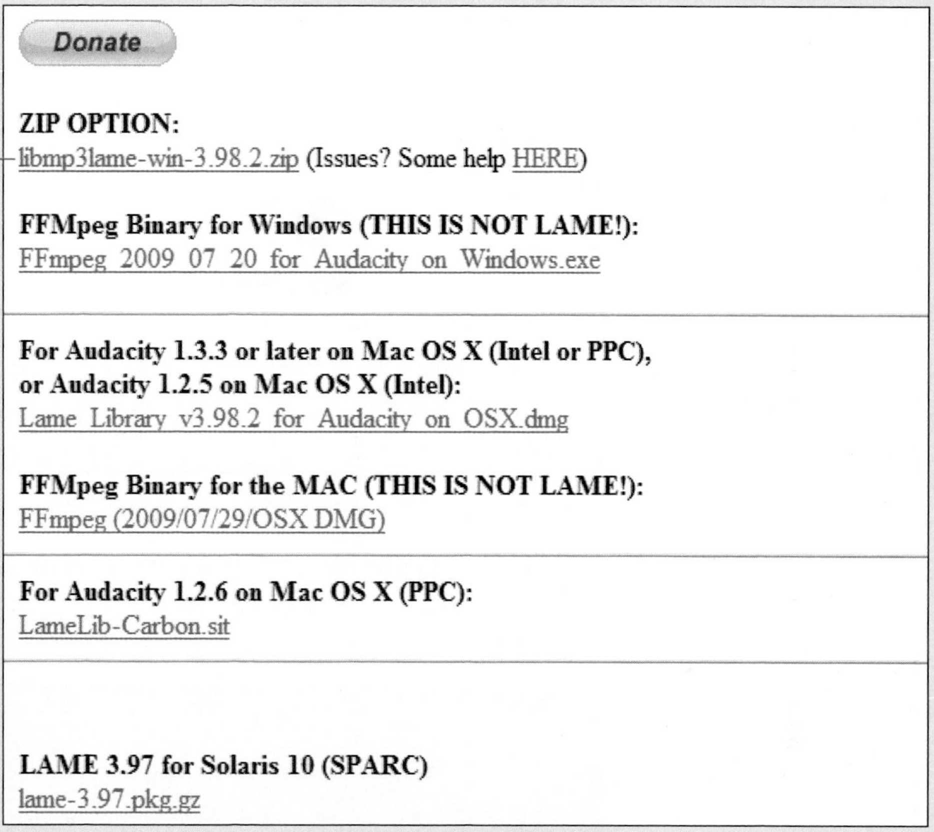

Donate

ZIP OPTION:
libmp3lame-win-3.98.2.zip (Issues? Some help HERE)

FFMpeg Binary for Windows (THIS IS NOT LAME!):
FFmpeg_2009_07_20_for_Audacity_on_Windows.exe

For Audacity 1.3.3 or later on Mac OS X (Intel or PPC), or Audacity 1.2.5 on Mac OS X (Intel):
Lame_Library_v3.98.2_for_Audacity_on_OSX.dmg

FFMpeg Binary for the MAC (THIS IS NOT LAME!):
FFmpeg (2009/07/29/OSX DMG)

For Audacity 1.2.6 on Mac OS X (PPC):
LameLib-Carbon.sit

LAME 3.97 for Solaris 10 (SPARC)
lame-3.97.pkg.gz

Figure 4.17 Hands-On Exercise 1, Step 3b.

c. When the **Windows Internet Explorer** dialog box appears asking how to handle the zipped file, click the **Save As** button to display the **Save As** dialog box.

Alert!

When downloading a file, if you click **Save**, Internet Explorer 9 saves the downloaded file to the Users\username\Downloads folder by default. To change the default location for all downloaded files, press **Ctrl+J** and click the **Options** link to select the desired location. To change the download location for an individual file, use the **Save As** option.

d. In the **Save As** dialog box, navigate to an appropriate place on your hard drive in which to save the zipped folder you are downloading. Your desktop is probably a convenient place.

e. Click the **Save** button to download and save the folder in the specified location. Once the download is complete, a **Download Complete** notification may appear at the bottom of your browser window. If necessary, click **Close** to dismiss this notification.

D – Navigate to an appropriate location to save the zipped folder

E – Click Save to download and save the folder

Figure 4.18 Hands-On Exercise 1, Steps 3d and 3e.

f. Locate the zipped folder on your desktop (or in the location where you saved it). The folder name is libmp3lame-win-3.98.2.

g. Right-click the zipped folder and select **Extract All** from the shortcut menu.

F – Locate the zipped folder

G – Right-click the folder and select Extract All

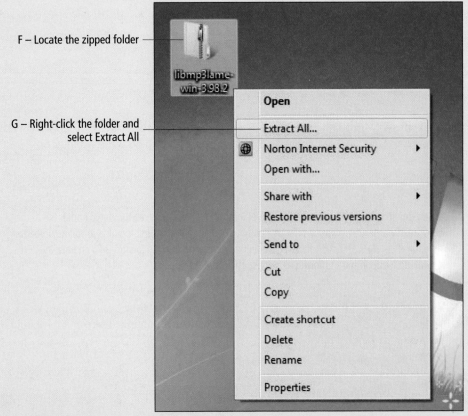

Figure 4.19 Hands-On Exercise 1, Steps 3f and 3g.

h. In the **Extract Compressed (Zipped) Folders** dialog box, click the **Browse** button to display the **Select a destination** dialog box.

i. In the **Select a destination** dialog box, navigate to the folder where you installed the Audacity files (such as C:\Program Files (x86)\Audacity 1.3 Beta (Unicode)). Click the **OK** button to return to the **Extract Compressed (Zipped) Folders** dialog box. Notice that the file path, showing the location of the selected folder, now appears in the **Files will be extracted to this folder** text box.

j. If necessary, click the **Show extracted files when complete** checkbox to place a check there. Click the **Extract** button to decompress the files and install them in the folder specified in the previous step.

Windows Vista and Windows 7 users may see a **Destination Folder Access Denied** dialog box. If you have administrator rights, click the **Continue** button to continue installing the files. If you do not have administrator rights, see your professor for instructions on how to proceed. You may also see the **User Account Control** dialog box. If necessary, click the **Allow** option to proceed.

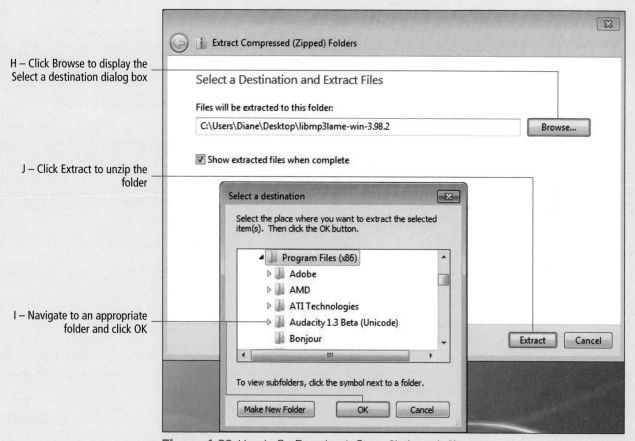

Figure 4.20 Hands-On Exercise 1, Steps 3h through 3j.

k. The extracted folder, named libmp3lame-3.98.2, should appear in a Windows Explorer window. If it doesn't, or if you need to find it later, right-click the **Start** button and select **Open Windows Explorer** from the shortcut menu to start Windows Explorer.

1. Navigate to the location where you extracted the zipped folder (known as the destination folder) and locate the folder named libmp3lame-3.98.2. Once you have located the folder, you can close the Explorer window.

   Remember where you placed this folder. You will need to tell Audacity where to find the files contained in it the first time you wish to export a sound file to an MP3 format.

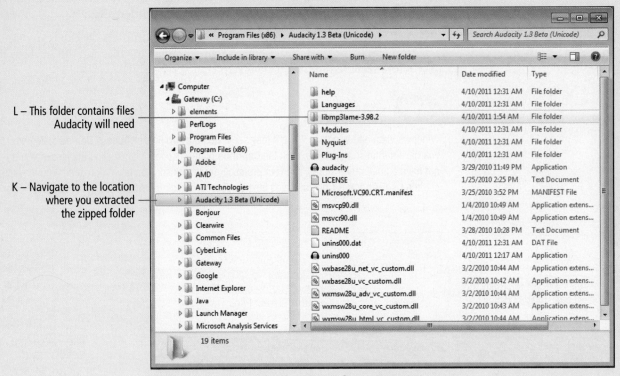

L – This folder contains files Audacity will need

K – Navigate to the location where you extracted the zipped folder

Figure 4.21 Hands-On Exercise 1, Steps 3k and 3l.

Congratulations! You now have the necessary software installed to record your first podcast.

Objective 6

Record an audio podcast

Now that you have installed the Audacity software, you are ready to record your first podcast. You may use a script of your own or you can follow the example of Professor Schmeckendorf's first podcast to his students.

For Professor Schmeckendorf's first podcast, he has decided to direct students to the Microsoft Office 2010 Ultimate Steal website in case they wish to purchase a discounted version of the Office 2010 software. For the podcast, he has developed the following script:

Microsoft is running an offer especially for college students called The Ultimate Steal. Students can obtain a copy of the Professional Academic version of Microsoft Office 2010 for only $79.95. To qualify for this offer, you must be enrolled at a U.S. educational institution and have a valid email address that ends with the domain suffix .EDU. Since GSU does provide you with an email address ending in .EDU, you all should be eligible. Considering this package sells for around $500 in stores, this is a fantastic deal for students. So go to theultimatesteal.com to check it out and save some money today!

Hands-On Exercises

2 | Record an Audio Podcast

Steps: 1. Ensure That Your Recording and Playback Devices Are Configured;
2. Start Audacity and Set Preferences; **3.** Record a Podcast; **4.** Export a Podcast to
an MP3 File.

Use Figures 4.22 through 4.34 as a guide to the exercise.

Step **Ensure That Your Recording and Playback Devices Are Configured**

Refer to Figures 4.22 and 4.23 as you complete Step 1.

a. Connect your microphone to your computer if you are using an external microphone. Turn on any external speakers that are connected to your computer or plug your headphones into the computer.

b. Click the Windows **Start** button and select **Control Panel** from the menu options.

c. In the **Control Panel** for Windows 7, click the **Hardware and Sound** icon and then click the **Sound** icon. If you are using Windows Vista, click the **Sound** icon. This will display the **Sound** dialog box.

> **Alert!**
>
> Depending upon your operating system and settings, the Control Panel may display in different ways—Category, Large Icons, Small Icons, Control Panel Home, Classic View, and so on. If your Control Panel does not match the one shown here, look for some variation of *Sound* or *Audio* to locate the correct setting.

The rest of this example will provide directions for configuring sound devices in Windows 7, but Windows Vista sound devices are configured in a similar manner.

d. In the **Sound** dialog box, click the **Playback** tab, if necessary. If you are currently playing music—or other audio—on your computer, the sound level bar should show green, indicating that the speakers or headphones are working. And, of course, you should hear sound coming out of the speakers!

D – When playing sound on your computer, the green bars indicate that the speakers are working

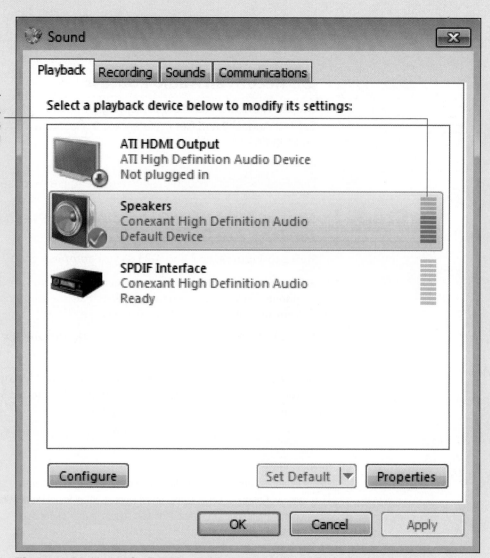

Figure 4.22 Hands-On Exercise 2, Step 1d.

e. Next, turn off any music or other sounds that you are currently playing through your computer. In the **Sound** dialog box, click the **Recording** tab. Speak into the microphone. The sound level bar should show green, indicating that the microphone is working properly.

f. After you've ensured that the recording and playback devices are working properly, click **Cancel** to close the **Sound** dialog box. You can also close the **Control Panel** at this time.

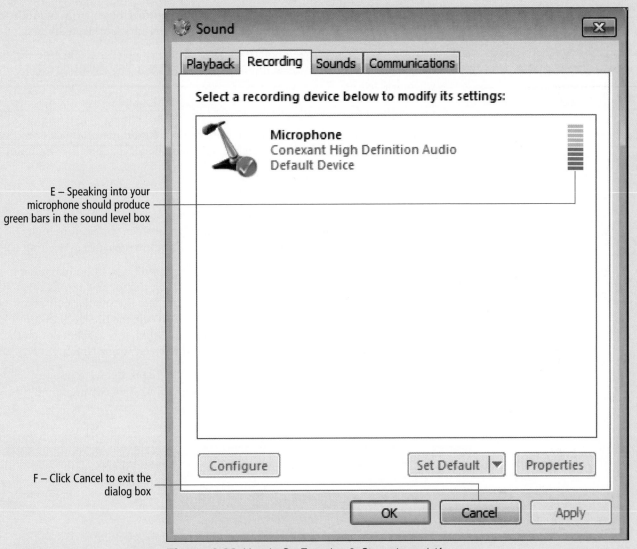

E – Speaking into your microphone should produce green bars in the sound level box

F – Click Cancel to exit the dialog box

Figure 4.23 Hands-On Exercise 2, Steps 1e and 1f.

 Alert

If your speakers or your microphone are not working properly, you may have a problem with the sound card in your computer, or the Windows sound drivers (special software that allows computer programs to communicate with hardware devices) may be improperly installed. Consult with your professor or a computer technician to resolve the problem.

Step 2 Start Audacity and Set Preferences

Refer to Figures 4.24 through 4.27 as you complete Step 2.

a. Click the **Start** button, select **All Programs**, and then select **Audacity** from the list of programs (or double-click the **Audacity** icon on your desktop) to start the Audacity software. If the **How to Get Help** window appears, click **OK** to bypass it. This window will appear each time you start Audacity. If you don't want it to appear again, simply check the **Don't show this again at start up** checkbox.

Figure 4.24 shows what the Audacity software should look like when the program is first launched. Your screen may look different if another student has changed the preferences on the computer on which you are working, but the functionality of the program should be the same. If necessary, click the **Maximize** button to view Audacity in full-screen mode. Some key features of the Audacity interface are as follows:

■ Pause button—Click to temporarily stop recording or playback. Clicking the Pause button a second time will resume the playback or the recording exactly where you left off.

■ Play button—Click to play back a sound file.

■ Stop button—Click to stop playback or recording. Resuming playback or recording after the Stop button is clicked will start the playback at the beginning of the file or begin recording a new audio file.

■ Record button—Click to record a new sound file.

■ Selection tool—When this icon is selected, the cursor will look like an I-beam when you are working in a sound file. Select this tool when you want to highlight a certain portion of a sound file to change its properties (such as deleting it).

■ Zoom tool—When this icon is selected, the cursor will look like a magnifying glass when you are working in a sound file. Clicking the sound file will zoom in on the file and spread out the time line so that there is a smaller portion of the sound file on the screen. This makes it easier to edit the file (such as cutting out pauses). Right-clicking while this tool is selected will zoom out on the time line to display more of the audio file on the screen at one time.

■ Time line—Shows (in seconds) how long the audio file is and what point in time you are at in the recording file. This is important when editing sound files.

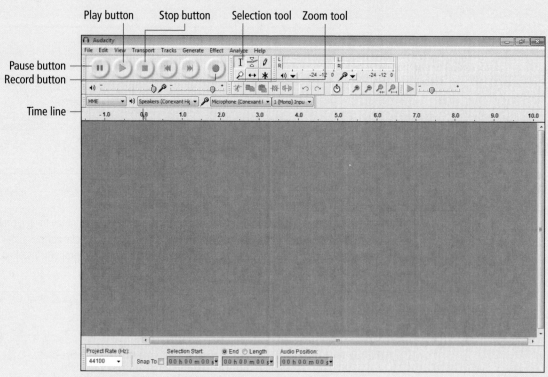

Figure 4.24 Hands-On Exercise 2, Step 2a.

b. From the **Edit** menu, select **Preferences** to display the **Audacity Preferences** dialog box. If necessary, select **Devices** from the list at the left of the dialog box.

Your default playback and recording devices should be showing in the device drop-down buttons, if they are properly configured and turned on. If they are not showing, click the buttons and select from the list of devices available.

Ensure that 1 (**Mono**) is selected as the format for channels. Mono means that only one channel of audio is recorded instead of two (the 2 (Stereo) setting). One channel is sufficient for voice recording and generates a smaller-size audio file. Your listeners should appreciate smaller files because they will take up less space on their PMPs when they download your podcast. Click **OK** to accept these settings.

 Tip

The most recent version of Audacity includes a Device toolbar that appears by default directly above the time line. This toolbar allows you to quickly change your input and output settings.

Now you need to set the preferences for exporting the audio files you will record to an MP3 format. You need to tell Audacity where to locate the LAME encoder file that you downloaded in Hands-On Exercise 1, Step 3.

Click here to display other output choices

Click here to display other input choices

Click here and select 1 (Mono) from the available choices

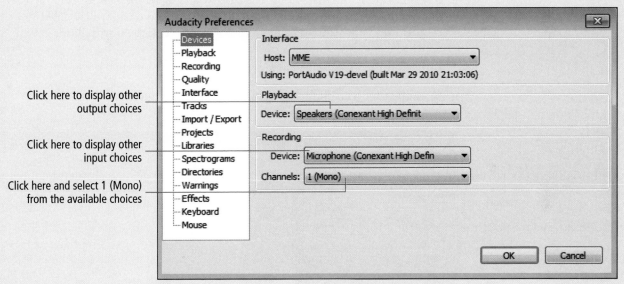

Figure 4.25 Hands-On Exercise 2, Step 2b.

c. If necessary, repeat Step 2b to open the **Audacity Preferences** dialog box and select **Libraries**.

d. Notice that under the section entitled *MP3 Export Library*, the MP3 export library is not found. Audacity has two options—you can either locate the LAME file on your computer or download it. Since you've already downloaded the file, click the **MP3 Library: Locate** button to display the **Locate Lame** dialog box.

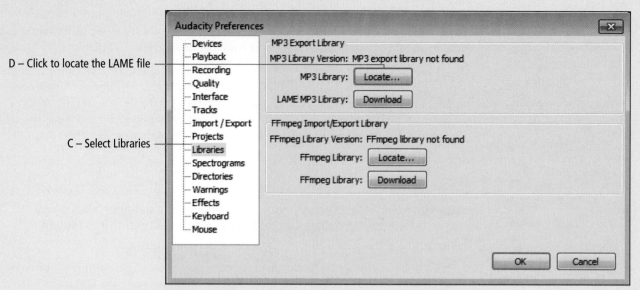

D – Click to locate the LAME file

C – Select Libraries

Figure 4.26 Hands-On Exercise 2, Steps 2c and 2d.

e. In the **Locate Lame** dialog box, click **Browse** to open the **Where is lame_enc. dll?** dialog box and navigate to the location where you unzipped the LAME encoder files folder, libmp3lame-3.98.2. Double-click the **libmp3lame-3.98.2** folder to display its contents.

f. Click the **lame_enc.dll** file to select it.

g. With the lame_enc.dll file selected, click the **Open** button to proceed.

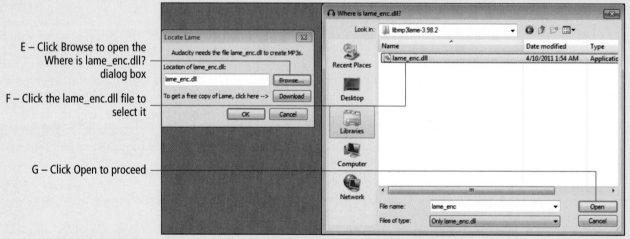

E – Click Browse to open the Where is lame_enc.dll? dialog box

F – Click the lame_enc.dll file to select it

G – Click Open to proceed

Figure 4.27 Hands-On Exercise 2, Steps 2e through 2g.

h. In the **Locate Lame** dialog box, click the OK button. Notice that in the **Audacity Preferences** dialog box, the MP3 Library Version now lists LAME 3.98.2. Click **OK** to exit the dialog box.

Step 3 Record a Podcast

Refer to Figures 4.28 through 4.32 as you complete Step 3.

You are now ready to record your podcast. There are two main issues that you must be concerned with while recording an audio file: (1) the recording sound level and (2) dealing with mistakes.

Sound level—Your podcast will be hard to understand if the sound recording levels are too high, as your voice will be distorted. Therefore, it is a good idea to test the levels at the beginning of your recording. The easiest way to vary the levels is to move closer to or farther away from the microphone or to speak in a softer or louder voice. Figure 4.28 shows a sample test recording to establish sound levels.

The recording level meter can be used as a guide for recording levels. It is active only while you are recording an audio track. The farther to the right the level meter goes, the more likely that the sound will be distorted.

The audio track window also gives you a clear indication of the suitability of your audio levels. The blue wavy lines represent the audio in the recording. When the blue lines bump up against the top or bottom edge of the audio track window, the recording levels are too high and the sound is most likely distorted. In Figure 4.28, the section of the recording shown outlined in the yellow box indicates recording levels that should be acceptable.

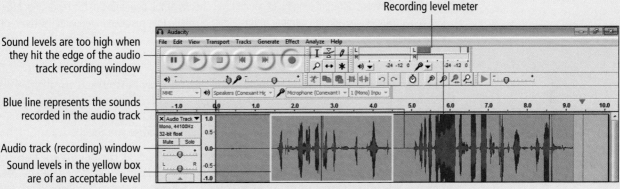

Figure 4.28 Sample test recording with sound levels displayed.

You should test the levels each time you begin to record to get the microphone positioned at an appropriate distance from your mouth. Remember to speak at the same general volume level throughout the recording. You can test the levels at the beginning of a podcast file and edit out the sound test later on. There is no need to create a separate file just for the sound test.

Mistakes While Recording—Even with a detailed script to follow, you are likely to make some mistakes while you are recording. Because you can easily edit a sound file, there is no need to stop the recording and start the entire file over again. Just pause, gather your thoughts, and go back to the sentence in your script that comes before you made the mistake. Repeat that sentence and continue recording. You can always edit out the mistake later on.

a. If you have not already done so, start the **Audacity** program.

b. Click the **Record** button and do a sound level check.

c. Record your podcast by speaking at a moderate pace (not too fast or too slow). If you are using Professor Schmeckendorf's script from earlier in the chapter, the beginning of your podcast may look something like Figure 4.29 after you record it.

d. When you are done recording, click the **Stop** button.

B – Click the Record button to begin

D – Click the Stop button when done

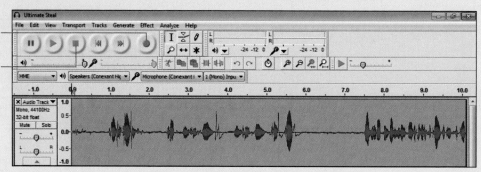

Figure 4.29 Hands-On Exercise 2, Steps 3b and 3d.

Alert!

Your recording won't look exactly like Figure 4.29. The differences result from different sound levels (voice levels), different lengths of sound level checks at the beginning of the recording, how fast you are speaking, and the number of mistakes you made that resulted in repeating portions of the recording.

You should play back your recording (by clicking the **Play** button) and see if it is of acceptable quality. If it isn't, just record it again using different sound levels. If the sound is acceptable, use the time line to review the recording and determine which portions you need to delete (such as the sound check and any mistakes you fixed).

In Professor Schmeckendorf's recording, the sound check at the beginning lasts for approximately 7.5 seconds and needs to be deleted. A mistake was made at 28 seconds into the recording and the correction began at approximately 34 seconds, so this portion (from 28 to 34 seconds) also needs to be deleted. The following steps demonstrate how to correct Professor Schmeckendorf's recording. Use these steps as a guideline when working with your own recording, keeping in mind that your adjustments will vary depending upon the changes you need to make.

e. Use the scroll bar at the bottom of the Audacity screen, or the **Skip to Start** button, to return to the beginning of the audio file.

f. Click the **Selection tool** to select it.

g. Click at the beginning of the area to be selected (in this case, the beginning of the recording).

h. While holding down the left mouse button, drag to select the appropriate area representing the sound check (in this case, the first 7.5 seconds of the recording).

F – Click the Selection tool

G – Click at the beginning of the area to be selected

H – While holding down the left mouse button, drag to select the appropriate area

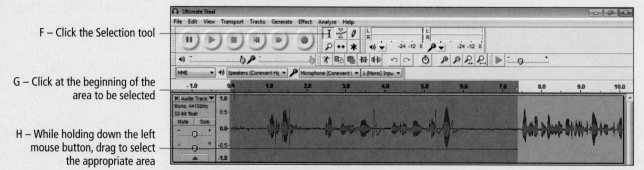

Figure 4.30 Hands-On Exercise 2, Steps 3f through 3h.

i. With the appropriate area selected, click the **Edit menu** and select **Delete** to remove the selected portion of the recording.

As you make changes to the sound file, the time line adjusts to display the new running time. Originally, the next portion to be deleted began approximately 28 seconds into the recording. Because the first 7.5 seconds of the recording were cut by deleting the sound check, the second portion to be deleted now begins approximately 20.5 seconds into the recording and ends slightly before the 26.5 second mark.

j. Play back the recording to locate the mistake that needs to be eliminated. Use the scroll bar to move to the appropriate portion of the time line.

k. Click at the beginning of the area to be selected and, while holding down the left mouse button, drag to select the appropriate area.

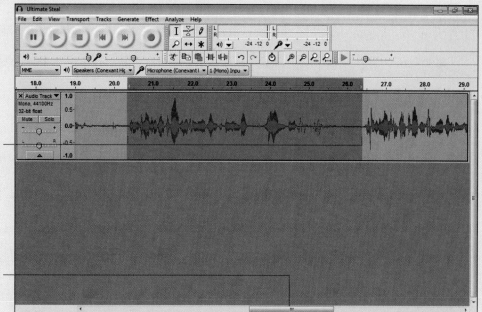

K – Click at the beginning of the area to be selected and drag to select the area to be deleted

J – Use the scroll bar to display the appropriate portion of the recording on the screen

Figure 4.31 Hands-On Exercise 2, Steps 3j and 3k.

l. With the appropriate area selected, click the **Edit** menu and select **Delete** to remove the selected portion of the recording.

m. Play back the recording a final time to ensure that all appropriate edits have been made and that you are happy with the final quality of the recording.

n. From the **File** menu, select **Save Project As** to display the **Save Project As** dialog box.

Alert!

A Warning box might be displayed, explaining that you will be saving the project in an Audacity file format (*.aup* file extension) and that this file format can't be played back by most other software. Click **OK** to proceed. You will export a file to an MP3 format in the next section.

o. Navigate to the folder where you wish to save the file—or create a new folder.

p. Type **Podcast_1_Your_Name** in the **File name** text box.

q. Click the **Save** button to save the file.

Alert!

Audacity projects actually consist of two components—the sound file (which uses the *.aup* extension) and a folder. The folder name includes the filename and _data. If you create a sound file and save it as **sample.aup,** the corresponding folder will be named **sample_data.** Audacity breaks the sound file into smaller components that are stored in the _data folder and reassembled when you play the file. To share an Audacity project file, you need to include the *.aup* file and the _data folder, or else the file will not open.

Click to create a new folder if you need one

O – Navigate to the folder where you wish to save the file

Q – Click Save

P – Enter a name for the file

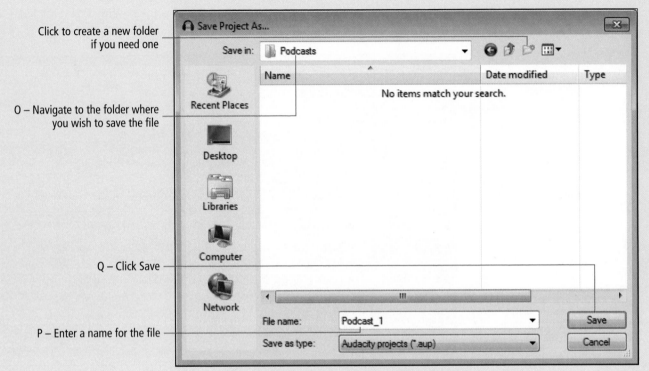

Figure 4.32 Hands-On Exercise 2, Steps 3o through 3q.

Step ④ Export a Podcast to an MP3 File

Refer to Figures 4.33 and 4.34 as you complete Step 4.

The most common format for audio podcasts is an MP3 file. MP3 files are used because most multimedia software and portable media players can play them back. Also, the MP3 format produces very efficient files that take up less space than many other formats. Therefore, you should distribute your podcasts in MP3 format.

a. If necessary, start Audacity. If the audio file you wish to export is not open, from the **File** menu, select **Open.** Browse to the folder where you saved the podcast file (**Podcast_1_Your_Name**) and select it to open it in Audacity.

b. Click **File** and select **Export** to display the **Export File** dialog box.

c. Navigate to the folder in which you wish to save the MP3 file.

d. Type **Podcast Volume 1-1_Your_Name** in the **File name** text box.

e. Click the **Save as type** drop-down arrow and select **MP3 Files,** if this isn't already selected.

f. Click the **Save** button to display the **Edit Metadata** dialog box.

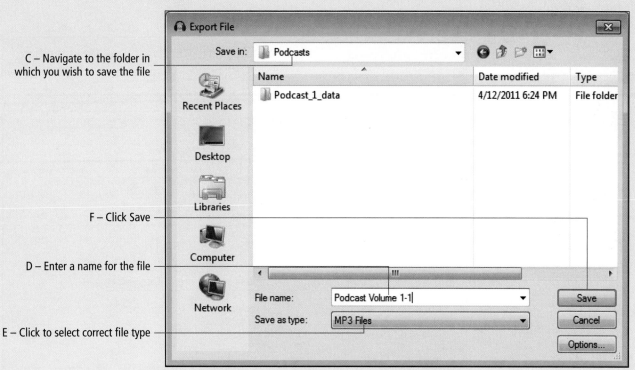

C – Navigate to the folder in which you wish to save the file

F – Click Save

D – Enter a name for the file

E – Click to select correct file type

Figure 4.33 Hands-On Exercise 2, Steps 4c through 4f.

ID3 tags Pieces of information that are attached to MP3 audio files.

The **Edit Metadata** dialog box allows you to specify *ID3 tags* for your podcast. ID3 tags are pieces of information that are attached to MP3 audio files. They display on the screen when the files are played back in software programs or on PMPs. You should fill in tags with descriptive information so that people who listen to your podcast know where it came from and who recorded it.

g. Fill in the appropriate information in each of the boxes in the **Edit Metadata** dialog box. Following are some suggestions:

- Artist Name—The name of the person (or organization) that distributes the podcast.

- Track Title—A descriptive title that informs the listener about the topic of this particular podcast.

- Album Title—The podcast series numbers (volume and episode numbers).

- Track Number—The volume and episode numbers again.

- Year—The year the track was recorded.

- Genre—The drop-down list in this text box contains a lengthy list of categories; however, *Podcast* is not one of them. You can choose another category, such as *Speech*, or you can simply type "Podcast" in the text box and bypass the drop-down list. To include "Podcast" as a permanent choice, click the **Edit** button in the **Genres** section to modify the category list.

- Comments—Consider including the URL where people can find your podcasts.

The **Add**, **Remove**, and **Clear** buttons allow you to create your own custom tags. The **Edit** and **Reset** buttons in the **Genres** section allow you to customize the genre categories for future use. The **Load**, **Save**, and **Set Default** buttons in the **Template** section can be useful if you want to apply the same tags to multiple recordings, rather than entering each tag for each recording.

h. Click the **OK** button to export the Audacity project file to an MP3 file.

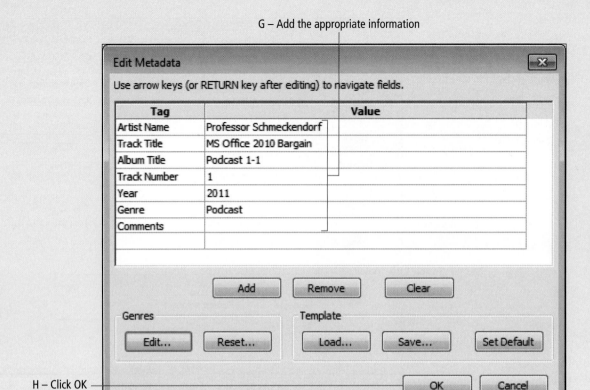

Figure 4.34 Hands-On Exercise 2, Steps 4g and 4h.

i. Open Windows Media Player or the media player of your choice, locate the MP3 file, and play it to ensure that the file sounds the way you intended. Alternately, you can also open Windows Explorer, navigate to the location where you saved this MP3 file, and double-click it to open it in Windows Media Player.

j. Close the media player and then close Audacity.

Objective 7

Import video to your computer

If you are recording video with a camcorder or other video capture device, you will need to transfer the video to your computer at some point so that you can use it to produce your podcast. This will require connecting your video capture device to your computer. Although some devices can connect to your computer wirelessly, most use a cable that connects to a USB or FireWire port.

Windows will recognize video devices as soon as you connect them to your computer and turn them on. You may have installed software that came with your video device to import video to your computer, or you can use the Windows video capture protocols. Capturing video works differently depending upon the video device used. In the examples that follow, we'll show you how to import video from a digital camera that is also capable of recording video. This process may vary slightly for your video device but should be similar enough for you to follow. Consult the manuals that came with your video device for complete instructions.

When you connect a video device to your Windows computer and turn it on, Windows displays the **AutoPlay** dialog box, which should look similar to the one shown in Figure 4.35. Your options may vary depending upon the device you have connected and the software available on your computer, but following are some possible choices:

- Import pictures and videos using Windows—This option will start a wizard (a programmed set of software steps) that will allow you to import video or pictures to your computer. Wizards usually require following rigid steps, so they may be cumbersome to use when importing large quantities of video clips or pictures. With a camcorder connected to the computer, selecting this option presents you with a wizard that has onscreen controls that mimic the controls on your camcorder for playback of video (play, stop, pause, fast forward, etc.), making it easy to capture the exact pieces of a video recording that you wish to download.

- Download using other software—Various programs can appear here, depending upon what software is installed on your computer or accompanied your video capture device.

- Open folder to view files using Windows Explorer—With cameras and cell phones, the video or still images are usually stored on flash memory cards. When viewed with Windows Explorer, the memory card appears as a new drive containing folders and files. This is a good option to select for downloading video from digital cameras or cell phones that can also record video, because the video is stored in discrete files as opposed to continuous segments on camcorders. We'll select this option for importing our video in this example.

Alert!

If the **AutoPlay** dialog box does not appear, you can open Windows Explorer by right-clicking the **Start** button, selecting **Open Windows Explorer** from the shortcut menu, and navigating to the location of the drive or folder containing the files you wish to download.

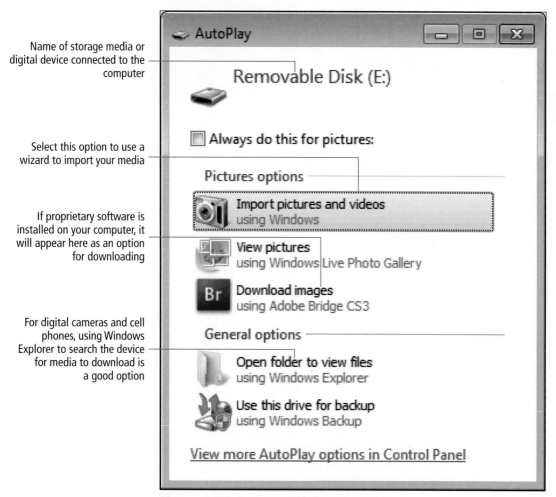

Name of storage media or digital device connected to the computer

Select this option to use a wizard to import your media

If proprietary software is installed on your computer, it will appear here as an option for downloading

For digital cameras and cell phones, using Windows Explorer to search the device for media to download is a good option

Figure 4.35 A sample AutoPlay dialog box.

When you select the option **Open folder to view files using Windows Explorer**, an Explorer window should open that looks similar to Figure 4.36. The digital device you are using should appear as a device connected to your computer (usually listed below the other devices on your computer, such as the hard drive or DVD drive). The digital device is assigned a drive letter such as *E*: or *F*:—the actual letter will vary depending upon the number of devices connected to your computer. Once you've located your digital device, you can browse through the storage media folders to find the folder that contains the video (or other digital media) that you wish to download to your computer. You can then copy the files to an appropriate directory on your computer's hard drive.

Again, these examples are for illustrative purposes only and will vary depending upon the type of digital device you are using. But once you have your digital video files downloaded to the computer, you are ready to begin producing your video podcast.

Copy the media you wish to download to a folder on your computer's hard drive

The storage media or digital device is assigned a drive letter

Locate the folder containing the media you wish to download

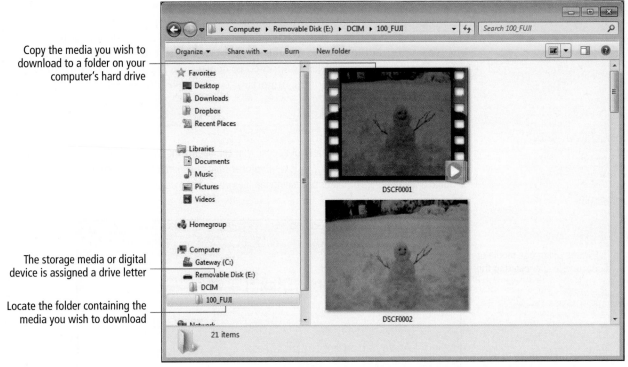

Figure 4.36 A sample Windows Explorer screen displaying two media files.

Objective 8

Create a video podcast using Windows Live Movie Maker

We are now ready to create Professor Schmeckendorf's first video podcast. All we need are the video clips that will comprise the podcast.

In the Hands-On Exercise that follows, you will need two video clips and a picture file (*.jpg*) that have been prepared for you. The first step of the Hands-On Exercise will detail how to download these files from the Internet. However, your instructor may have already downloaded these files and placed them on your school's network for your convenience. So check with your instructor before proceeding with Step 1.

Hands-On Exercises

3 | Produce a Video Podcast

Steps: 1. Download the Media Files to Your Computer; **2.** Download and Install Windows Live Movie Maker; **3.** Start Windows Live Movie Maker and Import the Media Files; **4.** Assemble the Components of the Podcast on the Storyboard; **5.** Apply an AutoMovie Theme to the Podcast; **6.** Export Your Podcast to a WMV File.

Use Figures 4.37 through 4.50 as a guide to the exercise.

Step 1 Download the Media Files to Your Computer

a. Open your web browser and type **www.pearsonhighered.com/nextseries** in the browser address bar. Press **Enter**.

b. From the list of books provided, locate this textbook and click the **Companion Website** link. This will take you to the companion website for the book.

   You will need to download two zipped files that contain the student files for this chapter.

c. Click the **Student Data Files** link.

d. Click the **Chapter 4 Part** 1 link to begin downloading the file to your computer. A **Windows Internet Explorer** dialog box will appear.

e. In the **Windows Internet Explorer** dialog box, click the **Save As** button to display the **Save As** dialog box.

f. Browse through the folders (or create a new folder) on your computer's hard drive or your flash drive to find an appropriate place to save the file.

g. Click the **Save** button to download the file and save it to your computer. A message bar may appear at the bottom of your screen indicating the download status. Once the download is complete, you can click the **Close** button to dismiss this message.

h. Repeat Steps 1d through 1g to download the Chapter 4 Part 2 student data file and save it to the same location as the Part 1 file.

i. After the files have been downloaded, close your browser.

j. Refer to Hands-On Exercise 1, Step 3, earlier in this chapter for guidelines for unzipping and extracting the files.

 Alert

Depending on the browser you are using, the file names may differ slightly from those shown here. An underscore symbol may replace a space between words.

Step 2 Download and Install Windows Live Movie Maker

Refer to Figures 4.37 through 4.39 as you complete Step 2.

Windows Live Movie Maker is part of Microsoft's Windows Live Essentials Suite. This video creating and editing application is available as a free download. A similar product, Windows Movie Maker, was provided in previous versions of Windows, but was removed from Windows 7. Windows Live Movie Maker allows users to create and publish videos. Although this new version does not include some of the advanced features that were previously available with Windows Movie Maker, it will be sufficient for our purposes.

You may already have Windows Live Movie Maker on your computer. To check, click the **Start** button; in the **Search** box, type **Windows Live Movie Maker**. If this program appears in the resulting list, you can skip this step and move on to Step 3. If you need to install Windows Live Movie Maker, follow these steps:

a. Open your web browser and type **http://explore.live.com** in the browser address bar. Press **Enter**.

b. On the **Windows Live** homepage, locate the **Essentials** link and click it to go to the **Windows Live Essentials** page. On this page, you have the option to download the full Essentials suite or individual components of the suite. At this time, you only need to download Movie Maker.

c. Click the **Movie Maker** icon to go to the **Windows Live Movie Maker** homepage.

d. Click the **Download now** button to begin the installation process.

e. If the notification bar appears, click **Run**. If the **User Account Control** dialog box appears, click **Yes** or **Allow** to proceed with the installation.

D – Click Download now

E – Click Run

Figure 4.37 Hands-On Exercise 3, Steps 2d and 2e.

f. The Windows Live Essentials 2011 installation wizard begins. You are asked again to select either the full installation or just the programs you wish to install. Be sure to read the disclaimer at the bottom of the screen. If you wish, you may also click the **Privacy, Service agreement**, and **Learn more** links for additional information. Once you've reviewed this information, click **Choose the programs you want to install**.

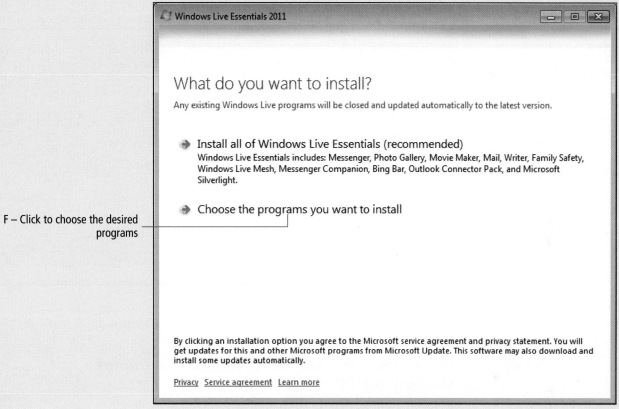

F – Click to choose the desired programs

Figure 4.38 Hands-On Exercise 3, Step 2f.

g. The next screen allows you to select one or more programs. In order to install Movie Maker, you also need to install Photo Gallery. If necessary, check the checkbox for these two programs. Be sure to uncheck the other programs.

h. Click **Install**. The installation process will begin. Once it has finished, click the **Close** button. At this time, you can also close your web browser.

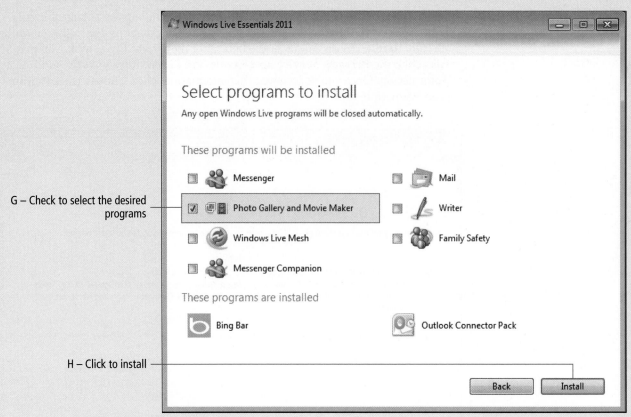

G – Check to select the desired programs

H – Click to install

Figure 4.39 Hands-On Exercise 3, Steps 2g and 2h.

Step ③ Start Windows Live Movie Maker and Import the Media Files

Refer to Figures 4.40 through 4.42 as you complete Step 3.

Professor Schmeckendorf is creating a video podcast to explain to his students how war driving works. War driving is an activity in which an individual drives around trying to locate a wireless network signal to which he or she can connect a computer for free. We'll use the media you just downloaded to create this podcast with Windows Live Movie Maker.

a. Click the **Start** button and select **All Programs**. Find Windows Live Movie Maker in the list of available programs and click it to launch the program.

b. If necessary, click the **Home** tab on the Ribbon.

c. From the **Add** group, click the **Add videos and photos** button or click on the right side of the screen to launch the **Add Videos and Photos** dialog box.

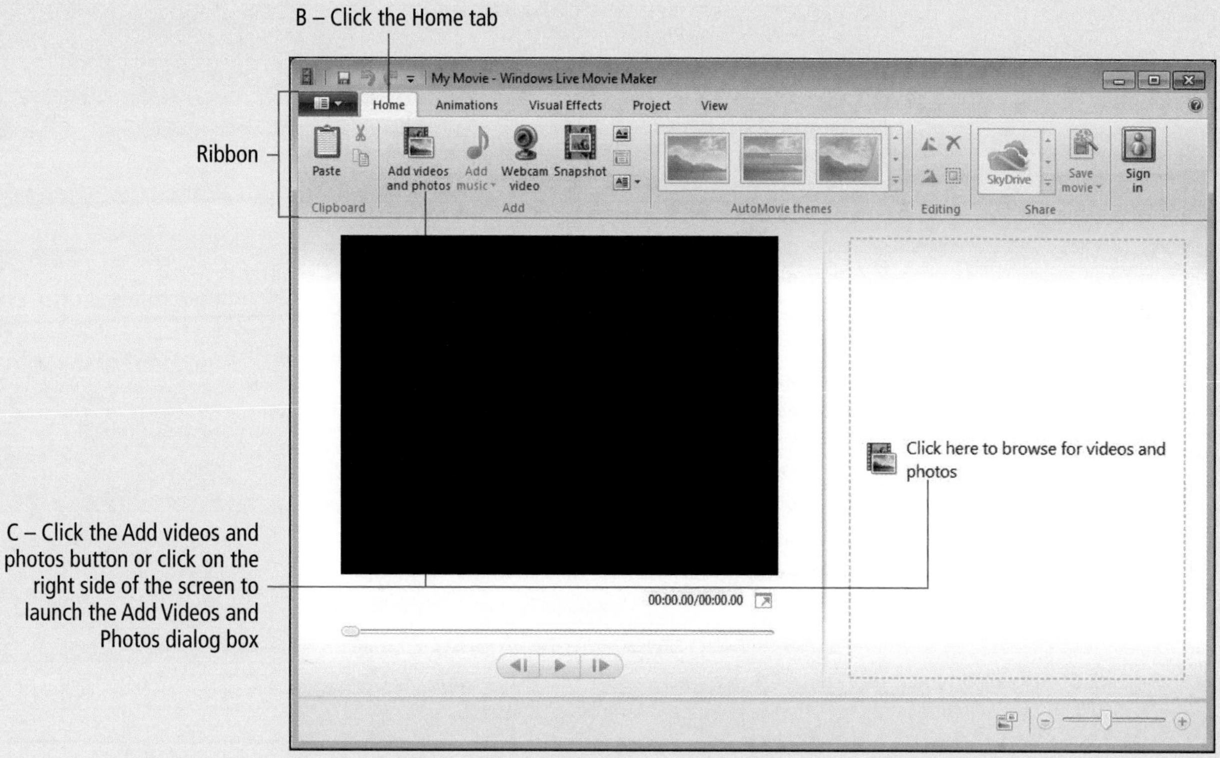

Ribbon

C – Click the Add videos and photos button or click on the right side of the screen to launch the Add Videos and Photos dialog box

Click here to browse for videos and photos

00:00.00/00:00.00

Figure 4.40 Hands-On Exercise 3, Steps 3b and 3c.

d. Browse to the folder where you saved the student data files for Chapter 4 that you downloaded in Step 1 of this Hands-On Exercise, and locate More Information on Wardriving.jpg, War Driver Signal Acquisition.avi, and War Driver Surfing.avi. Depending upon how the files were extracted, it is possible that the files required for this exercise are located in two separate folders—Chapter_4_Part_1 and Chapter_4_Part_2. Be sure to check both folders for the files you will need. You may also need to change the **Type of Files** option to **All Files**.

e. You may select each file individually, or Ctrl-click multiple media files to select them all.

f. Click the **Open** button to import the selected files into Movie Maker. If necessary, repeat Steps 3c through 3f until all three files have been imported.

The imported media should now appear in the hybrid Storyboard/time line area at the right side of the Movie Maker window. Clicking on one of the imported media clips will cause that item to be displayed in the preview window.

D – Browse to the folder where you stored the downloaded media

E – Select the required media files

F – Click Open to import the media into Movie Maker

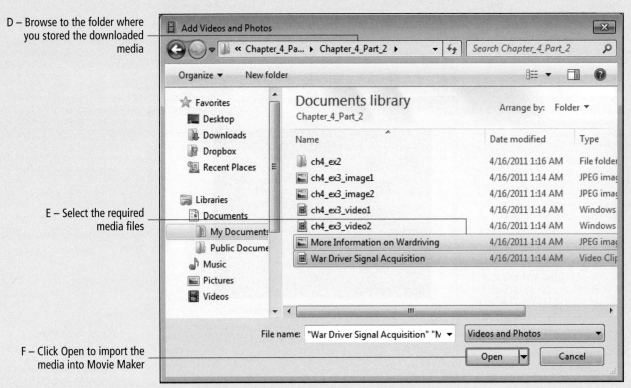

Figure 4.41 Hands-On Exercise 3, Steps 3d through 3f.

Storyboard A panel, or series of panels, arranged in sequence to portray the action or events that will occur in a video.

Transitions Effects that take place in between media clips.

The storyboard is where you construct your movie (video). A *storyboard* is a panel, or series of panels, arranged in sequence to portray the action or events that will occur in the video. You can click imported media and drag it into the proper sequence on the storyboard. The Zoom time scale at the bottom right of the screen can be used to display the media clips in longer or shorter time intervals, allowing you to see more details or get an overview of the whole project. The Movie Maker software allows you to add many kinds of effects to your videos. AutoMovie themes allow you to add titles, credits, transitions, and other effects quickly and easily. *Transitions* are the special effects that take place in between media clips. However, if you don't care for these pre-built themes, you can add these elements individually using the tools found on the various tabs on the Ribbon.

Imported media clips appear
in the storyboard area

The selected media clip appears
in the preview window

Use the preview bar slider and
playback buttons to preview
the movie

Use the Zoom time scale tool
to expand or collapse
video clips

00:07.00/00:44.67

Item 2 of 3

Figure 4.42 Windows Live Movie Maker screen displaying imported media clips.

Step 4 Assemble the Components of the Podcast on the Storyboard

Refer to Figure 4.43 as you complete Step 4.

The clips should be laid out on the storyboard in the order in which they should appear. The War Driver Signal Acquisition clip should come first, followed by the War Driver Surfing clip, and finally, the More Information on Wardriving image.

a. Click and drag the **War Driver Signal Acquisition** clip to the beginning of the storyboard. To determine which clip is the correct choice, simply hover over a clip. A screen tip will appear showing the name of the imported file and its duration, as well as any effects that may have been applied to it. Click and drag the **War Driver Surfing** clip to the second position and then click and drag the **More Information on Wardriving** image into the third position.

b. Click the first media clip to access the movie from the start.

c. Click the **Play (Space)** button to preview the movie you have created.

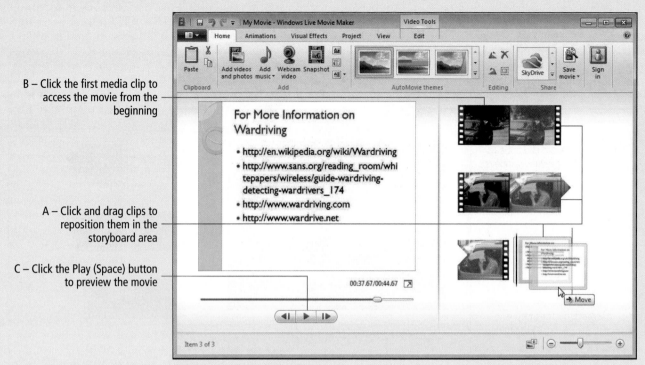

B – Click the first media clip to access the movie from the beginning

A – Click and drag clips to reposition them in the storyboard area

C – Click the Play (Space) button to preview the movie

Figure 4.43 Hands-On Exercise 3, Step 4.

Step 5 Apply an AutoMovie Theme to the Podcast

Refer to Figures 4.44 through 4.47 as you complete Step 5.

It is customary to add a title to the beginning of a podcast and credits at the end of the show. Similarly, adding transitions—those special effects that take place when moving from one media clip to the next—helps to make the shift from one clip to the next less jarring to the eye. Movie Maker's AutoMovie themes give you several easy options to work with.

a. On the **Home** tab in the **AutoMovie themes** group, click the **More** button to display the **AutoMovie themes** gallery. You can hover over the various choices to see how your movie will look using the **Live Preview** feature.

b. Click the **Fade** AutoMovie theme to apply this to the media clips.

c. A dialog box appears asking if you'd like to add music to your video. Although this might be a good choice if you were creating a video of still photos, since the video clips you've imported have sound, no music is necessary. Click **No** to proceed.

d. Click the **Play (Space)** button to preview your video with the AutoMovie theme. You'll notice that a title slide and several credit slides have been added to the media clips.

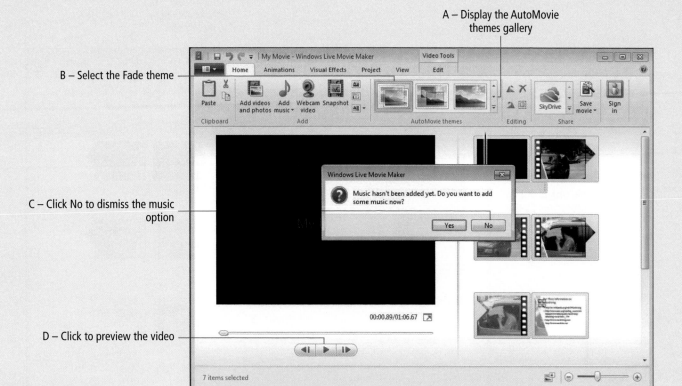

A – Display the AutoMovie themes gallery

B – Select the Fade theme

C – Click No to dismiss the music option

D – Click to preview the video

Figure 4.44 Hands-On Exercise 3, Steps 5a through 5d.

Title slides are useful for introducing your podcast and adding credits to the end of your podcast. Title slides can also be inserted before any media clip and modified accordingly. You can add additional slides by clicking the **Add title** or **Add credits** buttons found in the **Add** group on the **Home** tab. You will also find an **Add caption** button there, which allows you to superimpose text on any of the media clips. Since the title and credit slides were added when the AutoMovie theme was applied, Professor Schmeckendorf wants to remove the default text on these slides and replace it with text that is relevant to the podcast.

e. If necessary, scroll up to the beginning of the storyboard and click the title slide that was added when the AutoMovie theme was applied.

f. Double-click the **My Movie** text below the title slide icon to display the default text in the preview window. Notice that the **Text Tools Format** tab is now active on the Ribbon. You can use these tools to modify the text on the title slide and add special effects.

g. Delete the existing text and type **War Driving 101 Podcast** and then press **Enter.**

h. Type **Presented by Prof. Schmeckendorf** in the next line.

i. The text will automatically appear in the preview window so you can review the slide. Use the buttons on the **Text Tools Format** tab to make any changes you deem necessary. You can change the font type and the font size, add bolding and italics, and so on. However, any changes you make will be applied to all of the text on the slide. It is not possible to modify individual words. Notice that you can also resize the text box by using the sizing handles. As you make changes to the text, you may need to add or remove spacing to make the title flow properly on the slide.

j. With the title slide still selected, explore the choices found in the **Effects** group on the **Text Tools Format** tab. Apply the **Zoom in - big** choice.

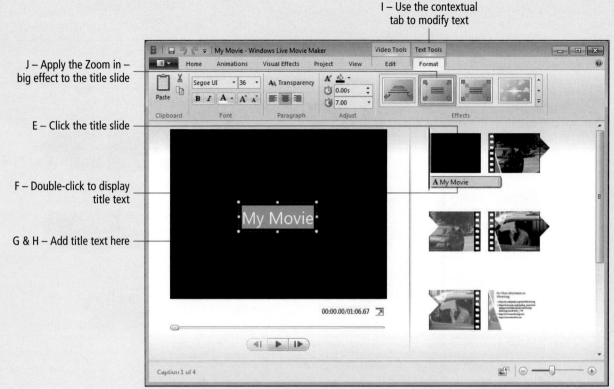

I – Use the contextual tab to modify text

J – Apply the Zoom in – big effect to the title slide

E – Click the title slide

F – Double-click to display title text

G & H – Add title text here

Figure 4.45 Hands-On Exercise 3, Steps 5e through 5j.

k. Scroll down to the credit slides at the end of the storyboard.

l. The AutoMovie theme has added three credit slides—Directed By, Starring, and Filmed On Location. You can delete any or all of these slides if you don't need them. You can also replace the sample text on these slides with whatever best suits your purpose. Professor Schmeckendorf wants to modify all three slides.

m. Select the Directed By credit slide and double-click the sample text. Replace the Directed By text with **War Driving 101 Podcast**. In the Starring credit slide, delete the text and replace it with two lines of text: **Presented by Prof. Schmeckendorf** and **Ginormous State University**. In the third credit slide, replace the Filmed On Location text with **For more podcasts, go to: http://pschmeckendorf.podbean.com**. Adjust the text box placement for each of these slides as necessary.

n. Review the credits in the preview window. To make changes, use the choices on the **Text Tools Format** tab and apply any effects you might wish to use.

o. Once you've finished adding or revising the credits, click the title slide at the beginning of the time line and click the **Play (Space)** button to preview the entire video.

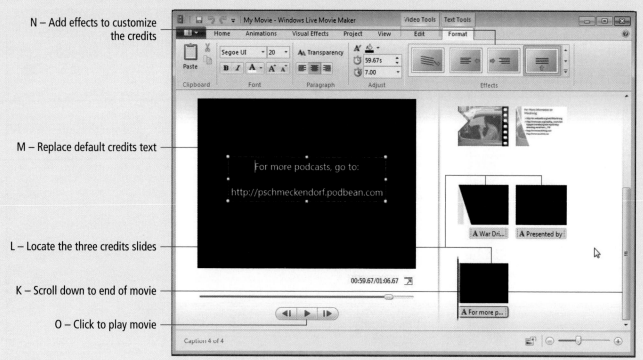

N – Add effects to customize the credits

M – Replace default credits text

L – Locate the three credits slides

K – Scroll down to end of movie

O – Click to play movie

Figure 4.46 Hands-On Exercise 3, Steps 5k through 5o.

Now that the movie is in final form (with titles and credits), it is possible to publish your video directly to video sharing sites like YouTube. However, Professor Schmeckendorf wants to save a copy of this video in case he decides to make changes later or needs to use it for another purpose. Additionally, you should save the file to avoid losing your work. You will be saving the movie file in the Windows Live Movie Maker Project file format (*.wlmp*), which is not a format that can be universally viewed by most media players. In the next step of the Hands-On Exercise, you'll convert the file to a format that is more useful to your viewers.

p. Click the **Movie Maker** tab on the left side of the Ribbon and select **Save project as** to display the **Save Project** dialog box.

q. Browse through the folders on your computer to find an appropriate place to save the file.

r. Type **War Driving 101 Movie Maker Format** in the **File** name text box.

s. Click the **Save** button to save the file.

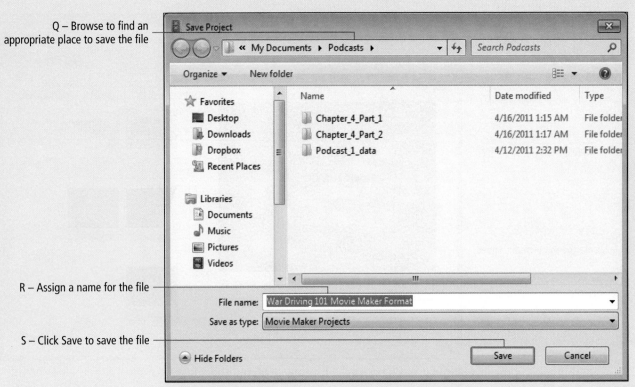

Q – Browse to find an appropriate place to save the file

R – Assign a name for the file

S – Click Save to save the file

Figure 4.47 Hands-On Exercise 3, Steps 5q through 5s.

Step 6 Export Your Podcast to a WMV File

Refer to Figures 4.48 through 4.50 as you complete Step 6.

To make it easy for subscribers to your podcast to view the file, you need to convert the movie you just made to a common video file format such as WMV. Fortunately, this is easy to accomplish in Windows Live Movie Maker.

a. On the **Home** tab, in the **Share** group, click the lower half of the **Save movie** icon and then click the **For computer** option to launch the **Save Movie** dialog box.

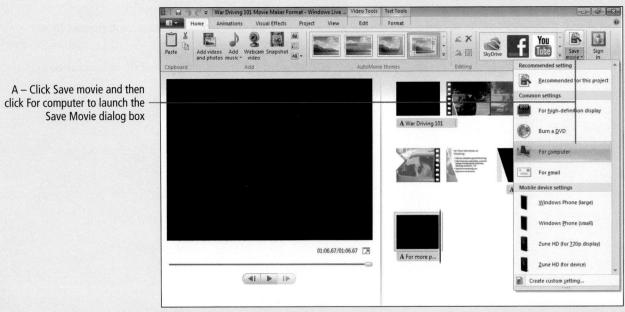

A – Click Save movie and then click For computer to launch the Save Movie dialog box

Figure 4.48 Hands-On Exercise 3, Step 6a.

b. In the **Save Movie** dialog box, navigate to the location where you are saving the files for this chapter.

c. Type **War Driving 101 Podcast** in the **File name** text box and click **Save.**

B – Navigate to the folder where you wish to save the file

C – Enter a name for the file

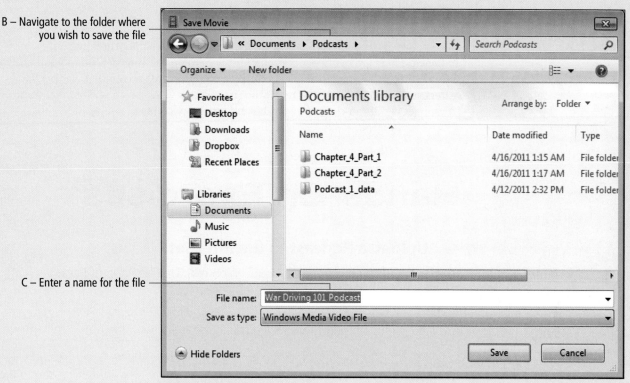

Figure 4.49 Hands-On Exercise 3, Steps 6b and 6c.

d. Depending upon the size of the file, you may experience a slight delay while the file is being converted. Once the file has been converted, a dialog box will appear with the option to play the movie or open the folder to which it has been saved. Click **Play** to view the finished movie in Windows Media Player. Close Windows Media Player when the video is done.

D – Click Play to view the movie in Windows Media Player

Figure 4.50 Hands-On Exercise 3, Step 6d.

e. Return to Windows Live Movie Maker and from the **Movie Maker** tab select **Exit** to close the program. If you are prompted to save changes, click **No.** You can also close Windows Media Player.

Congratulations! You now have a video podcast that is ready for posting on the Internet.

Objective 9

Upload a podcast to the Internet

Once you start creating podcasts, you need a way to distribute them to your audience. There are many podcast hosting services on the Internet, but a good one to start with is Podbean.com. This hosting service offers free accounts to get new podcasters started so that you can make sure its services work for you before you commit any money. Podbean can handle audio and video podcasts.

Hands-On Exercises

4 | Upload a Podcast to the Internet

Steps: 1. Create an Account at Podbean.com; **2.** Upload Podcast Files to Podbean.com.

Use Figures 4.51 through 4.58 as a guide to the exercise.

Step 1 Create an Account at Podbean.com

Refer to Figures 4.51 through 4.53 as you complete Step 1.

a. Open your web browser and navigate to **www.podbean.com**.

b. Locate the **Podcast Publishers** section and click the **Free Sign Up Now** link to begin the Podbean Basic Account creation process.

B – Click to create an account

Figure 4.51 Hands-On Exercise 4, Step 1b.

c. Ensure that the free **Podbean Basic Account** option is selected. Scroll down to the next section.

d. Type a member name for your account in the **Member Name** text box. This becomes part of the URL for your podcast site, so choose carefully.

e. Type your email address in the **Email** text box. You must use a valid email address because Podbean will send your initial password to this email account. You won't be able to access your Podbean account until you have retrieved the password.

f. Enter your personal information as required in the appropriate boxes.

g. Click the **Terms of Service** link. Podbean's Terms of Service will open in a new browser window. Review the terms and close the window when you are done. If necessary, click the **Service Agreement** checkbox to insert a check and agree to the terms of service for your Podbean account.

h. In the **Verification** section, type the text shown in the CAPTCHA box above. This text will be different than the text shown in Figure 4.52.

i. If you do not wish to receive the Podbean newsletter, click to uncheck the **Yes, email me Podbean newsletter** checkbox.

j. Click the **Sign Up Now** button to create your account.

D – Type a member name for your account

E – Type your email address

F – Enter your personal information in the appropriate boxes

G – Click the link to review the terms of service; then click the checkbox to agree to the terms

H – Enter the CAPTCHA text as shown in the box above (your text will vary)

I – To opt out of the newsletter, click the checkbox to uncheck it

J – Click the Sign Up Now button to create your account

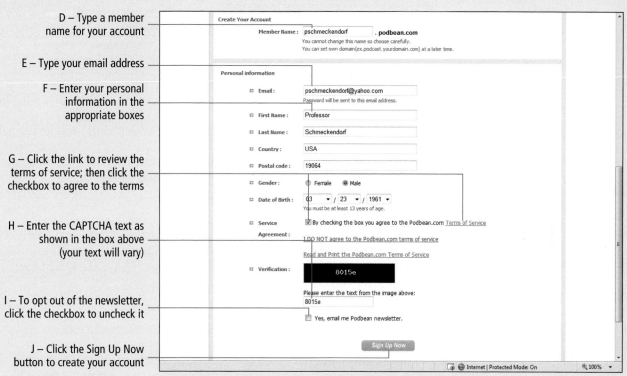

Figure 4.52 Hands-On Exercise 4, Steps 1d through 1j.

If you receive an error message, check to be sure that you have entered all of the required information. You will need to re-enter the CAPTCHA text because it will have changed. You may also need to uncheck the newsletter checkbox again.

In five to ten minutes, Podbean will send an email to the address you provided. The email will contain the password for your Podbean account. Retrieve your password and return to **www.podbean.com.**

k. Click the **Log In** link at the top-right corner of the site to display the login screen.

l. Type your username and password in the boxes provided.

m. Uncheck the checkbox next to **Remember me** if you are working on a public or shared computer, and click the **Login** button to access your account.

K – Click Log In

Uncheck this box if you are using a shared or public computer

L – Type your username and password

M – Click Login button

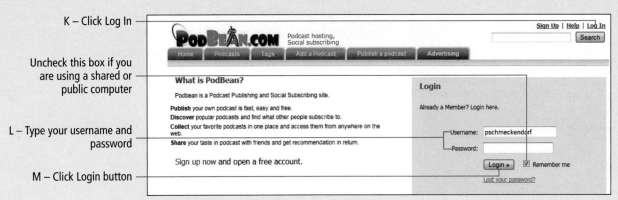

Figure 4.53 Hands-On Exercise 4, Steps 1k through 1m.

 Alert

The first time you log in to your account, you may be asked to upload a podcast logo (picture) to associate with your podcast. You can ignore this by clicking the **Skip for Now** link.

n. If you click the link provided in the email from Podbean and sign in, you will be taken to the **Dashboard** page automatically. For future visits, you will need to click the **Publish a Podcast** tab at the top of the page to go to the **Dashboard** page. This is the control center for your podcast site.

 Tip

When you first accessed your Podbean account, you used a password provided by Podbean. You should change this password to something that you will be able to remember but that will not be easily guessed by others. To change your password, click the **Profile** link at the top of the page; then click the **Change Password** link. In the **Update Your Password** section, type your new password. You must retype your password to ensure that it was entered correctly the first time. Click the **Update Account** button; then click the **My Podcast** link at the top of the page to return to the Dashboard.

Step 2 Upload Podcast Files to Podbean.com

Refer to Figures 4.54 through 4.58 as you complete Step 2.

You should have two files that you can upload immediately: the audio podcast you created in Hands-On Exercise 2 and the video podcast you created for Professor Schmeckendorf in Hands-On Exercise 3.

a. On the **Dashboard** screen, click the **Upload** link to begin the uploading process.

A – Click to begin uploading files

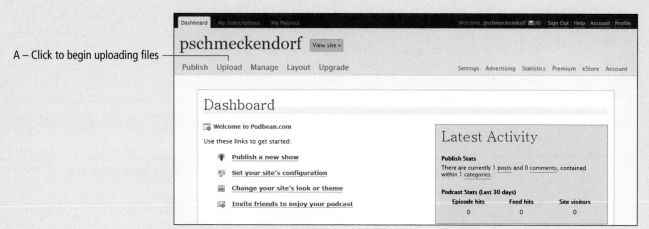

Figure 4.54 Hands-On Exercise 4, Step 2a.

b. On the **Media Manager** screen, click the **Upload** icon to proceed to the next screen.

B – Click here to proceed to the next screen

Figure 4.55 Hands-On Exercise 4, Step 2b.

The video podcast created in Hands-On Exercise 3 may be too large to post to the free Podbean account. Because the MP3 audio podcast created in Hands-On Exercise 2 is smaller, you will post this one to the account.

c. Click the **Browse** button to locate **Podcast Volume 1-1**, the audio podcast file created in Hands-On Exercise 2. Click the file and click the **Open** button to display the file in the **Upload files to your account** list.

d. Click the **Upload** button to transfer the audio file to your Podbean account. When the upload is complete, the filename will appear in the **Current Media** files list.

C – Click Browse to locate the audio podcast file created in Hands-On Exercise 2

D – Click here to upload the file

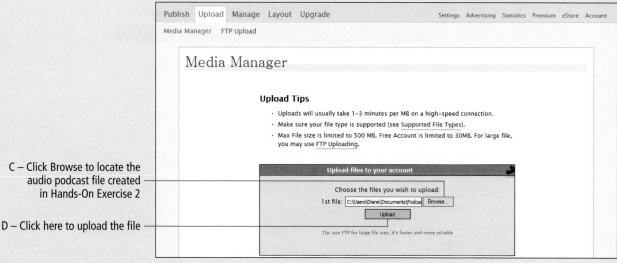

Figure 4.56 Hands-On Exercise 4, Steps 2c and 2d.

Your Podbean account has many features that are similar to a blog. One feature allows you to publish an entry similar to a blog post that describes the podcast episode you just uploaded.

e. Click the **Publish** link at the top of the Dashboard to proceed to the **Write Post/ Episode** screen.

f. Just as with blogs, you can create tags for your podcasts. You must create at least one tag consisting of two or more characters for the podcast. Type **Office 2010** in the **Tags** text box.

g. You also need to provide a title for your podcast. Type **Cheap MS Office 2010 Software** in the **Title** text box.

h. Similarly, it is helpful for your audience members to know what your podcast is about before they attempt to download it. Type the following description in the **Post** text box:

Volume 1 of the Professor Schmeckendorf podcast series contains information on how students can purchase the Academic Professional edition of Microsoft Office 2010 for only $79.95!

i. In this step, you will associate the audio file you have already uploaded with the post you are creating. In the **Podcasting** section, click the **Select From Account** drop-down arrow and select **PodcastVolume1-1.mp3**. This is the file that you already uploaded to the Podbean site.

j. Because there is a wide variety of file types that you can upload to Podbean, you also need to identify the file type. If necessary, click the **File Type** drop-down arrow and select **MP3 - Standard Audio (iPod Compliant)**.

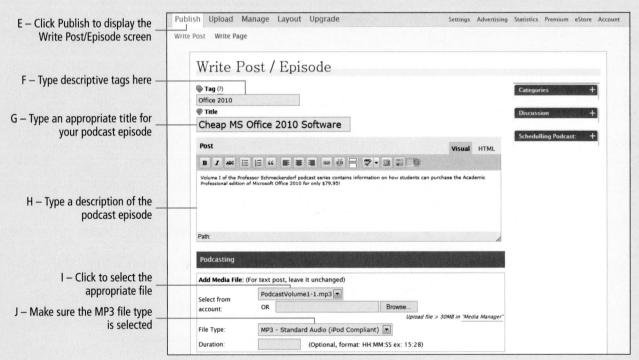

E – Click Publish to display the Write Post/Episode screen

F – Type descriptive tags here

G – Type an appropriate title for your podcast episode

H – Type a description of the podcast episode

I – Click to select the appropriate file

J – Make sure the MP3 file type is selected

Figure 4.57 Hands-On Exercise 4, Steps 2e through 2j.

k. At the bottom of the **Write Post/Episode** screen, click the **Publish** button to publish your episode on your Podbean site.

l. At the top of the **Dashboard** screen, click the **View Site** button to see what your podcast site looks like with your first episode posted (Figure 4.58).

There is a lot more you should do to enhance your Podbean site if you are planning to host regular podcasts. You should definitely provide a page on the site that describes your podcast and its theme. The **About page** option works well for this. You might even want to tell listeners a bit about yourself. So explore the options in Podbean and enhance your site. You might quickly develop a very loyal following if you are producing quality podcasts.

Loyal listeners can click here to subscribe to your podcasts in a reader

Anyone can click here and listen to your podcast episode

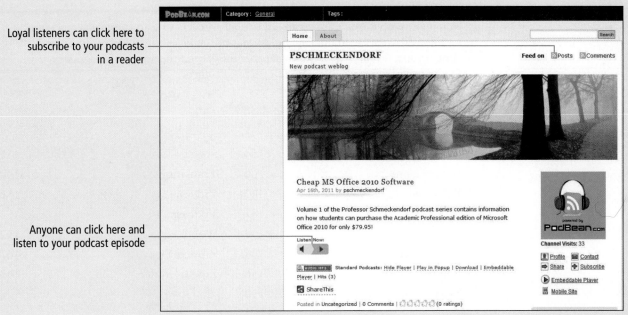

Figure 4.58 Hands-On Exercise 4, Step 2l.

Objective 10

Explore podcasting resources

Because podcasting has become quite popular, there is a wealth of information on the Internet that can help you learn more about creating effective audio and video podcasts. Here are some resources you may want to explore:

- How to Podcast (**www.how-to-podcast-tutorial.com**)—A well-written tutorial by Jason Van Orden who generates a number of his own podcasts. Jason takes the reader step by step through podcast planning and recording. He even has video files that demonstrate how to use Audacity.

- How to Create Your Own Podcast (**http://computer.howstuffworks.com/internet/basics/how-to-podcast.htm**)—This is another tutorial from the excellent How Stuff Works site. This tutorial covers the basics of podcasting and has links to additional technical articles for more in-depth information about how podcasts work.

- Podcasting Tools (**www.podcasting-tools.com**)—This site bills itself as a comprehensive podcasting resource containing everything you'd want to know about the topic. It includes an FAQ section, a blog, a wiki, user forums, and directories, as well as a number of other resources.

- Moving at the Speed of Creativity (**www.speedofcreativity.org/resources/podcast-resources**)—Written by an educator and digital learning consultant, this site contains many useful links to podcasting resources.

- Making a Podcast (**www.apple.com/itunes/whatson/podcasts/specs.html**)—Contains important information from the folks at Apple to help you understand how to create a podcast, as well as the process for submitting your podcast to Apple and getting it indexed in iTunes. You definitely want your podcast available in iTunes because it will help you build an audience quickly.

Summary

You have now learned many of the basic skills for creating engaging podcasts. The main thing that draws listeners to a podcast is interesting, original content. Adding cool features to your podcast like theme music, sound effects, and other gimmicks might be fun for you but won't always appeal to your listeners who are most likely looking for information or entertainment. So concentrate on generating well-produced podcast episodes on a regular schedule that support the general theme of your podcast, and you should be well on your way to building a loyal audience.

Key Terms

Multiple Choice Questions

1. To have data about a podcast appear on a PMP or on screen, the information should be added as a(n)

   (a) screen tip.

   (b) ID3 tag.

   (c) MP3 encoder.

   (d) web feed.

2. Which term describes software that is still in the testing stage and may not work as expected?

   (a) Aggregator software

   (b) Transitional software

   (c) Compressed file

   (d) Beta version

3. Which of the following statements is true about transitions?

   (a) Transitions are a series of panels arranged to portray action or events.

   (b) Transitions provide information about a podcast.

   (c) Transitions cannot be previewed in Windows Live Movie Maker.

   (d) Transitions are effects that take place in between media clips.

4. The software used to locate and collect new podcast episodes from the Internet is known as a(n)

   (a) aggregator.

   (b) extractor.

   (c) synchronizer.

   (d) pop filter.

5. Which of the following statements is *not* true about zipped folders?

   (a) Zipped folders are created with file compression software.

   (b) Zipped folders must be extracted before they can be used.

   (c) Zipped folders can be used only in Windows 7.

   (d) Zipped folders enable files to download quickly.

6. In order to use the files contained in a compressed folder, they must first be

   (a) debugged.

   (b) extracted.

   (c) associated with a file type.

   (d) compacted.

7. Which of the following is *not* an example of software that can be used when creating a podcast?

   (a) Sound Recorder

   (b) Sound card

   (c) Audacity

   (d) Windows Live Movie Maker

8. When planning a podcast, which of the following is *not* a step that needs to be considered?

   (a) Choose an aggregator.

   (b) Develop a schedule.

   (c) Consider the optimal length for the podcast.

   (d) Decide upon a topic or theme for the podcast.

9. Which of the following statements is *not* true about pop filters?

   (a) A pop filter is a mesh screen placed in front of a microphone.

   (b) A pop filter can help make your recordings sound more professional.

   (c) A pop filter helps to prevent popping sounds on a recording.

   (d) A pop filter is a software device attached to the computer's sound card.

10. Which of the following statements is *not* true about podcasts?

   (a) A vidcast is a video podcast.

   (b) A podcast is a group of audio or video media files.

   (c) A podcatcher or aggregator is required to locate podcasts.

   (d) Podcasts can be downloaded and saved for later use.

Fill in the Blank

1. A(n) _____ is an optional piece of equipment placed in front of a microphone to improve sound quality.

2. _____ are the special effects that take place in between media clips.

3. A(n) _____ is used to arrange a video's action or events in the proper sequence.

4. RSS is an example of a(n) _____ and is used to notify people when new podcast content is available.

5. To download a podcast to a PMP, you must connect, or _____, it to your computer.

Practice Exercises

1. **Creating a Podcast Script and Recording the Podcast**

   Prior to recording a podcast, it is a good idea to create a script. Creating a script helps you to organize your thoughts and cover all your key points. For this exercise, you will write a script explaining how to open a file using Microsoft Word. You will then record the podcast based on the script.

   (a) Open Microsoft Word.

   (b) Create a short script, in your own words, explaining how to open a file in Word.

   (c) Save your script as **Podcast Script 1_Your_Name**.

   (d) Print your script.

   (e) Check your recording and playback devices to be sure they are working correctly.

   (f) Start Audacity and record your podcast using the script you created. Be sure to perform a sound level check. You should also make one deliberate mistake and correct it verbally while you are still recording, using the technique explained in the chapter.

   (g) Review your recording once you've completed it. Do not edit the file at this time.

   (h) Save the file using the **Save Project As** option. Name the file **Podcast Practice 1_Your_Name**.

   (i) Submit the **Podcast Script 1_Your_Name** and **Podcast Practice 1_Your_Name** files to your instructor. Remember that the Audacity files consist of the *.aup* project file and the _data project folder.

2. **Downloading Compressed Files and Editing and Exporting a Podcast**

   A new podcast has been created for Professor Schmeckendorf's class; however, it has several errors that need to be fixed. The sound check should be deleted and the narrator has an error that occurs in the section beginning with "On the right side of the list…." You will need to delete this error. Remember that the time line will adjust as portions of the recording are edited. You will also need to export the edited podcast as an MP3 file.

   (a) Open **Audacity**.

   (b) Navigate to the location where you saved your student data files for Chapter 4. Open the **ch4_ex2 folder** and then open the **ch4_ex2.aup** file and review the podcast. Make note of the changes that need to be made to this recording and their location on the timeline.

   (c) Edit the podcast as needed. Use the **Save Project As** option and save the file as **ch4_ex2_Your_Name**.

   (d) Export the edited podcast as an MP3 file. Name the file **ch4_ex2_MP3_Your_Name**.

(e) Use the following information to create the ID3 tags:

Artist Name: Your Name

Track Title: ch4_ex2_MP3_Your_Name

Album Title: Podcast Practice Exercise 2

Track Number: 1

Year: 2011

Genre: Podcast

(f) Submit the edited Audacity files (project file and data folder sent as a zipped file) and the MP3 file to your instructor.

3. **Creating a Video Podcast**

Professor Schmeckendorf is working on a tutorial to show students how to use HTML to create web pages. You have been asked to create a video podcast using two video clips and two image files Professor Schmeckendorf has created.

(a) Start Windows Live Movie Maker and import the following two video clips and two image files from your Chapter 4 student data file downloads:

- ch4_ex3_image1.jpg
- ch4_ex3_image2.jpg
- ch4_ex3_video1.wmv
- ch4_ex3_video2.wmv

(b) Arrange the imported media clips on the storyboard in the following order:

- ch4_ex3_video1.wmv
- ch4_ex3_image1.jpg
- ch4_ex3_video2.wmv
- ch4_ex3_image2.jpg

(c) Play back the storyboard to ensure that everything is in place and then save the file in the Windows Live Movie Maker format (*.wlmp*) as **ch4_ex3_Your_Name**. Submit the file to your instructor.

4. **Applying an AutoMovie Theme and Publishing a Video Podcast**

In this exercise, you'll continue working with the video podcast created in Exercise 3. Professor Schmeckendorf would like you to add transitions in between the clips. He also wants you to add a title slide and credits at the end of the video. After these changes have been made, the video file must be converted to a Windows Media Video (WMV) file and published.

(a) Open Windows Live Movie Maker and locate the file you created in Exercise 3: **ch4_ex3_Your_Name**.

(b) From the **File** menu, select **Save Project As** and rename the file **ch4_ex4_Your_Name**.

(c) Apply the AutoMovie theme of your choice to the video. If the theme you pick does not include a title slide or credit slide, remember that these can be added by using the buttons found in the **Add** group on the **Home** tab.

(d) If necessary, create a title slide at the beginning of the video. Type **An Overview of HTML** on the first line. Add a blank line and on the next line, type **Presented by Professor Schmeckendorf**.

(e) Adjust the size of the text box and modify the font to suit your purpose.

(f) You will need only one credit slide at the end of the video. If the AutoMovie theme created multiple credits, simply click on the unwanted ones and delete them. If the theme you chose did not create a credit slide, use the **Credit** button in the **Add** group on the **Home** tab. Be sure to add your name as the assistant and the name of your institution. Use the following text, adjusting the text box and formatting as needed:

- **An Overview of HTML**
- **Presented by Professor Schmeckendorf**
- **Assisted by Your Name**
- **Your Institution Name**

(g) Play back the video to review your changes.

(h) Save the project as **ch4_ex4_Your_Name**. If you receive a message indicating the file already exists, click **Yes** to replace the file with this version.

(i) Next, you'll need to use the **Save movie, For computer** option to save the file. Save it to your computer as **ch4_ex4_WMV_Your_Name**. This step may take a while due to the size of the file.

(j) Due to the size of this video file, check with your instructor for instructions on how to submit the file.

Critical Thinking

1. Some podcasters like to add music to their podcasts—often as background music or as an introduction to the episode. It is important to be aware of the copyright issues that are involved when you add music to a podcast. Write a brief paper outlining the steps a podcaster should take to ensure that any music included in a podcast is in compliance with the current rules regarding copyright. Indicate your sources, and provide at least two or three Internet resources a podcaster can turn to for guidance.

2. A podcatcher, or aggregator, can be web based or installed on your computer. Research two examples of web-based podcatchers and two examples of aggregators that are installed on your computer. Write a short paper describing the advantages and disadvantages of each podcatcher.

Team Projects

1. This chapter explored the various items needed to produce audio and video podcasts. As a group, develop a list of the items you would need to equip your own podcast studio. Research the prices for these items. Create a chart listing the lowest and highest price for each item and where it can be obtained. Indicate which items you would choose and explain why you would choose them.

2. As a group, locate one video or audio podcast on each of the following topics:

- Music Industry
- Computers and Technology
- Hobby Tutorial or How-To
- Business Ethics

Create a table that lists the title and URL for each podcast and the topic it represents. Review the podcasts and rate them using the following criteria:

- How long was the podcast?
- How recent was the podcast?
- Was the podcast informative or entertaining? Did it stay on topic?
- How was the sound and video quality? How could it have been improved?
- Which of the four podcasts do you think is the best? Which is the worst?

Include your findings on the table and submit it to your instructor.

Credits

Figure 4.1, Courtesy of Channel 9/Microsoft.

Figures 4.2a–4.2b, © Podcast Pickle, Courtesy of Podcastpickle.com.

Figure 4.3, Courtesy of Google.

Figure 4.4, Adisa/Shutterstock.com.

Figure 4.5, Courtesy of Dean Sabatino.

Figures 4.6–4.17, 4.22–4.34, Screenshots retrieved from http://audacity.sourceforge.net, Copyright © 2011 Audacity Development Team. Courtesy of Audacity Software.

Figures 4.18–4.21, 4.35–4.50, Courtesy of Microsoft.

Figures 4.51–4.58, Reprinted by permission from Podbean.com. Courtesy of Podbean.com.

Student Data Files, Courtesy of Alan Evans.

CHAPTER 5

Wikis

Objectives

After you read this chapter, you will be able to:

1. Explain what a wiki is and why you would use a wiki

2. Describe Wikipedia and explain how to create and edit content on Wikipedia

3. Explain how to evaluate information found on the Internet

4. Discuss websites you can use to start a wiki

5. Set up an account and a wiki on PBworks

6. Edit a wiki page and add pages to a wiki

7. Add internal and external links to a wiki

8. Upload content to or embed content on a wiki

9. Explore wiki resources

The following Hands-On Exercises will help you accomplish the chapter objectives:

Hands-On Exercises

EXERCISES	SKILLS COVERED
1. Create an Account on PBworks and Configure a Wiki (page 224)	**Step 1:** Sign Up for an Account on PBworks **Step 2:** Configure a Wiki on PBworks
2. Edit a Wiki Page on PBworks and Add Pages to a Wiki (page 233)	**Step 1:** Log In to Your PBworks Account **Step 2:** Edit the FrontPage of Your Wiki **Step 3:** Add Pages to Your Wiki
3. Add Internal and External Links to Wiki Pages (page 242)	**Step 1:** Create a Navigation Scheme for a Wiki Using Internal Links **Step 2:** Insert External Links to Content on a Wiki Page
4. Upload Images to a Wiki and Embed Video on a Wiki Page (page 248)	**Step 1:** Upload an Image to PBworks **Step 2:** Embed a YouTube Video on a Wiki Page

Objective 1

Explain what a wiki is and why you would use a wiki

What is a wiki?

Chances are that you've looked at a website and noticed information that was incorrect or incomplete. When you found such a site, didn't you wish you had the ability to change the information on that website? This is the idea behind wikis.

Wiki A collection of web pages that are designed to be edited by groups of individuals.

A *wiki* is essentially a collection of web pages in which each page has its own edit button. Unlike a website, which is usually edited and maintained by a specially designated person or department, wikis were designed to allow groups of people to collectively generate and edit textual information. The text can be viewed by anyone with access to the wiki, which is often anyone with a browser who can find the URL of the wiki. An individual page on a wiki is known as a *wiki page*, whereas a group of related wiki pages is known collectively as a *wiki*. Wikis are a Web 2.0 application because they foster content creation and interaction among a group of people. Wikis are designed to be viewed and edited using nothing more than a web browser, and they require no knowledge of HTML coding.

Wiki page An individual page on a wiki.

Who invented wikis?

Ward Cunningham is generally credited as inventing the wiki in 1995 when he deployed the software to power the WikiWikiWeb on his company's website (www.c2.com). The WikiWikiWeb was designed to facilitate the sharing of information between programmers. *Wiki* is a Hawaiian word that means *fast*. The original wiki was named after the Wiki-Wiki Shuttle, a bus service that operates out of the Honolulu airport and provides a quick way to go from the airport to downtown Honolulu. Wikis grew quickly in popularity with computer programmers but did not become known to the mainstream public until the creation of Wikipedia in 2001.

Why would I use a wiki?

It is likely that you have already used one of the world's most popular wikis: Wikipedia. Wikipedia is basically an online encyclopedia, but its unique feature is that it is written by people just like you from all around the globe. Businesses and individuals are finding that wikis have benefits for many different purposes aside from encyclopedias.

Personal Uses of Wikis

- Note taking—Take notes in your college classes on your laptop and post them to your wiki (either during class or after class). Get your friends who are taking the same class to add their notes to the wiki. This will result in a collaborative study guide that should be more comprehensive than your notes alone. And most wikis have search features that facilitate locating specific information.

- Group projects—Students are often required to work in groups to complete assignments. Using a wiki facilitates communication and planning among group members. Wikis also can be used to keep track of who did how much work on a particular project. This is especially useful for providing objective evidence to your instructor when one group member is not doing a sufficient share of the work.

- To-do lists—We all have tasks to accomplish every day. A wiki is a great place to manage a to-do list because you can easily edit it as tasks change, and you can access it from any device (such as your phone, laptop, or iPad) that has access to the Internet.

- Event planning—Need to plan a 25th wedding anniversary party for your parents? How about a bridal shower for your best friend? Events are easy to organize through a wiki, as you can set up different parts of the wiki to handle various segments of the event: planning, physical location, gifts, decorations, seating charts, contact information, and so on.

- Creating a knowledge base—Perhaps you are passionate about a particular subject such as the *Star Wars* movies (Figure 5.1) or the television show *American Idol*. It is likely that there are fans throughout the world who share your interest. A wiki gives fans a chance to build a knowledge base and to speculate about developments in specific areas of interest.

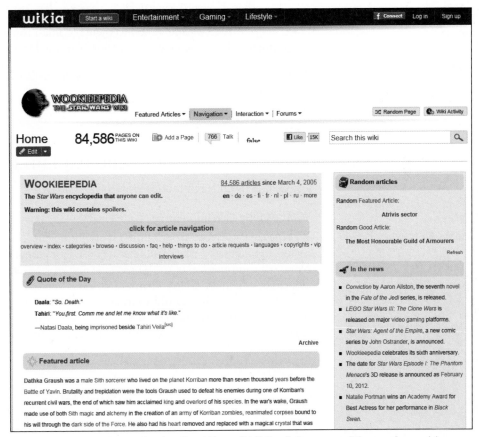

Figure 5.1 Wookieepedia, the *Star Wars* wiki (**http://starwars.wikia.com**), provides fans a place to share their knowledge and opinions about the official *Star Wars* universe.

Business or Organizational Uses of Wikis

- Project management and planning—Coordinating projects, especially when people who are involved in a project are located at widespread geographic locations, is often done through wikis. A wiki can provide everyone involved in a project with access to all planning documents, schedules, timelines, and images necessary to manage the project.

- Operations and training manuals—There is a great deal of documentation that workers consult to learn how to operate machinery or manage business processes. Distributing paper manuals is a waste of natural resources and time, especially if the manuals are frequently updated. Putting this information on a wiki makes it easier to access and also makes frequent updates simple. You'll always be looking at the current version of the manual if it is updated on the web whenever changes occur.

- Checklists—Operations with multiple steps are often repeated frequently. Having a checklist to refer to ensures that operations are carried out consistently and that the actions are taken in the correct order. Wiki checklists can be easily updated by multiple people.

- Development of business plans—Business plans (to launch a new business, product, or service) are developed by teams of individuals such as accountants, marketing professionals, attorneys, salespeople, manufacturing personnel, and logistics specialists. Coordination of complex business plans, where the input from many individuals is required, can be carried out more efficiently with the use of a wiki.

- Frequently Asked Questions (FAQ) documents—Time can be saved by generating answers to frequently asked questions and posting them on a wiki. Using a wiki allows people to easily generate new questions or post answers to questions that others have already asked.

- Community news and announcements—Small towns often start wikis to keep residents abreast of news and activities in the local community.

To understand how wikis work, we'll use Wikipedia as an example to explain the basic concepts.

Objective 2

Describe Wikipedia and explain how to create and edit content on Wikipedia

What exactly is Wikipedia?

Wikipedia An online encyclopedia that is deployed in many languages and is accessible at no cost to its users.

Wikipedia (www.wikipedia.org) is an online encyclopedia that is deployed in many languages and is accessible at no cost to its users (Figure 5.2). Wikipedia's name is a combination of the words *wiki* and *encyclopedia*. Unlike conventional encyclopedias, which are written by paid writers, Wikipedia's content can be generated by anyone who wishes to add to it, and the current content of Wikipedia has been written by unpaid volunteers. It was launched in January 2001 by Jimmy Wales and Larry Sanger, and it was originally supported by Jimmy Wales' company, Bomis.

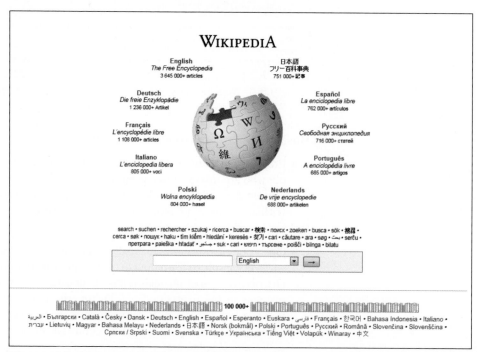

Figure 5.2 Wikipedia now features articles in over 270 languages, with over 3.6 million articles written in English.

Wikipedia is currently hosted, funded, and managed by the Wikimedia Foundation, Inc., a nonprofit organization located in San Francisco, California. The Wikimedia Foundation operates a variety of wiki projects in addition to Wikipedia. The foundation's mission is to encourage people to collaboratively develop information and provide that information to the general public free of charge. Although the foundation receives some grant money, it relies heavily on donations, which is why you will frequently see appeals for donations on Wikipedia pages.

What is the goal of Wikipedia?

Wikipedia strives to be a repository of factual knowledge. Its contribution guidelines state that topics submitted to Wikipedia must be encyclopedic in nature. To Wikipedia, this means that a topic must be *notable*, which is defined as having significant coverage in other reliable media sources (such as conventional media outlets or scholarly journals). In addition, Wikipedia is supposed to cover knowledge that is already established and recognized, in other words, facts. Wikipedia is not a forum for publishing new information, speculation, or original works (such as fictional stories). Wikipedia stresses that statements made in an article must be supported by appropriate references to other published sources of information that are deemed reliable.

Most importantly, since Wikipedia is designed to deal with facts, articles in Wikipedia should not express opinions or take sides. If an article is about a topic that has opposing views, each view should be given a roughly equal share of coverage.

How does Wikipedia differ from traditional encyclopedias?

Peer review, refereeing A process by which experts in a given field review another author's scholarly work to determine that the output is valid and substantially correct.

Traditional encyclopedias, such as *Encyclopedia Britannica*, have formal peer review processes to review content before it is published in the encyclopedia. *Peer review* (also called *refereeing*) is a process by which experts in a given field review another author's scholarly work to determine that the output is valid and substantially correct. For example, this textbook underwent a peer review process prior to publication. Professors with Web 2.0 expertise reviewed what the author had written to confirm its validity and to make suggestions about improvements (or corrections) to the content. Wikipedia has no such formal peer review process. Articles or edits to articles are published right after they are written and become available almost immediately on the Internet. Therefore, Wikipedia *does not guarantee* the validity or accuracy of the information it contains.

Ordinarily, the author or publisher of an article that is written for publication retains the copyright to the article, which means the right to copy, publish, or distribute the article remains with the author or publisher. In contrast, the copyright for articles on Wikipedia is not owned by the authors of the articles. When you provide content to Wikipedia, you surrender your rights to hold the copyright to your work. Also, Wikipedia is not censored. Therefore, content that some people may find objectionable or inappropriate may be published on the Wikipedia site.

Who enforces the guidelines for contributing articles to Wikipedia?

Wiki community The users and contributors to a wiki.

The users and contributors to Wikipedia make up its *wiki community*. A community is critical to a wiki because the community is what generates content for a wiki. Sometimes a community might consist of only three or four people, such as a group of students planning a project for their class. With large wikis like Wikipedia, the community is comprised of millions of people spread around the globe. Each person who visits Wikipedia can take on one or more of the following roles:

- Readers—Readers merely access Wikipedia, search for the information they need, and leave. Most people who visit Wikipedia are readers.

■ Writers—Some readers eventually choose to become writers by generating content for Wikipedia. Anyone can write for Wikipedia. There is no test or minimum standards for becoming a writer, and you can start writing for Wikipedia right now by generating a page. All you need to do to generate a new page for Wikipedia is create a free account.

■ Editors—Most pages in Wikipedia can be edited by anyone. Editors correct mistakes they see on a page or make additions and changes to content on a page. Regular editors and contributors often maintain watchlists of pages. A *watchlist* is a list of pages that are being monitored. Anytime updates are made to those pages, the person maintaining the watchlist is informed of the changes. A watchlist makes it easier to keep track of the pages that you are interested in monitoring. You can edit pages anonymously because editing does not require a Wikipedia account; however, you must have an account to create a watchlist.

■ Administrators—People who have been contributing to Wikipedia for a long time and who consistently do quality work either writing or editing articles are sometimes given administrator status on Wikipedia (currently about 1,800 people). This gives them the ability to delete or undelete pages, lock pages to keep them from falling prey to vandals, and block certain users from contributing to Wikipedia.

Aren't people tempted to put false information up on Wikipedia to further a cause or paint themselves in a positive light?

Human nature being what it is, this is not an infrequent occurrence on Wikipedia and other sites like it. Wiki vandals and Internet trolls sometimes post inappropriate information on Wikipedia. *Wiki vandals* deface pages in a wiki by one of these methods:

■ Deleting legitimate information

■ Inserting irrelevant or nonsensical information

■ Violating the policies of the wiki (such as adding content that is speculative on Wikipedia)

■ Inserting links to commercial sites in an attempt to sell products or services

Vandals are usually seeking amusement, furthering a political or hate-speech agenda, or just trying to see if their damage gets detected. *Internet trolls* are individuals who write inflammatory, controversial, or irrelevant content in online communities such as Wikipedia just to provoke emotional responses from readers.

The most famous case of vandalism on Wikipedia was false and defamatory content placed there about John Seigenthaler, an American journalist and political figure. The vandalism went undetected for four months but was finally reported and fixed. Mr. Seigenthaler then published an article criticizing Wikipedia for being inaccurate, which was certainly a justifiable reaction based on his experience.

How does Wikipedia prevent vandalism?

Community members take responsibility for policing the content and eliminating false or erroneous information. Certain pages that are subject to constant vandalism have been locked by administrators so that only approved individuals can edit them.

Watchlist A list of web pages that are being monitored.

Wiki vandals Individuals who deface pages in a wiki by deleting legitimate information, inserting irrelevant or nonsensical information, violating the policies of the wiki (such as adding content that is speculative on Wikipedia), or inserting links to commercial sites in an attempt to sell products or services.

Internet trolls Individuals who write inflammatory, controversial, or irrelevant content in online communities such as Wikipedia just to provoke emotional responses from readers.

Other pages that suffer from occasional vandalism are closely monitored by editors who are notified when changes are made so that they can review them for correctness and appropriateness. However, because the community can't be watching everything at once, incidents of vandalism or accidental additions of erroneous information aren't always detected right away on Wikipedia.

What does a Wikipedia page look like?

On Wikipedia's homepage (Figure 5.2), if you type the word *carousel* in the search box and click the search button, you will be taken to a wiki page about carousels (Figure 5.3).

Click here to edit this page

Information about carousels created by one or more contributors

Picture of carousel horses uploaded by a contributor

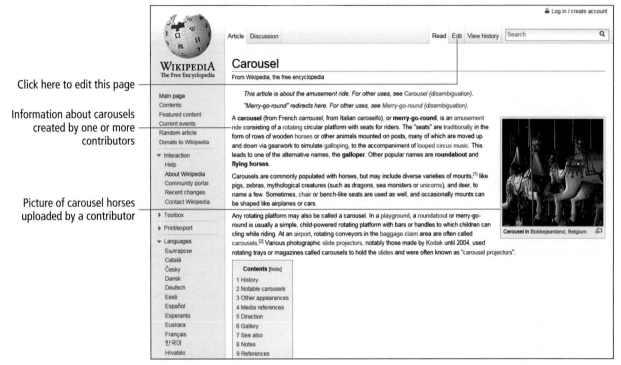

Figure 5.3 A wiki page about carousels from Wikipedia.

How do you edit a Wikipedia wiki page?

Wiki markup The extra symbols and keywords used by a wiki to display, categorize, and publish a wiki page.

At the top of most pages is an **Edit** tab. You may have new information about carousels that you wish to add to the page, or you may have a picture of a carousel figure that you want to upload to the page (uploading requires a Wikipedia account). If you click the **Edit** tab, you are taken to the editing page for the carousel wiki page (Figure 5.4). If you do not have a Wikipedia account, or are not logged in, an information area appears at the top of the page indicating how your edits will be identified. This area also provides links to other pages of interest to help you with the editing process. Below the information area is a text box containing the text you are able to edit for the carousel page, as well as wiki markup. *Wiki markup* consists of the extra symbols and keywords used by the wiki to display, categorize, and publish the page. Above the text box is a toolbar that provides additional functionality for editing the wiki page's content. You can add or change text wherever you need to on this page.

Professor Schmeckendorf knows quite a bit about carousels, and he has decided to expand the list of animals (other than horses) that are commonly found on carousels to include tigers. Below the editing area is a **Save page** button. Clicking this button will save the change Professor Schmeckendorf makes to the carousel page. The change will immediately be posted to the web, and the page will now include tigers in the list of animals.

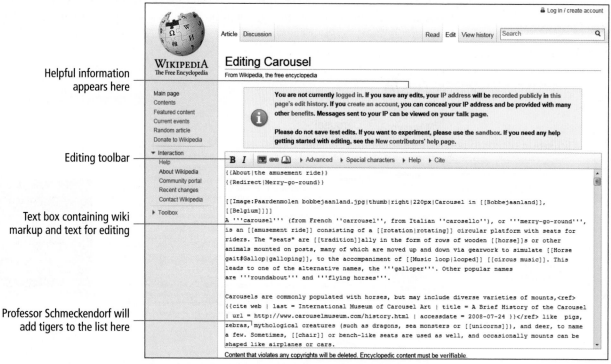

Helpful information appears here

Editing toolbar

Text box containing wiki markup and text for editing

Professor Schmeckendorf will add tigers to the list here

Figure 5.4 The carousel wiki page in the editing mode.

How do you know who has contributed to a page?

On Wikipedia, in most cases you will never know exactly who contributed to a page, because editing can be performed anonymously. However, wikis contain a feature called *revision history* that tracks which users (even anonymous ones) have made changes to a page. The *revision history page* (Figure 5.5) provides a chronological listing of the edits to the page, with the most recent edits appearing first. On Wikipedia, you can access this page by clicking the **View history** tab at the top of a wiki page. Edits made by contributors logged in to their Wikipedia accounts show the screen names for their accounts. Anonymous edits are identified only by the IP (Internet Protocol) address of the computer from which the edit was made. An *IP address* is a unique number assigned to devices connected to the Internet. The IP address is similar to the street address of your house. It helps data find its way from one device to another on the Internet.

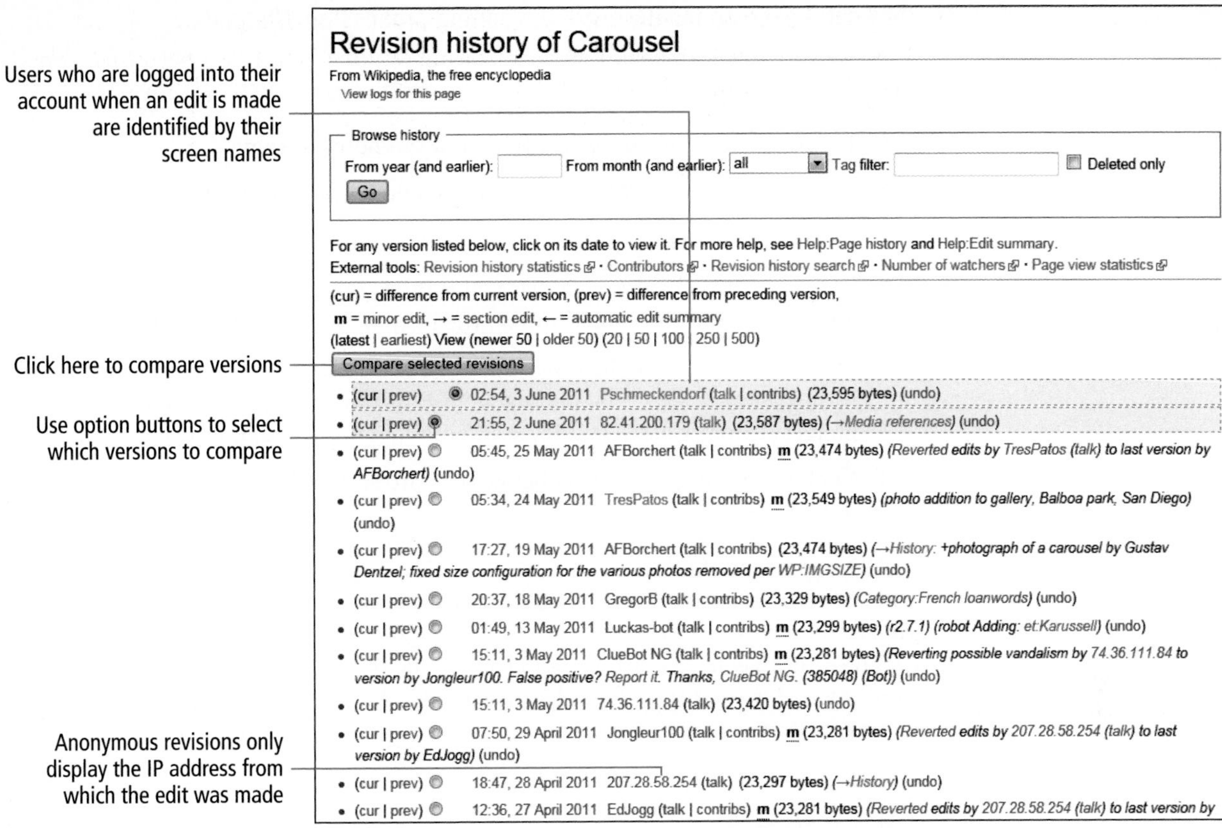

Users who are logged into their account when an edit is made are identified by their screen names

Revision history of Carousel

From Wikipedia, the free encyclopedia
View logs for this page

Browse history

From year (and earlier): ___ From month (and earlier): all ▼ Tag filter: ___ ☐ Deleted only
[Go]

For any version listed below, click on its date to view it. For more help, see Help:Page history and Help:Edit summary.
External tools: Revision history statistics ⚷ · Contributors ⚷ · Revision history search ⚷ · Number of watchers ⚷ · Page view statistics ⚷

(cur) = difference from current version, (prev) = difference from preceding version,
m = minor edit, → = section edit, ← = automatic edit summary
(latest | earliest) View (newer 50 | older 50) (20 | 50 | 100 | 250 | 500)

Click here to compare versions — [Compare selected revisions]

Use option buttons to select which versions to compare

- (cur | prev) ◉ 02:54, 3 June 2011 Pschmeckendorf (talk | contribs) (23,595 bytes) (undo)
- (cur | prev) ◉ 21:55, 2 June 2011 82.41.200.179 (talk) (23,587 bytes) (→*Media references*) (undo)
- (cur | prev) ○ 05:45, 25 May 2011 AFBorchert (talk | contribs) **m** (23,474 bytes) *(Reverted edits by TresPatos (talk) to last version by AFBorchert)* (undo)
- (cur | prev) ○ 05:34, 24 May 2011 TresPatos (talk | contribs) **m** (23,549 bytes) *(photo addition to gallery, Balboa park, San Diego)* (undo)
- (cur | prev) ○ 17:27, 19 May 2011 AFBorchert (talk | contribs) (23,474 bytes) (→*History: +photograph of a carousel by Gustav Dentzel; fixed size configuration for the various photos removed per WP:IMGSIZE*) (undo)
- (cur | prev) ○ 20:37, 18 May 2011 GregorB (talk | contribs) (23,329 bytes) *(Category:French loanwords)* (undo)
- (cur | prev) ○ 01:49, 13 May 2011 Luckas-bot (talk | contribs) **m** (23,299 bytes) *(r2.7.1) (robot Adding: et:Karussell)* (undo)
- (cur | prev) ○ 15:11, 3 May 2011 ClueBot NG (talk | contribs) **m** (23,281 bytes) *(Reverting possible vandalism by 74.36.111.84 to version by Jongleur100. False positive? Report it. Thanks, ClueBot NG. (385048) (Bot))* (undo)
- (cur | prev) ○ 15:11, 3 May 2011 74.36.111.84 (talk) (23,420 bytes) (undo)
- (cur | prev) ○ 07:50, 29 April 2011 Jongleur100 (talk | contribs) **m** (23,281 bytes) *(Reverted edits by 207.28.58.254 (talk) to last version by EdJogg)* (undo)

Anonymous revisions only display the IP address from which the edit was made

- (cur | prev) ○ 18:47, 28 April 2011 207.28.58.254 (talk) (23,297 bytes) (→*History*) (undo)
- (cur | prev) ○ 12:36, 27 April 2011 EdJogg (talk | contribs) **m** (23,281 bytes) *(Reverted edits by 207.28.58.254 (talk) to last version by*

Figure 5.5 The revision history page for the carousel wiki page.

The revision history page allows a user to compare two versions of a wiki page, such as the current version and a previous one. This makes it easy to see exactly what was changed on the page in the most recent edit (Figure 5.6). It also makes it possible for an editor to revert to the previous version of the page if the editor determines that the revisions were unnecessary, incorrect, or a result of vandalism. Professor Schmeckendorf's edit appears in red text in the right column of the page shown in Figure 5.6.

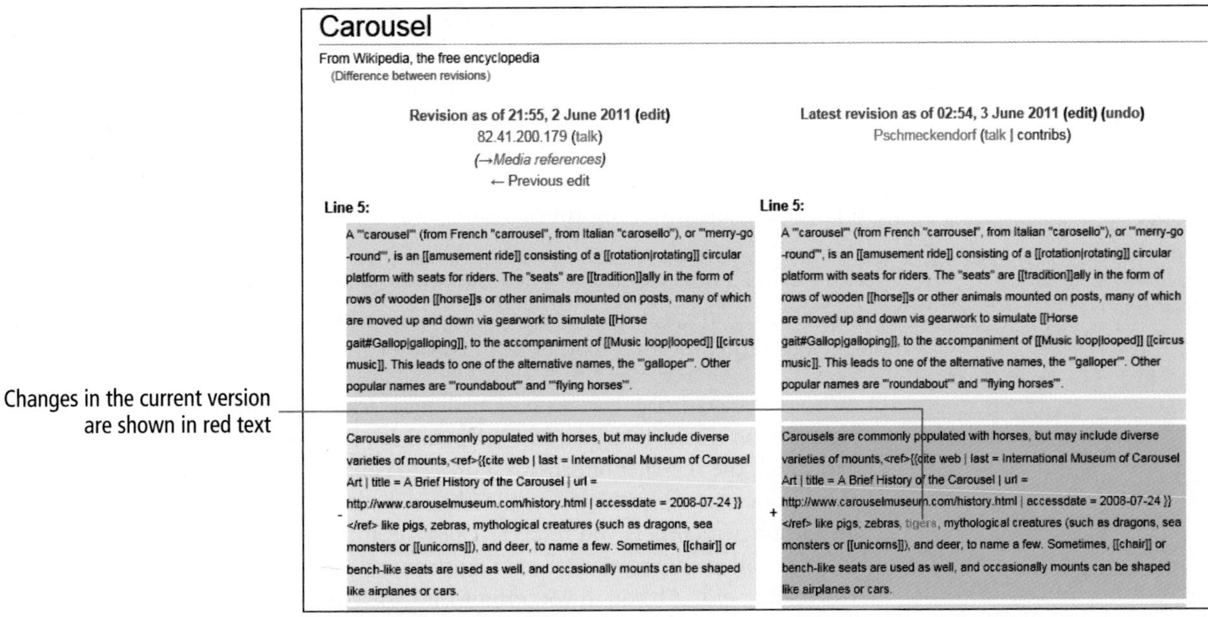

Carousel

From Wikipedia, the free encyclopedia
(Difference between revisions)

Revision as of 21:55, 2 June 2011 (edit)
82.41.200.179 (talk)
(→*Media references*)
← Previous edit

Latest revision as of 02:54, 3 June 2011 (edit) (undo)
Pschmeckendorf (talk | contribs)

Line 5:

A '''carousel''' (from French "carrousel", from Italian "carosello"), or '''merry-go-round''', is an [[amusement ride]] consisting of a [[rotation|rotating]] circular platform with seats for riders. The "seats" are [[tradition]]ally in the form of rows of wooden [[horse]]s or other animals mounted on posts, many of which are moved up and down via gearwork to simulate [[Horse gait#Gallop|galloping]], to the accompaniment of [[Music loop|looped]] [[circus music]]. This leads to one of the alternative names, the "galloper". Other popular names are "roundabout" and "flying horses".

Line 5:

A '''carousel''' (from French "carrousel", from Italian "carosello"), or '''merry-go-round''', is an [[amusement ride]] consisting of a [[rotation|rotating]] circular platform with seats for riders. The "seats" are [[tradition]]ally in the form of rows of wooden [[horse]]s or other animals mounted on posts, many of which are moved up and down via gearwork to simulate [[Horse gait#Gallop|galloping]], to the accompaniment of [[Music loop|looped]] [[circus music]]. This leads to one of the alternative names, the "galloper". Other popular names are "roundabout" and "flying horses".

Changes in the current version are shown in red text

Carousels are commonly populated with horses, but may include diverse varieties of mounts,<ref>{{cite web | last = International Museum of Carousel Art | title = A Brief History of the Carousel | url = http://www.carouselmuseum.com/history.html | accessdate = 2008-07-24 }} </ref> like pigs, zebras, mythological creatures (such as dragons, sea monsters or [[unicorns]]), and deer, to name a few. Sometimes, [[chair]] or bench-like seats are used as well, and occasionally mounts can be shaped like airplanes or cars.

Carousels are commonly populated with horses, but may include diverse varieties of mounts,<ref>{{cite web | last = International Museum of Carousel Art | title = A Brief History of the Carousel | url = http://www.carouselmuseum.com/history.html | accessdate = 2008-07-24 }} </ref> like pigs, zebras, tigers, mythological creatures (such as dragons, sea monsters or [[unicorns]]), and deer, to name a few. Sometimes, [[chair]] or bench-like seats are used as well, and occasionally mounts can be shaped like airplanes or cars.

Figure 5.6 A comparison of the current version of the carousel wiki page to the previous version of the page.

How can I become familiar with the editing process on Wikipedia?

The best way to become familiar with editing Wikipedia is to try it yourself. You can follow these steps as a guideline:

1. Think of a topic about which you are very knowledgeable.

2. Search for a page on Wikipedia that contains information about your topic.

3. Read the page carefully.

4. Locate a section of the page that you think might benefit from additional information, or find something on the page with which you disagree.

5. Click the **Edit** tab at the top of the page and make some changes to the page. If the page you select does not have an **Edit** tab, it may have been locked to protect it from vandalism. Try searching for another page instead.

6. Click the **Save page** button below the editing text box to submit your edits to Wikipedia.

Remember to check back in a couple of days to see what has happened to your edit. By then, the community should have responded in some way to your edit. An editor may have changed your wording slightly to make your meaning clearer. Or an editor may have deleted your change if he or she felt it was inappropriate or off topic. Or you might find that nothing has been changed, signaling that the community agrees with your edit.

Objective 3

Explain how to evaluate information found on the Internet

Because anyone can edit Wikipedia, how do I know that the information I find on it is accurate?

Wikipedia can be very accurate. At the end of 2005, the journal *Nature* conducted a study to compare Wikipedia's accuracy with that of *Encyclopedia Britannica*. The study found that for scientific articles, Wikipedia had about as many errors as the *Encyclopedia Britannica*. However, a similar study performed in 2009 by the journal *Reference Services Review* found that Wikipedia had an 80 percent accuracy rate, compared to a 95 to 96 percent accuracy rate from other sources. It is important to keep in mind that, at any given time, an article that you are reviewing on Wikipedia could be biased, factually incorrect, or contain outdated information. You need to evaluate the accuracy of what you find on Wikipedia in exactly the same way you would evaluate any other information you find on the Internet.

What criteria should you use for evaluating the suitability of a website?

Evaluation criteria are similar to those you use for printed resources that you would find in your school library. You need to consider the following:

- **Who is the author?** Is information about the author—including contact information—readily available on the site? If you know the author's name, you can search the Internet or other resources to consider the expertise of the author. Is the author a noted leader in the field he or she is writing about and recognized as an authority by others you respect? Does the author have appropriate credentials (such as college degrees or relevant work experience) that indicates expertise in that particular field? Although you might find what you consider to be good information on an anonymous blogger's website, you don't have any information about the blogger to consider that person an authority on a subject. Obviously, this isn't applicable to Wikipedia, where you never really know the author's name.

- **Who is the publisher of the information or the owner of the website?** Is the organization that owns or sponsors the website clearly identified? Is that entity an appropriate source of information for the topic you are researching? Is the publisher respected in the field and relied upon by others? Obviously, a respected journalistic body like the *New York Times* (www.nytimes.com) has more credibility than Billy Bob's Bodacious Blog!

- **What is the relationship of the author to the publisher?** Is the author an employee of the publishing entity? Or does the author have a more casual relationship with the publisher, possibly as a freelance author or independent contractor? Employees *might* be held to a more stringent level of competence and be required to have more appropriate credentials than freelancers or independent contractors.

- **Is the viewpoint biased?** Writers tend to use information that helps them make their points to the reader. A good writer is objective and provides different points of view, even when those points are detrimental to the writer's argument. The writer should also acknowledge when he or she is presenting an opinion as opposed to facts, and controversial theories should be identified as such. Consider the organization sponsoring the website and how it might be affected by the information. If you are reviewing information about products that the company publishing the website sells, be aware that the information presented may be intended to persuade people to buy the product. Corporate websites tend to paint the corporation in the most positive light, whereas a site not sponsored by the corporation might provide a more objective opinion about the company's operations and products. Also consider whether the publisher has a particular political, religious, or philosophical agenda that may encourage the author to slant the information that is presented to support the publisher's causes.

- **Does the work cite sources?** Just as your professors expect you to use footnotes and a bibliography in your research papers, scholarly publications on the Internet should also list their sources of information. When presented with a list of sources, check them. Are the sources respected publications or from authoritative and reliable authors on other websites? This is critical for evaluating information found on Wikipedia. Footnotes are located at the bottom of each wiki page on Wikipedia, so check them out for legitimacy.

- **Is the accuracy of the work verifiable?** Can you find the sources listed in the bibliography? Do hyperlinks to other articles work so that you can review the sources? For articles involving research, were the research methods, the collected data, and the interpretation of the results provided so that the research study could be reproduced if necessary?

- **Is the information presented current?** Are publication dates clearly indicated on the website? When the work is updated, are updates clearly identified and dated? Are the dates when research information was gathered presented (e.g., "based on a study conducted by XYZ Consultants in May, 2012")? You can check the history on Wikipedia to help determine how current the information is on that wiki page.

Finally, after following these steps, take a step back and consider what you have found. Decide why the page was placed on the web. Was the main goal of the page to inform, persuade, or sell? Consider whether the page was intended to be a parody or a satire. The best indicator for this is the tone of the writing. Was the writer sarcastic? Did the author tend to use a lot of humor or exaggerate to make points? Was the page supplemented with outlandish or humorous photographs? Decide if there are better places to find your needed research sources than on the Internet. Are the websites you are evaluating as credible as respected published periodicals or texts that you would consult in your college library? If, after all this analysis, you feel comfortable with the quality of the material you have reviewed, then you may have found a good source of reliable information on the web.

Objective 4

Discuss websites you can use to start a wiki

What do you need to start a wiki?

In the early days of wikis, you needed to install wiki hosting software on a *server* (a computer that provides services to other computers upon request) and connect that server to the Internet. Maintaining a wiki server is not a job for novices. Fortunately, the popularity of wikis gave rise to the creation of hosted wiki service providers, known as wiki farms, that can be used by individuals who lack technical knowledge.

A *wiki farm* is a server (or a group of connected servers) that runs wiki software and is designed to host multiple wikis at the same time. Some wiki farms charge a fee for hosting a wiki. However, many wiki farms offer free wiki hosting and support their companies by displaying advertising, such as Google AdSense ads, on the wikis they host. Often, you can pay a monthly fee to eliminate the ads placed by the hosting company and even place ads of your own on your wiki so that you can generate revenue for yourself.

Where can you find a wiki hosting service?

In an online search engine, just type in the phrase *free wikis* and you should find a long list of wiki hosting providers. Two popular sites for educators and students are PBworks (**http://pbworks.com**) and Wikispaces (**www.wikispaces.com**), as they offer free wiki hosting, a good range of features, and easy setup (Figure 5.7). Wikidot (**www.wikidot.com**) is another free wiki hosting provider that offers wikis with a more robust set of features and is a great place to set up a full-featured business wiki. However, the learning curve is a bit steeper for Wikidot, so it is not the best choice for setting up your first wiki.

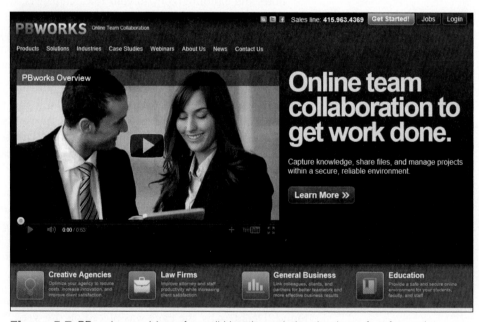

Figure 5.7 PBworks provides a free wiki hosting solution that is perfect for novice wiki designers.

How can you create a wiki that looks like Wikipedia?

In 2002, Wikipedia developed a software application called *MediaWiki* (Figure 5.8) to power its website. MediaWiki (**www.mediawiki.org**) is available free of charge under a *GNU General Public License* (GPL). A GNU GPL specifies that a software program can be distributed to and modified by anyone, even for commercial purposes (i.e., you are allowed to make money from it). The software is designed to run on large wiki farms and handle millions of user requests per day. MediaWiki requires technical expertise to deploy and maintain, so it is not used by beginners to host a wiki. But if you happen to develop a wiki that becomes wildly popular, with some help, you could eventually use the MediaWiki software to host your wiki.

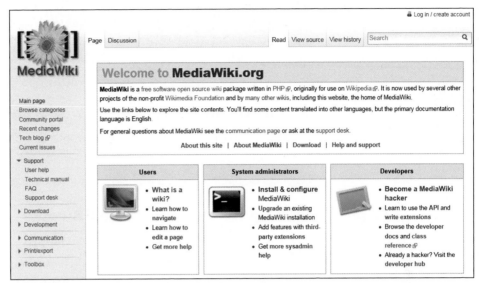

Figure 5.8 Although it requires technical expertise to deploy, MediaWiki is free, full-featured software that can be used to host a robust wiki site such as Wikipedia.

For the rest of this chapter, we'll be using PBworks to set up and host your first wiki.

Objective 5

Set up an account and a wiki on PBworks

What details should you consider before setting up a wiki?

Before taking the plunge and launching your first wiki, there are some decisions that you should make.

- **What is the purpose of your wiki?** Determining the goals for your wiki will help you decide if a wiki is really the best type of vehicle to accomplish your goals. Projects that involve collaborative writing (such as building a knowledge base), documentation that requires frequent revisions, providing information to employees who are geographically dispersed, or events that need planning are good candidates for a wiki. If you are merely trying to collaborate on joint projects and share files (such as spreadsheets and documents) with members of a group, an application such as Google Docs might be a better choice.

- **Should your wiki be visible to everyone?** Wikis do not have to be visible to everyone. A wiki can be made private so that only authorized individuals can view the wiki. This is often appropriate with proprietary information or a project that is not yet completed.

- **Who should be able to edit or add to your wiki?** Unlike Wikipedia, you can set up your wiki so that only authorized individuals have permission to edit it. In the case of a wiki that is used by a group of students to plan a class project, probably only the students in the group need the ability to edit the wiki.

- **Who will manage the wiki?** Although wikis can exist without formal management, setting responsibilities for certain wiki tasks can facilitate the completion of a project.

After you make the above decisions, you are ready to sign up for a wiki account on a hosting service and begin constructing your wiki.

Hands-On Exercises

Professor Schmeckendorf has decided to set up his first wiki to encourage research and information sharing for one of his computer literacy classes. In the Hands-On Exercises in this chapter, you'll recreate Professor Schmeckendorf's wiki on your own wiki site. You can always delete this site from your wiki account or change it to eliminate the wiki pages added in the Hands-On Exercises after you have completed the class for which you are performing these exercises.

1 | Create an Account on PBworks and Configure a Wiki

Steps: 1. Sign Up for an Account on PBworks; **2.** Configure a Wiki on PBworks.

Use Figures 5.9 through 5.20 as a guide to the exercise.

Step 1 Sign Up for an Account on PBworks

Refer to Figures 5.9 through 5.12 as you complete Step 1.

a. Turn on your computer and start your preferred browser (Internet Explorer, Firefox, Chrome, Safari, etc.). Type **http://pbworks.com** in the address bar of your browser and press **Enter**.

b. At the top of the page, click the **Get Started!** button to display the **Sign up to use PBworks** screen.

c. Click the **Personal User? Start here.** link to begin creating your account.

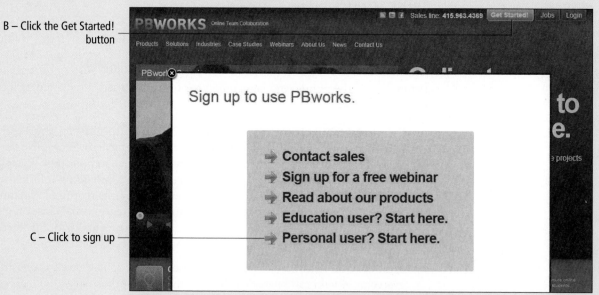

Figure 5.9 Hands-On Exercise 1, Steps 1b and 1c.

d. In the **Choose your address** text box, type a URL for your wiki. Because URLs are unique, you can't select something that is already in use. Since you are creating a wiki for your class, creating a URL that uses a combination of the course number for the course you are currently enrolled in, the first initial of your first name, and your full last name might be a good choice.

You cannot use cis110scfschmeckendorf as your URL. This URL is already in use by Professor Schmeckendorf's wiki. You will receive an error message if you try to use a URL that is already being used by someone else.

e. In the **Agree to non-commercial use** section, click the **For individuals** option to select it. Even though you are a student, the educational use option is geared toward teachers; so identifying yourself as an individual is appropriate.

f. Check the **I agree that this workspace is for non-commercial use only** checkbox.

g. In the **Create your account** section, in the **Your name** textbox, type your name. You do not have to use your real name if you are concerned about protecting your identity.

h. In the **Your email address** textbox, type your email address. This should be a current email address that you use and check regularly, as PBworks will be sending a confirmation email to this address.

i. Type a password in both the **Enter password** and **Confirm password** textboxes.

j. Click the **Next** button to continue the registration process.

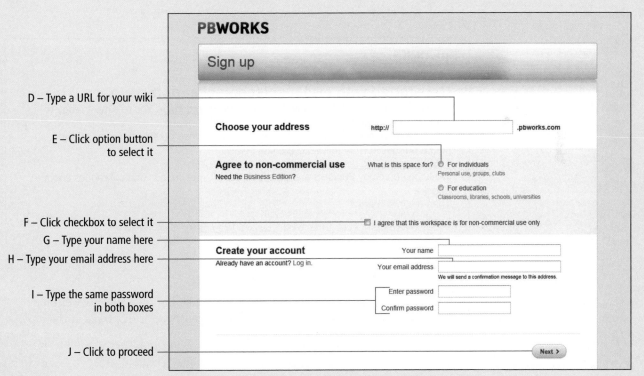

Figure 5.10 Hands-On Exercise 1, Steps 1d through 1j.

A new screen displays, as shown in Figure 5.11, instructing you to check your email account for your confirmation message from PBworks. You will need to click the link contained in this email message to activate your PBworks account. Note that PBworks uses the term *workspace* to describe its wikis.

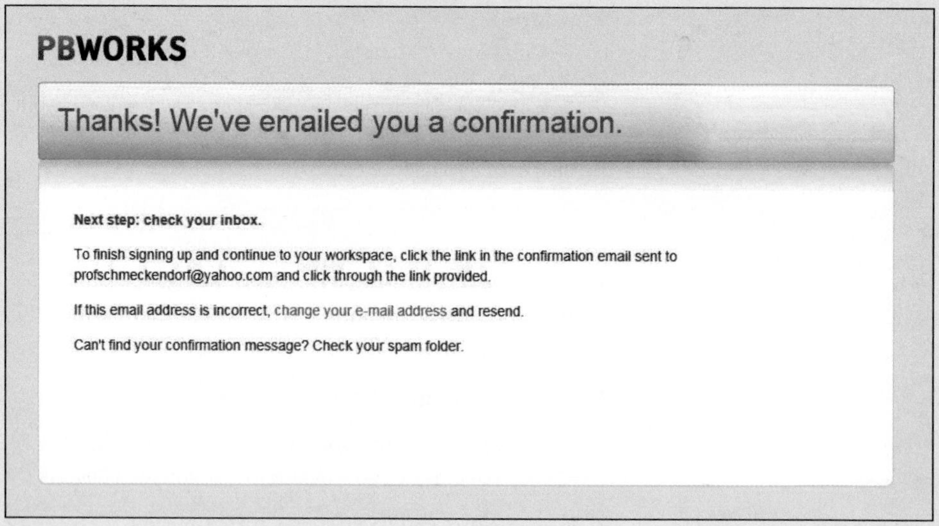

PBWORKS

Thanks! We've emailed you a confirmation.

Next step: check your inbox.

To finish signing up and continue to your workspace, click the link in the confirmation email sent to profschmeckendorf@yahoo.com and click through the link provided.

If this email address is incorrect, change your e-mail address and resend.

Can't find your confirmation message? Check your spam folder.

Figure 5.11 Confirmation screen showing that your wiki sign up information has been processed.

   k. Check your email account for an email message with the subject line "Confirm Your Account To Use PBworks" followed by the URL you selected for your wiki. If you don't see the email in your inbox, check your spam or junk mail folder.

   l. Click on the link in the email to activate your PBworks account.

PBWORKS

Get started with cis110scfschmeckendorf

Thanks for creating a PBworks workspace at **pbworks.com**. You're almost ready to start using your workspace!
We won't finish actually making your workspace until we verify your email address, so please do that now by following the link below:

L – Click to activate your account —— Activate your PBworks account now.

We hope you enjoy PBworks and please do tell all your friends and colleagues about it!
Thanks,
The PBworks Team

If you have questions or comments, contact support: http://pbworks.com/help.wiki?
wiki=cis110scfschmeckendorf.

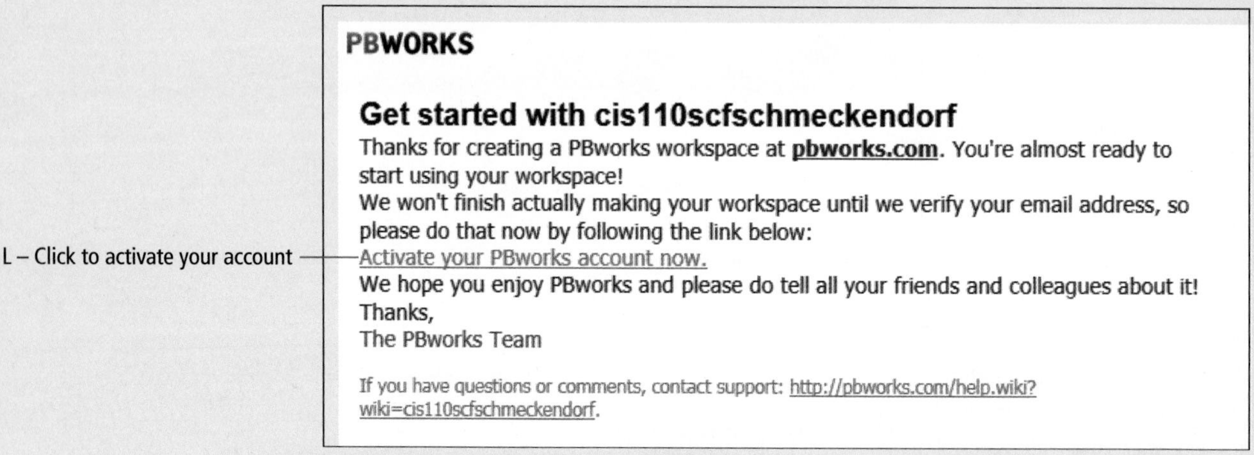

Figure 5.12 Hands-On Exercise 1, Step 1l.

A new tab or browser window should open, displaying the PBworks welcome screen for your wiki. Notice that the URL for your wiki is displayed at the top of this welcome screen (Figure 5.13).

Step 2 Configure a Wiki on PBworks

Refer to Figures 5.13 through 5.20 as you complete Step 2.

   a. If necessary, in the security settings section, click the **Anyone** option to make your wiki visible to anyone who wishes to see it, such as your professor. You can always change this setting later by selecting the **Only people I invite or approve** option to limit access to your wiki.

b. In the terms of service section, click the **terms of service** link to review this information. Click your browser's **Back** button to return to the welcome screen.

c. Click the **I agree to the PBworks terms of service** checkbox to select it and agree to the terms of service set by PBworks.

d. Click the **Take me to my workspace** button to view your wiki and continue configuring it.

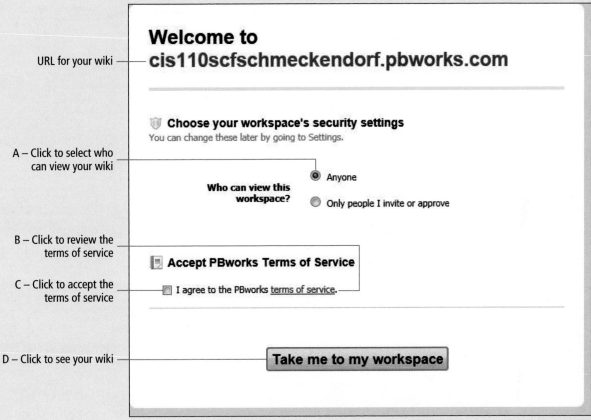

Figure 5.13 Hands-On Exercise 1, Steps 2a through 2d.

The wiki you created should look very similar to Figure 5.14. This is the basic wiki configuration that PBworks sets up when a wiki is first created. The only page that currently exists in the wiki is the FrontPage. It has text on it that was placed there by PBworks, but this can easily be edited or removed. By default, the title of the wiki is the URL, which is usually not very descriptive. You'll fix the title first and also edit some other settings for the wiki.

e. On the wiki, click the **Settings** tab to access the wiki settings screen.

Default title for wiki

E – Click to edit the wiki settings

Default text placed on the FrontPage can be edited or deleted

Contents of the SideBar can be edited just like other wiki pages

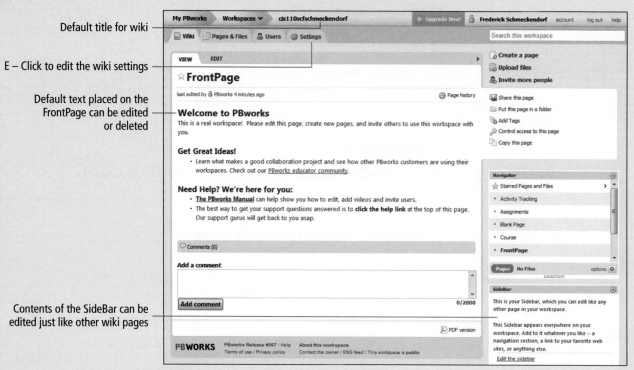

Figure 5.14 Hands-On Exercise 1, Step 2e.

 Alert!

When you enter the Wiki **Settings** screen, if the **About This Workspace** options are not displayed, click the **About This Space** link on the left side of the screen.

f. In the **Title** box, delete the default title and type **Professor Schmeckendorf's CIS 110 Wiki.**

g. In the **Description** box, type **A wiki created by Professor Schmeckendorf for his CIS 110 students at GSU.**

h. Check that the time and the keyboard language are correct for your wiki. If they are not, click the drop-down arrows next to the appropriate options and change them.

i. Click the **Save** button to save the changes you just made to the wiki. A notification will appear at the top of the screen to confirm that your settings were saved.

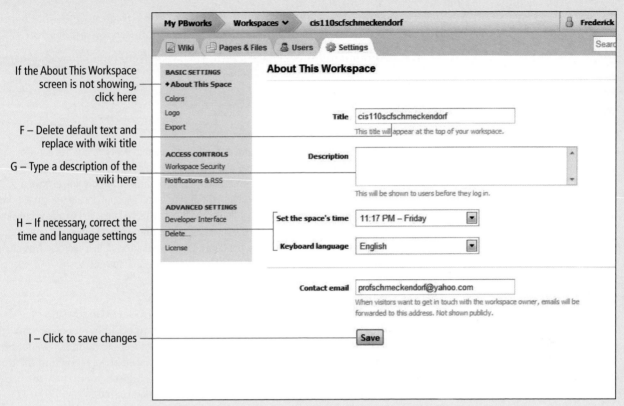

If the About This Workspace screen is not showing, click here

F – Delete default text and replace with wiki title

G – Type a description of the wiki here

H – If necessary, correct the time and language settings

I – Click to save changes

Figure 5.15 Hands-On Exercise 1, Steps 2f through 2i.

Professor Schmeckendorf wants to give access privileges to the wiki to one of his graduate students, Hannah Grindeldorf, who will be assisting him in maintaining the wiki. There are five different permission levels available for your wiki:

- Administrator—An administrator has the highest level of authority on a wiki. He or she can rename or delete anything on the wiki, add and delete users, modify settings, and change user permission levels. Administrators are the only users who have access to the wiki's **Settings** page. Use this level of permission carefully.

- Editor—An editor can rename or delete pages, files, and folders. Editors are able to make deletions that cannot be recovered, so they should be highly trusted individuals.

- Writer—A writer can edit pages, revert pages to previous versions, upload new files, and create new pages, but may not delete content. This is the recommended level of access for community members for a wiki, because writers cannot perform any action that cannot be undone.

- Reader—A reader cannot make any modification to the wiki, but is able to view and download the content.

- Page-level only—This is the most restrictive permission level available. Users with this permission level can access only the parts of the wiki for which you have granted them access. You can restrict their access to a particular page if necessary.

As the creator of your wiki, you have administrator-level permission, which gives you total access to the site. You can create and delete content, pages, and folders. You can even delete the entire wiki, if you so desire. Typically most wiki users are assigned writer-level permission so they will be able to create and edit content, but will not be able to make any changes that an administrator can't correct.

j. On the **About This Workspace** screen, click the **Users** tab to view and manage the current members of the wiki.

Alert

If an **Unverified** button appears next to your name, you may need to verify your email address. To do this, click the **account** link at the top right of the page to go to your **My PBworks** page. Click the **Email** tab on this page and locate your email address. Click the **Verify now** link to have a new email verification sent to your email account. Go to your email account, locate the email from PBworks, and click the link in the email to verify your address. This will take you to a new browser tab or window with the **My PBworks** page displayed. Click the **Home** tab and then click the name of your wiki to return to it. Once there, click the **Users** tab to continue with this exercise. You can close your email account and any extra PBworks windows or tabs that may be open.

k. Click the **Add more users** button to display the **Add Users** window and type the email address of one of your classmates into the **Users to add** box. If you are not working with classmates, use a friend or family member's email address. Do not type Professor Schmeckendorf's assistant's email address into the box as shown in the figure! Note that you can add multiple email addresses to register more than one person at the same time by adding each email address on a separate line.

l. If necessary, click the drop-down arrow and select **Writer** from the available permission levels. If you have added multiple email addresses, everyone you add will be assigned the same permission level. You can change individual permissions later, if necessary.

m. Click the **Add users** button to add this individual as a user to your wiki.

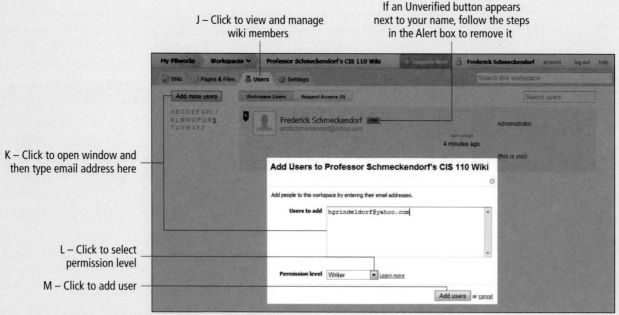

Figure 5.16 Hands-On Exercise 1, Steps 2j through 2m.

Figure 5.17 shows the results of adding two new users to Professor Schmeckendorf's wiki. Because Hannah already has a PBworks account, her name and email address are displayed. Professor Schmeckendorf added another user who does not yet have an account, so only the email address is displayed. The user's email address still needs to be verified as well. The users you just added should now be displayed under the list of users. Administrators on your wiki can change user permission levels for other users.

Administrators can change the permission level for an individual user

New users added to wiki

Email address has not been verified

Administrators can delete users

Figure 5.17 Users tab listing users authorized for a wiki.

The person you added to your wiki as a user will receive an email invitation to join the wiki (Figure 5.18). The new user will need to check his or her email inbox for this message (check the spam or junk mail folders if the message is not in the inbox). The email invitation contains a link to the PBworks site. Clicking the link will take the user to the PBworks log in page.

Sample email sent to user who does not have a PBworks account

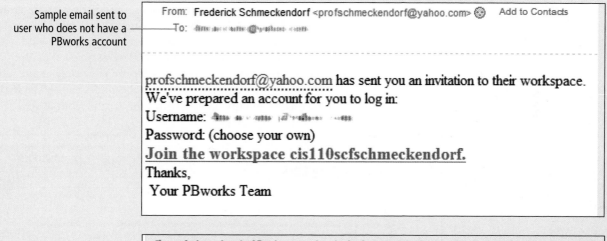

Sample email sent to user with existing PBworks account

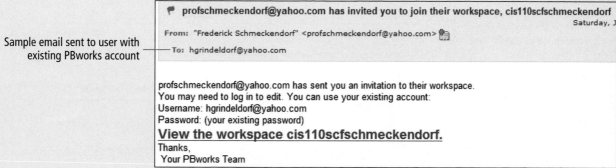

Figure 5.18 Sample wiki emails inviting a new user and a current PBworks member to join Professor Schmeckendorf's wiki.

After clicking on the link, the user you invited is taken to the **Set up your account** screen on PBworks (Figure 5.19). The user is asked to enter a name and password. Clicking the **Save** button takes the user to the next step in the sign up process.

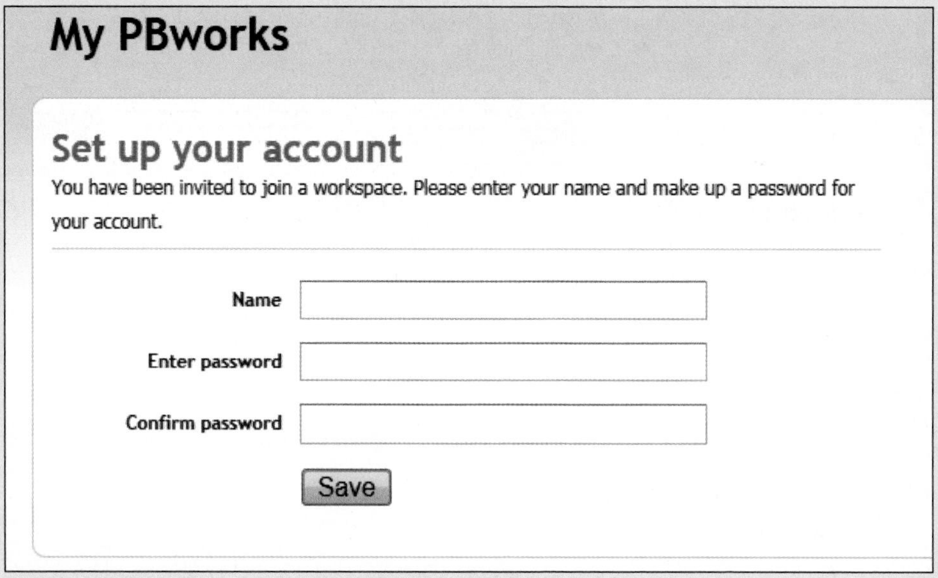

My PBworks

Set up your account

You have been invited to join a workspace. Please enter your name and make up a password for your account.

Name	
Enter password	
Confirm password	

Save

Figure 5.19 The user set-up screen on PBworks.

The user you invited has now established an account on PBworks. The **My Workspaces** page shows all the wikis that an account holder is a member of or has created. Since Hannah has not created or joined any wikis yet, only Professor Schmeckendorf's wiki will appear on this list (Figure 5.20). Clicking on the link to Professor Schmeckendorf's wiki will take Hannah to the wiki. Once the person you have invited to join your wiki follows the link in the email and creates a PBworks account, his or her My Workspaces screen should list your wiki on it. The **Preferences** section of the **My PBworks** homepage allows you to adjust how frequently you wish to receive email notifications about changes to the wiki. As you explore PBworks, you may find a public wiki that interests you. You can use the **Join a workspace** section of the **My PBworks Home** page to send a request to join someone's PBworks wiki, assuming you know the wiki's name. The **Profile** and **Email** tabs can be used to modify other settings for your account as well.

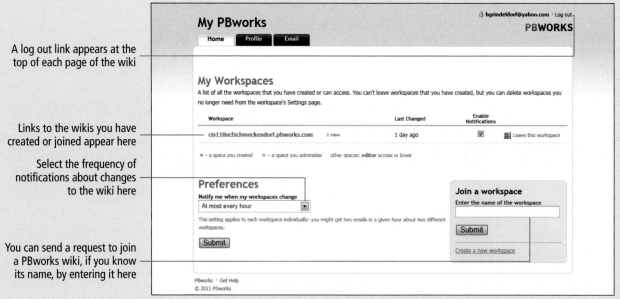

A log out link appears at the top of each page of the wiki

Links to the wikis you have created or joined appear here

Select the frequency of notifications about changes to the wiki here

You can send a request to join a PBworks wiki, if you know its name, by entering it here

Figure 5.20 The My Workspaces page for Hannah Grindeldorf, displaying the link to Professor Schmeckendorf's wiki.

n. Click the **Log out** link in the upper right corner to sign out of your PBworks account.

o. Close your browser.

Professor Schmeckendorf's wiki is now set up and configured. In the next Hands-On Exercise, you will modify Professor Schmeckendorf's wiki by editing the FrontPage and adding pages to the wiki.

Objective 6

Edit a wiki page and add pages to a wiki

In Hands-On Exercise 1, you set up Professor Schmeckendorf's PBworks account, created a wiki, and invited a user to join the wiki. Now it is time to start modifying the wiki to get the functionality that Professor Schmeckendorf requires. First, you'll edit the FrontPage to change the default text that PBworks places on all initial wiki pages. And then you'll add pages to the wiki to make it more functional.

Hands-On Exercises

2 | Edit a Wiki Page on PBworks and Add Pages to a Wiki

Steps: 1. Log In to Your PBworks Account; **2.** Edit the FrontPage of Your Wiki; **3.** Add Pages to Your Wiki.

Use Figures 5.21 through 5.33 as a guide to the exercise.

Step **1** **Log In to Your PBworks Account**

Refer to Figures 5.21 through 5.23 as you complete Step 1.

a. Start your preferred browser (Internet Explorer, Firefox, Chrome, Safari, etc.). Type **http://pbworks.com** in the address bar of your browser and press **Enter**.

b. At the top of the page, click the **Log in** link to sign in to your PBworks account.

B – Click to log in ———

PBWORKS Online Team Collaboration   Sales line: **415.963.4369** Get Started! Jobs Login

Figure 5.21 Hands-On Exercise 2, Step 1b.

 Alert!

The next screen may display a pink **Welcome back** box, depending upon the settings of your browser. If there is no pink box, just proceed normally with your log in. If you do have a Welcome back box and it is correct (i.e., the name showing is yours), just proceed to log in as normal. If the Welcome back box has a name other than yours, click the **[Not *person's name?*]** link to clear the other user's log-in information and then log in with your information.

c. Type your email address in the **Email address** box (or confirm that the address already showing in the box is yours).

d. Type your password in the **Password** box.

e. If the **Remember me** checkbox is checked, click to remove the check mark, especially if you are working on a public computer. This will help to protect your privacy and prevent others from possibly accessing your account or the wikis you have joined.

f. Click the **Log in** button to sign in to your account. The site opens with your **My PBworks** page displayed.

If the name and email address shown is not yours, click this link

C – Type your email address, if necessary

D – Type your password

E – Uncheck this box to ensure your privacy

F – Click to log in

Figure 5.22 Hands-On Exercise 2, Steps 1c through 1f.

Notifications Emails sent out by your wiki provider to alert you when changes are made to your wikis.

One of the preferences you can set for your wikis is the notification preference. *Notifications* are emails sent out by your wiki provider to alert you when changes are made to your wikis and are useful when you want to review changes that others have made. However, since you are going to be making a lot of changes to the wiki over the next few Hands-On Exercises, you probably don't want your email inbox filling up with notifications advising that you have changed your own wiki. Therefore, you should change the notification preference to **Never** to avoid this issue. You can always reset this preference at a later time.

g. On the **My PBworks** page, in the **Preferences** section, click the **Notify me when my workspaces change** drop-down arrow and select the **Never** option. Note that there are many other choices available.

h. Click the **Submit** button to save the change to your preferences.

i. Click the link to the wiki you set up in Hands-On Exercise 1 to access it. Note that the name of your wiki will not match the one shown in Figure 5.23, as you have created a unique URL for your wiki.

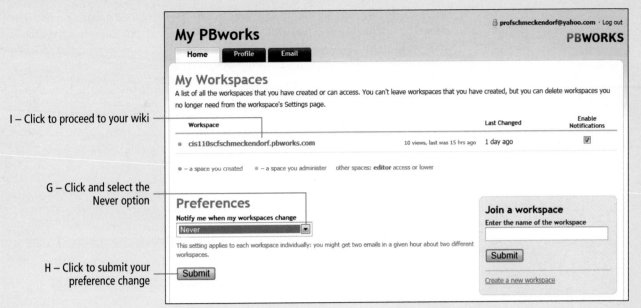

I – Click to proceed to your wiki

G – Click and select the Never option

H – Click to submit your preference change

Figure 5.23 Hands-On Exercise 2, Steps 1g through 1i.

Step 2 Edit the FrontPage of Your Wiki

Refer to Figures 5.24 through 5.28 as you complete Step 2.

The FrontPage is the first page you should see on your wiki, since you haven't created any other pages yet. PBworks creates this page when your account is first set up and adds the default text you see there to help you get started with your wiki. Take a few moments to review the information provided. The **PBworks Manual** can also be accessed by clicking the **help** link at the top of the page. In this exercise, you will be deleting the default text and replacing it with information about Professor Schmeckendorf's wiki.

a. Click the **Edit** tab to edit the FrontPage of your wiki.

Use this tab to access your My PBworks page

A – Click to edit this page

The help link provides access to the PBworks Manual

The default text provides useful information

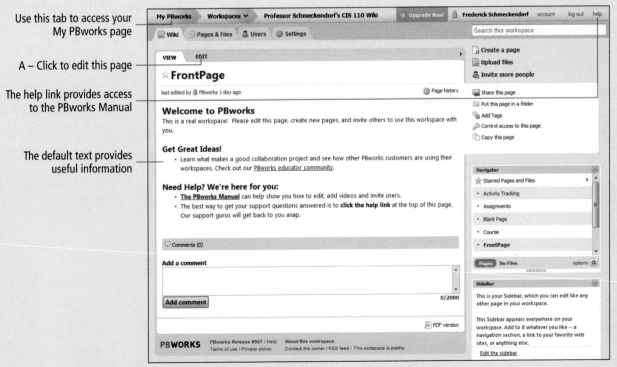

Figure 5.24 Hands-On Exercise 2, Step 2a.

The FrontPage of the wiki is now in edit mode. Notice that a group of icons representing various editing tools has appeared above a text box containing the default text. Many of these icons will look familiar, as they are very similar to icons used for editing in other software programs, such as Microsoft Word.

b. Click anywhere in the text. Press **Ctrl+A** to select all the text on the FrontPage. Press **Delete** to delete the text.

Editing tools —

B – Select and delete default text —

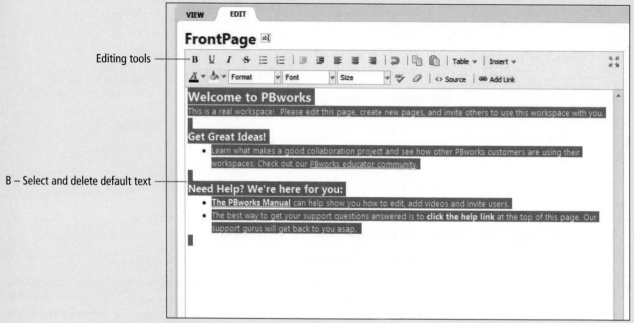

Figure 5.25 Hands-On Exercise 2, Step 2b.

c. Type the following in place of the text that you just deleted from the FrontPage.

Welcome to Professor Schmeckendorf's CIS 110 Wiki!

This wiki has been set up for the students in Professor Schmeckendorf's CIS 110 class to facilitate better communication by the class members and to help organize group research projects.

C – Type new text to replace deleted text —

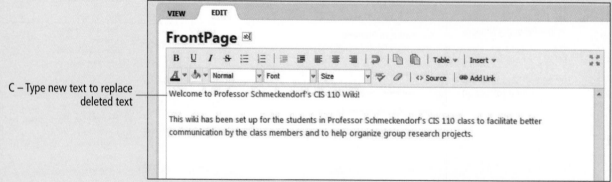

Figure 5.26 Hands-On Exercise 2, Step 2c.

Professor Schmeckendorf would like the first line of the text you just entered to be formatted as a heading. The heading should be enlarged so that it is more noticeable.

d. Click and drag to select the text in the heading.

e. Click the **Format** box drop-down arrow and select **Heading 1** from the available choices.

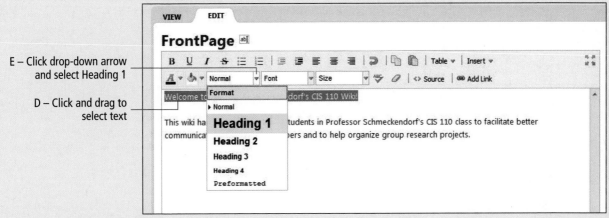

E – Click drop-down arrow and select Heading 1

D – Click and drag to select text

Figure 5.27 Hands-On Exercise 2, Steps 2d and 2e.

Notice that the heading of the page is now displayed in a much larger font (Figure 5.28). As more people join a wiki and begin editing it, it can be difficult to determine why some changes were made. The **Describe your changes** text box gives you a place to explain why certain changes were made. This is an optional feature, but it can be very helpful when you need to review page edits.

f. Click the **Describe your changes** text box and type **Removed default text and added Welcome message.**

g. Once you have completed your changes, you have three options—Save, Save and Continue, and Cancel. The **Save** option saves your changes and displays the newly edited page in view mode. **Save and Continue** saves your changes but leaves the page open in edit mode. **Cancel** undoes all your edits and returns you to the existing page in view mode. Click the **Save** button to save the edits that were made to the FrontPage.

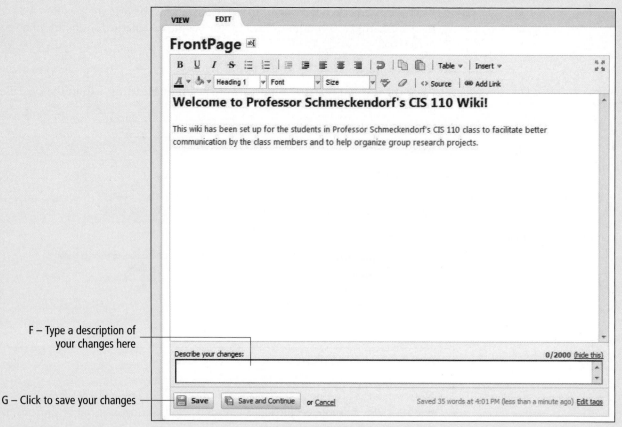

F – Type a description of your changes here

G – Click to save your changes

Figure 5.28 Hands-On Exercise 2, Steps 2f and 2g.

PBworks will occasionally display pop-up boxes containing tips for using the wiki. If a pop-up box appears suggesting you share this revised page with others, you can close it. You are now ready to increase the functionality of the wiki by adding more pages to it.

Step 3   Add Pages to Your Wiki

Refer to Figures 5.29 through 5.33 as you complete Step 3.

Professor Schmeckendorf wants to create two new pages for the wiki. The first is an information page that provides contact information for Professor Schmeckendorf. The second page is a research page where students can post abstracts of articles that they find on the Internet or provide links to videos that pertain to topics of study in the course.

a. If you have just completed Step 2, the FrontPage of your wiki should be displayed in the view mode. If you have logged out of your PBworks account, follow the directions in Step 1 of this Hands-On Exercise to access your wiki. On the **My PBworks** page, click the workspace link to go to your **FrontPage**.

b. Click the **Create a page** link to begin creating a new page for your wiki.

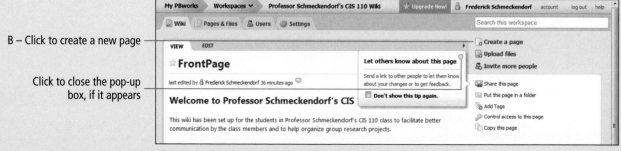

B – Click to create a new page

Click to close the pop-up box, if it appears

Figure 5.29 Hands-On Exercise 2, Step 3b.

c. In the **Name your page** text box, type **Contact Information**.

d. You can create a new page entirely from scratch by selecting the **Blank page** option. If you prefer, PBworks provides several templates that can be accessed by selecting the **Use a template** option and making a choice from the drop-down list that appears. Templates can help save time when setting up some types of pages. However, the **Contact Information** page Professor Schmeckendorf wants to create is fairly simple, so you should ensure that the **Blank page** option is selected. Since the wiki does not have any folders, you can skip the **Put this page in a folder** option for now.

e. Click the **Create page** button to create the page.

A new page titled **Contact Information** has now been created and opens in edit mode. Now you will add content to the page.

C – Type the page name here

D – Click to create a blank page

E – Click to create the page

Figure 5.30 Hands-On Exercise 2, Steps 3c through 3e.

f. Type Professor Schmeckendorf's contact information onto the **Contact Information** page:

Professor Frederick Schmeckendorf
Office: Founders Hall, Room 222
Office Hours: Monday, Wednesday and Friday -- 1 pm to 3 pm or by
    appointment
Email: profschmeckendorf@yahoo.com

g. In the **Describe your changes** text box, type **Created page and added contact information**.

h. Click the **Save** button to save the page.

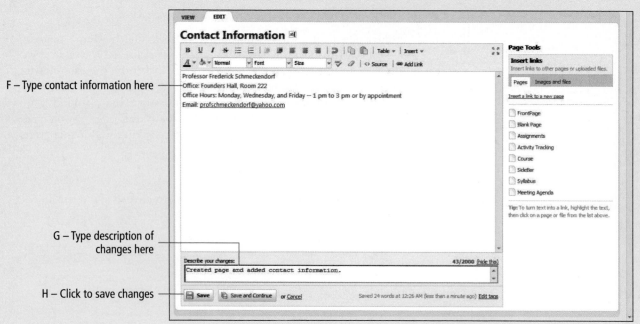

F – Type contact information here

G – Type description of changes here

H – Click to save changes

Figure 5.31 Hands-On Exercise 2, Steps 3f through 3h.

The **Contact Information** page should now display in the view mode. Now you'll create the second page that Professor Schmeckendorf wants for student research projects.

i. Click the **Create a page** link.

j. On the **Create a new page** window, use the skills you just learned in Steps 3c through 3e to create a new blank page titled **Student Research**.

k. Type the following description onto the page:

   On this page, please place links to articles or embed videos that pertain to topics we are covering in class. Sharing information with your classmates is part of your grade for the semester.

l. In the **Describe your changes** text box, type **Created new page and added instructions for sharing resources.**

m. Click the **Save** button to save the page and return to view mode.

K – Type page text here

L – Type description of changes here

M – Click to save changes

Figure 5.32 Hands-On Exercise 2, Steps 3k through 3m.

The **Student Research** page should now display in the view mode. It can be difficult to tell how many pages are in your wiki when looking at one page in the view mode. To review all pages currently on your site, you need to view the **Pages & Files** screen.

n. Click the **Pages & Files** tab near the top left of the page to access the **Pages & Files** page.

The **Pages & Files** page (Figure 5.33) shows you all the items that are currently part of your wiki. In addition to the pages you have already edited or created, there are several other pages—these are the templates that can be used to easily create a new page on your wiki.

The list on the left side of the page allows you to select which items you wish to view. You can choose **Pages & Files** to see all items, **All Pages** to see just the pages in the wiki, **All Files** to see all files (documents, images, etc.) that have been uploaded to the wiki, or **Unfiled Items** to view those items that have not yet been placed in a folder. Make sure the **Pages & Files** option is selected. From this page, you can edit, rename, delete, and move pages by clicking the **More** link and making the appropriate selection from the window that appears. You can also delete pages by clicking the checkbox next to the page name to select it and then clicking the **Delete** button or move a selected file into a folder by clicking the **Move** button at the top of the column. You can click the **New** button at the top left of the page to create a new page or a new folder, while the **Upload files** button right next to it helps you to add other items to your wiki.

o. Click the **Wiki** tab to return to the FrontPage of the wiki.

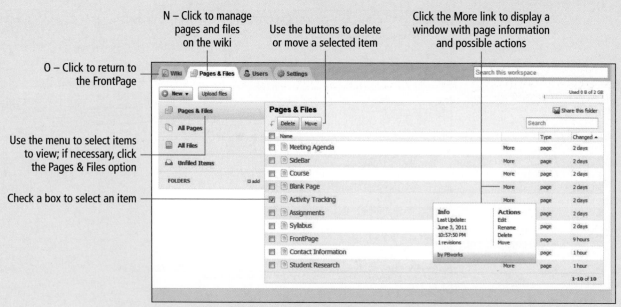

N – Click to manage pages and files on the wiki

Use the buttons to delete or move a selected item

Click the More link to display a window with page information and possible actions

O – Click to return to the FrontPage

Use the menu to select items to view; if necessary, click the Pages & Files option

Check a box to select an item

Figure 5.33 The Pages & Files page allows you to manage the pages on a wiki. Hands-On Exercise 2, Steps 3n and 3o.

You may now log out of the PBworks site or continue on to the next Hands-On Exercise. In the next section, you'll learn how to add clickable links to pages to improve their functionality and usefulness.

Objective 7

Add internal and external links to a wiki

Hyperlink A text or an image that connects to another document on the web or to another location on the same web page.

Internal links Hyperlinks that connect one wiki page to another location within the wiki.

External links Hyperlinks that connect to web pages located outside of the wiki.

A key feature of the World Wide Web is the hyperlink (or link). A ***hyperlink*** is a text or an image that connects to another document on the web or to another location on the same web page. Hyperlinks facilitate navigation on the Internet. Links are just as critical to wikis as they are to other web pages.

On wikis, ***internal links*** connect a wiki page to another location within the wiki. The link could connect to another location on the same wiki page or might connect to a different page of the wiki. Internal links are often used to facilitate navigation for users of a wiki. ***External links*** connect to web pages that are located outside of the wiki.

Hands-On Exercises

3 | Add Internal and External Links to Wiki Pages

Steps: 1. Create a Navigation Scheme for a Wiki Using Internal Links; **2.** Insert External Links to Content on a Wiki Page.

Use Figures 5.34 through 5.41 as a guide to the exercise.

Refer to Figures 5.34 through 5.39 as you complete Step 1.

Navigator A PBworks feature that is available on all pages, this section displays the wiki's site structure and allows users to view and access files and folders on the wiki.

A feature of PBworks is the *Navigator*, a small section that is always visible (by default) on the right side of your wiki no matter what page of the wiki you are viewing. The *Navigator* section cannot be edited, although you can expand or collapse it by clicking the arrow button on the title bar. Its main purpose is to display the site structure for the wiki. The Navigator's function is similar to that of Windows Explorer—you can use it to view and access all the files and folders on the wiki.

SideBar A feature of PBworks, this small section is always visible (by default) on the right side of your wiki and can be edited just like a full-size wiki page. It is often used to provide a list of internal links.

Directly below the Navigator is the *SideBar*, another small section that is always displayed on the right side of the wiki. Although it appears smaller than a conventional wiki page, it still has the same attributes as other wiki pages, so it can be edited. The **SideBar** can be used to display internal or external links, text, or images. It is often used to provide a list of internal links, similar to a table of contents or a favorites page, to help users navigate to the most frequently used pages of a wiki. Professor Schmeckendorf would like to use the **SideBar** for this purpose.

a. If you have just completed Hands-On Exercise 2, the FrontPage of your wiki should be displayed in the view mode. If you have logged out of your PBworks account, follow the directions in Hands-On Exercise 2, Step 1, to access your wiki.

b. On the **SideBar**, click the **Edit the sidebar** link to begin editing the SideBar wiki page.

Click to expand or collapse the section

The Navigator pane displays the wiki's files and folders

The SideBar can be edited to display text, links, or images

B – Click to edit the SideBar

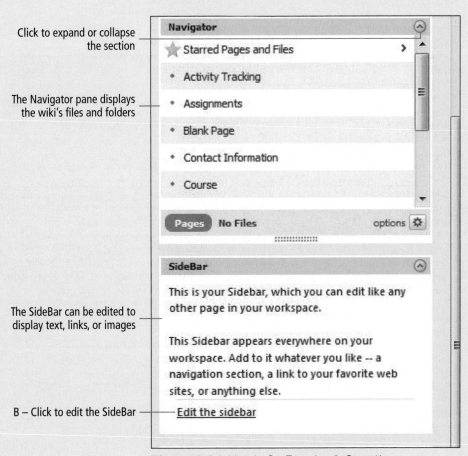

Figure 5.34 Hands-On Exercise 3, Step 1b.

c. Click anywhere in the text that is currently on the SideBar and press **Ctrl+A** to select it. Press **Delete** to delete this text.

Currently, there are only two pages in the wiki, besides the FrontPage, that Professor Schmeckendorf is using. You will create links in the SideBar to both of those pages, as well as a link to return to the FrontPage. We will explore several different methods to create these links in the next steps.

d. In the **SideBar** text box, type **Wiki Navigation** and then press **Enter** to place the insertion point on the line below this text.

e. In the **Insert links** section on the right side of the page, click the **Insert a link to a new page** link to display the **Insert Link** dialog box.

If a browser message appears asking if you want to leave this page, click the **Stay on this page** option.

D – Type page text here

E – Click to open the Insert Link dialog box

If a warning message appears, click button to stay on this page

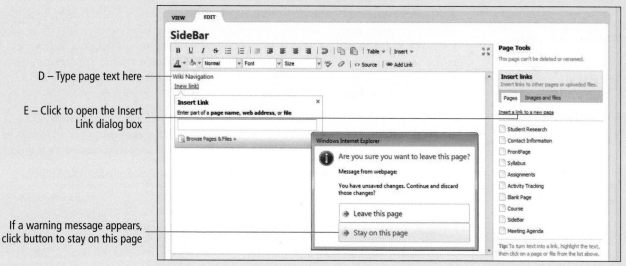

Figure 5.35 Hands-On Exercise 3, Steps 1d through 1e.

f. In the **Insert Link** dialog box, begin to type **Contact Information**. As you are typing, the PBworks auto-suggest feature attempts to match your text to the existing pages and displays the results below the text box.

g. Click the **Contact Information** result to insert the link.

G – Click the correct auto-suggest result here

F – Type page name here

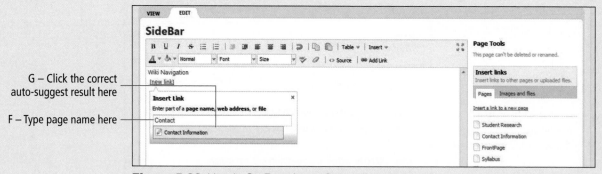

Figure 5.36 Hands-On Exercise 3, Steps 1f and 1g.

Notice that a hyperlink called *Contact Information* has been inserted on the **SideBar** page (Figure 5.37). Clicking this link will take you to the **Contact Information** page.

h. Position the insertion point on the line underneath the **Contact Information** link.

i. Notice that in the **Insert links** section, beneath the **Insert a link to a new page** link, there is already a list of the pages in the wiki. This list includes the pages you have created in these exercises, as well as the template pages provided by default from PBworks. Click the **Student Research** link to insert a link to the **Student Research** page on the **SideBar** page.

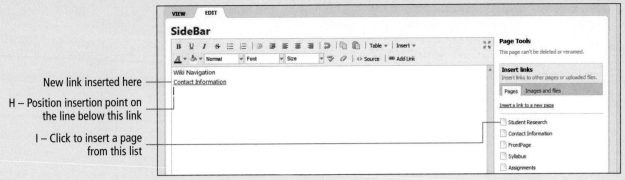

New link inserted here —

H – Position insertion point on the line below this link

I – Click to insert a page from this list

Figure 5.37 Hands-On Exercise 3, Steps 1h and 1i.

A link to the **Student Research** page has been inserted below the link for the **Contact Information** page (Figure 5.38). You also need to insert a link to enable users to return to the FrontPage. However, since *FrontPage* is a term unique to PBworks and may not be familiar to all users of the wiki, Professor Schmeckendorf feels that the link for the FrontPage should be called *Home* instead.

j. Below the **Student Research** link, add a new line and type **Home**. Click and drag to select the Home text.

k. With the Home text selected, from the **Insert links** section, click the **FrontPage** link. The word *Home* will become a hyperlink and its destination will be the FrontPage wiki page. Close the hyperlink toolbar if it appears after the link has been created. If necessary, click in a blank area of the page to deselect the Home link.

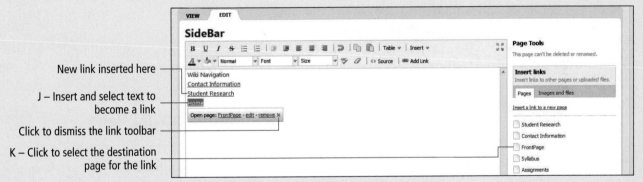

New link inserted here —

J – Insert and select text to become a link

Click to dismiss the link toolbar —

K – Click to select the destination page for the link

Figure 5.38 Hands-On Exercise 3, Steps 1j and 1k.

You should now have links to all three wiki pages on the **SideBar** page.

l. Click the **Describe your changes** text box and type a description of the changes you made.

m. Click the **Save** button to save the **SideBar** page.

The **SideBar** page will now display in view mode. Notice that the **SideBar** section on the right of the page now contains navigation links for the wiki (Figure 5.39). Clicking any of these links will take you to the appropriate page on the wiki. Confirm that all the links work correctly and then return to the FrontPage. As you add pages to your wiki, you should also add links to those pages in the SideBar so that users can locate pages easily.

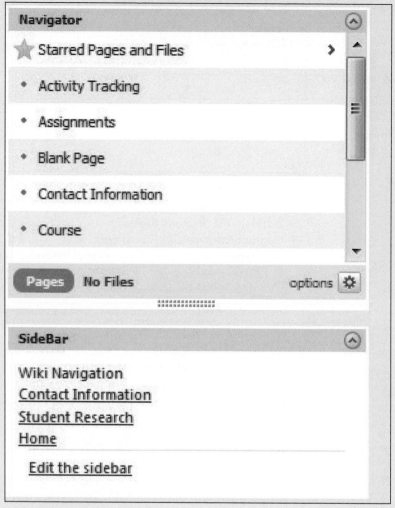

Figure 5.39 The SideBar with a wiki navigation scheme in place.

 Step 2 **Insert External Links to Content on a Wiki Page**

Refer to Figures 5.40 and 5.41 as you complete Step 2.

Professor Schmeckendorf has already set up the **Student Research** page so students can share information they locate on the Internet. He now decides to add an example on that page for them to follow.

a. Navigate to the **Student Research** page by clicking the link in the SideBar.

b. When the **Student Research** page is displayed, click the **Edit** tab at the top of the page to display the page in edit mode.

c. Type the following text beneath the existing text on the **Student Research** page. Use Figure 5.40 as a guide for text placement. Use the formatting buttons to bold the text *Surfing Safely on Wireless Hotspots*.

Here is an example of how I am expecting you to submit your information on this page:

Surfing Safely on Wireless Hotspots - Many people surf on wireless hotspots but are unaware of the precautions they need to take to protect themselves from hackers. This article from Microsoft contains eight good tips for protecting yourself while surfing (Submitted by Professor Schmeckendorf).

d. Select the text *article from Microsoft*. This text will be turned into a hyperlink to the article.

e. With the text selected, click the **Insert** button on the toolbar and, from the drop-down menu, click **Link** to display the **Insert Link** dialog box.

E – Click Insert and then click Link to display the Insert Link dialog box

C – Begin typing new text here

D – Select text for hyperlink

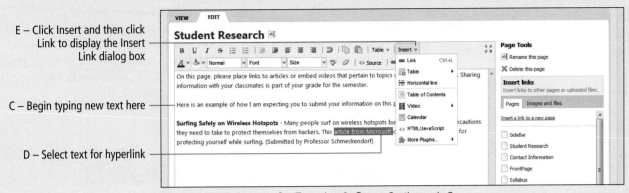

Figure 5.40 Hands-On Exercise 3, Steps 2c through 2e.

f. The **Insert Link** dialog box appears with the selected text in the text box. Delete this text and type the following URL for the article:

www.microsoft.com/atwork/remotely/hotspots.aspx

g. Press **Enter** to convert the text to a hyperlink on the wiki page. If a hyperlink toolbar appears, click the close button to dismiss it.

Notice that the text has now been turned into a hyperlink to the article on Microsoft's website.

h. In the **Describe your changes** text box, type **Added hyperlink to Microsoft site**.

i. Click the **Save** button to save your edits to the **Student Research** page and return to view mode.

G – Text becomes a hyperlink

F – Type URL here

H – Type description of changes here

I – Click to save changes

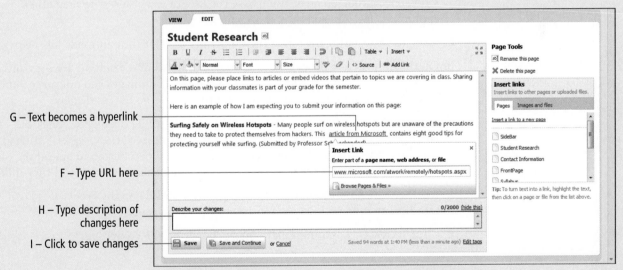

Figure 5.41 Hands-On Exercise 3, Steps 2f through 2i.

j. Click the link you just created to be sure it works correctly. If you have any problems switch back to edit mode, delete the link, and try again to ensure you typed the URL correctly. You may also want to type the URL directly into a browser address bar to be sure you are using the correct address.

You may now log out of PBworks or continue on to the next Hands-On Exercise. In the next section, you'll learn how to upload images to a wiki and display them and how to embed video on a wiki page.

Objective 8

Upload content to or embed content on a wiki

Like other web pages, wikis are more interesting and exciting when they contain relevant images or videos. Professor Schmeckendorf has decided that he should upload the logo for his university, Ginormous State University, to the FrontPage of his wiki. He also has found a video that he wants his students to view, so he needs to embed it on the Student Research wiki page.

Hands-On Exercises

4 | Upload Images to a Wiki and Embed Video on a Wiki Page

Steps: 1. Upload an Image to PBworks; **2.** Embed a YouTube Video on a Wiki Page.

Use Figures 5.42 through 5.49 as a guide to the exercise.

Step 1 **Upload an Image to PBworks**

Refer to Figures 5.42 and 5.43 as you complete Step 1.

a. Open your web browser, navigate to **http://pbworks.com,** and log in to your account. Make sure you are viewing the FrontPage of your wiki.

b. Download the Chapter 5 student data files from the companion website at **www. pearsonhighered.com/nextseries.** Instructions for downloading the files can be found on the companion website. Save the files to your hard drive or another appropriate location and then extract them.

c. Click the **Edit** tab at the top of the FrontPage to enter the edit mode for the page.

d. On the right side of the page, in the **Insert links** section, click the **Images and files** link. This area is used to work with the files and images you upload to your wiki. Since nothing has been added yet, this area has no files to display.

e. Click the **Upload files** link to display the **Upload a File** dialog box. Click the **Browse** button and navigate to the folder where you saved the Chapter 5 student data files. Select the **GSU_Logo.jpg** file. Click the **Open** button to upload the file to the wiki. A link for the file will appear in the area below the **Upload files** link.

f. Insert two blank lines above the heading that is already on the FrontPage. Position the insertion point at the top-left corner of the page.

g. Click the **GSU_Logo.jpg** link to insert the file on the FrontPage.

C – Click to edit page

E – Click to display dialog box and upload file

D – Click to upload files

F – Insert blank lines and position insertion point here

G – Click to add image to page

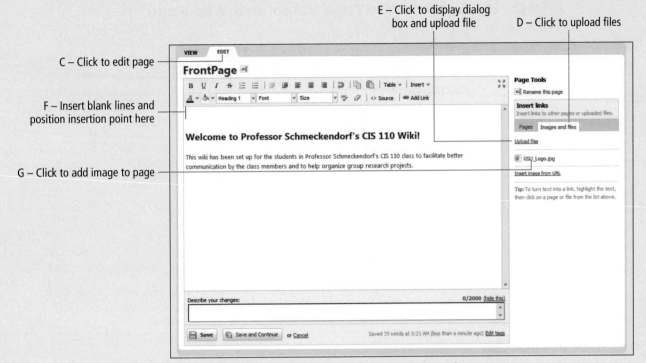

Figure 5.42 Hands-On Exercise 4, Steps 1c through 1g.

Tip

If the logo image is too large or looks disproportionate, click the image to select it and display the sizing handles. Click and drag a sizing handle to adjust the height and width of the image. Use a top or bottom handle to adjust the height, use a side handle to adjust the width, or use a corner handle to adjust height and width at the same time.

h. If necessary, adjust the height and width of the image.

i. Click the **Describe your changes** text box and type **Added GSU logo**.

j. Click the **Save** button to save your changes.

H – Click and drag sizing handles

I – Type description of changes here

J – Click to save changes

Figure 5.43 Hands-On Exercise 4, Steps 1h through 1j.

Step 2 Embed a YouTube Video on a Wiki Page

Refer to Figures 5.44 through 5.59 as you complete Step 2.

Professor Schmeckendorf located an interesting video on YouTube about increasing a Wi-Fi signal when using a laptop. This video is a few years old and some of the equipment is a bit outdated, but it introduces some interesting topics that can be used for class discussion. He has decided to embed the video on the **Student Research** page so that students can view it.

a. Open a new browser tab or window and type **http://youtu.be/LY8Wi7XRXCA** in the address bar. This will take you to the video on the YouTube site. You can watch the video or click the **Pause** button to stop it.

b. Click the **Share** button to display the various video sharing options.

c. Click the **Embed** button to display the embed code.

d. The current embed code may not be recognized as a video by PBworks. Click the **Use old embed code** checkbox to change the code in the **Embed** text box.

e. Click anywhere in the **Embed** text box to select the code. Right-click in the **Embed** textbox and select **Copy** from the shortcut menu to copy the code.

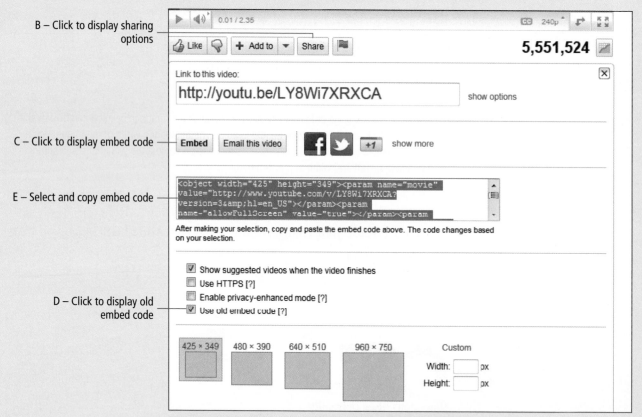

Figure 5.44 Hands-On Exercise 4, Steps 2b through 2e.

f. Return to the wiki and navigate to the **Student Research** page. Click the **Edit** tab at the top of the page to enter the edit mode.

g. Type the following text below the current text on the page:

Here is a helpful video on extending your Wi-Fi signal.

h. Position the insertion point two lines below the text you just typed.

i. On the toolbar, click **Insert**, select **Video**, and then **YouTube,** to display the **Insert Plugin** dialog box.

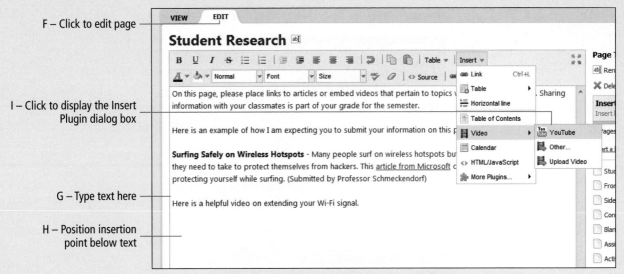

F – Click to edit page

I – Click to display the Insert Plugin dialog box

G – Type text here

H – Position insertion point below text

Figure 5.45 Hands-On Exercise 4, Steps 2f through 2i.

j. In the **Insert Plugin** text box, right-click and select **Paste** from the shortcut menu to paste the embed code that you copied from the YouTube site.

k. Click the **Next** button to preview the YouTube video. This ensures that the embed code is working properly.

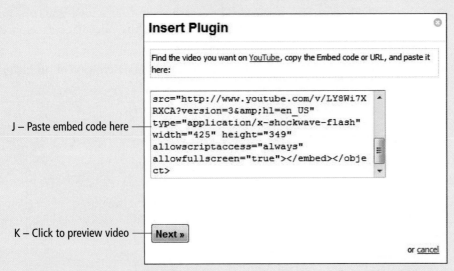

J – Paste embed code here

K – Click to preview video

Figure 5.46 Hands-On Exercise 4, Steps 2j and 2k.

The video should display in the **Insert Plugin** dialog box similar to how it appears on YouTube.

l. Click the **Play** button (large arrow) to test the video and ensure that it is working properly. If it does not work, click the **Back** button and try copying and pasting the embed code from YouTube again.

m. If the video appears to play properly, click the **Insert Plugin** button to embed the video on the wiki page.

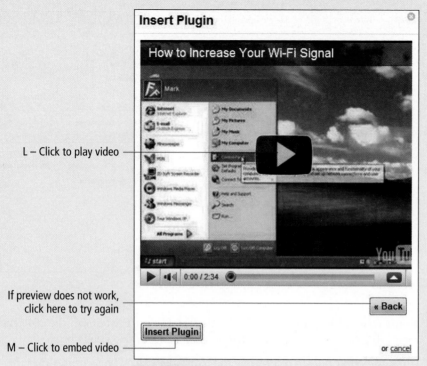

L – Click to play video

If preview does not work, click here to try again

M – Click to embed video

Figure 5.47 Hands-On Exercise 4, Steps 2l and 2m.

There should now be a large shaded box on the wiki page with a YouTube logo in the center of it (Figure 5.48). This indicates that the video has been embedded on the page.

n. In the **Describe your changes** text box, type a brief description of the changes you just made.

o. Click the **Save** button to save your changes to the page.

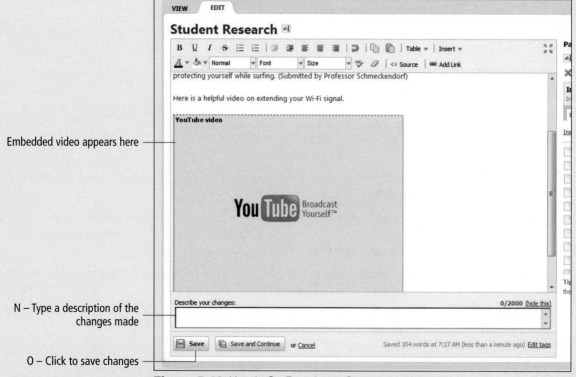

N – Type a description of the changes made

O – Click to save changes

Figure 5.48 Hands-On Exercise 4, Steps 2n and 2o.

The **Student Research** page should display in view mode (Figure 5.49). The video is embedded and ready to be viewed by anyone accessing the **Student Research** page.

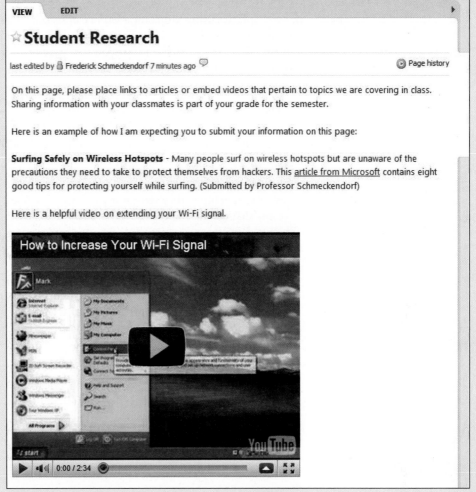

Figure 5.49 Student Research page with a YouTube video embedded and ready for viewing.

You may now log out of your PBworks account and close your browser.

Objective 9

Explore wiki resources

Many people are using wikis for a variety of reasons. Consequently, there is a wealth of information on the Internet that can help you learn more about creating wikis or help you locate wikis with information that may be of interest to you. Here are some resources you may want to explore:

- PBworks Educational Edition Manual (**http://usermanual.pbworks.com**)— There are other features available on PBworks that you can explore as you develop wikis for your own use. The *PBworks Educational Edition Manual* is a Help file that contains more information on using the PBworks site.

- Wikipatterns (**www.wikipatterns.com**)—A site geared toward making wikis viable business tools. The authors identify useful methodologies for increasing wiki readership and contributor participation. They also identify negative patterns that can drive people away from your wiki.

- Wikispaces Blog (**http://blog.wikispaces.com**)—Wikispaces is a free wiki hosting service. The information in this blog ranges from specific details for using the Wikispaces tools to general best practices for wiki users.

- Wikis in Education (**http://wikisineducation.wetpaint.com**)—A wiki that helps educators and students figure out effective ways to use wikis in the educational process. The wiki is hosted on Wetpaint, which is another free wiki hosting service that is easy to learn to use.

- Educause Wiki—132 Resources (**http://www.educause.edu/Resources/ Browse/Wiki/18426**)—The name says it all. This wiki from Educause has helpful information in a variety of formats including presentations, publications, podcasts, and blogs.

Summary

You have now learned many of the basic skills needed for creating and managing wikis. The main thing that makes a wiki effective is the community behind the wiki. If you attract committed, knowledgeable individuals who are willing to contribute to and edit information on your wiki, it can be very successful. Remember that the basis of most wikis is collaborating on the development of textual information. Yes, you can add images and videos to wikis, but use them sparingly and only when they are most effective for communicating information. Gratuitous use of multimedia can detract from an otherwise effective wiki.

Key Terms

Multiple Choice Questions

1. Links from one page on a wiki to another page on the same wiki are known as

   (a) internal links.

   (b) wiki links.

   (c) external links.

   (d) page links.

2. Wikipedia

   (a) is never accurate.

   (b) is an online encyclopedia written by unpaid volunteers.

   (c) can only be edited by people who have a Wikipedia account.

   (d) refuses to accept donations for funding.

3. A process by which experts in a given field review another author's scholarly work to determine that the output is valid and substantially correct is known as

   (a) wiki comparison.

   (b) peer review.

   (c) editing.

   (d) author review.

4. Individuals who write inflammatory messages on wikis just to provoke emotional responses from readers are known as

   (a) Internet vandals.

   (b) wiki wise guys.

   (c) wiki haters.

   (d) Internet trolls.

5. A group of computers set up to host multiple wikis at the same time is known as a wiki

   (a) forest.

   (b) farm.

   (c) community.

   (d) silo.

6. Which is the recommended permission level to grant to users of a PBworks account?

   (a) Administrator

   (b) Reader

   (c) Editor

   (d) Writer

7. Readers, writers, and editors are the basic people who make up a wiki

   (a) editorial team.

   (b) dream team.

   (c) commune.

   (d) community.

8. Erroneous information intentionally posted on a wiki is a type of wiki

   (a) error.

   (b) uncertainty.

   (c) vandalism.

   (d) validation problem.

9. Which of the following would *not* be acceptable to add to Wikipedia?

   (a) Speculation about the plot line of the next *Spiderman* movie.

   (b) Information about potential victims of the Holocaust who were rescued by German citizens during World War II.

   (c) The results of a research project that measured tidal flows at the New Jersey shoreline.

   (d) Blueprints of experimental weapons that were developed by the United States during the Vietnam War.

10. A common use for wikis by individuals is

    (a) note taking in a college class.

    (b) coordinating group projects for a college class.

    (c) planning a wedding.

    (d) All of the above.

Fill in the Blank

1. The word *wiki* is a Hawaiian word that means _____.

2. The page for a Wikipedia entry that shows which individuals have worked on writing and editing the page is known as the _____ _____ _____.

3. MediaWiki, the software that powers Wikipedia, is available to anyone who wants to use it because it is published under the _____ _____ _____ _____.

4. Links on a wiki that lead to web pages that are not part of the wiki itself are known as _____ _____.

5. The _____ is the first page that is set up on a wiki hosted by PBworks.

Practice Exercises

Note: Successful completion of these exercises assumes that the student has completed all of the Hands-On Exercises located in this chapter.

1. **Extending the Student Research Page of Professor Schmeckendorf's Wiki**

   Professor Schmeckendorf's vision for the **Student Research** page in his wiki is to make it a resource for students who want to learn more about information technology. In this exercise, you will add information to the **Student Research** page on the wiki you created in the Hands-On Exercises.

   (a) On the Internet, find an article on an information technology ethics issue (such as green computing, content filtering, plagiarism, or copyright infringement).

   (b) Search YouTube and locate one video that teaches about some aspect of information technology (such as how to build your own computer).

   (c) Open your preferred browser and navigate to PBworks.com.

   (d) Log in to your PBworks account and access your wiki.

   (e) Navigate to the **Student Research** page. Click the **Edit** tab at the top of the page to enter edit mode.

   (f) Write a short synopsis of the ethics article you found on the Internet and enter it on the **Student Research** page.

   (g) Create an external link to the article as a textual link in the synopsis.

   (h) Write a short sentence or two introducing the video you found and enter it on the **Student Research** page.

   (i) Using the techniques you learned in this chapter, embed the YouTube video on the **Student Research** page.

   (j) Type a brief description of the changes you made to the paper and click the **Save** button to save the edits you made to the page.

   (k) Print out the completed page and submit it to your instructor, or take a screenshot of the completed page and email it to your instructor. Log out of PBworks and close your browser.

2. **Create a New Page for Professor Schmeckendorf's Wiki**

   Professor Schmeckendorf has decided that each student in the class should introduce himself or herself to the other class members through the wiki. In this assignment, you will set up a new page on the wiki to facilitate this interaction.

   (a) Open your preferred browser and navigate to PBworks.com.

   (b) Log in to your PBworks account and access your wiki.

   (c) Click on the **Create a page** link.

   (d) Type **Student Introductions** in the **Name your page** box.

   (e) Click the **Blank page** option to select it.

(f) Click the **Create page** button to create the new page.

(g) Type the following at the top of the new page and format it using the Heading 1 style:

On this page you should write your name, explain your objectives for taking this class, and write a brief summary of your computer skills.

(h) On the second line (under the sentence you just typed), type your name and provide the information requested by Professor Schmeckendorf. Your goals should relate to the class for which you are completing this assignment.

(i) Add a brief description of the changes you made to the page and click the **Save** button to save your edits to the **Student Introductions** page.

(j) Print out the completed page and submit it to your instructor, or take a screenshot of the completed page and email it to your instructor. Log out of PBworks and close your browser.

3. **Add a Picture to Professor Schmeckendorf's Contact Information**

Professor Schmeckendorf has located an old picture of himself during his early days at GSU. He would like you to place it on his **Contact Information** page on the wiki.

(a) Open your preferred browser and navigate to PBworks.com.

(b) Log in to your PBworks account and access your wiki.

(c) Navigate to the **Contact Information** page in your wiki. Click the **Edit** tab at the top of the page to enter the edit mode.

(d) Click the **Images and files** link to display the **Upload files** link.

(e) Click the **Upload files** link to display the **Upload a File** dialog box. Navigate to the folder where you saved your Chapter 5 student data files and select the **Professor_Schmeckendorf.jpg** file. Click the **Open** button in the dialog box to upload the file to the wiki. A link for the file will appear in the area below the **Upload files** link.

(f) Insert two blank lines above the text that is already on the **Contact Information** page. Position the insertion point at the top-left corner of the page.

(g) Click the **Professor_Schmeckendorf.jpg** link to insert the file on the **Contact Information** page.

(h) Resize the photo as needed by clicking it and using the sizing handles.

(i) When you have adjusted the image to an appropriate size, type a brief description of the changes you made to the page and click the **Save** button to save your edits to the **Contact Information** page.

(j) Print out the completed page and submit it to your instructor, or take a screenshot of the completed page and email it to your instructor. Log out of PBworks and close your browser.

Critical Thinking

1. Including images on a wiki can help readers understand ideas and concepts. However, just taking images that you find on the Internet and using them is usually not appropriate, because most images are subject to copyright protections. Write a brief paper outlining the steps a wiki user should take to ensure that any images found on the Internet can be used on the wiki and do not violate someone's copyright.

2. There are numerous wiki hosting services that provide free wiki hosting to individuals and businesses. Other than PBworks, investigate at least two other free wiki hosting services. Write a short paper describing the advantages and disadvantages of each hosting service and compare and contrast their features to those of PBworks.

Team Projects

1. As a small group, consider how you could benefit from setting up a wiki as a study aid for a class that you are all taking. Write a short paper explaining how your wiki would be set up, what pages you would have in your wiki, and the duties and responsibilities of each member of the wiki community (frequency of contributions, expectations for editing other members' contributions, etc.).

2. As a group, locate at least four wikis (not including Wikipedia) that pertain to computers and technology. Create a table that lists the title and URL for each wiki and the main topics that it covers. Review the contents of the wiki, focusing on wiki pages that are up-to-date. Your instructor may determine a time frame for articles, but anything edited within the last six months may be acceptable. Remember that this can be determined by checking a wiki's history pages. Rate each of the wikis using the following criteria:

   - How current is the information on the wiki?

   - Does the wiki contain sufficient depth for all topics that it is supposed to cover?

   - Is the wiki well written? Are there a lot of spelling and grammatical errors? Is it easy to understand?

   - How would you suggest improving the wiki?

   - Which of the four wikis do you think is the best? Which is the worst?

   Include your findings on the table and submit it to your instructor.

Credits

Figures 5.7, 5.9–5.49, Screenshots retrieved from http://pbworks.com, reprinted by permission from PBWiki, Inc.
Exercises 1–4, Screenshots retrieved from http://pbworks.com, reprinted by permission from PBWiki, Inc.
Answer keys, Screenshots retrieved from http://pbworks.com, reprinted by permission from PBWiki, Inc.
Student Data Files, Courtesy of NASA.

CHAPTER 6

Additional Collaboration Tools

Objectives

After you read this chapter, you will be able to:

1. Explain what Twitter is and why you would use it

2. Create and use a Twitter account

3. Communicate with and expand your Twitter audience

4. Explore multimedia sharing sites

5. Manage multiple social media profiles

6. Explore resources for additional collaboration tools

The following Hands-On Exercises will help you accomplish the chapter objectives:

Hands-On Exercises

EXERCISES	SKILLS COVERED
1. Set Up a Twitter Account and Create a Profile (page 264)	**Step 1:** Start Your Browser and Navigate to Twitter **Step 2:** Create a Twitter Account **Step 3:** Complete Your Twitter Profile and Adjust Your Settings
2. Locate and Follow Useful Twitter Sources (page 274)	**Step 1:** Log In to Twitter and Use the Browse Interests Feature **Step 2:** Follow a User **Step 3:** Use the Search Tool to Locate and Follow a User
3. Send a Tweet, Reply to a Tweet, and Retweet a Tweet (page 281)	**Step 1:** Create and Send a Tweet **Step 2:** Reply to a Tweet **Step 3:** Retweet a Tweet
4. Create a YouTube Account and Upload a Video (page 285)	**Step 1:** Create a YouTube Account and Channel **Step 2:** Update Account Settings **Step 3:** Subscribe to a Channel **Step 4:** Upload a Video
5. Create a HootSuite Account (page 299)	**Step 1:** Create a HootSuite Account **Step 2:** Add Social Networks **Step 3:** Send an Update

Objective 1

Explain what Twitter is and why you would use it

What is Twitter?

Microblog A type of blog that is used to create very brief posts limited to a set number of characters per post; in Twitter's case, this limit is 140 characters.

Tweet A brief post created by users of Twitter.

Twitter is a type of Web 2.0 tool known as a microblog. Similar to blogs, a *microblog* permits users to share information, but the posts are limited in size. In Twitter's case, users can create a post, known as a *tweet*, which is up to 140 characters in length. These brief posts are similar to the status updates users create on social networks.

What is Twitter used for?

Many people are still trying to sort out how and why they would use Twitter. Describing itself as a "real-time information network," Twitter asks you, "What's happening?" Your response becomes your tweet. When Twitter first launched in 2006, it quickly became popular with celebrities and marketing people. Both of these groups see the value of being able to quickly share tidbits of information with a wide group of followers.

As Twitter use has grown, it has become involved in a number of breaking news stories. One of the most notable stories involved the raid on Osama bin Laden's compound in May 2011. The actual event was live-tweeted by a neighbor who was unaware of the significance of the night's activities until after the fact. The unofficial news of bin Laden's death was broken on Twitter by a government staffer, and Twitter reported that over 4,000 tweets per second were sent during President Obama's speech confirming the raid.

Novice Twitter users often take Twitter's "What's happening?" question literally, posting updates about their day-to-day, and sometimes minute-by-minute, activities. However, there are more productive uses for Twitter. Twitter, like all Web 2.0 tools, is a community, and communities work best when everyone communicates and provides worthwhile information. While Twitter is a good networking tool for promoting yourself and possibly your company or your services, you should be sure that you are also giving back to the community. Some of the ways you might use Twitter include:

- Gathering information—Are you looking for recommendations for a new computer or searching for a job? Posting a question on Twitter may provide you with some useful information.

- Staying current—Many organizations now use Twitter to post quick updates about newsworthy events, conferences, and product launches.

- Publicizing noteworthy activities—Send a tweet to notify your followers when you've updated your blog or podcast and include a link to your site.

- Sharing information—Have you found a useful article online? Are you stuck in the middle of a huge traffic jam? You can send a tweet to quickly share this information.

Twitter usage is increasing. A May 2011 study by the Pew Internet and American Life Project reveals that 13 percent of adults online are using Twitter, up from 8 percent in November 2010. The majority of Twitter users are between the ages of 18 and 49 and have attended at least some college.

Can anyone join Twitter?

Follow To select a specific Twitter user's account in order to receive that user's updates.

Anyone can create a Twitter account. Once you have an account, you can search for people you know and *follow* them, which means you will receive their Twitter account updates on your Twitter homepage. By default, your Twitter account is public and anyone can choose to follow you (Figure 6.1). You do not have to ask for, or give, permission to follow someone or to be followed, although you will receive an email notification when you have a new follower. Your tweets are also public by default, which means that anyone can search for and find your tweets. Unlike social networks, Twitter does not have reciprocal relationships, meaning it is possible to follow someone who does not follow you, as well as for others to follow you even if you don't follow them.

Click to follow this Twitter user —

Additional details about this Twitter user —

List of recent tweets —

Figure 6.1 The Twitter homepage for Pearson Learning shows the team's most recent tweets.

If you are concerned about privacy, you can take steps to protect your account. With a protected account, no one can follow you without your approval and your tweets will not be visible to anyone who does not already follow you. This also prevents your approved followers from sending your tweets to others and prevents you from replying to users who do not follow you.

Because of Twitter's inherent lack of privacy, think carefully about the personal information you provide in your profile and your tweets. You should never consider anything that you send by Twitter to be confidential or private.

Objective 2

Create and use a Twitter account

As with many Web 2.0 applications, there are two ways to use Twitter. You can be an active participant—creating and sending tweets, replying to tweets received from others, and sharing interesting tweets you receive. Or, you can choose to be an observer and simply follow the tweets of individuals and organizations that interest you. Whether you choose to be a participant or an observer, you don't have to use a mobile device, such as a smartphone, to use Twitter. You can create an account and use Twitter from your desktop or laptop computer. In fact, according to the Pew study, almost half of all users do just that.

Hands-On Exercises

Professor Schmeckendorf has decided to use Twitter to communicate with his students, network with his peers, and obtain up-to-date industry information. This Hands-On Exercise will create an account using Professor Schmeckendorf's information; you will be creating an account for yourself and should add your own information where appropriate.

1 | Set Up a Twitter Account and Create a Profile

Steps: 1. Start Your Browser and Navigate to Twitter; **2.** Create a Twitter Account; **3.** Complete Your Twitter Profile and Adjust Your Settings.

Use Figures 6.2 through 6.14 as a guide to the exercise.

Step 1 | Start Your Browser and Navigate to Twitter

Refer to Figure 6.2 as you complete Step 1.

If you already have a Twitter account, sign in to your account and skip to Step 3e to adjust your profile settings.

a. Turn on your computer and start your preferred browser (Internet Explorer, Firefox, Chrome, Safari, etc.).

b. Type **http://twitter.com** in the address bar of your browser and press **Enter**.

c. On the right side of the page, under **New to Twitter?**, in the **Full name** text box, type your name.

d. In the **Email** text box, type a valid email address. Twitter will send an email to this address to verify your Twitter account.

e. In the **Password** text box, type a secure password. Your Twitter password must be at least 6 characters and cannot contain any blank spaces. However, a secure password should be at least 8 to 12 characters in length and consist of a combination of upper and lowercase letters, numbers, and symbols. It should not be a word in a dictionary or something that someone who knows you can easily guess.

f. Click the **Sign up** button to proceed to the next step.

Figure 6.2 Hands-On Exercise 1, Steps 1c through 1f.

Step 2 Create a Twitter Account

Refer to Figure 6.3 as you complete Step 2.

The **Create an Account** page displays with the information you entered in Step 1. Twitter has added a comment at the end of each item to provide additional information.

a. Review the information in the first two text boxes to be sure your name and email address are correct.

b. Read the comment next to the **Password** text box. In Figure 6.3, you will see that Twitter indicates Professor Schmeckendorf's password is okay and the status bar is only half full. Ideally, the status bar should be completely green and Twitter's comment should indicate that your password is perfect. If necessary, follow the suggestions in Step 1e to create a more secure password.

c. In the fourth text box, Twitter has created a possible username for your account. If you are happy with this suggestion, proceed to Step 2d. Twitter also provides several other suggestions below the text box. You can click one of these if you'd like to use it. If you do not care for any of Twitter's suggested usernames, delete the suggested username in the text box and create one of your own. The comment next to the text box will let you know if the name you create is available. Your username must be unique and does not have to be your actual name. You can also change your username at any time, without having to create a new account. Since Professor Schmeckendorf does not like Twitter's suggestion, he will change his username to *PSchmeckendorf*.

d. Use the scroll bar to review the **Terms of Service** for Twitter.

e. Click the **Create my account** button to create your Twitter account.

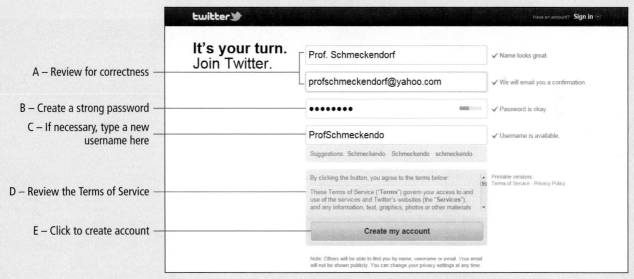

A – Review for correctness

B – Create a strong password

C – If necessary, type a new username here

D – Review the Terms of Service

E – Click to create account

Figure 6.3 Hands-On Exercise 1, Steps 2a through 2e.

Step 3 Complete Your Twitter Profile and Adjust Your Settings

Refer to Figures 6.4 through 6.14 as you complete Step 3.

a. The **Interests** page displays with suggested Twitter users and organizations, sorted by topic. Professor Schmeckendorf will not make any selections at this time, but he will revisit this information later. Click the **Next Step: Friends** button to proceed to the next page.

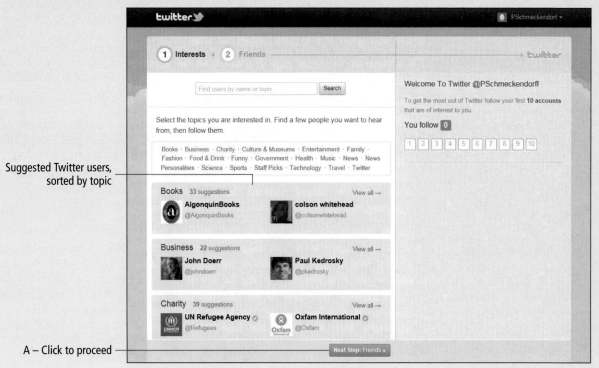

Suggested Twitter users, sorted by topic

A – Click to proceed

Figure 6.4 Hands-On Exercise 1, Step 3a.

b. The **Friends** page gives you the option to import Twitter users from your email account address book. Professor Schmeckendorf will skip this step also. Click the **Skip import** button to proceed to the next page.

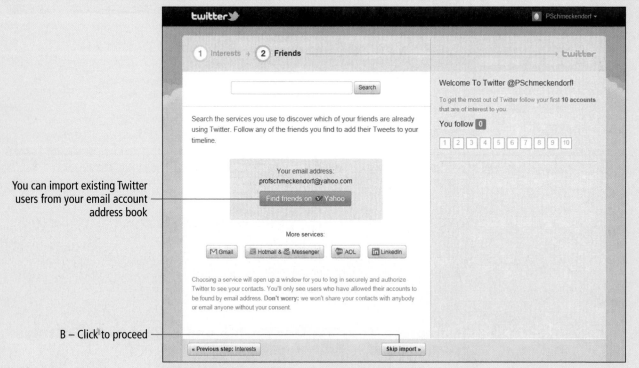

You can import existing Twitter users from your email account address book

B – Click to proceed

Figure 6.5 Hands-On Exercise 1, Step 3b.

Your Twitter homepage displays. Since you have not yet selected anyone to follow, there are no tweets on the left side of the page. The right side of the page contains a list of steps you can take to get started using Twitter. However, there are still some things that need to be done before you start tweeting.

c. At the top of the page you should see a notification bar indicating that you need to confirm your email change. The change Twitter is referring to is the addition of your email address to this account. Open a new browser tab or window and navigate to the email account you used when you created your Twitter account.

C – Message bar indicating email address has not been verified

Suggested tasks for getting started with Twitter

Type your own tweet here

Tweets will appear here when you begin following other Twitter users

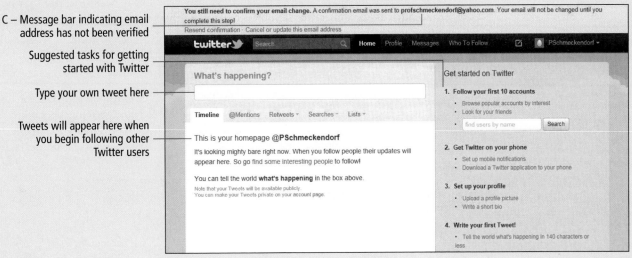

Figure 6.6 Hands-On Exercise 1, Step 3c.

d. In your email account, locate a message from Twitter with a subject line containing the phrase *Confirm your Twitter account* followed by your username. Open this email and click the link that it contains to confirm your Twitter account. Once you've confirmed your account, you will receive a Welcome email from Twitter providing some helpful tips for how to use this service. It is not necessary to read the Welcome email now.

e. Your Twitter homepage will open in a new browser tab or window. Sign out of your email account and close any other open browser tabs or windows. Click your username at the top right of the page to display a drop-down menu and click **Settings**.

Alert

If the notification message about your email address change still appears at the top of your homepage, try refreshing your page. If the message still appears, return to your email account and click the link in your email message again. When your homepage reopens, the message should be gone. Remember to close any extra browser tabs or windows that may be open.

E – Click username and then Settings

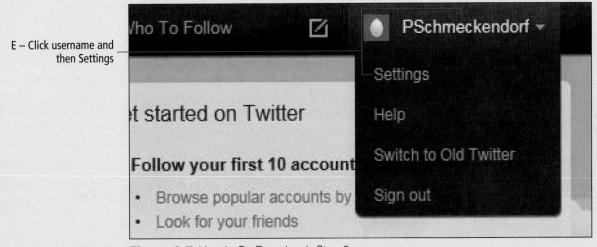

Figure 6.7 Hands-On Exercise 1, Step 3e.

The **Settings** page allows you to modify many different areas of your Twitter account, including your account privacy settings and notifications.

f. The **Settings** page should open with the **Account** tab already selected. Review the information displayed on this page. In the **Email** section, if you want people to be able to find you by your email address, leave the **Let others find me by my email address** box checked. If you do not want others to find you via your email address, click the checkbox to uncheck it.

g. If necessary, use the **Time Zone** drop-down box to select the correct time zone for your location.

h. The **Tweet Location** option is used to allow Twitter to track and store your location and share it with others when you send a tweet. It is disabled, and therefore unchecked, by default. If you want to turn this feature on, click the checkbox to add a check mark. Professor Schmeckendorf does not wish to use this feature, so he will leave it unchecked.

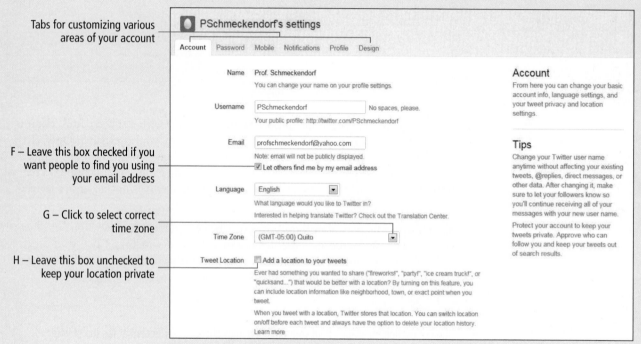

Figure 6.8 Hands-On Exercise 1, Steps 3f through 3h.

i. The **Tweet Media** option is used to reduce the risk of viewing objectionable or unwanted materials on Twitter. If the box is left unchecked, you will only be able to see photos and videos sent by people whom you are following. Professor Schmeckendorf will leave this box unchecked.

j. Remember that, by default, your Twitter account is public and viewable by anybody. The **Tweet Privacy** option allows you to make your Twitter account private. If you check this box, only followers whom you have approved will be able to see your tweets. At this time, Professor Schmeckendorf prefers to leave his account public, so this box will remain unchecked. Note that you can change this preference at any time. If you choose to make your account private at some later time, older tweets may still be publicly available, but future tweets will be private.

k. The **HTTPS Only** option provides a greater level of security, especially when using an unsecured wireless connection, such as a public Wi-Fi hotspot in a local coffee shop or restaurant. Click this checkbox to add a check mark and make your Twitter activity more secure.

l. Click the **Save** button to save the changes you have made to your **Account** settings.

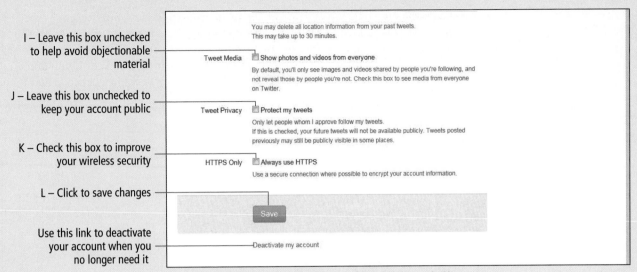

I – Leave this box unchecked to help avoid objectionable material

J – Leave this box unchecked to keep your account public

K – Check this box to improve your wireless security

L – Click to save changes

Use this link to deactivate your account when you no longer need it

Figure 6.9 Hands-On Exercise 1, Steps 3i through 3l.

The **Deactivate my account** link at the bottom of the **Account** tab on the **Settings** page enables you to close your Twitter account if you choose not to use it. Don't click this link now, but if you decide that you don't want to continue using Twitter at the conclusion of this course, you should return to the **Settings** page and deactivate your account, rather than simply abandoning it. This will help to prevent hackers from gaining access to your account and using it without your knowledge.

m. A **Save account changes** dialog box will display. In the **Password** text box, type the password for your Twitter account to confirm that you have requested these changes.

n. Click the **Save changes** button to save your account changes. A message indicating that your settings were saved will appear briefly at the top of the page.

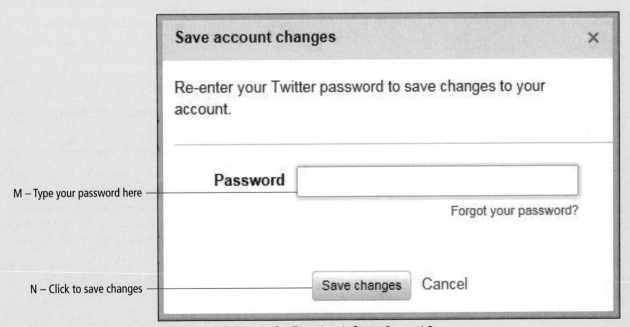

M – Type your password here

N – Click to save changes

Figure 6.10 Hands-On Exercise 1, Steps 3m and 3n.

o. Click the **Notifications** tab at the top of the page to review what types of email messages Twitter can send to you and how often these messages are sent. All the choices on this page are checked by default. Professor Schmeckendorf wants to receive these notifications; therefore he will leave them all checked. If you don't wish to receive an email for a specific item, simply uncheck the checkbox and then click the **Save** button.

O – Click to review how Twitter communicates with you

Uncheck the appropriate item to stop receiving notifications

Click to save any changes

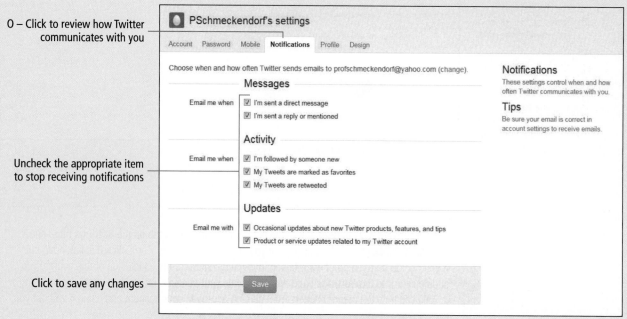

Figure 6.11 Hands-On Exercise 1, Step 3o.

p. Click the **Profile** tab at the top of the page. The items on this page help to personalize your Twitter account and help to identify you to people who may be searching for you. All these items are optional—you do not have to provide any of this information if you are concerned about security or privacy. These items will also appear in your public profile and include:

- Picture—Upload a picture to display alongside your tweets to help people identify you.

- Name—Twitter suggests adding your full name.

- Location—You can be as specific or as general as you like.

- Web—If you have a website or a blog, this is a good way to help publicize it.

- Bio—Add a little information about yourself, using fewer than 160 characters.

q. Professor Schmeckendorf has decided he wants to include some info in the **Bio** text box, but will not make any changes to any of the other options. You should update your profile according to your own preferences. Click the **Bio** text box and type your information. Professor Schmeckendorf will type **Computer Science instructor at Ginormous State University**.

r. Click the **Save** button to save your changes.

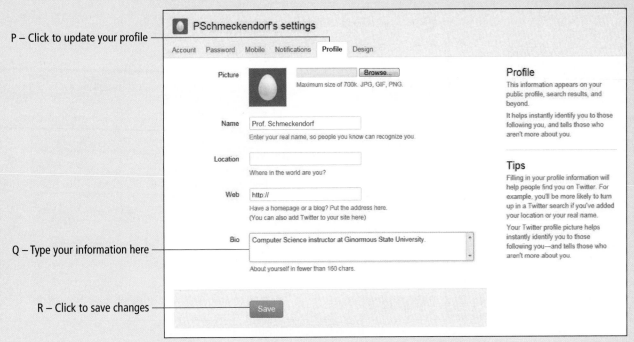

Figure 6.12 Hands-On Exercise 1, Steps 3p through 3r.

s. Click the **Design** tab. On this page, you can select a theme for your homepage. You can also upload a photo to use as your background image and change the design colors for various page components. Professor Schmeckendorf will choose one of the pre-designed themes.

t. Click on a theme to see how it will appear on your page. If you don't like your first choice, click another theme to see how that one will look. The theme you choose will be applied to most of the pages on your Twitter account, including the **Design** tab. However, the **Settings** section will continue to display the default Twitter theme on all tabs except the **Design** tab.

u. Once you've found a theme you like, click the **Save Changes** button to confirm your choice.

v. At the top of the page, click the **Profile** link (not the **Profile** tab) to view your Twitter profile page.

V – Click to view your profile page

S – Click to change your account's theme

T – Click a theme to apply it

U – Click to save changes

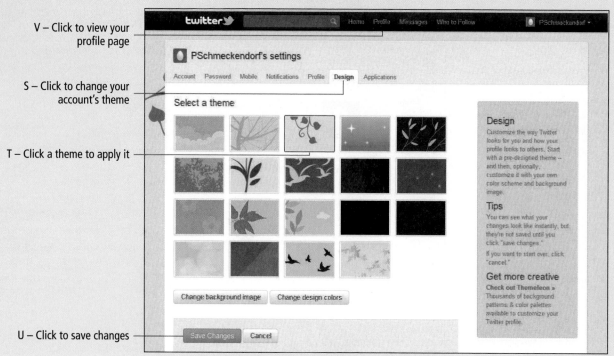

Figure 6.13 Hands-On Exercise 1, Steps 3s through 3v.

When you first create your Twitter account, you will see two other tabs for your Twitter settings. You can use the **Password** tab to create and confirm a new password and the **Mobile** tab to set up your Twitter account to use text messaging on your mobile phone. Professor Schmeckendorf does not intend to use Twitter on his phone and does not need to change his password, so he won't use these tabs now. However, you may want to review the information on each of these tabs for future reference. The **Applications** tab (shown in Figure 6.13) will not appear until you authorize a third-party application to access your Twitter account.

If you added a profile picture, website address, or bio, or if you changed your theme, you should see these changes on your profile page. Professor Schmeckendorf's profile page is shown in Figure 6.14. When you are done viewing your profile page, click on your username at the top right of the page and click **Sign out** to log out of your account and then close your browser.

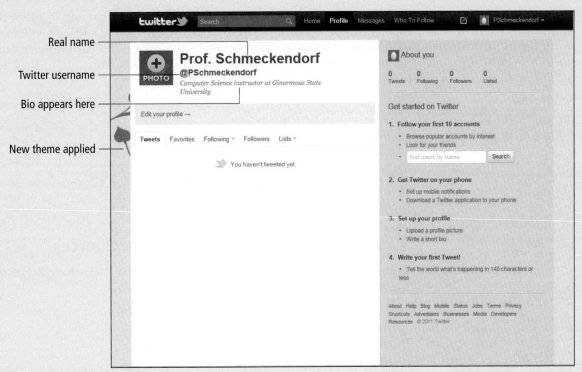

Real name

Twitter username

Bio appears here

New theme applied

Figure 6.14 Professor Schmeckendorf's profile page is shown with the bio he added and the new theme he applied.

Objective 3

Communicate with and expand your Twitter audience

Who should I follow on Twitter?

Now that you have a Twitter account, it is time to start interacting with other Twitter users. You will get the most value from your Twitter account if you are selective about whom you choose to follow. You might start out following other Twitter users whom you know personally, but you don't have to know someone to follow him or her. Here are some other types of Twitter accounts you should consider following:

- Organizations—Many businesses and charities now have Twitter accounts. You can follow a business to learn about new products, receive press releases, get news updates, and learn about sales or discounts for Twitter users. Don't forget to see if your school uses Twitter!

- Industry Leaders—Follow key people in your field of study or work to stay up-to-date on industry news and happenings. Consider following the CEO of a company, journalists in your industry, or a noted spokesperson.

- Hobbies—If you have a hobby—sports, music, dance, and so on—there's a good chance that someone involved in one of these areas has a Twitter account.

- Celebrities—Although Ashton Kutcher and Demi Moore may be the most widely known Twitter celebrities, they aren't the only ones. See if any of your favorites use Twitter and get the inside scoop on their activities.

- Other Followers—Once you start following a Twitter user, it can be useful to see who that user also follows. Similarly, once you start to get followers of your own, check to see who else they follow. You may find some interesting sources this way.

Many websites now include the Twitter icon to make it easy to follow the site. Twitter also wants to help you get started using its service, so it provides several different ways to locate other Twitter users. You can use Twitter's search tool that appears at the top of each page or use the **Who To Follow** link. In the next Hands-On Exercise, you will locate and follow some Twitter users.

Hands-On Exercises

2 | Locate and Follow Useful Twitter Sources

Steps: 1. Log In to Twitter and Use the Browse Interests Feature; **2.** Follow a User; **3.** Use the Search Tool to Locate and Follow a User.

Use Figures 6.15 through 6.22 as a guide to the exercise.

Step **1   Log In to Twitter and Use the Browse Interests Feature**

Refer to Figures 6.15 through 6.17 as you complete Step 1.

a. Start your browser and type **http://twitter.com** in the address bar.

b. In the **Username** text box, type your Twitter username or email address.

c. In the **Password** text box, type the password for your Twitter account.

d. Click the **Sign in** button to proceed.

Figure 6.15 Hands-On Exercise 2, Steps 1b through 1d.

e. Your Twitter account opens with your homepage displayed. From the menu bar at the top of the page, click the **Who To Follow** link.

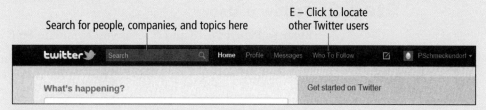

Search for people, companies, and topics here

E – Click to locate other Twitter users

Figure 6.16 Hands-On Exercise 2, Step 1e.

The **Who to follow** page has three tabs. The **View Suggestions** tab contains a list of accounts that might interest you. As you increase your use of Twitter and begin to follow others, Twitter will begin to provide suggestions that are related to your usage. The **Browse Interests** tab displays a number of categories, each of which has a selection of users suggested by Twitter. The third tab is the **Find Friends** tab, which allows you to search your email address book for existing Twitter users.

f. Click the **Browse Interests** tab and review the topics Twitter has selected.

g. Scroll down to the bottom of the page and locate the **Twitter** topic. Click the **20 suggestions** link to display the entire list.

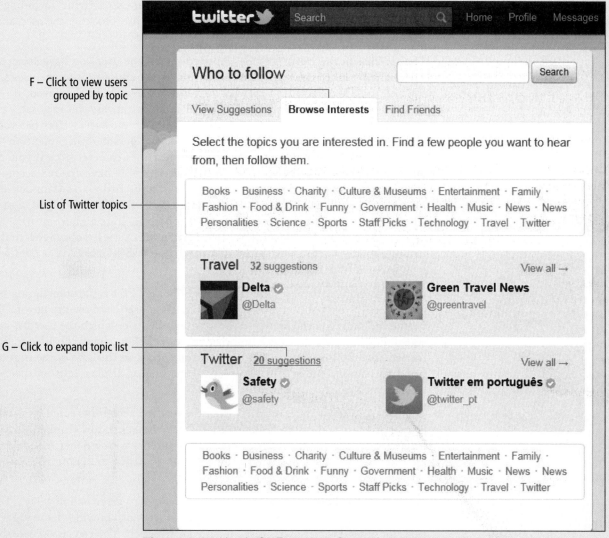

F – Click to view users grouped by topic

List of Twitter topics

G – Click to expand topic list

Figure 6.17 Hands-On Exercise 2, Steps 1f and 1g.

Step 2 | Follow a User

Refer to Figures 6.18 and 6.19 as you complete Step 2.

a. Locate the Twitter account named **Safety** and click the link to display a sidebar containing more details about this user on the right side of the page.

Due to the ever-changing nature of Twitter, some of the Twitter accounts used in this exercise may be listed in a different order or may have been closed. If you don't see a specific account, try to locate something similar and use that instead.

The left side of the page displays the expanded category list containing links to the Twitter accounts in the category, including the **Safety** account you just selected. If a user has uploaded a photo or added a bio, this information is also displayed on this side of the page. The **Follow** button allows you to quickly select those users you'd like to follow. To the right of the **Follow** button is a button showing the profile of a person, known as the **Person** icon. Clicking this icon displays a drop-down menu with options for that user account, including mentioning the user in a tweet, adding the user to a list, blocking the user, and reporting the user for spam.

The sidebar on the right provides an overview of the user you have selected. This pane includes the user's name and username, and a link to the user's full profile. The user's bio and website address may also be displayed, if the user has provided this information. In some instances, you may see a blue check mark next to a user's name. This indicates that Twitter has verified this account and that it belongs to the actual person or organization whose name is displayed. It can be difficult at times to determine if you have found the right person, especially if other people have created accounts with similar names. For example, a quick search for Bill Gates (founder of Microsoft) reveals multiple accounts, including Bill_Microsoft, BillGates-Zune, bill_gates, and BillGatess, many of which include a photo of Bill Gates and references to Microsoft. However, none of these accounts actually belongs to Bill Gates! Bill Gates' real username is BillGates and is confirmed by Twitter's blue check mark.

Below the user's name is a summary of his or her Twitter activity including how many tweets have been sent, how many people the user is following, how many people are following the user, and the number of lists to which the user has been added. Each of these items is a link that you can click to view additional information. The **Follow** button and **Person** icon appear on this side of the page also, below the summary area. The lower half of the sidebar displays a list of the most recent tweets by this user.

b. The **Safety** sidebar indicates that this is a verified account created to share Twitter's trust and safety updates. Professor Schmeckendorf thinks this may be a useful Twitter account, especially for students who are just learning how to use Twitter. Click the **Follow** button to begin following the **Safety** account.

Notice that the **Follow** button's appearance changes to green and now says "Following" once you have followed the account. Twitter also provides some suggestions for other Twitter users, based upon your selection. You can choose whether or not you want to follow any of the suggested users.

Account details appear here

User information and Twitter activity summary appear here

Verified account

A – Click to display additional details

B – Click to follow a user

Recent tweets appear here

Click to display a drop-down menu with other options

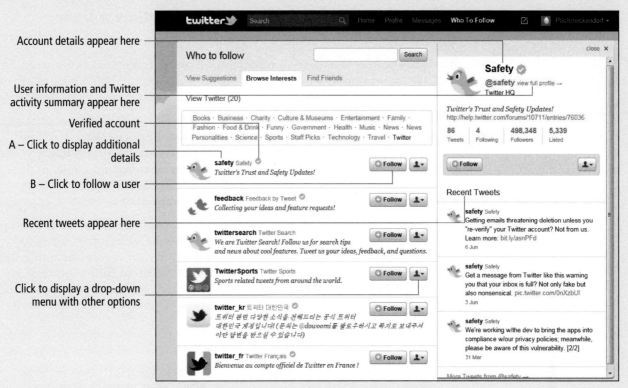

Figure 6.18 Hands-On Exercise 2, Steps 2a and 2b.

c. Repeat Steps 1f and 1g and Steps 2a and 2b to locate and follow two more individuals or organizations that interest you. Professor Schmeckendorf has chosen to follow **Read-WriteWeb** from the **Technology** category and **NASA** from the **Science** category.

d. On the menu bar at the top of the page, click the **Home** link.

Your homepage now appears with the **Timeline** tab displaying a list of tweets from the users you just followed, similar to the one shown in Figure 6.19. If you see tweets from other users that you haven't followed, they may be retweets—messages that someone you follow received from another user and subsequently shared with his or her followers.

D – Click to display the homepage

Tweets from users you are following appear on the Timeline

Figure 6.19 Hands-On Exercise 2, Step 2d.

Step 3 Use the Search Tool to Locate and Follow a User

Refer to Figures 6.20 through 6.22 as you complete Step 3.

The **Browse Interests** feature is useful for locating influential and interesting Twitter accounts, but is not very good at locating specific individuals or organizations. To locate someone in particular, Twitter's search tool might be a better choice.

a. At the top of the page, click the **Who To Follow** link. The **Who to follow** page displays with suggestions. Notice that since you have already followed some users, Twitter's suggestions may include Twitter users that are similar to those you have already selected. The right side of the page shows the users you are already following and again offers some related suggestions.

b. The left side of the page displays two search boxes. The search box at the top of the page can be used to search Twitter for people, companies, and places, as well as for specific words or phrases, and will return tweets containing the search results. The lower search box next to the **Who to follow** headline is used solely to locate Twitter users. You can search by username or topic. Click the lower search box and type **pearson_student** and then click the **Search** button.

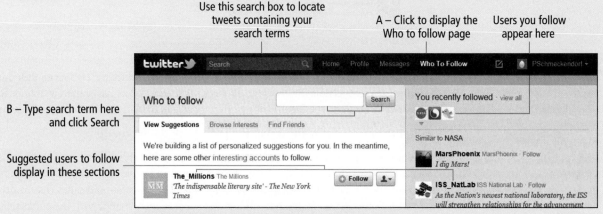

Use this search box to locate tweets containing your search terms

A – Click to display the Who to follow page

Users you follow appear here

B – Type search term here and click Search

Suggested users to follow display in these sections

Figure 6.20 Hands-On Exercise 2, Steps 3a and 3b.

c. The search results will display on the left side of the page. Locate the **pearson_student** account and click on the result to display the user details on the right side of the page. Note that your search results may vary and the **pearson_student** account may not be at the top of the results list.

d. Review the information to be sure you have selected the right account and click either of the **Follow** buttons for this user. Pearson is the publisher for this textbook. The **Pearson Students** account has been developed to help facilitate communication between Pearson and students, provide leadership opportunities for students, help students gain professional experience, and help students earn money.

New Twitter accounts and accounts with little or no activity may not appear in your search results. You may need to wait until the account becomes active before you can find and follow it.

User details appear here

D – Click either button to follow user

Search results appear here

C – Click to display user details

Figure 6.21 Hands-On Exercise 2, Steps 3c and 3d.

e. Repeat Steps 3a through 3d to locate and follow Professor Schmeckendorf's Twitter account, **PSchmeckendorf**.

f. On the menu bar at the top of the page, click the **Home** link to display your homepage with the **Timeline** tab displaying an updated list of tweets from the users you are following. The right side of the page shows the users you are following. If necessary, refresh the page to display this information. Each user is represented by an icon derived from the user's profile image. Hover over an icon to display the name of the user or click the icon to go to that user's profile page. Your Twitter account may have also been found by someone else who has chosen to follow you. If so, you will see a list of your followers, also represented by clickable icons.

F – Click to display the homepage

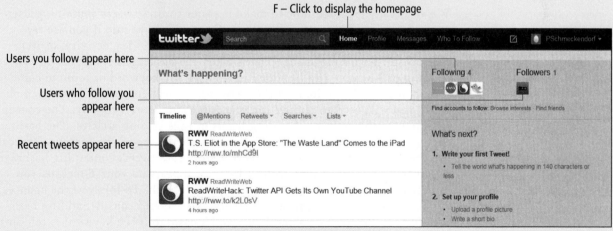

Users you follow appear here

Users who follow you appear here

Recent tweets appear here

Figure 6.22 Hands-On Exercise 2, Step 3f.

How do I begin to interact with other Twitter users?

Twitterverse, Twittersphere
The collection of individuals and organizations that make up the Twitter community.

Twitter provides many different ways to share information and interact with the *Twitterverse*, also known as the *Twittersphere*—the group of users that make up the Twitter universe. You can create your own post, or tweet, about anything you want. Ask a question, share a thought, make a comment, recommend a company, or share a link,

Message A short, private note sent to a follower of a Twitter user.

@Reply A tweet sent in response to another user's tweet.

@Mention A tweet that includes the username of a person or organization preceded by the @ symbol to draw attention to the user.

Retweet A tweet that was created by one user and then shared by the recipient with his or her followers.

Hashtag Created by adding the # symbol to a keyword; used to categorize tweets and make content searchable.

picture, or video—as long as it's 140 characters or less. Even if you don't have any followers yet, your message goes out to the Twitterverse and is available in search results. It is also possible to send a *Message* (formerly known as a Direct Message or DM) to individual users. A Message is a private note that can be sent only to someone who is currently following you. Messages are subject to the same size limitations as tweets.

But, the interaction doesn't end there. If you find a tweet that you want to respond to, you can send an *@Reply*. When you reply to a tweet, your response will always begin with the @ symbol followed by the username of the user. So, the reply from someone responding to a tweet from Professor Schmeckendorf would begin with *@PSchmeckendorf*. These types of replies are not visible to everyone. They will appear on your Timeline if you are following both the user and the responder. If someone replies to one of your tweets and you are not following that person, the response appears in another section of your Twitter homepage—the @**Mentions** tab. @Replies also belong to a broader category of tweets known as @Mentions. An *@Mention* is any tweet that includes a username preceded by the @ symbol and is used to help identify another user's Twitter account. Since a reply always begins with *@username*, it would also be an @Mention. However, an @Mention doesn't have to be a reply. If you wanted to send a tweet about Professor Schmeckendorf's class at Ginormous State University, you might write something like "Heading off to @GSU for computer class with @PSchmeckendorf." Someone receiving your tweet might then choose to investigate the Twitter account for GSU or Professor Schmeckendorf. If someone you are following mentions you, the tweet will appear on your Timeline. The @**Mentions** tab on your homepage will list any tweet that mentions you using the @username style, even if the tweet is from someone you do not follow.

Sometimes a tweet is so thought-provoking, funny, or useful that you want to share it with others. A *retweet*, sometimes abbreviated as *RT*, is similar to a forwarded email—if you receive a tweet that you want to share, you can click the **Retweet** link at the bottom of the post to send it to your followers. The original user's information continues to display on the tweet, but the top line of the tweet will also display the retweet symbol and the username of the person who sent it.

How can I find useful tweets and make my tweets more searchable?

We've already explored how to make it easier to find tweets containing usernames by using @Mention or @Reply. But what do you do if you are trying to find tweets that contain information about an idea, activity, or item that doesn't have a username? That's when the hashtag becomes useful. The *hashtag* or # symbol can be added in front of any keyword or topic to convert it to a searchable item. If the keyword or topic consists of more than one word, you will need to remove the spaces for it to work properly. The concept is similar to the practice of adding labels or tags to blog articles. The hashtag enables you to categorize tweets and search them for specific content. You can use the search tool at the top of the page to locate tweets containing hashtags. Alternately, if a tweet containing a hashtag appears on your Timeline, you can click the hashtag to automatically start a search. To improve the chances of your tweets appearing in search results, you should consider adding hashtags to your tweets. You should only add a hashtag if the keyword is relevant to the content of the tweet and you should try to limit yourself to adding no more than three hashtags per tweet. So a tweet that says "Can anyone recommend a good #digitalcamera?" would be a good use of a hashtag, while a tweet that says "Going to the #store to #buy a #digital #camera, then off to #lunch" would not be as effective.

Hands-On Exercises

3 | Send a Tweet, Reply to a Tweet, and Retweet a Tweet

Steps: 1. Create and Send a Tweet; **2.** Reply to a Tweet; **3.** Retweet a Tweet.

Use Figures 6.23 through 6.28 as a guide to the exercise.

Step 1 Create and Send a Tweet

Refer to Figure 6.23 as you complete Step 1.

If you are continuing from Hands-On Exercise 2, you should be viewing your Twitter homepage with the **Timeline** tab active. If you signed out of Twitter, follow the instructions provided in Hands-On Exercise 2, Step 1, to sign back in to your account.

a. Previously, Professor Schmeckendorf suggested that his students locate his Twitter account (@PSchmeckendorf) and begin following him. By doing so, they will receive any tweets he sends about the class. Today he would like to remind students about the link to the Companion Website for this textbook. Click in the **What's happening?** text box and type:

Consider adding the Companion Website for this book to your Favorites. http://www.pearsonhighered.com/nextseries

As you type your message, notice that Twitter counts the number of characters you have used and displays how many characters are remaining, or if you have exceeded the 140 character limit, below the text box. This makes it easier to know whether you will have to revise your tweet to make it shorter. Also, Twitter automatically shortens any URL that is longer than 13 characters and displays a message below the text box to indicate that the URL will be shortened. There are a number of link shortening services available. Third-party sites such as bitly (**http://bitly.com**) and TinyURL (**http://tinyurl. com**) became popular for their ability to convert long, complex URLs into something quick and easy to share. Using one of these services allows you to shorten a lengthy URL and share it on a blog, in an email, on a website, on a slideshow, or in a tweet. Twitter currently uses its own link shortening service. URLs are assigned a **t.co** link ID; however, the link will still appear as a slightly shorter version of itself. For example, the URL for NASA's Missions page is **http://www.nasa.gov/missions/index.html**, but when added to a tweet it displays as "nasa.gov/missions/index…" and the shortened URL from Twitter appears on the browser's status bar as **http://t.co/Pp9Crlv**. Most link ID services effectively hide the true URL address, which can cause people to unknowingly click on a link that leads to a malicious website. By displaying a recognizable portion of the URL, Twitter enables people to make informed decisions before they click on a link.

b. Click the **Tweet** button to send your first tweet. Your tweet will quickly appear at the top of your Timeline.

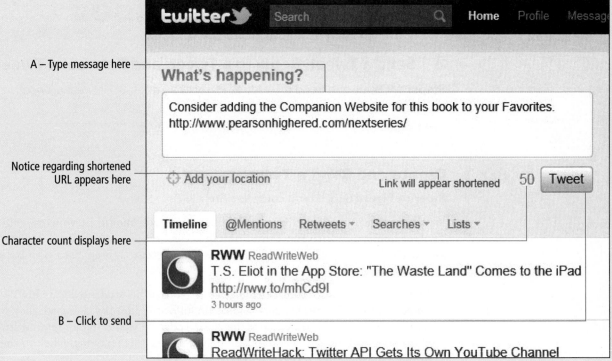

A – Type message here

Notice regarding shortened URL appears here

Character count displays here

B – Click to send

Figure 6.23 Hands-On Exercise 3, Steps 1a and 1b.

Tip

If you change your mind about a tweet that you have sent, or find you have made a mistake, it is possible to delete your tweet. Simply hover over your tweet when it appears on your Timeline and click the **Delete** link that will appear below it. However, be aware that the contents of your tweet may still appear in Twitter search results for an indefinite period of time.

Step 2 Reply to a Tweet

Refer to Figures 6.24 and 6.25 as you complete Step 2.

Keep in mind that when you reply to a tweet, your response is not private and may be seen by many people. If you are going to reply to a tweet, your response should contribute something to the conversation. For this step you should locate a tweet that you believe you can respond to with some useful information. The **pearson_ student** Twitter account often sends tweets asking for your opinion or feedback. This might be a good place to find a tweet you can reply to knowledgably.

a. Locate a tweet and click it to reveal a sidebar containing additional information. If the tweet included a photo or video, it will appear here. The tweet selected in Figure 6.24 contains an image, which you can see in the sidebar.

b. Click the **Reply** link below the tweet.

Tweet details appear in sidebar

A – Click tweet to display details

B – Click to reply

Image or video appears here

Figure 6.24 Hands-On Exercise 3, Steps 2a and 2b.

c. A **Reply to** pop-up window appears with the @username information already in the text box. Click in the box after @username and type your response. Remember to use hashtags where appropriate.

d. Click the **Tweet** button to send your response. The tweet you just sent will appear on your homepage in the Timeline.

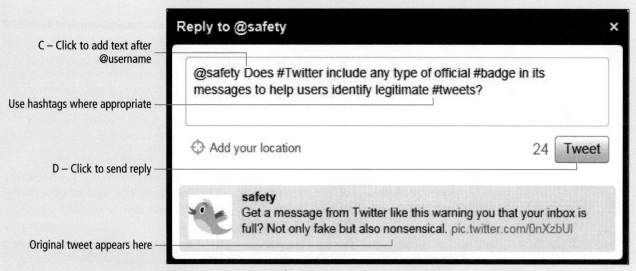

C – Click to add text after @username

Use hashtags where appropriate

D – Click to send reply

Original tweet appears here

Figure 6.25 Hands-On Exercise 3, Steps 2c and 2d.

 Step 3 **Retweet a Tweet**

Refer to Figures 6.26 through 6.28 as you complete Step 3.

In this step, you will share a useful tweet that you have received or located. If nothing on your Timeline appears worthwhile, try checking Twitter's **Safety** account. You may find a tweet about a serious hacking attempt or a malicious download that other Twitter users will appreciate knowing about.

a. Locate an appropriate tweet to share with your followers and click it to reveal the sidebar containing additional information.

b. Click the **Retweet** link below the tweet.

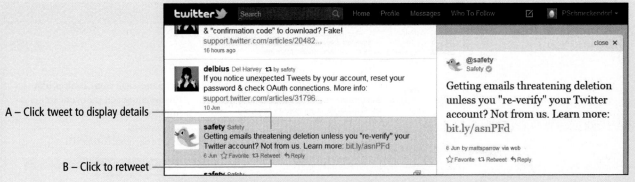

A – Click tweet to display details

B – Click to retweet

Figure 6.26 Hands-On Exercise 3, Steps 3a and 3b.

c. A **Retweet this to your followers?** pop-up window appears containing the original text from the tweet. Click the **Retweet** button to send it. When you retweet, you don't have the option to include a message of your own.

C – Click to send

Figure 6.27 Hands-On Exercise 3, Step 3c.

After you have retweeted the original message, the original tweet is modified, as shown in Figure 6.28. The top-left corner of the tweet is marked with a green triangle, as is the details pane. Additionally, the **Retweet** link has changed to an **Undo Retweet** link with a green icon next to it. If you have changed your mind about sending the message, you can simply click the **Undo Retweet** link to undo it.

d. Click the **Home** link to return to your homepage. Note that the message you retweeted does not appear on your Timeline. To see it, you need to click the **Retweets** tab. A drop-down list appears with the choice to see retweets that were sent by others, retweets that you have sent, or any of your tweets that have been retweeted.

D – Click to return to the homepage
Icon indicates message was retweeted

Click to undo tweet

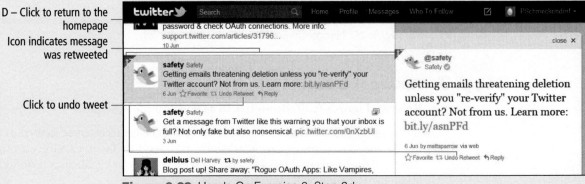

Figure 6.28 Hands-On Exercise 3, Step 3d.

You can now sign out of Twitter by clicking on your username at the top right of the page and selecting **Sign out** from the drop-down menu. You can also close your browser window.

Objective 4

Explore multimedia sharing sites

If a picture is worth a thousand words, imagine how much a site like YouTube or Flickr is worth! While it is possible to share photos, videos, and podcasts on a blog, wiki, or social network, sometimes it's more convenient to have one central repository for these items, especially if you have a lot of them.

With over 48 hours of video uploaded per minute and over 3 billion views per day, chances are good that you've viewed a video on YouTube. If you have a YouTube account, you can do even more. Having a YouTube account allows you to vote on a video and leave comments. You can also subscribe to a video channel that you enjoy, such as the popular Simon's Cat channel (**www.youtube.com/ user/simonscat**) that has close to a half million subscribers, and receive notifications when a new video has been added. When you sign up for a YouTube account, you create your own *channel*, which is similar to a profile page on other sites. It displays your user information, any videos you have uploaded to YouTube, information about anyone who has subscribed to your channel, your friends, your playlists, your favorites, and your recent activity. Other YouTube users can subscribe to your channel if they want to be informed when you post new videos. Subscribers do not need your approval to subscribe. Friends can also be added to your channel, but unlike subscribers, friends must be invited and friend requests need to be approved.

In addition to YouTube, there are other video sharing sites available. Sites such as Vimeo (**www.vimeo.com**), Dailymotion (**www.dailymotion.com**), and Viddler (**www.viddler.com**) have their own features and benefits and may be worth exploring.

Channel Similar to a profile page, a YouTube channel displays user information, videos, and other pertinent information.

Hands-On Exercises

Professor Schmeckendorf has decided to use YouTube to post some helpful tutorials for his students. This Hands-On Exercise will create an account using Professor Schmeckendorf's information; you will be creating an account for yourself and should add your own information where appropriate.

4 | Create a YouTube Account and Upload a Video

Steps: 1. Create a YouTube Account and Channel; **2.** Update Account Settings; **3.** Subscribe to a Channel; **4.** Upload a Video.

Use Figures 6.29 through 6.49 as a guide to the exercise.

 Step 1 Create a YouTube Account and Channel

Refer to Figures 6.29 through 6.34 as you complete Step 1.

If you already have a YouTube account, sign in to your account and skip to Step 2 to update your account settings.

a. Start your preferred browser (Internet Explorer, Firefox, Chrome, Safari, etc.).

b. Type **www.youtube.com** in the address bar of your browser and press **Enter**.

c. Click the **Create Account** button on the left side of the page or the **Create Account** link at the top right of the page.

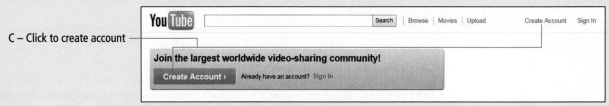

C – Click to create account

Figure 6.29 Hands-On Exercise 4, Step 1c.

d. The **Create a new YouTube|Google account** page appears. YouTube is owned by Google. Since you already have a Google account, click the **sign in here** link to proceed.

D – Click to sign in using your Google account information

Figure 6.30 Hands-On Exercise 4, Step 1d.

e. On the **YouTube Sign in** page, type the email address and password you used to create your Google account into the appropriate text boxes.

f. Click the **Sign in** button to proceed.

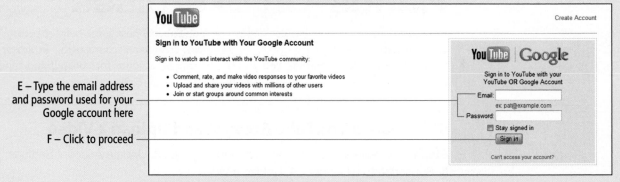

E – Type the email address and password used for your Google account here

F – Click to proceed

Figure 6.31 Hands-On Exercise 4, Steps 1e and 1f.

The next page displays several categories of videos, as well as a list of recommended channels. As you begin to use YouTube, this page will display your activity and any videos or channels to which you subscribe.

g. At the top-right of the page, locate your username and click the drop-down arrow next to it to display the **My Account** menu.

h. Click the **Channel** link to set up your YouTube channel.

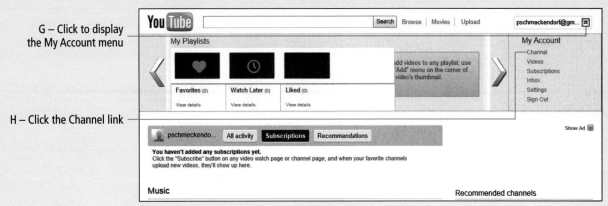

G – Click to display the My Account menu

H – Click the Channel link

Figure 6.32 Hands-On Exercise 4, Steps 1g and 1h.

i. The **Set up your YouTube username and channel** page displays. In the **Username** text box, type the username you want to use. Viewers of your videos or your channel will see this name. Note that it can contain only letters and numbers and it must be unique.

j. Click the **Check Availability** link to see if your username is available. If it is not, select one of the suggestions YouTube provides or create a new one and try again.

k. If necessary, click the **Location** drop-down box to select your desired location.

l. Click the appropriate **Gender** option button.

m. You should check or uncheck the next two checkboxes depending upon your personal preferences. Professor Schmeckendorf wants students to be able to find his YouTube channel if they know his email address, so he will leave this box checked; however, he would prefer not to receive product-related email from YouTube, so he will leave this box unchecked.

n. Click **Next** to proceed.

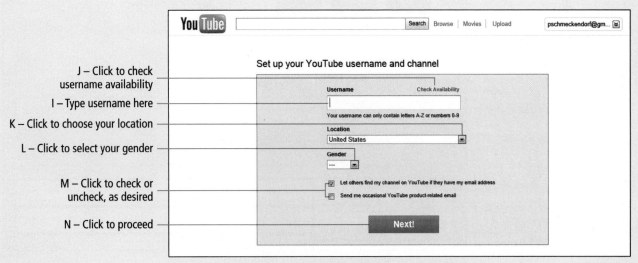

J – Click to check username availability

I – Type username here

K – Click to choose your location

L – Click to select your gender

M – Click to check or uncheck, as desired

N – Click to proceed

Figure 6.33 Hands-On Exercise 4, Steps 1i through 1n.

o. The next page displays a message at the top of the screen confirming the creation of your YouTube channel. By default, all your YouTube activity is displayed on your channel, but the **Privacy and Sharing** page allows you to modify these settings. Click the desired checkbox to select or unselect any of these choices.

p. Click the **All done!** button to view your channel.

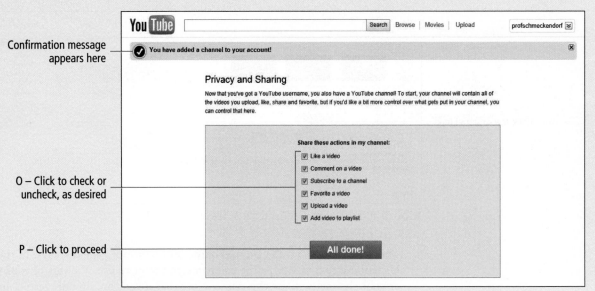

Confirmation message appears here

O – Click to check or uncheck, as desired

P – Click to proceed

Figure 6.34 Hands-On Exercise 4, Steps 1o and 1p.

Step 2 Update Account Settings

Refer to Figures 6.35 through 6.37 as you complete Step 2.

After clicking the **All done!** button, your YouTube channel will display. You will explore this channel in the next step, after you've adjusted the account settings.

a. Click the drop-down arrow next to your username and, from the **My Account** menu, click **Settings** to go to your **Account Settings** page.

A – Click to display menu and then click Settings

Your YouTube channel

Figure 6.35 Hands-On Exercise 4, Step 2a.

The **Overview** section of the **Account Settings** page displays a summary of your activity on YouTube, including information such as how many videos you've uploaded and how many times they have been viewed, how many videos you have marked as favorites, and how many people have subscribed to your channel. On the left side of the page is a list of other account settings you can adjust. Take some time to review these and make the adjustments you want to your account.

b. Click the **Privacy** link to adjust the privacy settings on your account.

Summary of your account activity

B – Click to change privacy settings

Figure 6.36 Hands-On Exercise 4, Step 2b.

c. Review the settings displayed on your **Privacy** page and make any necessary changes. Professor Schmeckendorf will make the following changes to his settings:

- **Advertising Settings**—Uncheck this box to turn off targeted ads.
- **Profile and Activity Settings**—Uncheck the **Friends** box to make this information private.

d. Click the **Save Changes** button, found at the top and bottom of the page, to save your new privacy settings. The page will refresh and display a message indicating that your changes were saved.

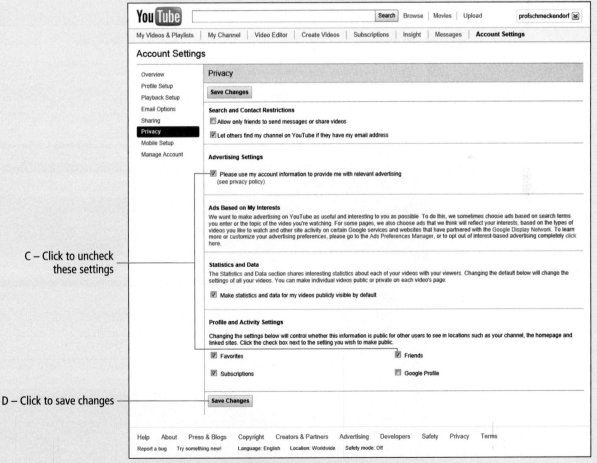

C – Click to uncheck these settings

D – Click to save changes

Figure 6.37 Hands-On Exercise 4, Steps 2c and 2d.

Step 3 Subscribe to a Channel

Refer to Figures 6.38 through 6.43 as you complete Step 3.

a. At the top of the **Account Settings** page, click the **My Channel** link.

A – Click to view your YouTube channel

Figure 6.38 Hands-On Exercise 4, Step 3a.

Your YouTube channel appears. If this is a new account, your channel won't have any content and may look similar to Professor Schmeckendorf's, as shown in Figure 6.39. If you have an existing account, your channel may look different depending upon your activity on the site. YouTube may display a message at the top of the page to alert you to changes or new features. There are also a series of tabs at the top of the page that allow you to customize how you communicate with subscribers, the way your channel looks, and the content that is displayed. You can also customize the individual modules, or sections, of your channel by clicking the **Edit** link or the positioning buttons found in the top-right corner of each module.

b. If necessary, close any messages from YouTube and click the **Close** link to close any open tabs.

c. At the top of the page, click the **Browse** link to start searching for content to add to your channel.

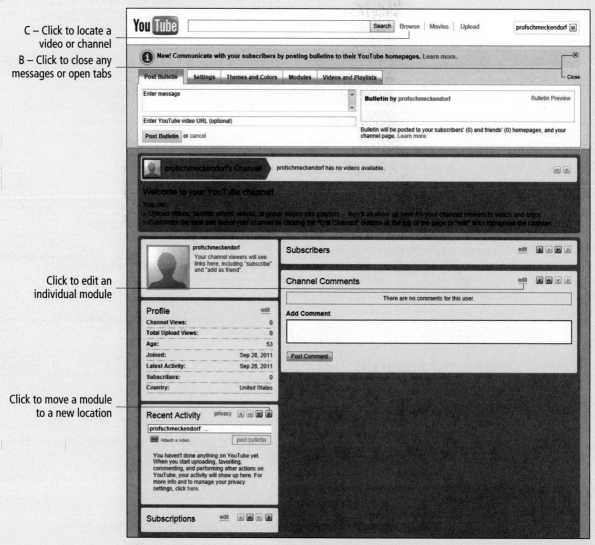

C – Click to locate a video or channel

B – Click to close any messages or open tabs

Click to edit an individual module

Click to move a module to a new location

Figure 6.39 Hands-On Exercise 4, Steps 3b and 3c.

d. YouTube displays a page of videos separated into various categories. Next to the **All Categories** heading, click the **Categories** drop-down arrow to display a list of YouTube categories.

e. Click the **Education** link to display videos related to education.

Figure 6.40 Hands-On Exercise 4, Steps 3d and 3e.

YouTube categories are useful for finding videos and channels related to a specific category. However, the actual content in each category changes as new videos are posted to YouTube and as new channels are added or old ones are removed. To ensure that his students can subscribe to the channel Professor Schmeckendorf has selected, he will provide them with a link to the channel.

f. In your browser's address bar, type **www.youtube.com/user/ NASAtelevision** to go to NASA's YouTube channel.

The top of the page features the most recent video posted by NASA. The video will begin playing as soon as the page opens. You can choose to watch the video or click the **Pause** button to stop the playback. Above the video is a **Subscribe** button. Other videos that NASA has uploaded appear on the right of the page. Approximately halfway down the page on the left, you will see the module containing NASA's profile information, with another **Subscribe** button. To the right of the profile is a module listing a number of other NASA channels.

g. Click either of the **Subscribe** buttons to add the NASA channel to the **Subscriptions** module of your channel. A pop-up window appears confirming your subscription. Click the **Close** button to dismiss this window. Also, notice that the **Subscribe** button has changed to a **Subscribed** button. You can click the drop-down arrow on this button and then click the **Unsubscribe** link to unsubscribe from the channel if you change your mind.

Figure 6.41 Hands-On Exercise 4, Step 3g.

h. At the top of the page, click the drop-down arrow next to your username to display the **My Account** menu.

i. Click **Channel** to return to your YouTube channel.

I – Click to return to your channel

H – Click to display My Account menu

Button indicates your subscription status

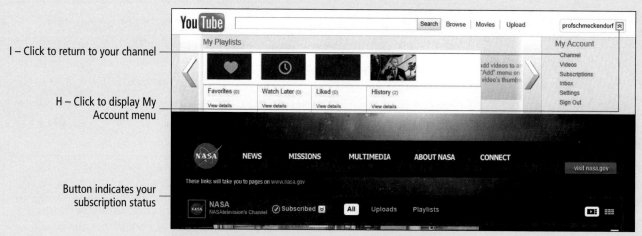

Figure 6.42 Hands-On Exercise 4, Steps 3h and 3i.

Your channel should now display information in your **Recent Activity** module and display the addition of the NASA channel in your **Subscriptions** module. Professor Schmeckendorf's channel with these changes is shown in Figure 6.43.

Details about new subscription appear here

New subscription appears here

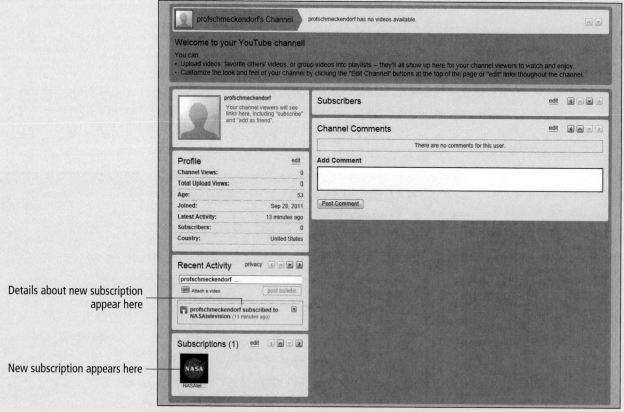

Figure 6.43 Changes to Professor Schmeckendorf's channel after subscribing to the NASA channel.

Step 4 Upload a Video

Refer to Figures 6.44 through 6.49 as you complete Step 4.

Professor Schmeckendorf has created a video tutorial that he wants to upload to YouTube. If you have a video that is suitable for uploading to your channel, go to your YouTube channel and skip to Step 4o. If you do not have a video, follow these instructions to download a sample video from the Companion Website.

a. Open a new browser tab or window and type **www.pearsonhighered.com/ nextseries** in the address bar and then press **Enter**.

b. From the list of books provided, locate this textbook and click the **Companion Website** link. This will take you to the companion website for this book.

c. Click the **Student Data Files** link and then click the **Chapter 6** link to start the download process.

d. In the **Windows Internet Explorer** dialog box, click the **Save as** button to display the **Save As** dialog box.

e. Browse through the folders (or create a new folder) on your computer's hard drive or your flash drive to find an appropriate place to save the file.

f. Click the **Save** button to download the file and save it to your computer. Be sure to remember where you saved the file.

g. A message bar may appear at the bottom of your screen indicating the status of the download. Once the download is complete, you can click the **Close** button to dismiss this message.

h. You can close all the Companion Website tabs or windows in your browser, but leave the browser window or tab containing your YouTube channel open.

i. The file you just downloaded is a zipped folder. Open Windows Explorer and browse to the location where you saved this file.

j. Right-click the zipped folder and select **Extract All** from the shortcut menu.

k. In the **Extract Compressed (Zipped) Folders** dialog box, there may already be a file path displayed in the **Files will be extracted to this folder** text box. If this is the location to which you wish to extract the file or files, proceed to Step 4l. If this is not the correct location, click the **Browse** button to locate the correct location.

l. If necessary, ensure there is a check in the **Show extracted files when complete** checkbox.

m. Click the **Extract** button to proceed. A new window appears showing the extracted folder.

n. Close Windows Explorer and return to your YouTube channel in your browser.

When you are logged in to your YouTube account, a menu bar appears at the top of each page. The menu bar includes a search box and links to help you browse videos and channels, purchase movies, and upload videos. Your username also appears here.

o. On the menu bar, click the **Upload** link.

Search for content and users on YouTube   Browse video categories   Search for movies to purchase and download   O – Click to begin uploading a video

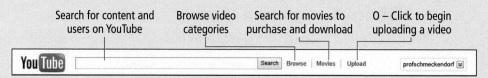

Figure 6.44 Hands-On Exercise 4, Step 4o.

p. The **Video File Upload** page appears. You can upload a variety of file formats to YouTube. Your video can be up to 2GB in size and up to 15 minutes long. You can even upload high definition video. Click the **Upload video** button to begin the process.

P – Click to begin the upload process

Figure 6.45 Hands-On Exercise 4, Step 4p.

q. The **Select files to upload** dialog box appears. Navigate to the location where you saved your video file or to the location where you downloaded and extracted the student data file for this chapter. Select the **Ch_6_Exercise_4.avi** file and click **Open**.

Navigate to the location of your video file

Select the video file to be uploaded

Q – Click to upload the file

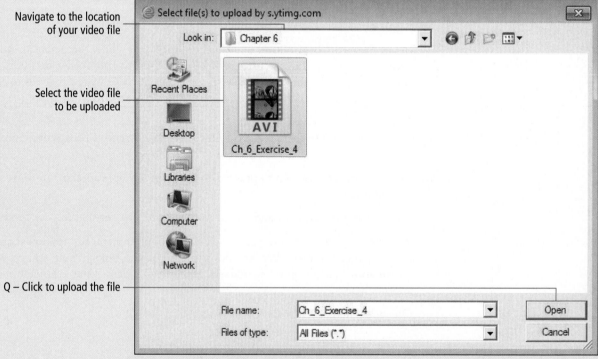

Figure 6.46 Hands-On Exercise 4, Step 4q.

As the video uploads, YouTube provides a status bar showing the upload progress, and also displays some sample frames from the video.

r. In the **Video information and privacy settings** section, click the **Title** text box. Delete the existing title and replace it with something more descriptive. If you are using Professor Schmeckendorf's video, type **How to Remove a USB Flash Drive**.

s. In the **Description** text box, type a brief description. Professor Schmeckendorf will provide the following description:

A brief tutorial demonstrating the correct way to remove a USB Flash drive.

t. In the **Tags** text box, type the tags that best describe your video. Tags should be separated by a space and tags consisting of multiple words should be enclosed in quotation marks. You can also click any of the tags that YouTube suggests to add them. Professor Schmeckendorf will add the following tags:

- **tutorial**

- **howto**

- **computer**

- **USB flash drive** (enclosed in quotation marks)

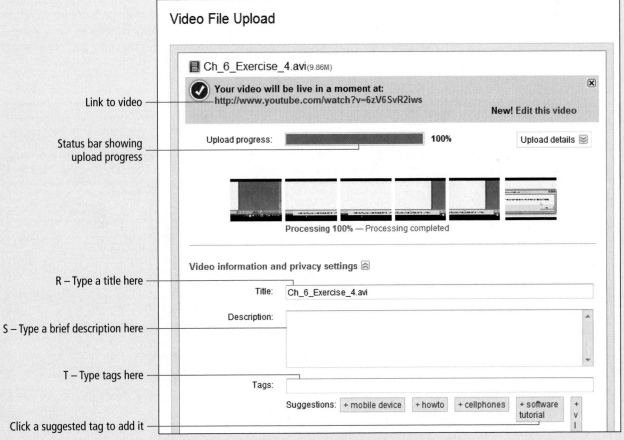

Figure 6.47 Hands-On Exercise 4, Steps 4r through 4t.

u. Click the **Category** drop-down list and select the appropriate category for your video. Professor Schmeckendorf will choose **Howto & Style**.

v. Professor Schmeckendorf will leave the default **Privacy** option—**Public**—selected. For the **License** section, he will select **Creative Commons- Attribution (CC-BY-reuse allowed)**, since he will be allowing his students to repost this video. For these two items, you should select the choices that are best for you.

w. Click **Save changes** to proceed. The page will refresh and display a message at the top confirming that the video settings were saved.

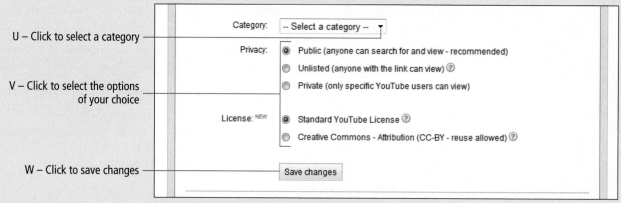

U – Click to select a category

V – Click to select the options of your choice

W – Click to save changes

Figure 6.48 Hands-On Exercise 4, Steps 4u through 4w.

x. Click your username and then click **Channel** to view the changes. The video you uploaded should appear in the main window with the title and description below it, similar to Figure 6.49. The module on the right side of the page will display a thumbnail of the video, and the **Recent Activity** module will reflect this new activity. Click the **Play** button to view your video on YouTube. Once you are done, log out of YouTube and close your browser.

A list of uploaded videos appears here

X – Click to play video

Video title and description appear here

Figure 6.49 Hands-On Exercise 4, Step 4x.

What other types of multimedia sharing sites are there?

In addition to the video sharing sites mentioned previously, you can also share photos and slides. Photo sharing sites have been around for many years and are quite popular. One of the most well-known sites is Flickr (**www.flickr.com**), which is owned by Yahoo! (Figure 6.50). Other sites include Google's Picasa (**http://picasa.google.com**), SmugMug (**www.smugmug.com**), Shutterfly (**www.shutterfly.com**), Snapfish (**www.snapfish.com**), and Photobucket (**http://photobucket.com**).

Figure 6.50 Photo-sharing sites like Flickr encourage collaboration by enabling members to share, search, and comment on the site.

Other sites focus on sharing presentations. The aptly named SlideShare (**www.slideshare.net**) is a good example. Members can upload their presentations to the site, search for presentations that were uploaded by other members, follow members, and comment on the presentations. SlideShare also allows members to upload PDF files, documents, and video presentations. Zoho Show (**http://show.zoho.com**) not only lets you display your presentation, it provides software to help you create it. Still other sites, like Animoto (**http://animoto.com**), provide the tools to turn your slideshows into video presentations.

Visit any of these sites and you'll find a thriving community of people sharing their artwork, ideas, and comments. Some sites are public, while others are set up to share content only with other members, or with people who have been invited to view a member's content. Many of these sites are free, although some offer premium accounts that provide extra features—such as no advertisements and additional privacy settings—for a fee.

Objective 5

Manage multiple social media profiles

Web 2.0 applications make it easy to share information and collaborate on projects. But there are so many different tools available, that it can be difficult to keep track of your online presence and manage all the information that is generated. Although no one has developed a way to manage everything from one central location, there are some tools available that can make it easier.

How can I keep track of all my online profiles?

It may not be possible to keep track of every profile you've ever created, but the website About.me (**http://about.me**) can help you to consolidate many of your online profiles in one place. Essentially, About.me is a free one-page website that you can quickly customize. The sign-up and profile creation process is simple. Pick a background color or image, write a brief blurb about yourself, and add links to your various social networks or to any web content you've generated. About.me lets you add links to many popular blogging sites, social networks like LinkedIn, Facebook, and Twitter, and several photo and video sharing sites by adding the site's icon to your page. It is up to you to choose which sites to include on your profile page and which sites to omit. If the site you want isn't listed, you have the option of adding the URL directly to your page. About.me provides you with a personalized URL for your page and encourages you to share it with others. Figure 6.51 shows Professor Schmeckendorf's About.me page with links to many of the sites in which he participates. Since About.me doesn't provide an icon for PBworks or Podbean, he has created his own links leading to his wiki and podcasting sites.

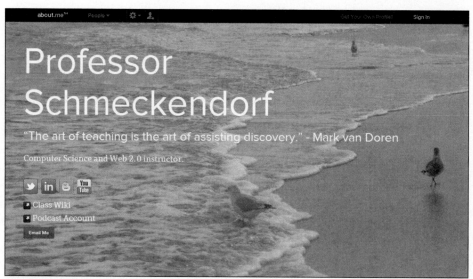

Figure 6.51 Professor Schmeckendorf's About.me page helps to consolidate his online presence.

About.me is a great way to group all your online sites in one place. It also makes it easy to share your information with others. Rather than giving people a list of the sites in which you participate, simply give them the URL for your About.me page and let them explore the many different facets of your online persona.

Is there a way to update all my sites at once?

Having one central web page to find all the sites in which you participate is handy, but what happens when you want to post an update? Although there are times when you need, or want, to update only one site, sometimes you have general information that is appropriate to share with all your sites. Currently, you would have to go to each site—LinkedIn, Twitter, Facebook, and so on—and post the news you want to share. This can be tedious and time-consuming. Fortunately, Web 2.0 tools have been developed to make this process easier. Sites like Ping.fm (**www.ping.fm**), Twitterfeed (**www.twitterfeed.com**), Atomkeep (**www.atomkeep.com**), FriendFeed (**www.friendfeed.com**), and HootSuite (**www.hootsuite.com**) are each designed to help you manage your social profiles. Each of these tools works slightly differently; you may want to explore some or all of them to see which one will work best for you.

Hands-On Exercises

Professor Schmeckendorf wants to be able to easily update his social media sites and has decided to use HootSuite. As you work through this Hands-On Exercise, remember to use your information to create your own account.

5 | Create a HootSuite Account

Steps: 1. Create a HootSuite Account; **2.** Add Social Networks; **3.** Send an Update.

Use Figures 6.52 through 6.62 as a guide to the exercise.

Step 1 Create a HootSuite Account

Refer to Figures 6.52 through 6.54 as you complete Step 1.

a. Start your preferred browser (Internet Explorer, Firefox, Chrome, Safari, etc.).

b. Type **www.hootsuite.com** in the address bar of your browser and press **Enter**.

c. Click the **Sign up now** button.

C – Click to proceed

Figure 6.52 Hands-On Exercise 5, Step 1c.

d. HootSuite offers a premium version, as well as a free version. You can manage up to five social media profiles with the free version. Professor Schmeckendorf believes this will be sufficient for his needs. Click the **Sign Up Now Always Free** button.

D – Click to proceed

Figure 6.53 Hands-On Exercise 5, Step 1d.

e. On the **Sign Up** page, in the **Create Your Account** section, enter the appropriate information into the text boxes.

f. Click the **Time Zone** drop-down arrow to select the appropriate time zone.

g. The **Subscribe to HootSuite newsletters** checkbox is checked by default. If you do not wish to receive the newsletters, click to uncheck this box.

h. Click the **Create Account** button to proceed.

E – Add the appropriate information here

F – Click to select time zone

G – Click to unselect newsletter option

H – Click to proceed

Figure 6.54 Hands-On Exercise 5, Steps 1e through 1h.

Step 2   Add Social Networks

Refer to Figures 6.55 through 6.59 as you complete Step 2.

A Welcome screen appears with a dialog box listing several social media sites with which you may want to connect. You may also see a pop-up window at the top of the screen. HootSuite will occasionally point out new features in this way. You can click the **Close** button to dismiss this window. Professor Schmeckendorf wants to connect to Twitter and LinkedIn. He will not connect to Facebook at this time.

a. Click the **Add a Twitter profile** button to connect to your Twitter account.

Click to dismiss message

A – Click to connect with Twitter

Figure 6.55 Hands-On Exercise 5, Step 2a.

b. The **Add Social Network** dialog box appears with a list of possible sites on the left side. The Twitter option should be active. There are two checkboxes in this dialog box. You should leave both of them checked to create a new tab for the profile and receive important information.

c. Click the **Connect with Twitter** button to give HootSuite access to your Twitter account.

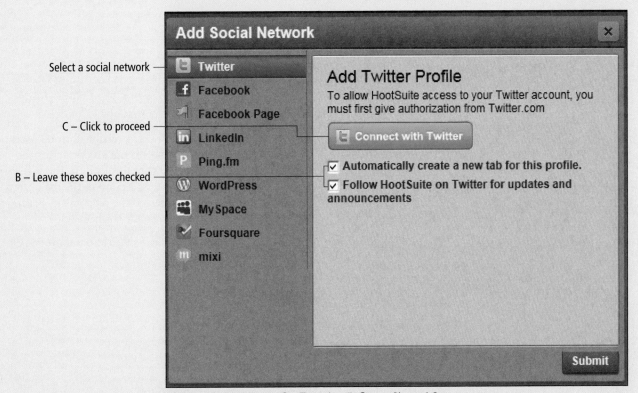

Select a social network

C – Click to proceed

B – Leave these boxes checked

Figure 6.56 Hands-On Exercise 5, Steps 2b and 2c.

Alert!

You may receive an error message when attempting to connect to a social network. Follow the instructions in the message. If you take too long while making the request, it may not go through. If this happens, you may have to log back in to your HootSuite account.

d. An **Authorize an application** pop-up window appears from Twitter. Review the information provided about how HootSuite will interact with your Twitter account. In the **Password** text box, type your Twitter account password.

e. Click the **Authorize app** button to proceed.

D – Type Twitter account password here

E – Click to proceed

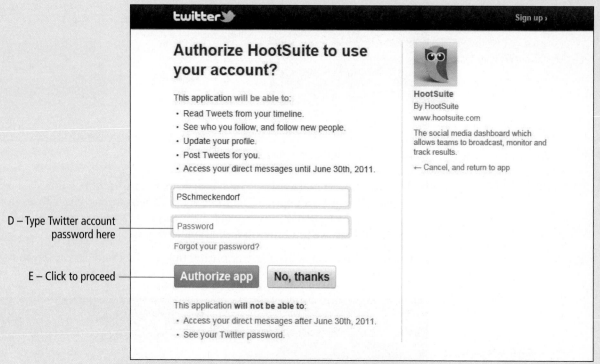

Figure 6.57 Hands-On Exercise 5, Steps 2d and 2e.

A **Settings** dialog box appears. The right side of the dialog box is for users who are collaborating with other team members. The HootSuite Pro version permits users to add other team members to the account; however, this is not an option for the free account. The list on the left side of the dialog box contains links to the various areas of HootSuite that you can customize. The center section of the dialog box displays the social media networks that have been added to the account. In Figure 6.58, notice that Professor Schmeckendorf's Twitter account has been added.

f. On the center section of the **Settings** dialog box, click the **Add Social Network** link to display the **Add Social Network** dialog box again.

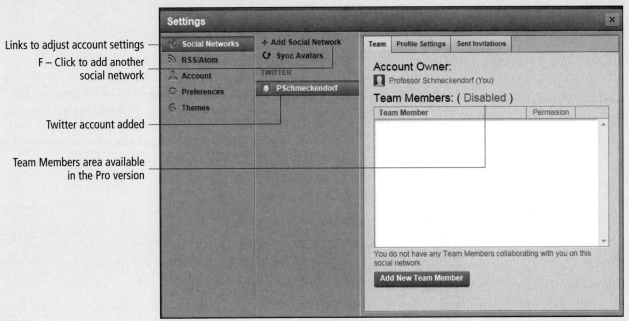

Links to adjust account settings
F – Click to add another social network

Twitter account added

Team Members area available in the Pro version

Figure 6.58 Hands-On Exercise 5, Step 2f.

g. Click the **LinkedIn** link on the left side of the dialog box. Repeat the actions in Steps 2b through 2e to authorize HootSuite's access to your LinkedIn account.

h. The **Settings** dialog box now lists Professor Schmeckendorf's Twitter account and LinkedIn account. Click the **Close** button on the dialog box.

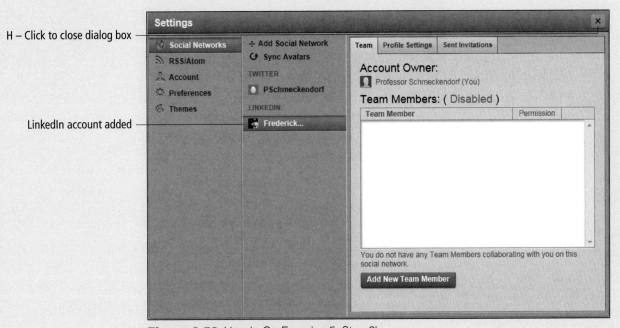

H – Click to close dialog box

LinkedIn account added

Figure 6.59 Hands-On Exercise 5, Step 2h.

Step 3 Send an Update

Refer to Figures 6.60 through 6.62 as you complete Step 3.

At the end of Step 2, the HootSuite **Welcome** tab appears with some suggested actions displayed. You may want to explore these later. On the left side of the page is a sidebar with a series of icons. Hover over an icon to have the sidebar pop out and display more information. At the bottom of the sidebar is the **Log Out** icon. At the top of the page is a text box that you can use to create and send status updates to the accounts you have linked to your HootSuite account. Below the text box is a series of tabs. In addition to the **Welcome** tab, you should see a tab for each of the social networks you added to HootSuite (Figure 6.60).

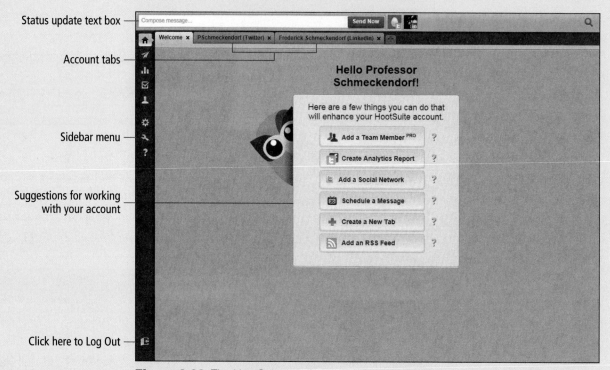

Figure 6.60 The HootSuite interface allows you to send status updates and monitor multiple social media sites.

a. Click the **Twitter** tab at the top of the page to display your Twitter feeds. By default, there are four columns displayed:

- **Home Feed**—This column displays all the tweets you would ordinarily see on the Timeline of your Twitter account's homepage.

- **Mentions**—If anyone has mentioned you in a tweet, those tweets are collected in this column.

- **Direct Message (Inbox)**—This column displays any direct messages you may receive; however, this functionality may be phased out of HootSuite.

- **Sent Tweets**—The tweets you have sent appear in this column on the far right of your screen.

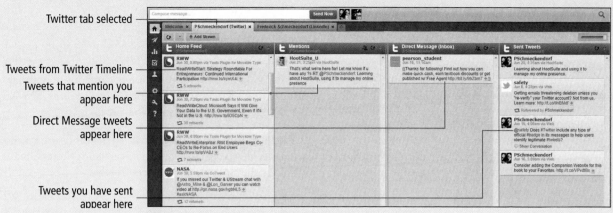

Twitter tab selected

Tweets from Twitter Timeline

Tweets that mention you
appear here

Direct Message tweets
appear here

Tweets you have sent
appear here

Figure 6.61 Hands-On Exercise 5, Step 3a.

b. Click the **LinkedIn** tab to review the content shown for this profile. If you have not used your LinkedIn account or are not connected with many people, you may not have anything on the HootSuite page. The more often you use the social media sites you've joined, the more information will be available to be displayed.

c. Click the **Compose message** text box at the top of the screen to create a status update. The text box expands and provides buttons for uploading an image or file, and scheduling your update for a later time. Type **Learning about HootSuite and using it to manage my online presence**.

d. Next to the text box are a group of icons representing your profile picture for the various sites you have joined. You can choose which sites receive your update by clicking the individual icons. If you want to update all your accounts, click the **Select All** button. To readjust your settings, click the **Select None** button and start over.

e. Click the **Send Now** button to send your first status update from HootSuite. If you are curious, log in to your Twitter or LinkedIn account and check your homepage to see how your update looks.

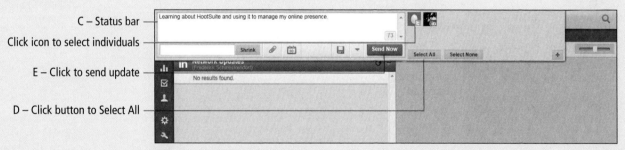

C – Status bar

Click icon to select individuals

E – Click to send update

D – Click button to Select All

Figure 6.62 Hands-On Exercise 5, Steps 3c through 3e.

You may now log out of HootSuite by clicking the **Log Out** link in the bottom-left corner of the screen. You can also close your browser.

Objective 6

Explore resources for additional collaboration tools

Web 2.0 tools are constantly changing and evolving. Some become more popular, while others fall out of favor or close down altogether. The following sites may help you to keep up with all these changes and stay ahead of the curve.

- **Social Media Today (http://socialmediatoday.com)**—This blogging community is composed of marketing, public relations, and advertising professionals, as well as anyone else who values the importance of social media.

- **Social Media (http://thenextweb.com/socialmedia)**—Part of The Next Web family, this blog about social media has a lot of good information. Use the search box on this site to look for the post titled "20 Slick YouTube Tips and Tricks You Need to Know" to learn about some interesting things to do with YouTube.

- **My Twitter Guide for Skeptics & Newbies (http://bit.ly/twitterideas)**—Sree Sreenivasan, the author of this site, is Dean of Student Affairs and a professor at Columbia Journalism School. He was also voted one of Ad Age's "25 Media People to Follow." This site provides many good resources for Twitter.

- **HootSuite Blog (http://blog.hootsuite.com)**—This blog from HootSuite explores various aspects of the site and provides information about new features, as well as more in-depth information about some of HootSuite's advanced features.

- **Mashable (http://mashable.com)**—Mashable has been reporting on web news, including social and digital media, since 2005. Visit this site for breaking news, trends analysis, reviews, and resources.

Summary

This chapter explored a variety of Web 2.0 tools. You learned the basic skills needed to set up a Twitter account and begin communicating with others using 140 characters or less. You also explored sites such as Flickr, SlideShare, and YouTube that let you share your ideas and information in ways that don't rely as much on words. And we looked at ways to help organize all your Web 2.0 profiles and manage your social media presence with sites such as About.me and HootSuite.

Key Terms

Multiple Choice Questions

1. On YouTube, you can save your playlists and your favorite videos to a central location known as a

    (a) network.

    (b) channel.

    (c) profile.

    (d) subscription.

2. Which of the following statements about Twitter is *not* true?

    (a) Twitter is a microblog.

    (b) Users send posts that are no more than 140 characters.

    (c) Users do not need permission to follow other Twitter users.

    (d) Users can send replies, known as *chirps*, to other users.

3. A private tweet sent to an individual user is a(n)

    (a) Message.

    (b) QuickPost.

    (c) Shush.

    (d) Update.

4. The Twitter community is often referred to as the

    (a) Cloud.

    (b) Tweeties.

    (c) Twitterverse.

    (d) Tweetdom.

5. Recent tweets from users you follow appear on your

    (a) Timeline.

    (b) Leaderboard.

    (c) Channel.

    (d) Tweetspot.

6. As a YouTube member, which of the following actions is *not* something that you can do?

    (a) Subscribe to a video channel.

    (b) Revise or annotate someone else's video.

    (c) Vote on a video.

    (d) Comment on a video.

7. On Twitter, an @Reply is also an example of a(n)

    (a) Message.

    (b) Retweet.

    (c) @Mention.

    (d) Chirp.

8. Which of the following sites is *not* an example of a video sharing site?

    (a) Viddler

    (b) Vimeo

    (c) Dailymotion

    (d) Picasa

9. When retweeting on Twitter, which of the following statements is *not* true?

    (a) Retweeting allows you to send someone else's tweet to your followers.

    (b) You can add your own message to a retweet.

    (c) It is possible to undo a retweet.

    (d) The original tweet displays a green triangle in the top-left corner.

10. Which of the following statements is a benefit of having a protected Twitter account?

    (a) Your followers cannot share your tweets with others.

    (b) Your tweets are visible to everyone who has a special passcode to your account.

    (c) You are able to reply to users who don't follow you, but they can't reply to you.

    (d) Your tweets display with a special padlock symbol to denote encryption.

Fill in the Blank

1. A(n) _____ is a combination of the # symbol and a keyword and is used to make tweets more searchable.

2. An original tweet that contains a username preceded by the @ symbol anywhere within the tweet is known as a(n) _____.

3. Twitter is an example of a(n) _____ because its posts, or tweets, are limited in size.

4. On YouTube, your _____ displays your user information, the videos you have uploaded, and your recent activity.

5. In order to receive a person's Twitter account updates on your Twitter homepage, you must _____ him or her.

Practice Exercises

1. **Customize Your Twitter Profile**

   In Hands-On Exercise 1, you set up a Twitter account and made some adjustments to your account settings. In this exercise, you will add a profile picture to your account. You will need an image to use for your profile picture. The file must be between 48k and 700k in size and can be a JPG, GIF, or PNG file type. You do not have to use a photo of yourself; in fact, you might decide to use a picture that represents something you like, such as your pet, a nature scene, or a hobby. Whatever image you select, remember that it must follow copyright guidelines and Twitter's rules (which can be found at **http://support.twitter.com/articles/18311**).

   (a) Open a web browser and navigate to **www.twitter.com**.

   (b) Log in to your Twitter account using your username and password.

   (c) At the top right of the page, click your username and then click **Settings**.

   (d) On the **Settings** page, click the **Profile** link.

   (e) In the **Picture** section, click the **Browse** button to navigate to the location of the image you wish to upload.

   (f) Select the desired image and click **Open** to insert the file path in the **Browse** text box.

   (g) Click **Save** to save your changes. It may take a few moments for the upload to complete. Once it does, a message will appear at the top of the page confirming that the changes have been saved. You will also see a thumbnail of your image appear next to your name at the top of the **Settings** page and next to the **Browse** text box.

   (h) At the top of the page, by the **Search** box, click the **Profile** link to view your profile page with your new image in place.

   (i) Take a screenshot or print out your **Profile** page and submit it to your instructor.

   (j) Log out of Twitter and close your browser.

2. **Use Hashtags to Find a New Resource**

   As discussed in this chapter, hashtags act as labels or tags, making it easier to locate tweets from many users on similar topics. Professor Schmeckendorf wants his computer science students to search Twitter and locate another individual or resource that is involved in computer science to follow. In this exercise, you will perform a search using a hashtag to locate an appropriate resource.

   (a) Open a web browser and navigate to **www.twitter.com**.

   (b) Log in to your Twitter account using your username and password.

   (c) At the top of the page, click in the **Search** box by the Twitter logo. Type an appropriate hashtag or combination of hashtags related to some aspect of computer science and press **Enter**. Suggested hashtags you might want to try include #computerscience, #Web2.0, #ITconference, and #ITcareer. Your instructor may also provide some suggestions or guidance.

   (d) Resulting tweets containing the hashtag(s) will appear on the left side of the page. People results will appear on the right side of the page.

   (e) Scroll through your results. If you find a possible resource, click the tweet to display its details on the right side of the page.

   (f) If you are satisfied with the individual or organization you have selected, click the **Follow** button to add them to your followers.

   (g) Print out the page or take a screenshot to submit to your instructor. Make sure the page or screenshot includes the **Search** results title containing the hashtag(s) you used to perform the search, and the person or resource you followed.

   (h) Log out of Twitter and close your browser.

3. **Explore YouTube's Insight Feature**

   To successfully complete this exercise, you must have already completed Hands-On Exercise 4. Have you ever wondered if anyone is watching the videos you post on YouTube? YouTube's **Insight** feature not only tells you how many times your video has been viewed, it can provide other useful details as well, such as where your viewers are located, their age, and how they found your video.

   (a) Open a web browser and navigate to **www.youtube.com**.

   (b) Log in to your YouTube account using your username and password.

   (c) At the top right of the page, click your username and then click **Settings**.

   (d) From the **Menu bar** at the top of the page, click the **Insight** link.

   (e) Insight's **Summary** page displays, showing various graphs indicating how often the video has been viewed, viewer demographics, and the popularity of your videos. Note that if your YouTube account is new and includes only the video posted in Hands-On Exercise 4, the data displayed by **Insight** may be incomplete. Print out this page or take a screenshot to submit to your instructor.

   (f) **Insight** includes links to various sections at the left of the page. Click the **Discovery** link to see how viewers have located your video. Print out this page or take a screenshot to submit to your instructor.

   (g) Review the other reports that **Insight** provides for your videos. The **Community** report lets you see how viewers are interacting with your video. This report lets you see if anyone has rated your video or left a comment. The **Subscribers** report provides information about who (if anyone) has subscribed to your channel.

   (h) Submit the printouts or screenshots you've taken of the **Summary** and **Discovery** pages to your instructor.

   (i) Log out of YouTube and close your browser.

4. **Create an About.me Profile**

   The About.me site mentioned in this chapter allows you to create a personalized page that includes links to many popular Web 2.0 and social networking sites.

   (a) Open a web browser and navigate to **http://about.me**.

   (b) The About.me website opens. You need to provide three key pieces of information:

   - Type your email address.
   - Create a password—Remember that secure passwords are 8 to 12 characters in length and include upper and lowercase letters, numbers, and symbols.
   - Type your own About.me URL.

   (c) Click the **Create Your Profile** button to go through the sign-up process.

   (d) Once you've added some information, your page will display your name and a brief bio. The **Edit Profile** dialog box appears so you can make other adjustments to your profile. You can add or change your background image or artwork, edit your bio, change your page's colors and font, and select the services you want to display on your page.

   (e) As you add services, you will be asked to allow About.me to access your other sites.

   (f) Your changes are saved automatically as you make them. Once you are done, close any dialog boxes or extra web pages that may have been opened.

   (g) Click on the icons you added to ensure they work as expected.

   (h) Once you are done, print out your About.me page or take a screenshot and submit it to your instructor.

   (i) Log out of the About.me site by clicking the **Account** link at the top right of the page and choosing **Logout**. Close your browser also.

Critical Thinking

1. Log in to your YouTube account and click the **Copyright** link at the bottom of the page. Review the information in the **Copyright Center**. YouTube takes copyright infringement very seriously. Were you aware that YouTube could block videos for copyright infringement? Have you ever known anyone whose video was blocked, or whose account was suspended or terminated? Have you ever reported a video for copyright infringement? How does YouTube help to prevent copyright infringement? Write a brief one- or two-page paper answering these questions and summarizing YouTube's copyright policy and submit it to your instructor.

2. When you created your HootSuite account in Hands-On Exercise 5, you gave HootSuite permission to access your LinkedIn and Twitter accounts. How does HootSuite handle your personal information? What are the concerns about allowing third-party applications to access users' information on other sites? What steps should you take to protect your privacy? Does HootSuite's usefulness outweigh any concerns you might have about granting it access to your other accounts? Create a short presentation outlining your findings and submit it to your instructor or present it to your class.

Team Projects

1. As a team, explore three other video sharing sites. Compare and contrast these sites to YouTube and create a table listing your findings. Consider items such as included features, number of members, site design, and ease of use. Include a brief review of your impression of each site. Would you consider using one of these sites? If so, would you continue to use YouTube? Explain your answers and submit your results to your instructor.

2. Add each of your team members to the list of people you follow on Twitter. Over the next three to five days (or a length of time specified by your instructor), use Twitter to communicate with your team and share ideas. You should send at least two or three tweets per day. In addition, you should reply to each team member at least once or twice over the course of this project and retweet any relevant tweets from non-team members you are following. Your tweets may be class-related, but can also be about other items you find interesting, funny, or useful. At the end of the time period, meet as a group and discuss your experience. What was the most useful thing you learned from this project? Would you consider using Twitter as a collaboration tool for other projects? Why or why not? Write a brief report detailing your experiences using Twitter and submit it to your instructor.

Credits

Glossary

@Mention A tweet that includes the username of a person or organization preceded by the @ symbol to draw attention to the user.

@Reply A tweet sent in response to another user's tweet.

Aggregator See *feed reader*.

Apps Applications or features that you can add to your social network. Also known as *widgets*.

Badge A small graphic or icon posted on a website or social networking site that links to another social network site.

Beta version Software that is still being tested and evaluated.

Blog Short for *web log*, a type of web page featuring multiple entries providing commentary on a topic of interest or a particular genre.

Blog archive A list of the posts added to a blog, organized by date.

Blog carnival A type of online magazine (or newsletter) that is usually published on a blog on a regular basis (weekly, monthly, etc.).

Blog comments Written commentaries left by blog readers pertaining to a specific blog post.

Blog directories Listings of blog sites, usually organized by topic.

Blog posts The text, images, and/or video that provide information to blog readers; appearing in reverse chronological order, each post includes a title and the date it was added to the blog.

Blog search engine A specialized type of search engine that focuses on indexing and returning search results from information posted on blogs.

Blog spam Comments designed to promote an often undesirable product or website that are posted to a blog by automated programs.

Blogger A person who creates and maintains a blog.

Blogosphere The entire collection of all blogs on the web.

Blogroll A list of hyperlinks to other blogs that the blog creator believes will be of interest to his or her readers.

CAPTCHA A program used to prevent software programs, or bots, from executing unauthorized procedures on websites.

Cease and desist letter A request to immediately stop an alleged copyright infringement.

Channel Similar to a profile page, a YouTube channel displays user information, videos, and other pertinent information.

Closed community A social network to which members typically must be invited by the site organizer or pre-existing members.

Cloud computing See *Web as platform*.

Contributory infringement A type of infringement in which you do not commit the original copyright infringement, but you link to copyrighted material that you are aware has been infringed upon and your link to the content materially contributes to the infringement.

Copyleft A licensing scheme that permits the creator of a work to retain the copyright while distributing the work freely to others with restrictions to limit the use of the work.

Copyright The legal protection granted to authors of "original works of authorship."

Copyright infringement The use of copyrighted material without the permission of the copyright holder.

Cyberbullying Limited to children, preteens, or teens, this type of bullying takes place via online tools such as email or social networks, as opposed to occurring face-to-face.

Cyber predator An adult who uses the Internet to prey on children or other hapless individuals, attempting to lure them into a sexual, or otherwise unsafe, situation.

Cyberstalking Threatening or harassing behavior that is facilitated by the use of the Internet and online tools such as email and online social networks.

Dot-com bust A period of time from late 2000 through 2002 during which many dot-com companies with unworkable business ideas went out of business.

Dot-coms Companies that do most or all of their business on the Internet.

Events Used to identify Google calendar entries, regardless of the duration or frequency of occurrence.

External applications Features that can be added to a social network that are created by third-party developers, sometimes for commercial purposes.

External links Hyperlinks that connect to web pages located outside of the wiki.

Extracted Files that have been unzipped, or restored, to their original size.

Fair use Permits the use of portions of copyrighted material for the purpose of commentary and criticism.

Feed reader Software designed to check the Internet for new content from sites that use web feeds and to which you have subscribed, and to gather the information in one central location for subsequent viewing. Also known as *aggregator*.

Follow To select a specific Twitter user's account in order to receive that user's updates.

Gadget A section of a blog that contains code resulting in some type of functionality for the blog.

GNU General Public License A license that specifies that a software program can be distributed to and modified by anyone, even for commercial purposes.

Hashtag Created by adding the # symbol to a keyword; used to categorize tweets and make content searchable.

Header A section of a blog that contains the title of your blog and possibly a subtitle.

Hyperlink Text or an image that connects to another document on the web or to another location on the same web page.

ID3 tags Pieces of information that are attached to MP3 audio files.

Internal applications Features that can be added to a social network that are developed by the creators of the network.

Internal links Hyperlinks that connect one wiki page to another location within the wiki.

Internet trolls Individuals who write inflammatory, controversial, or irrelevant content in online communities, such as Wikipedia, just to provoke emotional responses from readers.

IP address A unique number assigned to devices connected to the Internet.

Issues-focused network A social action network that provides members with information and opportunities to help with causes that range from global warming and animal rights to fair trade and peace in the Middle East.

Labels Topics or categories, similar to keywords, created by a blog's author and assigned to a blog post to help readers locate information on the blog.

Malware Malicious software designed to damage or disrupt a computer, often leaving it vulnerable to hackers; includes viruses, spyware, worms, and Trojan horses.

Message A short, private note sent to a follower of a Twitter user.

Microblog A type of blog that is used to create very brief posts limited to a set number of characters per post; in Twitter's case, this limit is 140 characters.

Moderator A social network role responsible for maintaining the network's standards.

Navigator A PBworks feature that is available on all pages, this section displays the wiki's site structure and allows users to view and access files and folders on the wiki.

Notifications Emails sent out by your wiki provider to alert you when changes are made to your wikis.

Open community A social network in which anyone is free to join, regardless of his or her interests or who he or she might know.

Page views The number of times a web page is loaded in a browser.

Peer review A process by which experts in a given field review another author's scholarly work to determine that the output is valid and substantially correct. Also known as *refereeing*.

Phishing A type of social engineering in which a fake website attempts to trick you into revealing private and personal information, such as passwords and account numbers, in order to steal your identity.

Podcast A group of audio or video files, usually issued in a series or sequence, that can be subscribed to and downloaded from the Internet.

Podcatcher Software that is specially designed to go out and check the Internet for new episodes of the podcasts to which you subscribe.

Pop filter A mesh screen that is placed directly in front of a microphone to disrupt the fast flow of air as it speeds toward the microphone.

Professional network A social network that connects businesspeople and other professionals in an online community and allows them to showcase their talents and skills.

Profile A feature of a social network that is used to provide information about a member.

Promoter A person who actively markets and promotes a social networking site, encouraging others to help spread the word.

Public domain The realm containing works that are not protected by intellectual property laws.

Really Simple Syndication (RSS) A popular type of web feed used to syndicate content on the Internet.

Recurring event An event that takes place more than once.

Refereeing See *peer review*.

Retweet A tweet that was created by one user and then shared by the recipient with his or her followers.

Revision history page A chronological listing (most recent first) of the edits to a wiki page.

Server A computer that provides services to other computers upon request.

SideBar A feature of PBworks, this small section is always visible (by default) on the right side of your wiki and can be edited just like a full-size wiki page. It is often used to provide a list of internal links.

Site administrator A social network role with responsibilities for determining which features appear on the site, approving photos and videos prior to posting, approving member requests to join the site, deleting offensive comments or materials, and banning members who act inappropriately.

Social network A community made up of people, groups, or organizations that are connected by one or more common interests.

Storyboard A panel, or series of panels, arranged in sequence to portray the action or events that will occur in a video.

Sync The process of connecting your PMP to your computer to update its contents.

Terms of use The terms governing the use of copyrighted material.

Transitions Effects that take place in between media clips.

Tweet A brief post created by users of Twitter.

Twittersphere See *Twitterverse*.

Twitterverse The collection of individuals and organizations that make up the Twitter community. Also known as *Twittersphere*.

Unique visitors The number of different people, as identified by their IP addresses, who visit a website within a specific time period.

Venture capitalists Investors who specialize in funding new, high-growth ventures in exchange for shares of stock in a company.

Vidcast A video podcast. Also known as *vodcast*.

Vodcast See *vidcast*.

Watchlist A list of web pages that are being monitored.

Web 2.0 An expression that is used to describe the changes that have taken place in the usage and applications available on the Internet (specifically the World Wide Web) since 2004.

Web as platform A concept in which users are not tied to a specific application or computing device; rather, users access their information via services available over the Internet. Also known as *cloud computing*.

Web feed A specialized type of web page written in XML code, enabling it to be updated whenever the website's content is updated.

Widgets See *apps*.

Wiki A collection of web pages that are designed to be edited by groups of individuals.

Wiki community The users and contributors to a wiki.

Wiki farm A server (or a group of connected servers) that runs wiki software and is designed to host multiple wikis at the same time.

Wiki markup The extra symbols and keywords used by a wiki to display, categorize, and publish a wiki page.

Wiki page An individual page on a wiki.

Wiki vandals Individuals who deface pages in a wiki by deleting legitimate information, inserting irrelevant or nonsensical information, violating the policies of the wiki (such as adding content that is speculative on Wikipedia), or inserting links to commercial sites in an attempt to sell products or services.

Wikipedia An online encyclopedia that is deployed in many languages and is accessible at no cost to its users.

Zipped files See *zipped folders*.

Zipped folders Groups of files that have been compressed using a special file compression software to condense the files so that they are smaller in size and can be downloaded quickly. Also known as *zipped files*.

Index

@Mention, 280
@Reply, 280

A

About.me, 298
Access, limiting, 56
Account settings, modification on
  LinkedIn, 75–82
Administrators
  social network sites, 84
  Wikipedia, 216
Advertising, 4
Aggregator, 32–33, 154
Amazon.com, 2
Animoto, 297
Antispyware software, 6
Antivirus software, 6
Apple iPod, 152, 154
Apple iTunes, 153, 203
Applications (apps), 52
Archives, blog, 92, 126
Atomkeep, 299
Attribution—CC BY, 12
Attribution-NonCommercial-
  NoDerivs—CC BY-NC-ND, 12
Audacity
  download and install, 160–170
  overview, 157
  recording podcasts, 170–182
Audio files
  Audacity, downloading and installing,
    160–170
  playing, 154
  podcasts, hardware and software,
    154–158
  podcasts, hosting services, 198–203
  podcasts, use in, 152–154
  recording, 170–182
AutoPlay, Windows, 182, 183

B

Badge, 84
Bebo, 50
Berners-Lee, Tim, 2
Beta version, 160
Birthdate, 15
Bitly, 281
Blog/blogging
  adding features to, 126–140
  characteristics, 94
  copyright concerns, 7, 9, 11, 114
  corporate, 93
  defined, 92
  free hosting, 96–97
  media, 93
  personal, 93
  planning, 95–97
  political, 93
  publicizing, 140–144

social awareness, 93
Blog archive, 92, 126
Blog carnival, 142
Blog comments, 92, 94, 96, 141
Blog directories, 94
Blogger
  adding features, 126–140
  adding labels, 126–129
  creating blogs on, 97–103
  creating URL, 96
  editing blog post, 104–113
  modifying layouts, 130–136
  writing and publishing blog post,
    104–113
Bloggers, 92
Blogger Tips and Tricks, 144
Blogging Tips, 144
Blogosphere, 92
Blog posts, 92
  adding features to, 126–140
  adding images and video to, 114–126
  creating, 104–113
  editing, 104–113
  publishing, 104–113
Blogroll, 92
Blog search engine, 142
Blog spam, 96
Business plans, wikis, 214
Business use, wikis, 213–214

C

Camcorder, 157. *See also* Video
CamStudio, 158
CAPTCHA (Completely Automated
  Public Turing Test to Tell Comput-
  ers and Humans Apart), 16
Carnival, blog, 142
CC BY license, 12
Cease and desist letter, 9–10
Celebrities, on Twitter, 273
Celebrity blog, 93
Change.org, 51
Channel, 285
Checklists, wikis, 213–214
Classmates, 50
Closed community, 51. *See also* Social
  network
Cloud computing, 12–13
Coffee Break Spanish, 152
Comments, blog, 92, 94, 96, 141
Community news and announce-
  ments, wikis, 214
Compression software, 167
Computer
  importing video to, 182–184
  security, 6
Connections, adding to LinkedIn,
  69–75
Contributory infringement, 10

Cookie file, 98
Copyleft, 11–12
Copyright, 7–12
  defined, 7
  Wikipedia, 215
Copyright infringement
  alternatives to avoid, 11
  cease and desist letter, 9–10
  defined, 9
  embedding video and, 10
  rules to avoid, 11
Copyright law, 7–12
Corporate blog, 93
Creative Commons, 12, 114
Credits, posts, 194
Cunningham, Ward, 212
Cyberbullying, 55
Cyber predator, 55
Cyberstalking, 55

D

Daily Blog Tips, 144
Dailymotion, 285
Data breaches, 6
David Lee King, 84
Digg, 143
Direct Message. *See* Message
Domain names, 96–97
Donations, on Wikipedia pages, 215
Dot-com bust, 3
Dot-coms, 2–3

E

Editing
  blog post, 104–113
  wikis, 217–218, 220, 233–242
Editors, Wikipedia, 216
Educause Wiki, 254
Embed code, 84, 125
Embedding video
  copyright concerns, 10
  on wikis, 248–253
Enter The Group, 51
Event planning, wikis, 213
Events, 25
Exporting podcast, 196–197
External applications, 52
External links, 242
Extracted Files, 167

F

Facebook, 9, 50, 52, 57, 84
Fair use, 11
FAQ (Frequently Asked Questions),
  wikis, 214
File compression, 167
Flickr, 51, 104, 285, 297
Feed reader. *See* Aggregator

Follow, 262–263, 273–279
Formatting text, Blogger, 109–112
Free wikis, 222
FriendFeed, 299
Friends, social network sites, 52, 54
Friendster, 50

G

Gadget, Blogger, 130
    adding Subscription Links, 137–140
    page layout, 130–136
GNU, 12
GNU General Public License (GNU
    GPL), 12, 222
Google Account, creating, 12–21
Google Blog Search, 142
Google Calendar, creating and
    sharing, 21–32
Google's Picasa, 297
Google Reader, 33
Group projects, wikis, 212
Grou.ps, 51

H

Hackers, 6
Hardware
    creating podcasts, 155–157
    viewing podcasts, 154–155
Hashtag, 280
Header, 130
Headphones, 156
Hit list, 142
Hobbies, on Twitter, 273
HootSuite, 299
    adding social networks, 301–303
    creating account on, 299–305
    sending update, 304–305
HootSuite Blog, 306
Hyperlink, 242
    adding to blogs, 109–113
    adding to wikis, 242–248
    blogroll, 92

I

IceRocket, 142
Identity, protecting, 54–58
ID3 tags, 181
IE9 (Internet Explorer 9.0), 7
Images
    in blogs, 92, 104, 114–126, 144
    copyright, 7–12
    podcasting, 159, 183
    privacy concerns, 5
    in wikis, 248–249
Importing media files, 188–191
Importing video, to computer,
    182–184
Industry leaders, on Twitter, 273
Internal applications, 52
Internal links, 242
Internet resources, 41
    blogging, 144
    podcasting, 203

social networking, 84–85, 305
    wiki, 254
Internet trolls, 216
Invitations
    LinkedIn, 71–73
    social networks, 71–73, 84
    wikis, 229–231
IP address, 218
iPod. *See* Apple iPod
iTunes. *See* Apple iTunes,
    153, 203
Issues-focused networks, 51. *See also*
    Social network

J

Jumo, 51

K

Knowledge bases, wikis, 213
Kutcher, Ashton, 273

L

Labels, 126–140
LAME MP3 Encoder, installing,
    166–170
Layout, blogs, 130–136
Legal concerns, 7–12
LinkedIn, 51
    account and profile on, 58–69
    adding connection to, 69–75
    modifying account settings on, 75–82
Links
    adding to blogs, 109–113
    adding to wikis, 242–248
    blogroll, 92

M

Malware, 6
Mashable, 85, 306
Match.com, 51
Media blog, 93
Media files. *See* Audio files; Images;
    Video
MediaWiki, 222–223
Message, 280
Microblog, 262. *See also* Twitter
Microphone, 156, 262
Microsoft Office 2010, 170
Microsoft Safety and Security Center,
    5, 7, 85
Microsoft's Channel 9, 152
Moderators, 84
Moore, Demi, 273
MorgueFile, 104
MP3 files, 166–170, 175, 180–182
Multimedia sharing sites, 285–297
    photo sharing, 296
    presentation sharing, 297
    video sharing. *See* YouTube
Multiple social media profiles,
    managing, 298–305
MySpace, 50, 54, 83

N

Navigation schemes, wikis, 243–247
Navigator, 243
News events blog, 93
The Next Web, 306
Ning, 51, 84, 85
Note taking, wikis, 212
Notifications, 234

O

OnGuard Online, 5
Open community, 51. *See also* Social
    networks
Open source software, 157, 158
Operations manuals, wikis, 213
Organizations, on Twitter, 273
Orkut, 50

P

Page views, 94
Passwords, 5, 7, 15, 57, 58
PBworks, 222
    adding pages, 238–242
    configuring wiki, 226–233
    creating account, 224–226
    editing wiki page, 233–238
    uploading image, 248–249
PBworks Educational Edition Manual, 254
PD Photo, 114
Pearsonified, 144
Peer review, 215
Personal blog, 93
Personal Development for Smart
    People, 144
Phishing, 57
Photobucket, 297
Ping.fm, 299
Plaxo, 51
PlayStation Network, 6
PMP (Personal media players), 152,
    154, 155. *See also* Audio files
Podbean, 198–203
Podcast Alley, 153
Podcast Pickle, 153–154
Podcasts
    creating, 156–158
    defined, 152
    importing video, 182–184
    listening, 154–155
    overview, 152–154
    planning, 158–159
    recording audio, 170–182
    resources, 203
    uploading to Internet, 198–203
    video, using MovieMaker, 184–197
    viewing, 154–155
Podcatcher, 154
Political blog, 93
Pop filter, 156
Privacy, protection, 5–7
Problogger, 144
Professional network, 51. *See also*
    Social network

Wikis (*continued*)
    Wikipedia, 214–220
Wikis in Education, 254
Wikispaces, 254
Wiki-Wiki Shuttle, 212
WikiWikiWeb, 212
Windows Live Movie Maker, 158
    creating video podcast using,
        184–197

WMV file, 196–197
Writers, Wikipedia, 216

Y

Yahoo!, 297
YouTube, 10, 51
    creating account and channel, 285–288
    embeding video on wiki, 250–253

subscribing channel, 289–292
update account settings, 288–289
uploading video, 293–296
YouTube Blogger Help, 144

Z

Zipped folders, 167
Zoho Show, 297